Organizational Dignity and Evidence-Based Management

Maria Luisa Mendes Teixeira ·
Lucia Maria Barbosa de Oliveira
Editors

Organizational Dignity and Evidence-Based Management

New Perspectives

Springer

Editors
Maria Luisa Mendes Teixeira
Universidade Presbiteriana Mackenzie
São Paulo, Brazil

Lucia Maria Barbosa de Oliveira
Universidade Presbiteriana Mackenzie
Espinheiro, Pernambuco, Brazil

ISBN 978-3-030-68559-1 ISBN 978-3-030-68560-7 (eBook)
https://doi.org/10.1007/978-3-030-68560-7

This Springer imprint is published by the registered company Springer Nature Switzerland AG
The registered company address is: Gewerbestrasse 11, 6330 Cham, Switzerland

In memoriam

Claudia Adler and Hajnalka Gati who did not have time to see the end of the work. With love and gratitude.

Contents

List of Figures

Part I
Organizational Dignity: Different Perspectives

Chapter 1
From Dignity in Organizations to Dignity Between Organizations

Maria Luisa Mendes Teixeira

Abstract This work aims to present an organizational dignity (OD) theory and discuss its usefulness in guiding the relationships between organizations, stakeholders and B2B relationships. The main question that drove the construction of OD theory was "what do stakeholders review when they evaluate the consequences of the actions that organizations for the stakeholders' dignity carried out?" Then the answer to this main question is that stakeholders evaluate the consequences of the actions that are carried out by organizations for their dignity in terms of cultural elements (practices supported by values); ethics orientation (deontological or teleological); focus more personal or social-oriented focus (stakeholders focus), and classifying the OD of an organization from high to low, as moral, legal, or pragmatic. Stakeholders evaluate the dignity of a firm according to its practices toward them. It is in this sense that organizational dignity means the dignity of a firm is evaluated by stakeholders. The evaluation results of each element address the stage in which the organizations can be allocated and receive the degree of dignity for their relations with the stakeholders.

Keywords Organizational dignity · Dignity inter-organizations · Stakeholders

1.1 Introduction

This work aims to present an organizational dignity (OD) theory and to discuss its usefulness in guiding the relationships between organizations and stakeholders and B2B relationships. Dignity has been studied so far in connection with work and workers in the internal organizational environment. Other stakeholders, like clients or suppliers, have not been usually taken into account by scholars in their studies on dignity. Nonetheless, all of the stakeholders can be affected by the organizations, and stakeholders are able to evaluate the organization and act toward them.

M. L. M. Teixeira (✉)
São Paulo, Brazil
e-mail: marialuisa.teixeira@mackenzie.br; malluluisa@gmail.com

M. L. Mendes Teixeira and L. M. B. de Oliveira (eds.), *Organizational Dignity and Evidence-Based Management*, https://doi.org/10.1007/978-3-030-68560-7_1

Some would argue "What do we need the OD concept for? Hasn't the relationship between organizations and their stakeholders been sufficiently discussed under the concept of organizational ethics and corporate social responsibility? Aren't those concepts strong enough to discuss that relationship?" Ethics refers to the reasons for the intentionality of actions (Abbagnano, 2007). Organizational ethics has been translated as corporate social responsibility (Davidson & Griffin, 2000), and corporate social responsibility has been conceived as a way to achieve a better corporate performance, or the counterpart of the economic power that organizations exert over society, either as an important issue that business operations need to consider due to their legitimacy, or the morality of acting toward society (Okoye, 2009). OD does not discuss the consequences of organizational actions for economic performance or the intentions of their actions. OD treats the consequences of the actions that are carried out by the organizations for the dignity o f their stakeholders that can only be evaluated by them.

The main question that drove the construction of OD theory was "what do stakeholders review when they evaluate the consequences of the actions that are carried out by organizations for the stakeholders' dignity?".

The OD theory was developed based on facet theory. Facet theory claims that the concept needs to come before measurement. The concept needs to be defined in substantive terms in order to make it clear what will, in fact, be studied. Facet theory provides a framework for hypothesizing structural relationships among substantive variables defined to integrate the concept (Guttman & Greenbaum, 1998).

Facet theory was first defined by Guttman in 1954 as "an outline of some new methodology for Social Research" (Guttman & Greenbaum, 1998, p. 15). It comprises a set of tools that support theory development: mapping sentences, facets, and variables relationships structure.

Mapping sentence is "a verbal statement of the domain and of the range of a mapping, including verbal connectives between facets as in ordinary language" (Shye, 1978, p. 413). Mapping sentences consist of two parts: one part comprises the facets of the construct and the other the phrases that connect those facets (Shye, 1978). Three types of facets are necessary for one mapping sentence: respondents (population facet), stimuli (content facet), and responses (response facet). Mapping sentences help researchers to identify and explain at the same time the theoretical constructs and the types of observations that are necessary to test them (Guttman & Greenbaum, 1998).

In this work, the concept of OD is proposed considering its different facets. The possibility of attributing dignity to organizations is discussed. The different aspects of the OD construct are presented in connection with other related constructs such as ethics and social responsibility. An empirical study shows the first results of testing the facets proposed.

The OD theory is two-fold: one practical and the other theoretical. The practical approach contributes to the organizations in order to learn how organizations are evaluated by their stakeholders in terms of the consequences of their actions for stakeholders' dignity. The theoretical approach proposes another theory, which would be better specified than organizational ethics or corporate social responsibility.

1.2 Historical Uses of Dignity

Dignity is a term that can be viewed in many ways (Mattson & Clark, 2011), as different meanings lie in its multiple conceptions (Mitchell, 2017). One meaning of dignity has its roots in Greek and Roman civilizations and denotes social status due to someone occupying a high position in society. The use of this meaning has endured for centuries. It can be found in the medieval, Renaissance, and modern periods and not only in Western cultures but also in Eastern ones (Rosen, 2012). The term "dignity" has its origin in the Latin term "dignitas," which means prestige (Bal & Jong, 2016). Another conception of dignity is based on meritocracy and has its roots in Greece and in the Aristotelian thoughts. In this sense, dignity is a result of one's behavior and includes a virtue perspective. Dignity is deserved by people whose actions are respectable and praiseworthy (Bal & Jong, 2016).

However, dignity has acquired other meanings throughout history (Seery, 2014). From the Christian perspective, human dignity is inherent to human beings, since they are shaped in the image and likeness of God. This meaning was born with Christianity and has endured till the modern era. The Renaissance period produced the first questions regarding the nature of the inherent dignity as the Christian dignity conception. Piccolo Della Miranda in Oration claimed that human beings are able to choose their destiny and not simply fulfill a predestinated order, as God gave them that capacity. However, it was in modernity that inherent dignity as a rationale for human beings' capacity to make moral choices emerged with Kantian thoughts. Dignity is central to the Western discussion about what dignity means and its practice over the centuries. Kant's core concept of dignity is a human value that is inner and unconditional. For that thinker, everything has either a price or dignity. What cannot have a price accepts no equivalent for replacement, and what is raised above all prices has dignity. Autonomy is, for Kant, the ground of dignity, as God created humans as free beings. After Kant, one can consider dignity as a matter of human dignity (Rosen, 2012), and its principle has had a deep influence on the contemporaneous world, especially regarding human rights (Bal & Jong, 2016).

1.2.1 Beyond Kant's Dignity Conception: Influences and Contrapositions

Kant's conception of human dignity as an inner human characteristic that cannot be violated or lost has influenced human rights, as in the Universal Declaration of Human Rights and the constitutions of nations like the USA and Brazil, among others (Sarlet, 2012). In spite of this, some concepts of dignity have emerged from critiques related to human dignity.

Hodgkiss (2013) resorts to sociology founders Marx, Durkheim, and Weber to weave some criticism to Kant dignity concept. In spite of the different ontological and epistemological perspectives related to human beings, all of them regarded people as social human beings living and working under the society forces.

Marx opposes Kant's idea of dignity because dignity and human significance are equivalent, and dignity is a dynamic property of the free creativity in the labor process carried out by conscious people in a community of cooperation and common objectives (Hodgkiss, 2013). Self-actualization by productive experiences is the fundamental requirement for worker dignity, which means autonomy (Hodson, 2001). Marx argued that it is through the work process that people transform themselves and dignity is an important element of that process (Healy & Wilkowska, 2017); however, this is a condition that cannot be sought under capitalism, as workers and their work are subordinated to the rule of making profits for companies (Hodson, 2001). According to Hodgkiss (2013, p. 420) for Marx "The fullest development of human dignity itself is contingent upon total emancipation from an iniquitous mode of production".

Hodgkiss (2013) contrasts Durkheim dignity conception to Kant conception of human dignity in spite of being partially inspired by Kant who championed the rights and human freedom, although under the umbrella of moral individualism. This means that those rights and freedom, based on principles of equality and social justice, must not be subordinated to the social order. Dignity is a moral concept that is not only obligatory but must also be desired and socially desirable. Human beings are moral agents, and to act as such, they ought to have developed rational awareness of their conduct and morality parameters. These societal parameters are diffused within society and are not inner to individuals. However, human beings develop a process of individuation inside collectivities that leads to a conscious process and autonomy. Autonomy is possible even through pathological processes, such as anomy and suicide (Hodgkiss, 2013).

Max Weber's disillusion about the power of reason to make moral choices as proposed by Kant steered him in new directions regarding the dignity conception (Hodgkiss, 2013). Max Weber considers that it is not an absolute system of values but a competing system of values that compels individuals to make choices for their life in order to make it meaningful. Dignity consists of self-realization of values that are related to an individual's life. In line with Durkheim, Max Weber agrees that human beings need to be aware of the social forces that they are instruments of, but this is not enough. Individuals facing the meaninglessness of objectivity and the world feel forced to attempt their own construction of the meaning for their life and context (Hodgkiss, 2013).

Jacobson (2009) criticized the concept of human dignity as transcendental and universal for being vague and contradictory. Under the symbolic interactionism paradigm, Jacobson (2009) proposed that dignity be understood as having two distinct but complementary forms: human dignity, which is abstract and universal, and social dignity, which is generated in the interactions between individuals and among them within collectivities and societies. Social dignity may be divided into the dignity of self and dignity in relation, both being socially constructed. The former is a quality of self-respect and self-worth, and the latter refers to ways of conveying respect through individuals and collectivities. Interactions occur in encounters between or among individuals or collective social actors who are embedded in the social order. These encounters have the potential to promote or violate dignity according to the sets of conditions. Inequality substantiated by asymmetry can put one social actor in a position of vulnerability and subject him to violation of his dignity. By contrast, dignity promotion becomes more likely when the encounter is based on solidarity, according to which one actor is in a position of confidence and the other in a position of compassion.

Another criticism of human dignity as a universal transcendence concept came from the epistemological approach. The transcendent nature of dignity brings epistemological problems. Dignity must be investigated as a result of interactions, and it is a matter of relations between individuals and the group or broader groups with which they interact. Dignity is culturally rooted and translated into a notion of individual worth shared in a specific context (Mitchell, 2017).

The Kantian concept of dignity is limited to understanding what the term means in everyday life. "Dignity depends not only on words but on deeds and material conditions" (Sayer, 2007, p. 567). Dignity is fragile. It depends on how one is treated by the others as an end (substantive) or mean (instrumental). Dignity is related to autonomy, dependence, seriousness, and trust. To have dignity means to have self-command, to be in control of oneself, as it means not attempting to control the lives of others and respecting differences. Humans are social beings, so they are vulnerable and depend on others throughout their lives. Autonomy is fragile. One's autonomy needs to be accepted by others (Sayer, 2007).

In sum, dignity has taken many meanings throughout history. It can mean social status; to be related to someone's merit of acting in a respectable way; a property of human beings as they are made in the image of God; the human capacity of rationality choices; self-actualization of values; or a result of interactions supported by respect between or among individuals or collectivities. In most dignity concepts, autonomy is a central point, that is, the autonomy of action and respect of the autonomy of others.

1.3 Dignity in Organizations

Dignity has been studied in several contexts, and among them is the organizational framework as dignity related to workers and organizations. Hodson and Roscino (2004) are the authors of one of the classic and most influential studies about dignity at work. They discussed the meaning of dignity and the strategies that workers have at their disposal to defend their dignity in the work-life environment. According to those authors, "Dignity is the ability to establish a sense of self-worth and self-respect and to appreciate the respect of others" (Hodson & Roscino, 2004, p. 3). It is about exercising agency (Hodson, 2001). Autonomy is the "Individual's will to be self-determining, to have their own space and privacy to make their work more meaningful" (Yalden & Mccormack, 2010, p. 141), and it is one's capacity to shape his/her action Margolis (1997). Dignity at work is related to the happiness of being motivated/inspired and having the freedom to make choices and achieve goals, which can be understood as a flourishing process and the ultimate aim in life underpinned by the personhood notion, a principle of *Eudemonia* (Yalden & Mccormack, 2010).

Starting from the points of view of Marx, Durkheim, and Weber about the Industrial Revolution and its undesirable consequences for workers, Hodson and Roscino (2004) demonstrated that dignity in the workplace varies as to the degree of control that allows workers to fulfill a sense of self-worth and self-respect from their jobs. Control depends on the degree of direct supervision, task segmentation, automation, rules, on-the-job training, and participation in the workplace (Crowley, 2013) as well as management competence (Hodson, 2001). Among the negative consequences of control, Hodson (2001) emphasizes abuse and inequality, mismanagement, overwork, a low level of autonomy, and untruthful employee involvement. Other negative consequences are gender inequality (Crowley, 2013) and loss of motivation (Parandeh et al., 2016).

To protect their dignity, employees can overcome obstacles by creating alternatives such as resistance, citizenship, independent meaning systems, and the development of social relations at work (Hodson, 2001). On the other hand, organizations can develop organizational and job-level practices to gain competitiveness power and employees' well-being (Margolis, 1997; Hodson & Roscino, 2004). To improve competitiveness and well-being, organizations need to fulfill three dignity conditions: autonomy, respect for contributions, and the opportunity of learning and growing (Margolis, 1997). Those conditions cannot be separated from the dynamic relationship between workers and management (Yalden & Mccormack, 2010). This dynamic is of an interdependent, relational, and intersubjective nature in which the ethical habits of relationships, transparency, and trust have to take place in a process of workers' dignity construction. That process shapes the self and personhood of workers and, by extension, the team dignity (Yalden & Mccormack, 2010). Workers feel their sense of dignity as they perceive themselves to be trusted by others and feel that others are confident that they will use their autonomy in a way that will not take advantage of others and that managers will not take advantage on them (Sayer, 2007). Thus, trust is the sewing thread of worker dignity inside the organizations.

1.3.1 Defining Organizational Dignity

Facing societal challenges and the necessary dignified relations between organizations and their stakeholders, studies on dignity in the workplace have evolved toward organizations and their relationships with stakeholders other than employees,

The first question to be answered when defining OD is whether it is appropriate to attribute dignity to organizations. Organizational scholars rarely discuss what makes an organization a social actor, i.e., an entity that is capable of intentional purpose and action (King & Whetten, 2010). Because of this lack of discussion, the possibility of attributing OD to organizations ought to be justified.

Organizations as a social actor

The main reason why the conception of the organization as a social actor has not been widely discussed is that an organization is usually conceived as a collection of individuals that interact with each other (organizing). For scholars who advocate this conception, i.e., that "an organization acts" means that the individuals are, in fact, the ones who perform a role. Other than this, the organization is an abstraction that makes no sense. For those scholars, to attribute dignity to organizations means to attribute dignity to a collection of individuals who are social entities and act performing roles as social actors (King & Whetten, 2010). To argue that the organizations have dignity implies another conception of organization: organization as a social entity, as a social actor.

To conceive organizations as social actors implies that they are [social entities] perceived by stakeholders as capable of making decisions and of assuming the responsibility for their decisions and practices. Thus, the organizational social actor conception is characterized by (1) external attributions given by the stakeholders and (2) legal responsibility taken by the organizations for the impact of their actions (King & Whetten, 2010). Stakeholders are audiences that are able to perceive the organizations' decisions and actions, evaluate whether they are affected by them, and decide whether or not to try to modify them (Freeman, 1984). OD relates to the relationship between organizations and their stakeholders.

Organizational dignity can be characterized as social dignity which is "generated in the interaction between and among individuals, groups or collectivities" that can be promoted or violated (Jacobson, 2009, p. 589) in their relationship between organizations and their stakeholders.

Stakeholders' influence on organizations

The relationships between organizations and their stakeholders have been studied during the last five decades. During this period, scholars have devoted a lot of attention to discussing the concept. Furthermore, they have discussed how these relations should be (normative), have been (descriptive), and could be (instrumental) (Donaldson & Dunfee, 1999; Donaldson & Preston, 1995; Hendry, 2001; Friedman & Miles, 2006). The importance of these discussions is underlined by the influence that organizations exert or can exert on stakeholders and vice versa (Fassin, 2009).

One of the most classic categorizations of stakeholders with respect to influence postulates two types: those that exert direct influence on organizations and whose relationships are contractual (primary), and those that exert indirect influence without contractual connections (secondary) (Clarkson, 1995; Collier & Roberts 2001; Carroll, 1991).

The distinction of direct *versus* indirect stakeholders' influence is still intensively used in [stakeholders] research. Between 2010 and 2015, the primary *versus* secondary [stakeholders] classification could be found in the EBSCO database in 148 articles, almost 50% of the academic papers on stakeholders since 1983. The use of this classification seems to increase in the studies regarding the relationships between organizations and stakeholders.

Regarding the stakeholders' concept (Freeman, 1984), the indirect or direct influence stakeholders have on organizations (Clarkson, 1995), and the concept of organization as social actor (King & Whetten, 2010), it is possible to say that stakeholders are able to perceive and evaluate the OD of organizations and act toward them in a direct or indirect way.

1.4 Organizational Dignity: Facets and Concept

Cultural elements and focus on organizational dignity

Organizational dignity is embedded in the organizational practices and values. As the OD is social, according to the concept of social dignity proposed by Jacobson (2009), it stems from the interactions between organizations and their stakeholders. Those interactions are mediated by organizational practices and organizational values perceived by stakeholders (Guardani et al., 2013). Therefore, it is possible to say that OD is reflected in organizational values and practices that are perceived by stakeholders. Organizational practices are "'theories in use' which represent the typical behaviors/procedures adopted by members of an organization" (Verbek, 2000, p. 589). Those practices reflect how organizations interact with the market and are shaped by the core organizational values (Verbek, 2000). Practices and values are elements of organizational culture (Hofstede et al., 1990).

Organizational values guide organizational members' behavior and represent what an organization considers important for achieving its goals (Bourne & Jenkins, 2013). Values can emphasize either self-expression and the achievement of one's own interests and dominance over others (personal focus) or the concern for interests of the others and for regulation of collective behavior (social focus) (Schwartz, 2006). As the structure of values is the same for individuals and organizations (Bilsky & Jehn, 2008), organizations can be self-oriented by their organizational values giving priority to the fulfillment of self-interests or can be socially oriented regarding the stakeholder's interests.

Organizational dignity can be understood as a specific kind of organizational culture that can be perceived by stakeholders when they interact with the organization and can evaluate whether the organization is more self-interests oriented or more oriented to stakeholders' interests.

Ethical orientation

Because organizations are conceived as social actors (King & Whetten, 2010), intentions are embedded in organizational practices shaped by core organizational values. Ethics is related to the intentions that underlie human conduct (Abbagnano, 2007), and ethics and business cannot be treated as separate subjects (Allinson, 1998). Ethics is related to moral principles that guide organizations in relationships with stakeholders (Chakrabarty & Bass, 2015). There are several approaches to studying ethics; however, the most common in business ethics are deontological and utilitarian ethics. Deontological ethics prescribes what is right or wrong in absolute terms while for utilitarian ethics or consequentialism (teleological ethics) the actions' consequences are what matters (Allinson, 1998). Thus, it means that organizations can have their values and practices oriented by deontological or utilitarian ethics. In this sense, ethics is embedded in OD.

Standards of dignity

Tadd et al. (2010) identified four types of dignity which were classified following Spiegelber (1970) classification in two categories of dignity: "dignity in **general**" and "**human** dignity". The first one comprises three dignity types: **merit**, **moral status,** and **identity**. The second one, ***Menschenwuerde***, the only one that cannot be evaluated or alienated from the human beings, because it means the worth possessed by every human being. The dignity of merit is related to social status or position in society that can be gained or lost. This kind of dignity can be reached by social heritage, e.g., when a person is born, that person receives a title of a social position or strives for it. This kind of dignity has its roots in the Roman Empire, and it was related to the senators' position (Abbagnano, 2007). Other authors named this kind of dignity "distinction" inside society (Gosdal, 2007; Jacobson, 2009). The dignity of moral status corresponds to moral autonomy guided by moral principles, which can be preserved or not by people. The dignity of identity is related to self-respect and identity. This type of dignity can be violated emotionally, psychologically, or physically (Tadd et al., 2010) or promoted in encounters between individuals or collectivities (Jacobson, 2009). This type of dignity comprises moral and legal aspects. The moral aspect means that people should not be violated emotionally, psychologically, or physically. The legal aspect means that people legal rights should not be violated.

After the Second World War, dignity based on the defense of human rights has gained space in the social and legal realms (Sarlet, 2009). Since moral dignity cannot be considered separately as one specific type of dignity (for it is also related to the dignity of Identity), we suggest the redefinition of the three types proposed by Tadd et al. (2010) into: distinction, moral, and legal dignity. With respect to OD, we labeled distinction dignity as pragmatic dignity. Persons can have social, economic, and political status; however, organizations can only have economic status, and this cannot be achieved by heritage but only by strategic plans and actions.

Organizational dignity concept

Considering the different dignity aspects, we propose that OD is the dignity of an organization which is reflected in its values and practices, and it is slanted toward stakeholder's interests, justified by deontological or teleological ethics, and this ethics is evaluated in terms of moral, legal, or pragmatic standards by the stakeholders who exert direct or indirect influence on such ethics. This concept includes four facets: cultural elements, focus on these elements, ethical justification, and standards of OD (Fig. 1.1).

Mapping Sentence for Assessing Organizational Dignity

	X: influence		
	(x1 direct	)	
A stakeholder that exerts	(x2 indirect	)	**influence on an organization**
	(x3 an unspecified	)	

Evaluates the dignity of this organization

	A: cultural elements		
	(a1 values	)	
which is reflected in	(a2 practices	)	**that**
	(a3 unspecified	)	
	B: focus		
	(b1 personal	)	
have a	(b2 social	)	**focus and are**
	(b3 unspecified	)	
	C: ethics		
	(c1 deontological	)	
justified by	(c2 teleological	)	
	(c3 unspecified	)	

	D: standards		
	(d1 moral	)	
in terms of	(d2 legal	)	**standards**
	(d3 pragmatic	)	
	(d4 unspecified	)	

	R		
	(high	)	
On a scale from	(…	)	**with respect to these standards.**
	(low	)	

Fig. 1.1 Mapping sentence for assessing OD (Teixeira & Bilsky, 2015)

1.5 Why Developing the Organizational Dignity Concept

The study of dignity associated with organizations is not new and has been improved in the last two decades. The focus of these studies has been the worker and the work environment inside organizations, regarding the worker dignity (Ross, 2013) and dignity at work (Hodson, 2001; Hodson & Roscino, 2004).

The OD concept was first used for organizations by Margolis (1997) who proposed this concept as the condition offered by an organization to dignify employees. For Margolis (1997), dignity is the capacity of a person to shape his/her own actions, and OD is the dignifying condition that organizations offer to promote the workers' dignity. This concept has its roots in Kantian approach to dignity. The dignifying conditions are autonomy, respect for workers' contributions, and opportunity to learn and grow.

The first questions facing those approaches to dignity and organizations are: Why study only the workers' dignity? Why not the dignity of other stakeholders like clients, suppliers, government, and society? Is it possible to attribute dignity to organizations? Who attributes and evaluates the dignity of organizations? What is the usefulness of this evaluation?

The importance of dignity practices for the competitiveness of organizations has been demonstrated, at least since Hodson and Roscino (2004). Moreover, as the organization's practices dignity, they contribute to people's well-being (Mattson & Clark, 2011). We believe that developing a measurement instrument that enables stakeholders to access organizations may contribute to the improvement of their practices and act in an increasingly dignified manner, respecting the stakeholders as people.

Another issue that comes up when dealing with the importance of developing the concept of OD is related to the superposition of concepts such as ethics and social responsibility. As mentioned above, ethics refers to the reasons for intentionality of actions (Abbagnano, 2007) while dignity does not discuss neither the causes of intentions nor the intentions themselves. OD treats the consequences of actions for those who act and for the others (Jacobson, 2009). There is an interface between ethics and dignity, since ethics is one of the facets of dignity, but dignity is more than just ethics.

Another superposition that could be evoked is related to OD and corporate social responsibility. Corporate social responsibility in the business world has been conceived as ethics exerted by organizations (Davidson & Griffin, 2000). Despite more than 50 years of scientific research, the concept of social responsibility remains unclear. Four strands seem to bring together different approaches to corporate social responsibility: a way to achieve better economic performance; responsibility toward society as counterpart of the economic power exerted over it; the importance of taking into account the social demands to the business operation due to their legitimacy; and the morality of acting before the society (Okoye, 2009).

The concept of OD takes distance itself from the first three strands by not considering any relations to the organizational performance, nor being the counterpart of the economic power of the organizations or meeting the different demands of society. The only social demand considered is the dignity of stakeholders as people that have to be respected when organizations interact with them by their practices. The concept of OD has a connection only with the latter strand of CSR, the morality before society, since one of the dignity's standards is moral dignity. It is important to notice that OD is not only moral dignity; it encompasses three different types of standards: moral, legal, and pragmatic.

Another key question to be answered is whether it is possible or not to assign dignity to organizations. The answer was found in the concept of an organization as a social actor according to King and Whetten (2010).

To summarize, one can say that the concept of OD should not be confused with the concepts of ethics or social responsibility, although it could have some affinity with them.

1.6 Evidences of OD Applicability

To verify the applicability of OD theory's proposal, a scale was elaborated regarding the facets of the construct. Facet is a category of attributes that represent an aspect of the construct under investigation. The facets that explain the construct must be mutually exclusive. Facets represent conceptual unmatched elements of the construct. We can attribute one and only one element of each facet to each variable (Bilsky, 2003).

In the OD theory, stakeholders that exert direct, indirect, or unspecified influence on an organization represented the population facet. Content facets were represented by cultural elements, focus, and ethics. Response facet was represented by OD standards and a scale from high to low with respect to those standards.

In social sciences, several methods are available to identify variables relationships structures. Facet theory uses the smallest space analysis that is a non-metric method for multidimensional scaling analysis (MDS). Applying MDS to the data, a regional space is specified by a set of variables that represent a one-facet element (Bilsky, 2003). In our work, MDS was applied to content facets and response facet in terms of OD standards.

The design of space regions corresponds to the variable's relationship structure. Facets could be ordered or qualitative. An ordered facet is that which groups of elements are organized in a progressive way either in modular space partitions (circles) or axial organized side by side. It is possible to predict a hierarchal correlation between variable correlation pairs. On the other hand, the elements of qualitative facets are organized in cuneiform regions, which have a common origin in a circumplex design with no order between. The elements of a qualitative facet are displayed in angular regions so that elements that are in adjacent regions are more similar than in the others (Bilsky, 2003).

To develop and test OD theory, a mapping sentence served as a frame of reference for categorizing the items of a provisional OD questionnaire. Those items were selected from a qualitative research about what dignity means for Brazilian employees (Teixeira et al., 2010) and were classified by four specialists in each element of each facet. Item profiles (structuples) resulting from those independent categorizations were the basis for composing a faceted 47-item OD questionnaire. Regional hypotheses based on the item profiles were tested by reanalyzing a comprehensive data set of 407 employees. Ordinal and interval MDS analyses were applied to the correlation matrix of OD items.

The results indicated that the facet cultural elements were perfectly identified in modular space partitioning, with core values and practices around, which makes sense, as these are values that support practices. Values are in the culture core (Hofstede, 2011).

Deontological ethics and teleological ethics divided space in diagonal, which means that these elements of the ethics facet are opposite. This result is in line with Allinson (1998): Deontological ethics prescribe what is right or wrong, while from the teleological ethics the consequence of actions is what matters in a process decision.

Focus facet was not perfectly identified. Nevertheless, two important results can be observed in the space partition: first, the design—modular; second—personal focus appeared in the center. This result means that organizations giving priority to the personal focus less than the social focus (stakeholders' focus). One possible reason for the deviations found could be the item's classification as it was done by four investigators.

OD standards facet was not perfectly identified either. However, two important results were found for OD theory development: Legal standard and pragmatic standard were perfectly located in the space. Only a few moral standards items appeared misplaced mainly in the legal standard space. One reason could be a superposition of meanings: legal standard OD items that can be understood as moral standard items.

Despite two partially identified facets, the results indicated that all four content facets proposed as OD facets were found with the previewed elements. Then it is possible to answer the main question that drove this work: Stakeholders evaluate the consequences of the actions that are carried out by organizations for their dignity in terms of cultural elements (practices supported by values); ethics orientation (deontological or teleological); focus (more personal or social-oriented focus (stakeholders focus), and classifying the OD of an organization from high to low, as moral, legal, or pragmatic. Stakeholders evaluate the dignity of a firm according to its practices toward them. It is in this sense that OD means the dignity of a firm evaluated by stakeholders. The combination of the content facets results in stages in which the organizations can be allocated and receives the degree of dignity for their relations with the stakeholders.

Aguado et al. (2017), based on the Integrative Social Contracts Theory (ISCT), on Maslow's hierarchy of needs, on Herzberg's two-factor theory, and on stakeholders theory, proposed a theoretical approach for dignity analysis at the firm level. According to the authors, human dignity is a fundamental element that should permeate strategies, operations, and daily decisions in order to align social interests and organizational actions in the form of social macrocontracts. Social macrocontracts, in turn, must be guided by hypernorms, which must be aligned with the declaration of human rights and other initiatives permeated by humanistic values. Macrocontracts are operationalized through microcontracts between specific communities.

Aguado et al. (2017) argue that in order for the firm's dignity model to materialize, it is necessary to create conditions for people who integrate organizations to develop their potential and propose that the dignity of the organization be evaluated according to the levels of needs proposed by Maslow et al. (1970). The evolution of the firm would take place from the level of physiological needs to self-actualization. At the level of physiological needs and safety needs are companies that seek to correct their actions in terms of dignity. At the level of social needs and esteem needs would be those organizations that promote dignity, and at the highest level of needs (Self-actualization), those organizations that keep the terms of dignity.

Aguado et al. (2017, p. 81) proposed their model considering that dignity at a firm level needs to be "beyond stakeholder approach" and proposed that organizations dignity needs to be evaluated regarding the human dignity in the microcontracts and the stages of dignity based on Maslow et al. (1970) hierarchy needs. However, those authors did not explain which the audience is capable of making the evaluation and how to make such an evaluation. The model proposed in this chapter suggests that the dignity of the firm—organizational dignity—should be evaluated by stakeholders considering practices supported by values, ethics, focus, and parameters.

1.7 Implications for Management

The OD theory introduced in this chapter has several implications for management. The first is the fact that the assessment that each stakeholder makes about the dignity of an organization is influenced by the dignity practices he/she perceives in relation to other stakeholders. Therefore, the assessment that employees make about the dignity of the organization is influenced by the practices of dignity they perceive to be performed in relation to customers, suppliers, and society. In turn, customer's assessment of the organization's dignity is also influenced by the practices that customers perceive in relation to employees and suppliers. The same occurs with the assessment made by suppliers.

A second implication concerns what stakeholders take into account when assessing the dignity of a company: the practices, the ethical orientation, the focus oriented toward the interests of the organization itself, or oriented toward the social, and the legal, moral, or pragmatic parameters. These assessment contents show that corporate social responsibility practices are not sufficient for stakeholders to assess the dignity of an organization, nor the perceived ethics. It is necessary that the organization meets all the contents of the OD and in relation to all stakeholders so that it can be considered a worthy organization.

Another implication concerns the measurement and monitoring of OD. An organizational dignity measurement scale should include values related to dignity, dignity practices that reflect ethics, focus, and evaluation parameters. Bearing in mind that the stakeholders have different interests from each other, scales directed to each type of stakeholders are necessary, but covering all OD content. These scales must be applied periodically to monitor the status of OD, generate feedback for management, allowing the steering of efforts to raise the level of OD practiced. Throughout the different chapters that make up this book, we can identify scales for measuring OD from the point of view of employees (Chap. 7), customers (Chap. 12), and suppliers in the B2B relationship (Chap. 14).

Finally, considering that OD consists of a type of culture, it is essential to monitor how organizational culture is impregnated with values related to OD and apply efforts so that an organization's culture be essentially an OD culture. OD practices need to be emphasized, disseminated, and enhanced in the organizations' day-to-day activities, least the results of an organization's dignity assessments be short-lived.

1.8 Final Remarks

Managers have been pressured by different demands from society and its stakeholders, whether they are employees, customers, suppliers, shareholders, social institutions, and class associations. To meet these demands, managers have resorted to corporate social responsibility (CSR) practices; however, the variety of CSR concepts has resulted in different sets of practices, which make it difficult for stakeholders to assess.

In addition to CSR practices, managers have been demanded regarding the ethics that permeates the actions and decisions that steer management. Much has been written about business ethics, but little practical guidance has been offered to the organizations' management. In addition, CSR and business ethics practices do not, by themselves, account for the preservation and promotion of human dignity.

Human dignity consists of the deepest respect for the autonomy of moral action of human beings, their right to be, to develop, and to act (Margolis, 1997). A worthy company is one that is assessed by its stakeholders as such. The violation of dignity can lead to the rupture of the relationship with the organization and to the loss of competitiveness (Jones, 2012).

The OD theory presented in this chapter allows managers to know how stakeholders assess the dignity of the organization in which they operate and outline strategies to raise the level of OD, through the development of an organizational culture that contemplates dignity in its essence.

References

Abbagnano, N. (2007). *Dicionário de Filosofia.* Martins Fontes.
Aguado, R., Retolaza, J. L., & Alcañiz, L. (2017). Dignity at the level of the Firm: Beyond the stakeholder approach. In M. Kostera & M. Pirson (Eds.), *Dignity and the organization.* (Humanism in Business Series). London: Palgrave Macmillan. https://doi.org/10.1057/978-1-137-55562-5_9.
Allinson, R. (1998). Ethical values as part of the definition of business enterprise and part of the internal structure of the business organization. *Journal of Business Ethics, 17*(9/10), 1015–1028.
Bal, P. M., & Jong, S. D. (2016). From human resource management to human dignity development: A dignity perspective on HRM and the role of workplace democracy. In M. Costera & M. Pirson (Eds.), *Dignity and organizations* (pp. 173–1950). Palgrave McMillan.
Bilsky, W., & Jehn, K. A. (2008). Cultura organizacional e valores individuais: evidências de uma estrutura comum. In M. L. M Teixeira (Ed.), *Valores humanos e gestão: novas perspectivas.* São Paulo: Senac.
Bilsky, W. (2003). A Teoria das Facetas: Noções básicas [Facet Theory: Basic notions]. *Estudos De Psicologia, 8*(3), 357–365.
Bourne, H., & Jenkins, M. (2013). Organizational values: A dynamic perspective. *Organization Studies, 34,* 495–514.
Carrol, A. B. (1991). The pyramid of corporate social responsibility: Toward the moral management of organizational stakeholders. *Business Horizons, 34*(4), 39–48.
Chakrabarty, S., & Bass, A. E. (2015). Comparing virtue, consequentialist, and deontological ethics-based corporate social responsibility: Mitigating microfinance risk in institutional voids. *Journal of Business Ethics, 126*(3), 487–512.
Clarkson, M. B. E. (1995). A stakeholder framework for analyzing and evaluating corporate social performance. *The Academy of Management Review, 20*(1), 92–117.
Collier, J., & Roberts, R. (2001). Introduction: An ethic for corporate governance? *Business Ethics Quarterly, 11*(1), 67–71.
Crowley. M. (2013, May). *Gender, the labor process and dignity at work. Social Forces, 91,* 1209–1238.
Davidson, P., & Griffin, R. W. (2000), *Management: Australia in a global context.* Brisbane: Wiley.
Donaldson, T., & Dunfee, T. (1999). *Ties that bind: A social contracts approach to business ethics.* Boston: Harvard Business School Press.
Donaldson, T., & Preston, L. E. (1995). The stakeholder theory of the corporation: Concepts, evidence and implications. *Academy of Management Review, 20*(1), 65–91.
Fassin, Y. (2009). The stakeholder model refined. *Journal of Business Ethics, 84,* (1), 113–135.
Freeman, R. (1984). *Strategic management: A stakeholders approach.* Boston: Pitman.
Friedman, A. L., & Miles, S. (2006). *Stakeholders: Theory and practice.* Oxford: Oxford University Press.
Gosdal, T. C. (2007). *Dignidade do trabalhador: Um conceito construído sob o paradigma do trabalho decente e da honra.* São Paulo: LTr.
Guardani, F., Teixeira, M. L. M., Bido, D. S., & Mazzon, J. A. (2013). A relação entre valores, práticas organizacionais e confiança de clientes no setor de serviços. *Produção, 23*(4), 806–817.
Guttman, R., & Greenbaum, C. W. (1998). Facet theory: Its development and current status. *European Psychologist, 3,* 13–36.
Healy & Wilkowska. (2017). Marx, alienation and the denial of dignity of work. In M. Costera & M. Pirson (Eds.), *Dignity and organizations* (pp. 173–1950). Palgrave McMillan.
Hendry, J. (2001). Economic contracts versus social relationships as a foundation for normative stakeholder theory. *Business Ethics: A European Review, 10*(3), 223.
Hodson, R., & Roscino, V. (2004). Organizational success and worker dignity: Complementary or contradictory? *The American Journal of Sociology, 110*(3), 672.
Hodgkiss. (2013, August). A moral vision: human dignity in the eyes of the founders of sociology. *The sociological review, 61*(3), 417–439.
Hodson, R. (2001). *Dignity at work.* Cambridge: Cambridge University Press.

Hofstede, G. (2011). Dimensionalizing cultures: The Hofstede model in context. *Online Readings in Psychology and Culture, 2*(1).

Hofstede, G., Neuijen, B., Ohayv, D. D., & Sanders, G. (1990). Measuring organizational cultures: A qualitative and quantitative study across twenty cases. *Administrative Science Quarterly*, 35, 286–316.

Jacobson, N. (2009). A taxonomy of dignity: A grounded theory study. *BMC International Health and Human Rights, 9,* 1–9.

Jones, J. (2012). Human dignity in the EU charter of fundamental rights and its interpretation before the European Court of justice. *Liverpool Law Review, 33,* 281–300.

King, B. G., & Whetten, D. A. (2010). Finding the organization in organizational theory: A meta-- Theory of the organization as a social actor. *Organization Science, 21*(1), 290–305.

Margolis, J. (1997). *Dignity in balance: Philosophical and practical dimensions of promoting ethics in organizations* (p. 307p). Massachusetts: Harvard University.

Maslow, A. H., Frager, R., & Cox, R. (1970). *Motivation and personality* (Vol. 2). In: J. Fadiman, & C. McReynolds (Eds.) New York: Harper & Rowa.

Mattson, J. D., & Clark, S. (2011). Human dignity in concept and practice. *Policy Sciences, 44,* 303–319.

Mitchell, L. (2017). Dingity and membership: A route to the heart of how dignity is done in everyday interaction. In M. Costera & M. Pirson (Eds.), *Dignity and organizations* (pp. 173–1950). Palgrave McMillan.

Okoye, A. (2009). Theorising corporate social responsibility as an essentially contested concept: Is a definition necessary? *Journal of Business Ethics, 89*(4), 613–627.

Parandeh, A., Khaghanizade, M., Mohammadi, E., & Mokhtari-Nouri, J. (2016). Nurses' human dignity in education and practice: An integrated literature review. *Iranian Journal of Nursing Midwifery, 21,* 1–8.

Rosen, C. (2012). *Dignity: Its history and meaning.* Cambridge, MA: Harvard University Press.

Ross, R. J. S. (2013, March). Women workers and the struggle for dignity and respect. *The Journal of Labor & Society, 16*, 59–68.

Sarlet, I. W. (2012). *Dignidade da pessoa humana e direitos fundamentais na Constituição Federal de 1988.* 9. Ed – Livraria do advogado. Porto Alegre.

Sarlet, I. W. (2009). *A eficácia dos direitos fundamentais: Uma teoria geral dos direitos fundamentais na perspectiva constitucional* (10th ed.). Porto Alegre: Livraria doAdvogado.

Sayer, A. (2007). Dignity at work: Broadening the agenda. *Organization, 14,* 565–581.

Schwartz, S. H. (2006). Les valeurs de base de la personne: Théorie, mesures et applications [Basic human values: Theory, measurement, and applications]. *Revue Française De Sociologie, 42,* 249–288.

Seery, J. (2014). *George Katteb: Dignity, morality, individuality.* London: Routledge Innovators and Political Theory.

Shye, S. (Ed.). (1978). *Theory construction and data analysis in the behavioral sciences.* San Francisco: Jossey-Bass.

Spiegelber, H. (1970). Intention and 'Intentionality' in the scholastics; Brentano and Husserl. In L. L. McAlister (Ed.) (pp. 108–28).

Tadd, W., Vanlaere, L., & Gastmans, C. (2010). Clarifying the concept of human dignity in the care of the elderly. *Ethical Perspectives, 17*(2), 253–281.

Teixeira, M. L. M., Dias, S. M. R. C., Araujo, B. F. B., Paz, M. G. T., & Oliveira, L. M. B. (2010). O conceito de empresa digna na percepção de trabalhadores brasileiros. In Anais do Congreso de la asociaci6n latinoamericana de sociología del trabajo, Anais ALAST, Ciudad do México, México.

Teixeira, M. L. M., & Bilsky, W. (2015). Faceting organizational dignity. *International Facet Theory Conference.* Presentation, not published.

Verbek, W. (2000). A revision of Hofstede et al.' s (1990) organizational practices scale. *Journal of Organizational Behavior, 21*(5), 587–602.

Yalden & Mccormack. (2010). Constructions of dignity: A pre-requisite for flourishing in the workplace? *International Journal of Older People Nursing, 5*(2), 137–147.

Chapter 2
Organizational Dignity, Corporate Social Responsibility, and Business Ethics

Vanessa Custódio Zorzetti Pollon, Francilene Araújo de Morais, and Maria Luisa Mendes Teixeira

Abstract This study aims to investigate the relationship between organizational ethics, business ethics, and social responsibility. The research was carried out in three steps. The first step was to review the relationship between organizational dignity and business ethics. Next, it reviewed the relationship between organizational dignity and corporate social responsibility. In a third stage, it identified the relationship between business ethics and corporate social responsibility. Finally, it investigated the relationship between all constructs. Each step corresponded to one study. The first study collected data from 214 administrative employees. The results showed that business ethics presented a predictive power of 28.1% in relation to the organizational dignity. The second study was carried out with 140 unspecified employees and 214 administrative employees. The results of both samples showed that corporate social responsibility explains more than 50% of organizational dignity. Finally, the third study showed that the business ethics mediates the relationship between corporate social responsibility and organizational dignity. It was possible to conclude that the three constructs are not interchangeable. The absence of organizational dignity practices may lead to the rupture of the relationship with the company, and the consequent loss of customers.

Keywords Organizational dignity · Corporate social responsibility · Business ethics

2.1 Introduction

The society is increasingly demanding business organizations to use more sensitive means to run their businesses. Corporations are required to move away from management based on profits at any price, mainly considering the scandals (Carroll & Buchholtz, 2009), resulting in protective laws to several segments of the society considered to be part of the partially disadvantaged group. It is illustrated by the

V. C. Z. Pollon · F. A. de Morais · M. L. M. Teixeira (✉)
São Paulo, Brasil
e-mail: malluluisa@gmail.com

M. L. Mendes Teixeira and L. M. B. de Oliveira (eds.), *Organizational Dignity and Evidence-Based Management*, https://doi.org/10.1007/978-3-030-68560-7_2

protection to workers' rights by the labor laws, and to consumers' rights through the consumers' rights code.

This matter, however, is not new. It has been investigated in different lights such as businesses ethics and corporate social responsibility (CSR), dignity in organizations, and dignity of organizations. Teixeira (2016) argues that dignity of organizations, or organizational dignity, social responsibility, and business ethics are interrelated but not interchangeable concepts. The author, however, did not present any empiric study substantiating this theoretical proposition. This study aims to investigate the relationship between organizational ethics, business ethics, and social responsibility. The first step was to review the relationship between organizational dignity and business ethics. Next, it reviewed the relationship between organizational dignity and social responsibility. In a third stage, it identified the relationship between business ethics and corporate social responsibility. Finally, it investigated the relationship between all constructs.

The theoretical purpose of this study was to advance knowledge about organizational dignity. In practical terms, it aimed to warn managers about the difference between the constructs, so they can better evaluate which construct would better fit to assess the relationship between the organization of their stakeholders.

2.2 From Dignity in Organizations to Dignity of Organizations

In light of dignity in organizations, the studies have considered issues related to employees, approaching worker's and labor's dignity like, for example, Hodson and Roscigno (2004), Berg and Frost (2005), Brodie (2004), Mattson and Clark (2011), health and sanitation (Auerbach, 1998; Agassi, 1986), safety at work (Ghai, 2003); equal rights for men and women (Ghai, 2003), downsizing implementation (Greenspan, 2002; Barbee, 2001; Brodie, 2004); low wages, risks inherent to work, and stress (Zeytinoglu et al., 2004); alienating work and its impacts on the worker's life at the workplace (Agassi, 1986).

The study about dignity of organizations, known as DO, is recent. Although the term DO has been coined for the first time by Margolis (1997) as the people's capacity of shaping their own action, referring to the autonomy every human being should have, the author's approach to DO is limited to the conditions organizations should offer to let their employees act with autonomy, recognizing the contributions they offer, and providing them with the required conditions to develop their potential. Teixeira (2008) supports that DO should consider not only the employee, but also other stakeholders:

Organizational dignity "[...] consists in the relationship between the organization's personnel and others, herein referred to as stakeholders, oriented by the communicative action, where people say what they think in an intelligible way, and where agreements are made based on understanding and, therefore, there is no intention of using the other to reach one's own purposes" (Teixeira, 2008, p. 86).

Later, Teixeira et al. (2014), based on empirical research and for the purpose of studying the DO, propose ranking stakeholders in two groups: (a) stakeholders that directly influence the organization, with whom the organization establishes formal relationships, such as employees, customers, and vendors; (b) stakeholders that indirectly influence the organization, and with whom the organization establishes non-formal relationships.

One issue that Margolis (1997) failed in solving was that related to the DO designation. DO implies assigning dignity to organizations, while dignity is traditionally assigned to individuals. Teixeira et al. (2014) resorted to King and Whetten (2010) to advocate for the term DO. They argue that, in order to be considered a social player, an entity must receive attributions from other social players and must be acknowledged as capable of legally responding for its actions. These conditions are met by organizations when stakeholders perceive them as having the ability to act, and taking on legal liability.

The advocacy for the expanded concept of DO gave rise to works devoted to studying the dignity of organizations: Louback (2012), Araujo (2013), Malini (2014), Medeiros and Teixeira (2011), Mott (2015).

Based on literature and empirical data, Teixeira and Bilsky (2015) proposed a Theory of Organizational Dignity that involved four elements: cultural elements; focal orientation of cultural elements; ethical orientation; and organizational dignity standards.

According to Teixeira and Bilsky (2015), DO is embedded in the practices and values shared in the organization and is experienced by stakeholders when they interact with the organization. In this sense, the DO can be considered as a type of culture. Therefore, the organizations' practices and values would be oriented by dignity. These values and practices could be primarily oriented to the company's interests (personal focus), or to meet the stakeholders' interests (social focus). The authors claim that organizations could be understood as social players and, as such, capable of action and intention. Therefore, the DO necessarily has an ethical element, and its practices can be oriented by deontological or utilitarian ethics.

Teixeira and Bilsky (2015) propose three standards for the DO: pragmatic, moral, and legal. These three standards are rooted in the western history. Distinction-based dignity (pragmatic) dates back to the Ancient History, in Greece and in the Roman Empire, where one of the versions of dignity concerned the social status held. This dignity standard changed over time (Sarlet, 2010) and still exists in the contemporary societies (Tadd et al., 2010). Moral dignity refers to the commitment to moral action, and to not causing damages to the other (Tadd et al., 2010), while legal dignity concerns the human rights. These elements are present in the concept of DO:

Organizational dignity is the dignity of an organization and is reflected in the organization's values and practices oriented to the stakeholders' interests. They are justified by the deontological or teleological ethics, being assessed by stakeholders in terms of moral, legal, or pragmatic standards (Teixeira & Bilsky, 2015).

It is worth noticing that the concept proposed by Teixeira and Bilsky (2015) is a descriptive rather than a prescriptive concept. It allows reviewing the stages of the DO in a given organization, ranging from low level to high level of practice of dignity. The organizations whose values and practices are oriented to stakeholders' interests, justified by a deontological ethics, and valued by stakeholders in moral terms, are inserted in the highest level.

The first question posed by the concept proposed by Teixeira and Bilsky (2015) regards the interface between organizational dignity and ethics. Teixeira (2016) argues that ethics and DO should not be confused, since ethics deals with the reasons of intentions, while the DO deals with the consequences of the actions on the organizations and the stakeholders. Literature does not make clear what business ethic is about. The term seems to be interchangeable with corporate social responsibility (CSR) (Ferrell et al., 2000).

At least four strands approach ethics and/or corporate responsibility: (a) ethics in the business world is the exercise of social responsibility; (b) social responsibility deals with the impact of business activities on the society, and ethics deals with the impact of those activities on the internal audience; (c) non-existence of connection between ethics and social responsibility; (d) social responsibility has several dimensions, and ethics is one of them (Fisher, 2004). One example of the last one is the traditional proposal by Carroll (1979) that splits corporate social responsibility (CSR) into four categories: economic, legal, ethical, and discretionary. Economic responsibility concerns the corporation's obligation toward sustaining the economic growth, and meeting the needs of consumption. Legal responsibility refers to the obligation of running the business in compliance with legal requirements. Ethical responsibility refers to the commitment toward the society's moral rules to be respected when doing business. The discretionary responsibility, in turn, concerns deliberate actions that promote the employees' well-being, and help the disadvantaged ones. When reviewing the literature on business ethics, Tseng et al. (2010) identified three sets of articles: (a) approaching ethics in decision-making; (b) corporate governance, and the company's performance; and (c) ethical principles and codes of conduct.

The overlapping of ethics and CSR, and the conceptual inaccuracy, mainly of the last, were confirmed by Freeman et al. (2010) when they affirmed that, even after more than half century of studies, no CSR concept is largely accepted. O'berseder et al. (2014) turns to Dahlsrud (2008), Matten and Moon (2008) to affirm the existence of more than 35 different concepts for corporate social responsibility. In brief, we could say that business ethics and corporate social responsibility (CSR) are not clearly defined.

If on the one hand, the concept of ethics and corporate social responsibility (CST) seems quite obscure in literature, on the other hand the scale of organizational dignity practices developed by Teixeira et al., (2011), and further refined (Teixeira et al., 2014) presents one factor named social responsibility among its five factors, comprising: "Put charity actions into practice"; "Invest in the environment"; "Comply with obligations before the society"; "Offer products and services helpful to the environment" (Teixeira, et al., 2014, p. 9).

The conceptual inaccuracy of CST, added to the partial overlapping with the concept of business ethics and DO, justifies investigating the relationship between these concepts.

2.3 The Relationship Between Business Ethics and Corporate Social Responsibility

To review the relationship between business ethics and corporate social responsibility, the electronic corporate ethical values (CEV) scale, developed by Hunt et al. (1989), and the consumer perception of corporate social responsibility (CPCSR) scale, developed by O'berseder et al. (2014), were applied to a convenience sampling made up by 140 unspecified employees from different segments, Brazilian geographic regions, and hierarchical levels. Of the employees, 55% were women younger than 40 years (79%), with high school diploma (53%), holding non-managerial offices (82%), working for up to five years (61%) for big-size (74%) private corporations (82%).

The CEV scale was elected because it is a scale of organizational values aimed to measure the ethical culture of organizations, free of the social responsibility bias. The CEV scale measures to what extent organizations act in an ethical way and prioritize interests on ethical issues over the concerns related to products and services alone. It also incorporates the system of award to ethical behaviors and punishment to non-ethical behaviors (Hunt et al., 1989). It is a one-dimensional scale, with good level of reliability (Cronbach's alpha = 0.78), explaining 43% of the variance (Hunt et al., 1989). In other studies, however, it is considered a two-dimensional scale (Singhapakdi et al., 2008; Obalola et al., 2012). In this study in the Brazilian context, the scale proved to be one-dimensional after the review of the main components, supporting the finding by Hunt et al. (1989).

The consumer perception of corporate social responsibility (CPCSR) scale developed by O'berseder et al. (2014) proved to be suitable to the assessment of employees. That is so because the content and wording of the items are not consumer-specific, being applicable to any stakeholder, and because when it assesses the corporation, it considers the practices oriented to the remaining stakeholders. A third reason to pick this scale was because it does not consider the traditional dimensions proposed by Carroll (1979), where ethics is one of the dimensions of corporate social responsibility. And a fourth reason: organization is considered as a social player capable of action. Another reason for selecting this scale is based on the concept of CSR proposed by O'berseder et al. (2014), according to which "the corporation social responsibility integrates social and environmental topics into the business activities and acts with responsibility regarding employees, customers, the environment, vendors, the local community, its shareholders, and the society at large" (p. 103). Lastly, the author's suggestion of applying the scale in other countries and with other stakeholders, such as employees, also supports the selection.

The analysis of the relationship between business ethics and CSR considers the first as antecedent of the last, and data were processed through the PLS-PM. The PLS-PM measurement model implies assessing the construct validity, through the assessment of convergent validity and discriminant validity. The convergent validity is assessed through the explained mean–variance (EMV) that must be equal to or higher than 0.5 (Fornell & Larcker, 1981); compound reliability equal to or higher than 0.7 (Bido, 2012); and *t* value for each indicator and related latent variable at a minimum level of 0.5 (Gefen & Straub, 2005). The discriminant validity, in turn, is assessed by means of the analysis of each item' load, which must be higher in the latent variable to which it belongs, and lower in the other variables. Gefen and Straub (2005) mention, for illustration purposes, that if the load of an item is 0.7 in the expected variable, it should be no more than 0.6 in the remaining variables. Another analysis is through the VME square root for each LV, which must be higher than the correlation between the LVs (Chin, 1998). Gefen and Straub (2005) refer to the non-existence of a standard to be followed regarding the amplitude of this difference. Both the CEV and the CPCSR scales present convergent validity and discriminant validity.

The result of the sampling data processing pointed out that business ethics, measured by the CEV, explained 31.6% of the variance of social responsibility and, therefore, these constructs are not interchangeable.

2.4 The Relationship Between Business Ethics and Organizational Dignity

For the analysis of the relationship between organizational dignity and business ethics, data from 214 administrative employees of an educational institution were collected by electronic distribution of a questionnaire made up by the CVS scale developed and validated by Hunt et al. (1989), and by the DO practices scale, the *Escala de Práticas de Dignidade Organizacional*—EPRA-DO Teixeira et al. (2014). The sampling was made up by 52% of male individuals, mostly aged from 31 to 50 years (56%), with graduation degree (89%), mainly holding non-managerial positions (52%) at private corporations (80%).

The EPRA-DO scale was applied in the format shown in Teixeira et al. (2014). This scale comprises 24 items pooled in five factors:

F1—Practices of Promotion of Employees: gathers managerial practices oriented to the valuation, development, and promotion of the employee;

F2—Practices of Social Responsibility: practices of care with environment, and with minorities less protected in social terms;

F3—Practices of Respect to the Rights of Employees: practices that guide the protection of the employees' legal rights;

F4—Practices of Offer of Quality Products and Services: practices referring to the respect for consumers and customers;

F5—Non-misleading Practices (Transparency): practices that promote transparent relationship with the many stakeholders.

As can be observed from the scale factors, when the employees assess the DO of the organization to which they work, they assess not only the practices oriented to them, but also those practices oriented to customers, and transparent relationships with several stakeholders. In a study carried out by Teixeira et al. (2014) with 2509 employees, the factors reported Cronbach's Alphas higher than 0.7, the desirable index to assess the reliability of a pool of items (Hair et al., 2005), and explained 58.66% of the variance.

The analysis of the relationship between business ethics and DO considers the first as antecedent of the last, and data were processed through the PLS-PM. The PLS-PM measurement model implies assessing the construct validity, through the assessment of convergent and discriminant validity. To this sampling, the CVS and EPRA-DO scales reported convergent validity and discriminant validity.

The data processing result showed that business ethics presented a predictive power of 28.1% in relation to the DO. It is worth noticing that business ethics has stronger power of explanation in relation to the CSR (31.6%) than in relation to DO (28.1%).

2.5 The Relationship Between Corporate Social Responsibility and Organizational Dignity

Since social responsibility is one of the factors of organizational dignity, i.e., when stakeholders assess the dignity of an organization they consider the social responsibility, but organizational dignity comprises the relationships of dignity with other stakeholders in addition to society. In this study, the corporate social responsibility was elected as an antecedent of DO.

For this analysis, the CPCSR and the EPRA-DO scales were applied to both samplings that participated in the previous studies. Data were processed with PLS-PM. The convergent validity of the CPCSR scale was tested in the second sampling, and the same validities were tested to the EPRA-DO scale. Both scales got satisfactory results.

The results indicate that in the first sampling, the CSR explained 52% of DO, while in the second sampling, explanation was 57%. In both samplings, the power of explanation of the CSR in relation to DO exceeded 50%. The comparison of the results of the explanation (predictive) power of business ethics and CSR in relation to DO showed that in both samplings, the CSR predictive power in relation to DO is higher than that of business ethics. This result can be potentially explained by the fact that CSR practices are better known to employees than the ethical values that are more abstract.

2.6 The Relationship Between Organizational Dignity, Business Ethics, and Corporate Social Responsibility

Previous results point out significant relationships between three variables (CSR, business ethics, and DO) reviewed two by two, it indicates the usefulness of testing the relationship between the three variables. Since values stand for a more abstract variable than the CSR practices and also concern the way organizations are run, the relationship between CSR and DO mediated by ethical values was selected to be tested. To perform the mediation test, the structural coefficients were calculated using the PLS-PM, and the VAF formula was applied, as recommended by Hair et al. (2005). A VAF result lower than 20% signalizes the absence of mediation. A result ranging from 20 to 80% is a sign of partial mediation, and above 80% indicates full mediation.

VAF Formula

$$\text{VAF} = \frac{\beta 12.\beta 13}{(\beta 12.\beta 23) + \beta 13}$$

where:

- $\beta 12$: The effect of the relationship between the antecedent variable (CSR) and the mediator variable (ethical values);
- $\beta 13$: The effect of the relationship between the antecedent variable (CSR) and the final variable DO;
- $\beta 23$: The effect of the relationship between the mediator variable (ethical values) and the final variable (DO);

Data processing resulted in the following structural coefficients: $\beta 12 = 0.563$; $\beta 13 = 0.676$; and $\beta 23 = 0.140$. When the formula is applied, it results in a 24% mediation, corresponding to a partial mediator effect (Hair et al., 2005).

The research results suggest that business ethics and CSR are not interchangeable constructs, neither is the DO. This means to say that corporations that have high levels of ethical values intertwining business, and put the CSR into practice, are not necessarily considered worthy, but just partially worthy.

2.7 Implications for Management

Considering the social pressure on companies to avoid profits at any price, (Carroll & Buchholtz, 2009) managers have sought alternatives to add social value to their businesses. One of these alternatives is to incorporate social responsibility practices into the business practice, and another is to promote ethics in the relationship with stakeholders (Freeman et al., 2010). Simultaneously, there is the debate about dignity in organizations, notably workers' dignity (Mattson & Clark, 2011). More recently, we find the scope of dignity of companies in the relationship with stakeholders (Teixeira & Bilsky, 2015; Teixeira, 2016), and to the B2B relationship (Aguado et al., 2017). However, a question posed to the corporate practice is why to have an additional concept? How should it be used? What is the advantage?

In this chapter, we analyzed the relationship between CSR, ethical values, and DO, to learn if the three constructs were equivalent. Results pointed out they are not equivalent. The research participants tended to relate ethical values to DO more weakly than ethical values and CSR. Practicing CSR is half-way for stakeholders to perceive the company as worthy, since it explains more than 50% of the DO, more than the ethical values perceived in business management. This result, however, does not allow managers to move business ethics to the back burner, not only because it affects the company's dignity perceived by stakeholders, but because there is no reason for an action that is not guided by ethics.

However, resuming the issue, why should dignity be practiced in the business scope? Practicing CSR and business ethics would not be enough? The answer is "no"! A review of the literature about dignity shows a core element in that concept, which is translated into autonomy. We could say the dignity of a relationship is affected when a party inhibits the other's autonomy of action in relation to something valuable that affects the other's identity or self-respect. This core element is shown in Chapter 11 about the relationship of dignity with a call center company's customer. The affected dignity may lead to the rupture of the relationship with the company, and the consequent loss of customers. Chapter 14, that discusses dignity in the B2B relationship, shows that a consequence of not respecting the partner manager's autonomy is an increase in the operational costs of the business that had its dignity affected.

Considering dignity in the relationship with stakeholders is a factor that increases the business competitiveness.

2.8 Final Remarks

The results found in previous studies (Teixeira et al., 2014; Teixeira & Bilsky, 2015) were the driving reason for this study. Those studies, aimed at developing a Theory of Organizational Dignity. The theory development left two unanswered questions: if the construct of DO, CSR, and CVS (business ethics) were overlapping, and if a new construct like the DO was really needed and for what.

The studies results presented in this chapter demonstrated that, respecting the limits of the samplings, the three concepts are not interchangeable, i.e., DO practices cannot be replaced by CSR practices, or CVS-oriented operations. CSR and CVS make the DO but are far from exhausting it. DO goes much farther. It implies respect to the dignity of all stakeholders, mainly respect to their autonomy of acting on what they consider valuable to their identities and self-respect.

Although other chapters show that violation of dignity practices can affect the operational costs and retention of customers, worthy relationships between organizations and stakeholders should exist regardless the business results. Therefore, dignity in relationships should be preserved no matter the impact on businesses.

References

Agassi, J. B. (1986). Dignity in the workplace can work be dealienated ? *Journal of Business Ethics, 5,* 271–284.

Aguado, R., Retolaza, J. L., & Alcañiz, L. (2017). Dignity at the level of the Firm: Beyond the stakeholder approach. In M. Kostera & M. Pirson (Eds.), *Dignity and the organization* (Humanism in Business Series). London: Palgrave Macmillan. https://doi.org/10.1057/978-1-137-55562-5_9

Auerbach, J. (1998). Organized labor: Toward a new dignity in the workplace. *Journal of Career Development, 15*(01).

Araújo, B. F. B. A (2013). Construção dos Significados de Dignidade no âmbito da relação entre Empresas e Comunidade. In: *XXXVII ENANPAD.* Rio de Janeiro.

Barbee, G. E. L. (2001). Downsizing with dignity: Easing the pain of employee layoffs. *Business and Society Review.*

Berg, P., & Frost, A. (2005). Dignity at work for low wage, low skill service workers. *Industrial Relations, 60*(04).

Bido, D. S.(2012). Modelagem de Equações estruturais com estimação PLS. *ANPAD.*

Brodie, D. (2004). Protecting dignity in the workplace: The vitality of mutual trust and confidence. *Industrial Law Journal, 33,* 349–354.

Carroll, A. (1979). Three-dimensional conceptual model of corporate social performance. *Academy of Management Review, 4,* 497–505.

Carroll, A. B., & Buchholtz, A. K. (2009). *Business and society: Ethics and stakeholder management*, 7th edn. Mason, OH: SouthWestern Cengage Learning.

Chin, W. W. (1998). The partial least squares approach for structural equation modeling. In G. A. Marcoulides (Ed.), *Modern methods for business research* (pp. 295–236). London: Lawrence Erlbaum Associates.

Dahlsrud, A. (2008). How corporate social responsibility is defined: An analysis of 37 definitions. *Corporate Social Responsibility and Environmental Management, 15,* 1–13.

Ferrell, O. C., Fraedrich, J., & Ferrell, L. (2000). *Business ethics: Ethical decision making and cases* (4th ed.). Boston: Houghton Mifflin.

Fisher, A. (2004). *The logic of real arguments.* Cambridge: Cambridge University Press.

Fornell, C., & Larckel, D. F. (1981). Evaluating structural equation models with unobservable variables and measurement error. *Journal of Marketing Research, 18*(1), 39–50.

Freeman, R. E., Harrison, J. S., Wicks, A. C., Parmar, B., & Colle, S. (2010). *Stakeholder theory.* The state of the art. Cambridge: Cambridge University Press.

Ghai, D. (2003). Decent work: Concept and indicators. *International Labour Review, 142*(02), 113–145.

Gefen, D., & Straub, D. (2005). *A practical guide to factorial validity using PLS-graph: Tutorial and annotated example.* Communications of the Association for Information Systems, Vol. 16.

Greenspan, D. S. (2002). *Downsizing with dignity.* Wiley InterScience.

Hair, J. F., Tatham, R. L., Anderson, R. E., & Black, W. C. (2005). *Análise multivariada de dados. Translated into Portuguese by Adonai Schlup Sant'Anna;Anselmo Chaves Neto Anselmo Chaves Neto* (5th ed.). Porto Alegre: Bookman.

Hunt, S. D., Wood, V. R., & Chonkp, L. B. (1989). Corporate ethical values and organizational commitment in marketing. *Journal of Marketing, 53,* 79–90.

Hodson, R., & Roscigno, V. J. (2004). Organizational success and worker dignity: Complementary or contradictory? *The American Journal of Sociology, 110*(3), 672–708.

King, B. G., & Whetten, D. A. (2010). Finding the organization in organizational theory: A meta—Theory of the organization as a social actor. *Organization Science, 21*(1), 290–305.

Louback, J. C. (2012). *Dignidade e Relações de Poder: Um estudo em um call center à luz de Foucault.* Tese (Doutorado em Administração de Empresas): Universidade Presbiteriana Mackenzie. São Paulo.

Malini, E. (2014). Cultura Organizacional e Práticas de Dignidade Organizacional: Uma análise por meio de Equação Estrutural. In *XXXVIII ENANPAD.*

Mattson, J. D., & Clark, S. (2011). Human dignity in concept and practice. *Policy Sciences, 44,* 303–319.

Matten, D., & Moon, J. (2008). Implicit" and "Explicit" CSR: A conceptual framework for a comparative understanding of corporate social responsibility. *Academy of Management Review, 33*(2).

Margolis, J. D. (1997). *Dignity in the balance: Philosophical and practical dimensions of promoting ethics in organizations* [Doctoral dissertation]. Cambridge: Harvard University.

Medeiros, A. L., & Teixeira, M. L. M. (2011). Emancipação e Dignidade nas Práticas de Gestão em Universidades brasileiras: uma reflexão à luz de Boaventura Santos. In *ENGPR,* João Pessoa.

Mott, M. M. (2015). *Caminhos da adaptação intercultural na expatriação: uma cartografia simbólica da dignidade de latino-americanos no Brasil.* Tese (Doutorado em Administração de Empresas). Universidade Presbiteriana Mackenzie, SP.

Obalola, M., Yaba, A, Aduloju, K., Akoka, Y. & Olowokudejo, F. (2012). Organizational commitment and corporate ethical values: Exploring the Nexus between employees' psychological contract and firms' ethical behaviour in the Nigerian insurance industry. *Journal of Management and Sustainability, 2*(1).

O"Berseder, M. et al. (2014). Consumers' perceptions of corporate social responsibility: Scale development and validation. *Journal of Business Ethics, 124*(1), 101–115.

Sarlet, I. (2010). *Dignidade da Pessoa Humana e Direitos Fundamentais na Constituição Federal* (8a ed.). Porto Alegre: livraria do advogado.

Singhapakdi, A., Gopinath, M., Marta, J., & Carter, L. L. (2008). Antecedents and Consequences of Perceived Importance of Ethics in Marketing Situations: A Study of Thai Business People. *Journal of Business Ethics, 81,* 887–904.

Tadd, W., Vanlaere, L., & Gastmans, C. (2010). Clarifying the concept of human dignity in the care of the elderly: A dialogue between empirical and Philosophical Approaches. *Ethical Perspectives, 17*(1), 253–281.

Teixeira, M. L. M. (2008). Dignidade Organizacional: valores e relações com *stakeholders.* In: *Valores Humanos e Gestão: novas perspectivas.* Sao Paulo: SENAC.

Teixeira, M. L. M., Domenico, S. M. R., & Dias, S. M. R. C. (2011) Proposta e validação de um modelo de Dignidade Organizacioanal. *Relatório parcial de pesquisa (Tech. Rep.).* Mackenzie Presbyterian University.

Teixeira, M. L. M., Domenico, S. M. R., Dias, S. M. R. C., & Mendes, L. H. L. (2014). Práticas de Dignidade Organizacional Percebidas por Trabalhadores na Relação entre Organizações e Stakeholders. *XXXVIII ENANPAD,* Rio de Janeiro/RJ.

Teixeira, M. L. M., & Bilsky, W. (2015). *Faceting organizational theory.* In 15th Facet theory conference. New York.

Teixeira, M. L. M. (2016). Organizational dignity: A proposal. In Seminários em Administração – SEMEAD, São Paulo, SP, Brazil, 19.

Tseng, H.-C., Chou, L.-Y., & Yu, K.-H. (2010). Current research paradigms in expatriate(s) research: A bibliometric approach. *The International Journal of Organizational Innovation,* n. 2, *3,* 19–44.

Zeytinoglu, I. U., Lillevik, W., Seaton, M. B., & Moruz, J. (2004). Part-time and casual work in retail trade-stress and other factors affecting the workplace. *Relations Industrielles/ Industrial Relations, 59*(3), 516–544.

Chapter 3
Organizational Dignity in the Light of Boaventura Souza Santos Thoughts

Ana Lúcia de Medeiros

Abstract The objective of this work is to study the organizational dignity from the theoretical perspective of Boaventura Sousa Santos. The chapter brings up the debate on this construct from a mixed epistemology that is situated on the frontiers of modern thought. The discussion starts from the idea that organizations are spaces of production that have a power structure, which manifests itself in the form of the exploitation of labor by capital, which is supported by the law of production and by scientific knowledge that guides towards productivism and for the management culture that as a rule produces absences of dignity in organizations. The production space is the locus where social interactions take place with absences and/or presences of dignity and which can be determined by the lack of recognition of the different knowledge and rights of workers.

Keywords Organizational dignity · Absences · Presences

3.1 Introduction

With regard to the concept of the word dignity, we may say that it is quite controversial. Generally, it is assumed that it concerns the human condition, thus maintaining a close relationship with the complex and unpredictable manifestations of human personality (Kim & Cohen, 2010). According to Bolton (2007), there are two conceptions of dignity, one based on external characteristics, which involve the human being, such as the social proposition, hierarchy, family inheritance; and the other, in which dignity appears as attributed and inherent to the human species and, therefore, is universal.

Still according to Brennan and Lo (2007), human dignity in classical antiquity was determined by the external attributes of the individual, thus those occupying a prominent position in society being more dignified In the following historical period, when the Christian faith prevailed, the construction of an understanding of

A. L. de Medeiros (✉)
Palmas, Brazil
e-mail: analucia@mail.uft.edu.br

M. L. Mendes Teixeira and L. M. B. de Oliveira (eds.), *Organizational Dignity and Evidence-Based Management*, https://doi.org/10.1007/978-3-030-68560-7_3

human dignity concept was based on the valorization of man insofar as the salvation promised by the Christian doctrine could be obtained by everybody (Rosen, 2012).

It can be said that man's distinction and, in turn, what accredited him to be perceived in his human dignity, was associated with the assumption that man was made *Imago Dei* and, therefore, should be worthy (Puffer, 2017). In the Renaissance period, the central question for those days' thinkers was to find ways to synthesize the relationship between faith and reason. We understand that the need to perform such synthesis was connected with people's distinction and social classification (Puffer, 2017).

According to Bayefsky (2013), the concept of human dignity, on the threshold of modernity, began to acquire an updated profile and gradually abandoning the notion of dignity dependent on ecclesiastical issues, as it occurred in the Middle Ages. It is reasonable to say, then, that, in the light of the Renaissance thinking, persons' worth should be measured by their ability to develop the virtues of their human condition (Bolton, 2007).

The concept of dignity, as a distinction, originates in antiquity as something inherent to human beings, and has assumed different meanings over time (Bayefsky, 2013). In the Middle Ages, because man was conceived as the image of God, he was worthy and, later, in the Enlightenment, particularly with Kant, as inherent to the human being but only because the human being is endowed with reason and is capable of moral choices (Kant, 2008). This conception of dignity, as a moral foundation, is inherently linked to the human person and is the source and reason for human rights in the universalist conception (Rosen, 2012).

Although human dignity is associated with moral and universal law, it has been and is currently violated by belligerent actions that slaughter innocent people. Such acts are conceived by Heads of State who wish to build power to achieve control over a territory or nation, and the Second World War can be marked as the classic example of this question, and it was only after that event that the State took responsibility for ensuring the protection of human dignity through the Universal Declaration of Human Rights (Beitz, 2013; Habermas, 2012).

In the preamble of this work it is stated that the recognition of dignity is inherent to all members of the human family, and that their rights, equal and inalienable, constitute the foundation of freedom, justice and peace in the world. Article 1 of the Universal Declaration of Human Rights (1948), states that "all human beings are born free and equal in dignity and rights. They are endowed with reason and conscience and should act towards one another in a spirit of brotherhood" (Beitz, 2013).

The thought of sociologist Boaventura Sousa Santos gained notoriety in much of the world for presenting a proposal aimed at a new understanding of social reality. Over the past few years, the author has dedicated himself to the development a set of epistemologies that constitute the emerging paradigm that fits, not as an opposition to the dominant and hegemonic, but that indicates that it is possible to think the world from a *mestizo* epistemology within the boundaries in which modern thought is situated. The objective of this work is to study organizational dignity from the theoretical perspective of Boaventura Sousa Santos.

The discussion in this chapter is grounded on the idea that organizations are productive spaces that have a power structure, which manifests itself in the form of the exploitation of labor by capital, which is supported by production right and scientific knowledge that guides towards productivism and to management culture.

Thus, it is understood that the production space is the *locus* where social interactions take place with absence and/or presence of dignity and that can be determined by the lack of recognition of different knowledge and rights. There is a need for a debate about the construction of a paradigm grounded on multiculturalism and counter-hegemony that serves as a guideline of social and managerial practices. This chapter aims to review what the thoughts of Boaventura Sousa Santos can add to the debate about organizational dignity.

3.2 Dignity in Organizations

Studies on human dignity have been gaining space in the field of Social Sciences, and, especially, among those who investigate organization-oriented subjects and also investigators from different areas of knowledge who discuss relationships in the workplace where it is understood that dignity of the worker is an end in itself (Lucas, 2015).

The economic, social, behavioral and political dynamics unfold in the global space that demands an increasingly higher level of competitiveness and efficiency by the market and organizations, from the perspective of business and economy. Driven by the price mechanisms and management practices that seek to ensure the permanence of organizations in the competitive space guided by productivism and the free interplay of the market forces, rights are relativized and the logic of competition and competitiveness determines what to produce, and how to produce, without the guarantee of promoting workers' well being and not considering them as a social and interactive being, but as a commodity that can be exchanged (Doherty, 2011; Crowley, 2012; Lucas, 2015; Zawadzki, 2018; Melé, 2014; Friedman et al., 2015).

The development of capitalism changes the structure and human relations, and the interactions among workers are carried out as if they were inside the "satanic mill", which represents the synthesis of social displacement caused by market mentality (Wreen, 2018). It is in this sphere that moral harassment and the denial of workers' rights in organizations occur (Friedman et al., 2015; Healy & Milkwoska, 2017) and the violation of organizational dignity and in the workplace (Lucas, 2015; Hodson, 2001; Hodson & Roscigno, 2004).

When subjugated by the managerial gears of the organizations, workers lose the space for dialogue and the ability to mobilize and fight against actions that violate their dignity in the work environment (Melé, 2014). Workers' discussions around working conditions are associated not only to obtaining better wages and job security, but also to recognition and respect, so that moral harassment, poor management, lack of autonomy, non-recognition of knowledge and persecution are factors that condition the presence of dignity in the organization (Sayer & Botton, 2007).

Dignity at work requires not only the absence of moral harassment and persecution, but respect for the worker and his autonomy and, in addition, it is desired that the worker be treated as an end in itself (Sayer, 2007). To be worthy, or to be treated with dignity, the individual must be in self-control and guided by values related to moral and ethics, considering that dignity is also associated with autonomy and self-command. Respect not only what there is in common, but, mainly, recognize the differences, because dignity concerns not only the behavior of workers in the workplace, but how they are treated in their daily life and how they are perceived by colleagues and by those in the highest management positions. It is true that work relations, especially vertical ones, are generally not harmonious, but conflicting and disrespectful, which demands from organizations a section that is in charge of creating playful and pleasant spaces within corporations (Sayer & Botton, 2007).

The study by Lucas (2015), which was performed with employees of different cultures working for different American companies, showed that labor relations in the workplace produce violations and denials of the worker's dignity.

Considering the vast literature (Hodson, 2001; Hodson & Roscigno, 2004; Sayer & Botton, 2007; Lucas, 2011, 2015; Melé, 2014; Thomas & Lucas, 2019; Healy & Wilkowska, 2017) already available about workers' dignity, in the workplace and in the organizations, the term dignity has already been the object of research, especially considering that in the production domain, it is observed that the interactions experienced there cause absences of dignity. The literature on the subject, produced in Brazil, addresses organizational dignity and inserts in the debate, as a core element, the dignity of expatriate workers, banking organizations, factories and companies from the most different fields, including the dignity of public and private universities' teachers.

Medeiros and Teixeira (2017) studied teachers' dignity in Brazilian universities from the theoretical perspective of the sociology of absences, of emergences and of the ecology of knowledge of the Portuguese philosopher Boaventura Sousa Santos. The authors assumed that the managerial practices established within these organizations revealed the production of dignity absences and presences, and that they are associated with the lack of recognition of different knowledge and rights.

In this connection, reviewing organizational dignity, in the light of Boaventura Sousa Santos concepts, is an exercise that makes us reflect on some sociological categories that are intrinsic in social practices, which are manifested in their relevant structural spaces, such as the acceptance of multiculturalism and ecologies as elements that should be catalysts of a political, economic and cultural paradigm. We would understand organizational dignity better if we understood it from a conception of the world that is: *mestizo*, multicultural, counter-hegemonic and based on ecologies. The term ecology is the practice of aggregating diversity by promoting sustainable interactions among partial and heterogeneous entities (Santos, 2010).

3.3 Spaces of Social Action: The Dignity *Topoi*

According to Lucas (2011), dignity, in the denotative sense, refers to a value inherent to the human being that must be present in the work environment. Baker and Lucas (2017) conducted a study with LGBT employees to identify whether the dignity of these workers was violated, and the data showed that LGBT employees felt indeed insecure and with threatened autonomy, requiring at all times the search for protection and for safer spaces in the workplace. Hence the need to find out under what conditions and why dignity is violated in the organizational spaces. The condition of being a worker and the position held in the hierarchy of a company's organizational architecture is what will determine whether or not your dignity will be violated. Does the condition of being a man, woman, homosexual, heterosexual, black, white, ignorant, educated, native or foreigner define the limit of organizational dignity?

Hicks (2016) shows that the violation of dignity does not happen only in the workplace, but in all spaces where there are people relating with each other. As a space for carrying out social practices, and where power relations stand out among those who are in charge and those who do, the workplace produces forms that violate people's dignity and, consequently, organizational dignity. Organizations seeking to maximize profits and to increase ever more their control over the market tend be places where dignity is degraded and violated (Pirson et al., 2015; Zawadzki, 2018).

In the wake of Hicks' (2016) thinking, issues associated with the violation of dignity are present in several spaces in which discussions on dignity and emancipation in the sense that will be given in this text, are suitable. There are many *topoi* where social practices occur with (in)dignity and emancip(action).

In this work, we bring up Boaventura Sousa Santos thoughts and we define that the presence or absence of dignity comes from respecting or not the differences that translate into: we have the right to be equal when our difference makes us inferior; and we have the right to be different when our equality de-characterizes us (Santos, 2009a, 2009b).

The term *topoi* comes from the diatopic hermeneutics There are finishes tough and arises from the idea that each region has the right to have its idiosyncrasies, and, as such, should be respected, having as reference the concept of multiculturalism. In this connection, *topoi* is understood as a common place and thus discussing the *topoi* of dignity is a way of saying that the spaces where there is no respect for differences bring together the conditions for violation, both of the acquired right and of that inherent to the human being (Santos, 2010).

The *topoi* of dignity gain meaning when the author demonstrates that the conception of the modern world and of the organizations have been guided by the scientific rigor of monoculture, linear time, social classification and productivism. This categorization allows us to understand that, in environments oriented by this way of world thinking, is conducive to the production of absences of dignity and emancipation that are forged in structural spaces, guided by three theoretical orientations: power, rights and knowledge (Santos, 2009a, 2009b).

In the structural spaces, six forms of power are also generated: in the home space, the form of power is patriarchy, in the production space, the form of power is exploitation, in the market space, the form of power is the commodity fetichism, in the community space, the form of power is the unequal differentiation between those who belong to the community and those who do not; in the citizenship space, the form of power is domination, and in the world space, the form of power is unequal exchange. (Santos, 2005a, 2005b, 2007, 2009a, 2009b).

In the production space, the institution dimension is represented by companies that are driven by the organization of production and work. Thus, it can be said, in the light of Boaventura Sousa Santos thoughts, that companies are units of social practices constituted by relations regulated by production right, where the predominant form of power is exploitation and the epistemological form is represented by the productivist conception, technologism, professional training and entrepreneurial culture (Santos, 2005a; 2009a).

With regard to the establishment of power in this space, Boaventura Santos thoughts stem from the premise that in any social relationship the exercise of power is reflected in the intensity with which the interested parties who share the same relationship are unequally treated, that is, the degree in which that specific group affects another in an inverse way to the interests of the latter (Santos, 2005a, 2009a).

Social and labor relations in capitalistic organizations obey a hierarchy that is delimited by the exploitation of labor, the right of production and the form of knowledge aimed at productive scientific management.

The form of power in these organizations is in charge of the exploitation of work, that of knowledge prioritizes hegemonic knowledge, present in modern science, which is the knowledge of scientific management that is based on laws, rules, clearly defined principles (Santos, 2009a, 2009b).

In the light of Boaventura Sousa Santos conception (2009a, 2009b), the form of the production right, in these spaces or organizations, establishes the regulations and normative standards that organize the daily relations of wage labor and its codes of conduct.

This is a right that can be imposed by the boss or the administration. When this right is unilateral, it is up to the workers to get organized to fight for guaranteeing their right and their dignity. According to Boaventura Sousa Santos (2009a, 2009b), the production right defines the routines within the company and the sanctions for their violation; it also exerts a tight and detailed control over the workers and managers' life during the working day and sometimes even beyond it.

Regulations on production are generally imposed on workers in this space, but they can affect their daily lives through restrictions on freedom of expression, in making political choices and in having greater public interactivity (Santos, 2009a, 2009b).

We can infer that organizations, when submitted to well-defined laws, rules and principles, which are presumptions of monocultural and hegemonic knowledge, can cause absence of dignity and emancipation in the same space where goods and services are produced.

It can be seen that these work and production spaces are isomorphic, since the standards and procedures adopted by companies are unified, both with regard to the epistemic form and to the law. In the organizations, knowledge and right employed in labor and production relations follow the universal and hegemonic conception.

3.4 Dignity as a Process of Emancipation and Recognition of Knowledge

Boaventura Sousa Santos thoughts are based on the assumptions of the emerging paradigm, which purpose is to understand the world on a counter-hegemonic conception, which is based on a set of epistemologies called ecologies of knowledge (Sousa Santos, 2007, 2009a, 2009b, 2010). In addition to ecologies, the sociologist uses the sociologies of absences and emergences and the translation work to give theoretical consistency to the support of ideas about the need for a new paradigm that is able to find alternatives for the design of a prudent science for a decent life and, especially, to criticize modern thinking, which is constituted by an indolent reason. In his terms: To combat the waste of social experience, it is not enough to propose another type of social science, but more than that, it is necessary to propose a different model of rationality (Sousa Santos, 2006).

It is in the light of this rationality that the thinking of Boaventura Sousa Santos will provide the basis for understanding the different conceptions of emancipation and dignity. This thinker's contribution to this theme is associated with the way he understands the world, from a counter-hegemonic and cosmopolitan perspective, from the principle of difference and equality. The recognition of the rights and knowledge of the community opens space for scientific knowledge, as well as the productivist logic, takes distance from knowledge monoculture and scientific rigor and capitalist productivism, respectively.

There are several themes associated to social and political issues analyzed by Boaventura Sousa Santos, considering that he believes in social transformation as a way to build a new social reality (Nunes, 2006; Sousa Santos, 2009a, 2009b). The thinker reviews the socio-political aspects of society and seeks to understand it in the light of the recognition of knowledge and the community rights.

According to Boaventura Sousa Santos (2010), the way in which human rights have changed, in the last two decades, in the language of progressive politics and almost synonymous with social emancipation causes some perplexity. The concept of human rights is grounded on a set of suppositions, all of which are typically Western, in which it is evidenced that universal human nature can be rationally known and that it is superior from that of other beings; individuals have an absolute and irreducible dignity and their autonomy require that society be organized in a non-hierarchical way, as the sum of free individuals (Santos, 2009a, 2009b).

The sociologist makes an extensive criticism of human rights conception from the perspective of the Western thoughts, especially because, in the author's understanding, it is not conceivable to treat different communities within a universalist perspective. Boaventura Sousa Santos (2009a, 2009b) understands that the main task of the emancipatory policy of our time is to transform the practice of human rights into a project in which the different knowledge and rights of social groups are recognized.

In his view, in order to understand the concept of human rights, in a perspective that goes against the Western thought, it is necessary to establish the premises for overcoming the debate on universalism and cultural relativism, that is, that all cultures have conceptions of human dignity, but that they do not conceive it in terms of human rights, and that all cultures are incomplete and problematic in their conceptions of human dignity, that no culture is monolithic.

All cultures have different versions of human dignity and, finally, all cultures tend to distribute people and social groups between two competitive principles of hierarchical belonging, and these premises are a starting point for an understanding of how Boaventura Sousa Santos conceives dignity. In stating that there are different conceptions of human dignity, that there is incompleteness of culture, that it is necessary to overcome the debate on universalism and that in some cultures dignity is not understood as an appendix to human rights, the author sheds light on a new conception of dignity and emancipation facing the universal conception.

The critic conceives emancipation and human dignity from the perspective of ecologies, of the recognition of knowledge and of rights from the perspective of multiculturalism. We can infer that he defends the need to establish an intercultural dialogue on human dignity and that, from there, a mixed (*mestizo*) understanding of human rights ensues (Sousa Santos, 2009a, 2009b). In this line of thought, for a new emancipation conception, the creation of new political common sense is required to be anchored to the pillar of solidarity, to the principle of community, to the idea of autonomy and to the birth of a new citizenship. This, in turn, constitutes the vertical obligation among citizens and the State, as well as the political obligation among citizens (Sousa Santos, 2005a, 2007). It can be seen that the author understands that there is a need to establish a high-intensity democratic culture.

Still following the footsteps of Boaventura Sousa Santos, this democratic process will only occur through its radicalization, which occurs through the replacement of power relations by shared authority relations. This, in turn, in order to materialize, ought to be supported by the principle of recognition of differences (Sousa Santos, 2006, 2007, 2010). We believe, however, that Boaventura Sousa Santos thoughts indicate an aspiration to a new process of social organization and to a new model of collective coexistence, which may demand from individuals new alternatives for living, as well as for the organization of work, of production and of doing science (Sousa Santos, 2007).

It can be inferred that this new social reality should be based on the principle of emancipation and the dignity of the community. To discuss issues such as emancipation and dignity, in the light of the modernity paradigm, is to address the issue in an incomplete way, because this singularizes and universalizes the debate. We understand that the concept of emancipation and dignity, for example, should be translated into the different cultures; further, when Boaventura Sousa Santos discusses the concept of human rights, he disagrees that it should be universalized (Sousa Santos, 2010).

Northern epistemology corresponds to the hegemonic thinking that was responsible, not only to support the scientific-cultural paradigm, but also to impose economic domination over most countries, especially those located in the southern hemisphere of the continent. This phenomenon can be called globalization, which, according to Boaventura Sousa Santos (2010), is the process by which a given condition or local entity extends its influence to the entire globe and, in doing so, develops the ability to designate another social condition or rival entity as local.

Considering the concept of globalization, Boaventura Sousa Santos (2005b, 2010) says that human rights will tend to operate as a form of hegemonic globalization, and such is true that four international human rights regimes are considered worldwide: the European, the Inter-American, the African and the Asian (Sousa Santos, 2010). Thus, it is understood, in the light of the author's concepts, that if a society wishes to develop an emancipatory human rights policy, it will have to make a counter-hegemonic movement. However, this movement will only be considered when all nations understand that knowledge is not universal and complete.

In addition, it will be necessary for everyone to learn to respect and recognize the different knowledge, the different cultures, both in the North and in the South, since as the debate triggered by human rights evolves into a global dialogue between different cultures on the principles of human dignity, it is imperative that such competition leads to the formation of wordwide coalitions that struggle for maximum values or demands, and not for minimum values or demands (Sousa Santos, 2010).

Another point to be discussed, about human dignity from the perspective of Boaventura Sousa Santos (2010), is that all cultures have conceptions of human dignity, but not all of them have conceptions in terms of human rights. This issue enhances the idea that human rights cannot be treated in an isomorphic way, nor can dignity. Bearing in mind that cultures are incomplete, one can deduce that human dignity should be understood according to how each culture perceives it.

According to Boaventura Sousa Santos (2010), increasing awareness of cultural incompleteness is one of the tasks prior to the construction of an emancipatory and multicultural conception of human rights. Thus, one must realize that human rights are not to be understood as universal—hegemonic conception—, but in a perspective of cosmopolitanism.

We can say that this process represents the reverse of hegemonic globalization, given that, as stated by Boaventura Sousa Santos (2004), it is a very vast and heterogeneous set of initiatives, movements and organizations that share the struggle against exclusion and social discrimination. The Portuguese critical theorist follows the same line of thought of Habermas, when he advocates the idea that dignity as the foundation of right must be earned. While Habermas believes that the achievement comes from communicative action and in the democratic process, Boaventura Sousa Santos seeks to explain that this process should not be a struggle just for equality, but, above all, for the recognition of differences and knowledge and, to that effect, it is necessary to think about human rights in a multicultural perspective (Sousa Santos, 2010).

In extolling multiculturalism, we assume that there are different grammars and languages that are used to express different meanings. From the moment that society understands that differences must be recognized, it will be possible to talk about respect for dignity, since it is a *sine qua non* condition for achieving human emancipation (Sousa Santos, 2004). For these reasons, it seems correct to state, in the wake of the author's thoughts, that organizational dignity is a process of emancipation complying with the principles of equality and difference, the recognition of the different knowledge and rights that are projected in the production space [emphasis added by the author].

3.5 Implications for International Management

The industrial revolution was responsible for the growth of companies, and as a result, there was a need to create methods and management practices that could ensure the maintenance of the production of goods and, in addition, foster their growth. Thus, it can be said that the industrial revolution historically represents the beginning of the instrumentalized organization of an economic production system.

After a few centuries, today we live in a space represented by the world which is global and interconnected by knowledge and business networks. Companies, in order to meet global demand, have expanded their businesses to a good part of the world through the creation of their subsidiaries. Along with the transnationalization of business came the challenges associated with the countries' culture, management knowledge and management practices in a multicultural world with different knowledge and rights (Stahl et al., 2017).

In those companies, management positions are held by expatriates who take "**management practices and knowledge, imagined as being universal**" [emphasis added by the author] to a new reality and a new world. This is one of the difficulties of setting up a transnational plant in which the distance of the countries' culture can generate violence and / or violations of the workers' dignity in the production space as well as foster the implementation of management knowledge; however, the subsidiary presents loss of competitiveness vis-à-vis the parent company (Bebenroth & Froese, 2020).

Studies have revealed "agency" problems between subsidiary companies and parent companies because there are diverging interests among them, and as a rule, the principal (parent company) has no major concern understanding the agent (subsidiary), since expatriates or those who manage the subsidiaries have to face conflicts of interest, both internally and externally (Kostova et al., 2018; Pak et al., 2019). According to Schmitz et al. (2018) the cultural element exhibits a strong relationship with the management and performance of companies In his study, Schmitz et al. warn of organizational cynicism as a cultural element that manifests itself in different ways, such as in the expression of criticism, sarcastic humor and pessimistic predictions about the organization and the workers.

Studies show that the cultural dimension has an important role in the management of organizations, so it is necessary to observe the extent to which the expatriation process and international management models produce presence or absence of organizational dignity. Considering the concept of organizational dignity used in this work and understanding that management, as a social and knowledge practice is conceived as universal and hegemonic knowledge, it is understood that the recognition of different knowledge and cultures is a step that needs to be taken to improve the organizational environment and the management practices.

3.6 Final Remarks

What is reiterated here is that the thoughts of Boaventura Santos present theoretical assumptions capable of pointing out alternatives for the understanding of organizational dignity. As Santos presents a counter-hegemonic theoretical construction, this makes it even more necessary for analyzing organizational dignity, especially because, even today, the paradigms that seek to understand dignity were disseminated by natural thinkers from the nations that hold the hegemony of scientific thought and economic power.

The objective of this work is to study the organizational dignity from the theoretical perspective of Boaventura Sousa Santos and bring to light the conception that it is possible to foster worthy management practices based on the recognition of the knowledge and rights of those who constitute the organizations. What is advocated here is that the management and social practices based on the assumptions of the sociologies of absences and emergences and of the set of epistemologies of knowledge ecologies can contribute to the broadening of the dignity field of study, highlighting the need to bring to the debate a look beyond the dichotomies still used in studies on dignity in its broadest aspect.

References

Baker, S. J., & Lucas, K. (2017). Is it safe to bring myself to work? Understanding LGBTQ experiences of workplace dignity. *Canadian Journal of Administrative Sciences/Revue Canadienne Des Sciences De l'Administration, 34*(2), 133–148.

Bayefsky, R. (2013). Dignity, honour, and human rights: Kant's perspective. *Political Theory, 41*(6), 809–837.

Bebenroth, R., & Froese, F. J. (2020). Consequences of expatriate top manager replacement on foreign subsidiary performance. *Journal of International Management, 26*(2), 100730.

Beitz, C. R. (2013). Human dignity in the theory of human rights: Nothing but a phrase? *Philosophy & Public Affairs, 41*(3), 259–290.

Bolton, S. C. (2007). *Dimensions of dignity at work*. London: Elsevier.

Brennan, A., & Lo, Y. S. (2007). Two conceptions of dignity: Honour and self-determination. In *Perspectives on human dignity: A conversation* (pp. 43–58). Dordrecht: Springer (The US. Panoeconomicus, 2018).
Crowley, M. (2012). Control and dignity in professional, manual and service-sector employment. *Organization Studies, 33,* 1383–1406.
Dalles, R. C. (1977). A medieval view of human dignity. *Journal of the History of Ideas, 38*(4), 557–572.
Doherty, E. M. (2011). Joking aside, insights to employee dignity in 'Dilbert' cartoons: The value of comic art in understanding the employer–employee relationship. *Journal of Management Inquiry, 20,* 286–301.
Friedman, S., Rossi, D., & Ralón, G. (2015). Dignity denial and social conflicts. *Rethinking Marxism, 27*(1), 65–84.
Habermas, J. (2012). The concept of human dignity and the realistic utopia of human rights. In *Philosophical Dimensions of Human Rights* (pp. 63–79). Dordrecht: Springer.
Healy, M., & Wilkowska, I. (2017). Marx, alienation and the denial of dignity of work. In *Dignity and the organization* (pp. 99–124). London: Palgrave Macmillan.
Hicks, D. (2016). A culture of indignity and the failure of leadership. *Humanistic Management Journal, 1*(1), 113–126.
Hodson, R. (2001). *Dignity at work.* New York: Kindle First Edition.
Hodson, R., & Roscigno, V. J. (2004). Organizational success and worker dignity: Complementary or contradictory? *American Journal of Sociology, 110*(3), 672–708.
Kant, I. (2008). *A metafísica dos costumes* (2a ed.). São Paulo: Edipro.
Kim, Y. H., & Cohen, D. (2010). Information, perspective, and judgments about the self in face and dignity cultures. *Personality and Social Psychology Bulletin, 36,* 537–550.
Kostova, T., Nell, P. C., & Hoenen, A. K. (2018). Understanding agency problems in headquarters-subsidiary relationships in multinational corporations: A contextualized model. *Journal of Management, 44*(7), 2611–2637.
Lucas, K. (2011). Blue-collar discourses of workplace dignity: Using outgroup comparisons to constructo positive identities. *Management Communication Quarterly, 25,* 353–374.
Lucas, K. (2015). Workplace dignity: Communicating inherent, earned, and remediated dignity. *Journal of Management Studies, 52*(5), 621–646.
Medeiros, A. L., & Teixeira, M. L. M. (2017). Limites da dignidade de docentes nas práticas de gestão em universidades brasileiras. *Revista Gestão Universitária Na América Latina - GUAL, 10*(2), 134–154.
Melé, D. (2014). "Human Quality Treatment": Five organizational levels. *JournalofBusiness Ethics, 120*(4), 457–471.
Nunes, J. A. (2006). Um discurso sobre as Ciências 16 anos depois. In B. S. Santos. (Org.),*Conhecimento prudente para uma vida decente: "um discurso sobre as ciências revisitado* (pp. 59–84). 2 ed. São Paulo: Cortez
Pak, Y. S., Sun, Q., & Yang, Y. (2019). Influences of expatriate managerial styles on host-country nationals' turnover intention. *Asian Business & Management, 18*(4), 263–280.
Pirson, M., Dierksmeier, C., & Goodpaster, K. E. (2015). Human dignity and business. *Business Ethics Quarterly, 24*(3), 501–503.
Puffer, M. (2017). Human dignity after Augustine's Imago Dei: On the sources and Uses of two ethical terms. *Journal of the Society of Christian Ethics, 37*(1), 65–82.
Rosen, M. (2012). *Dignity: Its history and meaning.* US: Harvard University Press.
Sayer, A. (2007). Dignity at work: Broadening the agenda. *Organization, 14*(4), 565–658.
Schachter, O. (1983). Human dignity as a normative concept. *The American Journal of International Law, 77*(4), 848–854.
Schmitz, M. A., Froese, F. J., & Bader, A. K. (2018). Organizational cynicism in multinational corporations in China. *Asia Pacific Business Review, 24*(5), 620–637.
Sousa Santos, B. (Org). (2004). Reconhecer para libertar: os caminhos do cosmopolitismo multicultural. Porto: Edições afrontamento.

Sousa Santos, B. (2005a). *Pela mão de Alice: O social e o político na pós-modernidade (10aed).* São Paulo: Cortez.
Sousa Santos, B. (2005b). Os processos da globalização In_B. Sousa Santos (Org.) *Globalização: Fatalidade ou utopia?*(3aed). Porto – PT: edições afrontamento.
Sousa Santos, B. (2006). *Conhecimento prudente para uma vida decente: "um discurso sobre as ciências" revisitado* (2nd ed., p. 2006). São Paulo: Cortez.
Sousa Santos, B. (2007a). Para além do pensamento abissal: Das linhas globais a uma ecologia de saberes. *Revista Crítica De Ciências Sociais, 78,* 3–46.
Sousa Santos, B. (2007b). *Renovar a teoria crítica e reinventar a emancipação social.* São Paulo: Boitempo.
Sousa Santos, B. (2009a). *A crítica da razão indolente: contra o desperdício da experiência* (7a ed, Vol. 1). São Paulo: Cortez.
Sousa Santos, B. (2009b). *Um discurso sobre as ciências*(7aed). Porto – PT: Edições afrontamento.
Sousa Santos, B. (2010). *A gramática do tempo: uma nova cultura política* (3a ed., v. 4). São Paulo: Cortez.
Stahl, G. K., Miska, C., Lee, H. J., & De Luque, M. S. (2017). The upside of cultural differences. *Cross Cultural & Strategic Management, 24*(1), 2–12.
Thomas, B., & Lucas, K. (2019). Development and validation of the workplace dignity scale. *Group & Organization Management, 44*(1), 72–111.
Zawadzki, M. (2018). Dignity in the workplace: The perspective of humanistic management. *Journal of Management and Business Administration., 26*(1), 171–188.

Chapter 4
Refuses to Be Governed as Discourses of Dignity: Dignity in the Foucauldian Perspective

Jones Carlos Louback

Abstract In this chapter, we proposed thinking dignity in a Foucauldian light, in the sense that refusals to be governed are a way of expressing discourses of dignity, or even better, that discourses of dignity underlie the refusals to be governed. Refusals to be governed are expressions of discourses of dignity. These refusals are refusals to a government that does not recognize rights, demanding the recognition of non-recognized rights. The discourses of dignity are discourses that claim the recognition of rights, ultimately the right of not being governed. Therefore, refusals to be governed are not synonym to discourses of dignity. Rather, they are expressions of those underlying discourses, discourses about recognition of rights that effectively are synonyms to dignity. Not only discourses on legal rights, but any and all rights. Reading dignity in the Foucauldian light means discussing dignity in the scope of the power relationships. As organizations are social, political, and economic entities, understanding dignity in the organization's context in the light of governmentality assumptions enables an analytical differential of dignity in the intra- and inter-organization relationships, opening new perspectives to management.

Keywords Refuses · Dignity · Governamentality

4.1 Introduction

According to Foucault, the issue of resistance has always been associated to power. In fact, it is far beyond associated since wherever there is power there is resistance. Power relationships comprise a wide range of resistance points (Foucault, 1988). There is no power without resistance and resistance, in turn, assumes freedom. In the absence of freedom, relationships become states of domination (Foucault, 2006a). Resistance always present in power relationships does not stand for a counterpower, or a strategy to take over and hold the place of power, a prevailing power, since when it becomes strategy, it ceases being resistance and becomes power. Resistance

J. C. Louback (✉)
São Paulo, Brazil
e-mail: jonesclouback@gmail.com

M. L. Mendes Teixeira and L. M. B. de Oliveira (eds.), *Organizational Dignity and Evidence-Based Management*, https://doi.org/10.1007/978-3-030-68560-7_4

operates in different ways that are not a strategy to rule the others (Souza et al., 2006, p. 9).

Foucault tries to depict the different means through which human beings become subjects through ways of objectivation (Foucault, 1995). In this light, resistance can be better understood on the grounds of the notion of governamentality no longer as a diffused resistance, but as the art of governing, always associated to the offset of how not being governed (Fonseca, 2002), to the art of not being governed like that and at that price (Foucault, 1990).

The refusal of being governed by others is a critical attitude, and a critical attitude is close to what Kant understood as enlightenment (Foucault, 1990). For Kant, enlightenment is the emergence from nonage, i.e., the inability to use one's own understanding without another's guidance (Kant, 2012).

In Kant, dignity is focused on the individuals' autonomy and right to self-determination, inherent to rational beings. Because of this condition, rational beings should refuse living in a nonage status, not being governed this or that way, seizing their own understanding, and should make moral decisions about what they consider to be the best for their lives, although respecting the decisions of the others for themselves (Kant, 2008). Considering this, and considering that Foucault advocates for the critical attitude as a decisive willingness of not being governed (Fonseca, 2002), we propose thinking dignity in a Foucauldian light, in the sense that refusals to be governed are a way of expressing discourses of dignity, or even better, that discourses of dignity underlies the refusals to be governed.

Reading dignity in the Foucauldian light means discussing dignity in the scope of the power relationships. As organizations are social, political, and economic entities, understanding dignity in the organization's context in the light of governmentality assumptions enables an analytical differential of dignity in the intra- and inter-organization relationships, opening new perspectives to management.

4.2 The Omnipresence of Power

Power is not a reality with a nature, an essence defined by its universal characteristics, but it is materialized in a social practice. Power is everywhere, omnipresent, and comes from everywhere, intertwined with a social network or social body.

The two models typically available to analyze power relationships, namely the law model and the strategic model, cannot cope with the complexity of power. Power as law, as prohibition, as institution, as proposed by Law, has proved to be unsuitable, and the warrior, strategic model is nothing but words (Foucault, 1979). Power is not a form of subjugation, or a system for subjugating individuals or groups by others. Rather, it is a multitude of power correlations (Foucault, 1988). Power is omnipresent not because it embraces everything, but because it is manifested everywhere. It is not an institution, and not a structure, neither a strength, but it is the name that one attributes to a complex strategical situation in a particular society with some remarkable features (Foucault, 1988), among which, the following stand out:

a. Power is no longer object of possession (acquire, overwhelm, share) and, as such, cannot be kept or lost. Within the mobile relationships, power is exercised from several points, rather than just one.
b. Power relationships are inherent to other types of relation such as knowledge relations and sexual intercourses, neither are in a position of superstructure, playing a role of prohibition or reconduction.
c. Power comes from bottom, not making part of any hierarchized structure; on the contrary, correlations of power serve large fragmentation effects crossing the social body.
d. Power relations are intentional, crossed by a calculation, having objectives, although they do not result from individual choice, or from the choice of a team.
e. Power and resistance are intertwined; therefore, resistances are always present in power relations, but never in a position of exteriority.
f. As regards power, we should refer to resistances, in the plural, not a place of the great refusals. Resistances exist in the strategic field of power relations, never externally to it.

Power relationships assume perpetual confrontation of the concerned parties through tactics and techniques. The idea of resistance is a core issue in these relationships, as much as freedom, since there is no power without freedom and potential resistance.

Resistance is not the reversed image of power, the opposite of power; rather, resistance is some way like the power itself. Just like power, it is inventive, mobile, productive, strategically distributed. To Foucault (1979a), there is no substance of resistance in face of a substance of power, but resistances exist wherever power relations exist and, therefore, power never imprisons.

Power is exercised as a mode of action on the others' action, assuming the existence of freedom. Ultimately, slavery is not a relation of power, but a physical relation of coercion (Foucault, 1995).

4.3 From Diffuse Resistance to Governmentality and Counter-Conduct

When proposing the construction of a power analytic, Foucault moves from the axis of history of knowledge and wisdom toward a review of the matrices that rule the behavior. This displacement consisted in reviewing techniques and procedures that drive the others' conduct, rather than the general and institutional forms of dominance (Foucault, 2010). This displacement consisted: in moving from the analysis of rule to the analysis of power exercise, of the governmentality procedures, opening in governmentality the possibility of thinking resistance as a refusal to be governed as such, this way, for those purposes, by those subjects (Foucault, 1990).

Previously to the concept of governmentality, resistance was thought in the disciplinary perspective, in the limits of power diffusion and capillarity, where individuals have little or nothing to do (Alcadipani, 2008; Fonseca, 2002; Branco, 2001), that is, with no refusal to be governed. In "Will of Knowledge," Foucault (1988) states que resistances would be unique, isolated and spontaneous cases.

Ortega (1999) recalls that in the Ethic of Care for the Self as a Practice of Freedom (an interview in 1984), Foucault also speaks about power relationships as "mobile, reversible, and instable," like in Lectures on The Will to Know (a book), but making it conditional to the existence of free subjects, since "if one of them was completely at the other's disposal and became his thing, an object on which he could wreak boundless and limitless violence, there would not be any relations of power," differentiating power relationships from states of domination. Power relationship demands two sides and some freedom, even in uneven power relationships. This means to say that there is always room for resistances (Foucault, 2006a).

The evolvement of the concept of resistance toward governmentality passes by the process of rethinking the issue of capillary resistance to a ruling power late in the 1970s and early in the 1980s, including revisiting the concept of enlightenment discussed by Kant.

In 1978, Foucault approached for the very first time a text by Kant (2012) about Enlightenment (*Aufklärung*), discussing the concept of critical attitude (Senellart, 1995; Fonseca, 2002). He argued that since the fifteenth century, there was a veritable explosion of the art of governing men both in civil society, through a process of secularization, and proliferation of this art of governing into a variety of areas. In that text, Foucault (1990) approaches the government of children, poor people, beggars, the family, the armies, of the body and soul themselves. In the fifteenth century, the issue about how to govern became central, leading to the spread of the arts of governing (Foucault, 1990). In that text and in other revisits to Kant's texts, like in 1983 in the course **The Government of Self and Others** (Foucault, 2010), Foucault argues that besides or interwoven with how to govern, there will always be a how not to be governed.

This critical attitude is not about a gesture of rejection. We have to move beyond the outside–inside alternative; we have to be at the frontiers, transforming the Kantian critique conducted in the form of necessary limitation into a practical critique that takes the form of a possible crossing-over (Foucault, 2008). According to Senellart (1995), it is in this connection of the Foucauldian thinking that we perceive the link between the critical issue, as he reformulates it, and the government issue (Senellart, 1995) both introduced in 1978.

According to Foucault (2008), the modern state is born in light of governmentality as a calculated and reflected political practice" (Foucault, 2008, p. 219), with a government willing to rule men's conduct when conflicts of conduct arise on the side of political institutions. Quoting some examples, Foucault (2008) places the exercise of governmentality taking on former pastoral functions, taking care of the human herd, by the end of the seventeenth century, beginning of the eighteenth century.

Secret societies, as the Freemasonry with its dogmas, rites, hierarchy, ceremonies, hold political objectives. These are revolutions and plots, but always seeking a different form of conduct: "wanting to be conducted differently, by other men, toward other objectives that that proposed by the official, apparent and visible governmentality of the society" (Foucault, 2008, p. 262). In medical institutions, there is certain refusal to a given allopathic rationality, with people using of homeopathy, herbs, and other resources instead (Foucault, 2008).

These are refusals against this way, against these principles, against these objectives, against these procedures, against this government (Foucault, 1990), a sort of specific web of resistance to forms of power that do not exercise sovereignty and do not exploit, but conduct (Foucault, 2008). But Foucault questions how these should be designated: revolt of conduct, disobedience, defiance, dissidence or counter-conduct? (Foucault, 2008).

Foucault (2008) is not satisfied with the phrase "revolt of conduct," although he uses it sometimes, because it is extremely precise and strong. On the other hand, the word "disobedience," although central to governmentality, strikes him as too weak since the historical movements of disobedience went farther than disobedience, having their productivity, way of existing, enduring and advancing over time on new paths and new governments. He wonders about the word "defiance," but it seems to be linked to military issues.

The word "dissidence" seems compelling to define resistances that have opposing objectives and adversary power to those who assume the task of conducting men in their lives and daily existence (Foucault, 2008). This can be found in the post-war Eastern Europe and the Soviet Union after 1945, powers fought by dissidents like the Soviet author and activist Soljenitsin. These would be the pastoral powers of a state as a generalized system of obedience. Despite resembling the resistance being defined, the word "dissidence" is not adopted because it is located in the aforementioned political context, which was a n inconvenient (Foucault, 2008).

Finally, he elects the word "counter-conduct" as it refers to conduct, prevents some associations of the word "dissidence," avoids the elation of some dissident personalities, and avoids the limits of "dissidence" when applied to crazy and delinquent people. Counter-conduct effectively means a family of counter-conducts (Foucault, 2008).

For Foucault (2006b), the power exercised by a man over another man is always dangerous, since the other's action restricts his freedom, and no one has the right to say "revolt for me, is the final liberation of each man," neither has the right to say that ranging is useless (Foucault, 2006). Revolting, rebelling, refusing is always a possibility. Therefore, powers are not "absolutely absolute," and counter-conducts are always possible.

4.4 From Nonage to Enlightenment and Dignity

In 1784, Immanuel Kant answers to the question asked in the previous year by the Berlinisch Monatschrift newspaper, "What is enlightenment?" with an assay of the same name: "Enlightenment (*Aufklärung*) is man's release from his self-incurred immaturity". But what is this self-incurred immaturity? "It is the inability to make use of his understanding without direction from another. It is the non-courage or cowardice of not making use of one's understanding" (Kant, 2012).

Being not of age stands for being governed: being governed by a book that takes over my understanding, being governed by a pastor who takes over my consciousness; being governed by a physician who decides my diet, because it is more comfortable, easier, more natural, not using one's understanding. Being not of age is to accept the tutelage of this or those who want to be a guardian, refusing what is yours by nature (Kant, 2012).

In the text Grounding for the Metaphysics of Morals that approaches human dignity, Kant (2008) presents how human being should be treated as an end in itself by virtue of his autonomy as a rational being. Therefore, if that human being has dignity, being able to do without any government willing to prevail over his capacity of acting based on his own understanding, he is able to refuse a book, a pastor or a physician that govern him, depriving him from his natural ability of acting rationally. This ability known as dignity belongs to a rational being that does not obey any rule but only their ruling will, and, thus, autonomy to comply with a universal law (Kant, 2008). This dignity bears absolute rather than relative value, belongs to every human being, is inherent and non-negotiable, is priceless, but is something above price, above valuation.

The conception of a rational dignity born from Enlightenment, based on Kant's philosophy, assigns to man an inherent, non-negotiable value as rational being, as moral agent. It is part of a concept of modernity that affects several areas of the society including arts, philosophy, and sciences, grounded on the assumption of escaping from tutelage self-incurred due to laziness or cowardice.

Foucault approached Kant's text in 1783 "What is Enlightenment?" (*Aufklärung*) in many opportunities (Senellart, 1995). Two Kantian heritages are present in the approximations and separations between Foucault and Kant: a "transcendental heritage" and a "critical heritage." Transcendental heritage deals with the establishment of "rules of universal truths to prevent the derangements of a dominant reason," a heritage that Foucault would refuse to subscribe. The second heritage, the critical heritage, tries to "provoke the present based on the diagnosis of 'what we are'," and Foucault would subscribe to it (Gros, 2010, p. 345). This critical attitude is not far from what Kant used to define as Enlightenment (*Aufklärung*). Conversely, it gets closer as it implies self's will that is not driven by the other (Fonseca, 2002).

Kant proposes breaking away with a tradition that located man in relationships where his decisions, and therefore his life and dignity as human being, depended on something external, be it the divine, assigning it value as created being; be it the human, telling him how to think and act, with precepts and rules as in the example of governors at large, and in specific cases of spiritual leaders or guiders, physicians, and books.

The man that lives in nonage, being governed by everything and everyone, having his dignity as moral rational being reduced, only needs freedom to re-learn thinking for himself, with no government. However, despite being a rational being this is not that simple, as immaturity became nearly a nature to man, a nature we feed and love (Kant, 2012).

The Enlightenment (*Aufklärung*) motto was "*Sapere aude*! Daring to think" (Kant, 2012, p. 64). However, according to Kant, even a revolution that breaks dominant tyrannical oppression and personal despotism "may be accomplished by revolution, but never a true reform in ways of thinking" (Kant, 2012, p. 65), as new prejudices and domains will arise. The conclusion is that the way out, regardless if facilitated by freedom or not, is on abandoning the non-decision and cowardice to take on what belongs to the person, what is theirs for its own nature, i.e., their condition of free moral rational being.

Hence, we could say that dignity for Kant is centered on individuals' autonomy and right to self-determination, inherent to rational beings. Because of this condition, rational beings should refuse living in a nonage status, governed this or that way, seizing their own understanding, and make moral decisions about what they consider to be the best for their lives, although respecting the decisions of others human beings for themselves.

To illustrate his idea about refusal to be governed, Kant (2012) advocates for the legitimacy of a next-generation to refuse the laws enacted in an incompetent or unlawful way by a previous generation. Likewise, citizens can legitimately challenge the laws passed by a ruler that are not acknowledged as pertinent to all, or to a share of the people. Despite its transcendental grounds inherent to human reason, Kant's human dignity is expressed in an effective refusal to be governed.

Considering that Foucault advocates for critical attitude as a decisive willingness of not being governed (Fonseca, 2002), an art of not being governed like that and at that price (Foucault, 1990), and that he subscribed a Kantian critical heritage, provoke the present based on the diagnosis of 'what we are' (Gros, 2010), and that "the issue of Enlightenment was to revisit the question: how not to be governed? (Gros, 2010), we propose thinking dignity in a Foucauldian light, considering that the discourses of dignity underly the discourses of refusals to be governed. What would be these discourses of dignity? What would be dignity in this case? What would be the refusal to be governed? In the following topics, we will try to answer these questions.

4.5 Discourses of Dignity as Discourses of Recognition of Rights

For Habermas (2010a), the use of pre-modern concepts of dignity entailed a sense of "honor" in different lights, a connotation of a "*ethós* dependent on the social status" similar to the king's dignity, as own style of thinking and behaving differently from the typical life of married women, craftsman, and the hangman (Habermas, 2010a).

Likewise, in the aristocratic system, Waldron (2007) says that dignity belonged to the nobleman, imposing respect to be recognized by all, diversely from the ordinary, non-noble man whose dignity was to not to be respected, but the obligation of respecting that dignity, depending on the context, could be punished if they did not pay the due respect to the one who was worth of it. Respecting the honor due to someone with dignity would be an adequate behavior.

Habermas (2010a) asserts that this root of the link between dignity and honor was an earmark in the understanding of the meaning of dignity leaving a trail in the semantic of the term dignity (Habermas, 2010a).

In a yearning to defend dignity in a universal concept, Waldron (2007), quoting Vlastos (1984), proposed the need for considering the social status system existing in the society, sharing the highest social privileges among all.

Waldron's (2007) understanding about dignity for all is not that of inversing the social hierarchy neither of extinguishing social privileges, but of a democratization of the "privileges" of the noblemen. However, he emphasizes that this concept bears in itself a contradiction since it implies depriving some from differentiation in face of the democratization of privileges. It also implies, in some circumstances, that the rights of some will damage the rights of others, such as in daily situations when, in group, the right to speech implies the obligation of the others to listen.

In his proposal of universalizing dignity based on the sharing of the highest social privileges for all, Waldron (2007) fails in approaching the power relationships. However, the contradictions in his proposal, and acknowledged by him, indicate their existence, thus challenging his proposal of universal dignity.

Habermas (2010a) goes farther than Waldron (2007) proposing his concept of human dignity. Much like Waldron (2007), and differently from Kant (2012), he recognizes that the human being is involved in social relationships; however, Habermas highlights their physical vulnerability and social dependence.

He agrees with Waldron (2007) that human dignity is rooted in social dignity, in the sense of honor in a hierarchy-based society. This "*status-dependent*" social dignity becomes universal when it is shared by all. Habermas (2010b), however, highlights that this dignity preserves the inference of self-respect that depends on social recognition (Habermas, 2010b). He proposes the construction of a dignity entailing from respect and mutual recognition of rights in democratic societies with symmetric relationships (Habermas, 2010a; 2010b).

However, Habermas (2010b) recognizes that building this mutual recognition ensues from fights and resistances as civil and human rights that are in constant tension.

One could say that the concept of human dignity proposed by Habermas encompasses two dimensions: universality, and recognition of civil and human rights. On the other hand, when he points out that rights are recognized through resistance and fights, he implies power relationships. The fights Habermas refers to are those in the light of Foucault, i.e., refusals to be governed in face of the existing government. If fights are fights for the recognition of rights, and in Foucault's perspective, these are refusals to be government, then these are refusals to a government that does not recognize rights and demands the recognition of non-recognized rights.

Therefore, refusals to be governed are expressions of discourses of dignity underlying them, in the sense of recognizing whichever rights of any nature.

When we advocate that refusals to be governed are expressions of discourses of dignity, we consider these refusals as refusals to a government that does not recognize rights, demanding the recognition of non-recognized rights; the discourses of dignity are discourses that claim the recognition of rights, ultimately the right of not being governed.

Therefore, refusals to be governed are not synonym to discourses of dignity. Rather, they are expressions of those underlying discourses, discourses about recognition of rights that effectively are synonyms to dignity. These are discourses not only discourses on legal rights, but any and all rights.

4.6 Discourses of Dignity and Implications on Management

Dignity in the Foucauldian light has implications on management and on the organizational structures. Organizations consist in structures of power, and the power relationships are inserted in the everyday life through the technique of power that makes individuals subjects, enforcing on them a law of truth that must be acknowledged by all (Foucault, 1995). In an organization, individuals are categorized by their offices and hierarchical position. The individual becomes subject, in the sense of being subjected to someone, attached to his own professional identity.

The issue of obedience should be added to the professional identity, since workers are constituted to accept the organization's guidelines. No discourse of dignity is found in this obedience, since the claim for rights is not contained in obedience.

However, it does not rule out the dignity of individuals working in an organization. Nogueira (2001) emphasized the relevance of consciousness about the action of the government's power in the practice of resistance. In principle, dignity is always possible considering that, in the Foucauldian perspective, dignity resides in the counter-conducts. These counter-conducts can be expressed in many ways, even though the rupture with the company, the decision to leave it. However, most times the counter-conducts are expressed through visible actions like inquiries, or less perceptible like boycotting.

Managers should be aware that exercising dignity through counter-conducts is part of the organizational life. That some workers will always challenge the way they are governed. Co-existing with this reality implies opening management to the leading role of workers, so they can actively participate in the decision-making mainly regarding decisions that directly affect their lives. Dignity inspired by a Foucauldian perspective demands new organizational models in which hierarchical structures make room to circular management, and shared government.

In the organizational context, counter-conducts are not a privilege of workers, but of all stakeholders. Customers discontented with the government intended by the organization on them can also make use of counter-conducts to refuse that government, on a par with vendors and other stakeholders. The main lesson managers can learn from the concept of dignity in the light of governmentality is that there is power in the relationship that, therefore, is bilateral. In the same way that managers try to exercise government over stakeholders, trying to make them docile, the clients, vendors, employees and the society, try to exercise power on the organizations through counter-conducts.

4.7 Final Remarks

Dignity, a Kant's enlightenment conception, can be discussed and rethought in a Foucauldian post-modern perspective, based on Foucault's approach to the power relations, "a way of action on actions" (Foucault, 1995, p. 245) that permeate and are intertwined in the whole society (Foucault, 1988), in such a way that a "society 'without power relations' can only be an abstraction" (Foucault, 1995, p. 246). The omnipresence of power is "not because it has the privilege of consolidating everything under its invincible unity but because it is produced from one moment to the next, at every point, or rather in every relation from one point to another" (Foucault, 1988, p. 103).

We could also figure the dignity construct in a Foucauldian light when we consider that power relations assume the existence of resistance. Therefore, there is no power relation without resistance (Foucault, 2006a), even if these are resistances in plural, even if these are unique cases: possible, necessary, improbable, spontaneous, wild, solitary, planned, dragged, violent, irreconcilable, ready to compromise, interested or doomed to sacrifice" (Foucault, 1988).

However, to fulfill the concept of dignity in the Foucauldian perspective, we should pass by the concept of dignity in Habermas, who advances in relation to Kant (2008) when he advocates for a detranscendentalized (*detranszendentalisierte*) version of Kant's "free will." Habermas advocates that this is not a natural feature of intelligible beings, but that autonomy is rather a precarious conquer of finite existences (Habermas, 2010a). Finally, rather than a gift, autonomy happens through means of social movements and political fights (Habermas, 2010b) implying fights for the recognition of rights.

Therefore, in Foucault, we should also advance to the approach of governmentality, making room to a resistance that is no longer diffuse, but a resistance as a refusal to be governed "in the name of those principles, with such and such an objective in mind and by means of such procedures, not like that, not for that, not by them" (Foucault, 1990, p. 3).

Considering that Foucault upholds the critical attitude as an art of not being governed as such, this way (Foucault, 1990, p. 4), we propose thinking dignity in a Foucauldian light, considering that the discourses of dignity underly the discourses of refusals to be governed. Yet, the discourses of refusal to be governed are not synonym to the discourses of dignity. As synonyms, the discourses of dignity would be the discourses of recognition of rights, of any and all rights.

References

Alcadipani, R. (2008). A Dinâmicas de poder nas organizações: A contribuição da governamentalidade. *Comportamento Organizacional E Gestão, 14*(1), 97–114.
Branco, G. C. (2001). As resistências ao poder em Michel Foucault. *Trans/Form/Ação,* São Paulo, *24*, 237–248.
Fonseca, M. A. (2002). *Michel Foucault e o direito.* Sao Paulo: Editora Max Limonad.
Foucault, M. (1979). Não ao sexo rei. *Machado* (pp. 229–242). Edições Graal: R. Microfísica do poder. Rio de Janeiro.
Foucault, M. (1988). *História da sexualidade I: A vontade de saber.* Rio de Janeiro: Edições Graal.
Foucault, M. (1990) Qu'est-ce que la critique? In: Conférence du 27 mai 1978. Bulletin de la Société Française de Philosophie 2, avril-juin. Armand Colin.
Foucault, M. (1995) O sujeito e o poder. In H. Dreyfus & P. Rabinow (Eds.), *Michel Foucault, uma trajetória filosófica*: para além do estruturalismo e da hermenêutica (pp. 231–249). Rio de Janeiro: Forense Universitária.
Foucault, M. (2006a). A ética do cuidado de si como prática da liberdade. In M. B. Motta (org). *Ditos e Escritos* V: estratégia, poder-saber (pp. p. 264–287). Rio de Janeiro: Forense Universitária.
Foucault, M. (2006b).É inútil revoltar-se? In M. B. Motta (org). *Ditos e Escritos V*: Ética, sexualidade, política (pp. p. 77–81). Rio de Janeiro: Forense Universitária.
Foucault, M. (2008). *Segurança, território, população: Curso no Collège de France (1977–1978): Curso no Collège de France (1977–1978).* São Paulo: Martins Fontes.
Foucault, M. (2010). *O governo de si e dos outros.* São Paulo: Editora WMF Martins Fontes.
Gros, F. (2010). Situação do curso. *Foucault* (pp. 343–356). Editora WMF Martins Fontes: M. O governo de si e dos outros. São Paulo.
Habermas, J. (2010a). *O futuro da natureza humana.* Sao Paulo: Martins Fontes.
Habermas, J. (2010b). The concept of human rights and the realistic utopia of human rights. *Metaphilosophy, 41*(4), 464–480.
Kant, I. (2008). *Fundamentação da metafísica dos costumes.* Portugal: Edições 70.
Kant, I. (2012). Resposta à pergunta: Que é "Esclarecimento"? (*Aufklärung*). In: *Immanuel Kant*: textos seletos. Petrópolis, RJ: Vozes, p. 63–71.
Nogueira, C. (2001). Análise do Discurso. In L. Almeida & E. Fernandes (Eds.), *Métodos e técnicas de avaliação: novos contributos para a prática e investigação* (pp. 15–48). Braga: CEEP.
Ortega, F. (1999). *Amizade e estética da existência em Foucault.* Rio de Janeiro: Edições Graal Ltda.
Senellart, M. (1995). A crítica da razão governamental em Michel Foucault. *Tempos Social,* V. 7, n. 1–2.
Souza, E. M., Bianco, M. F., & Machado, L. D. (2006). *Análises sobre poder: comparativo entre a perspectiva foucaultiana e funcionalista.* In Meeting of the National Association of Graduate Course in Administration and Research in Administration, 30, 2006, Salvador/Ba. *Minutes.* Salvador/BA.
Vlastos, G. (1984). Justice and Equality. In: Louis P. Pojman & Robert Westmoreland (eds.), *Equality: Selected Readings.* Oup Usa (1984)
Waldron, J. (2007). Dignity and rank. *Archive Européenne de Sociologie, XLVIII*, 201–237.

Chapter 5
Organizational Dignity in the Interpretative Perspective

Bruno Felix von Borell de Araujo

Abstract The objective of this chapter is to present organizational dignity from the interactionist perspective and to propose a theory capable of explaining the relationships between companies and the communities located in their geographical surroundings. The investigation was carried out through grounded theory in a community called here by the fictitious name "Litoral," using as object of analysis the relations between members of the community and two companies—one national (Modelo), the other multinational (Capixaba). The residents' expectations in relation to the company's eager interest for the community of its geographic surroundings and the way it responds was at the central core of the proposed theory. The expectations of the community are shaped and reformatted in a dynamic relationship with the concrete or abstract tangibility of the company, the critical situations experienced and the business actions in response to these situations. The company's zeal for the community is represented by symbols of dignity and objects of economic, environmental, socio-cultural or psycho-social dignity. The theory that emerged from the data address some important issues in order companies can trace strategies to cope to community expectations.

Keywords Organizational dignity · Community · Objects of dignity

5.1 Introduction

Recurrent conflicts between companies and communities involve issues such as environmental sustainability, cultural heritage and jobs offer and have been studied by several authors (Salzmann & Prinzhorn, 2006; Santos, 2004). Despite the importance of the concept of dignity as a guiding principle in the relationships between different social actors (Sarlet, 2001), this principle has been scarcely explored in the organizational literature.

B. F. von Borell de Araujo (✉)
Vitoria, Brazil
e-mail: bfelix@fucape.br

M. L. Mendes Teixeira and L. M. B. de Oliveira (eds.), *Organizational Dignity and Evidence-Based Management*, https://doi.org/10.1007/978-3-030-68560-7_5

The objective of this chapter is to present organizational dignity from the interactionist perspective and to propose a theory capable of explaining the relationships between companies and the communities located in their geographical surroundings.

The relationship between business organizations and communities is, in part, regulated by positive law, a field in which the aim of ensuring people's fundamental rights led by human dignity is advocated. However, Sarlet (2001) points out that dignity is often not expressly recognized in positive law. Also, on no rare occasions what is legal is not carried out according to the law. If the legal domain shows inadequacy to review the existence of dignity in the relationship between companies and communities, what alternative would be appropriate to understand this phenomenon? A clue is given by the path adopted by Beyleveld and Brownsword (2001) and Pullman (2001) for the study of dignity in the field of bioethics. By adopting an interactionist perspective of dignity, these authors were able to understand the definitions that people in different frameworks construct regarding what dignity is when it comes to ethical issues related to human life. They understand that dignity refers to what is valued by social entities, so that each social group is able to define what dignity is in its own context.

Urban communities can be seen as an interactional space in which several belief systems coexist (Cohen, 1960). Therefore, the interactionist approach, mainly the symbolic structural interactionism (Stryker, 1980), can be an adequate way to understand the dignity relationships between companies and communities. Stryker (1980) developed structural symbolic interactionism with the purpose of presenting an interactionist approach that would allow developing a discussion about the interdependence between the social structure and the individual. It is in this connection that the discussion on the dignity relationship between companies and communities' members takes place.

Organizations are assumed here as social actors. Conceiving organizations as social actors implies recognizing them as social entities that are perceived by stakeholders as being able to make decisions and assume responsibility for them and for the practices they perform. Thus, the organizational social actor conception is characterized by external attributions made by the stakeholders and the legal responsibility for the impact of their actions taken by organizations (King et al., 2009).

The investigation was carried out through Grounded theory approach in a community in the State of Espírito Santo (Brazil), called here by the fictitious name "Litoral," using as object of analysis the relations between members of the community and two companies—one national (Modelo), the other multinational (Capixaba).

We hope that the proposed theory can contribute to the management of dignity relations between companies and their communities.

5.2 Structural Symbolic Interactionism

Stryker's (1980) proposal assumes integration between the theoretical basis of symbolic interactionism and the theory of roles. Stryker (1980) argues that behavior depends on a classified universe, that is, the names that we give to different elements in the environment imbue them with meaning and raise our expectations about how to act before them. When interacting, people learn what symbols are used to designate positions of the relatively stable components of social structures, which have shared expectations of behavior derived from existing roles.

When acting in the context of the same structure, people designate each other and themselves according to their position and create mutual and individual expectations of behavior. Such qualifications are used as guides for the organization of the action. Although Stryker (1980) highlights the influence of structure on individual behavior, he does so by placing these ideas within the framework of Mead's (1972) symbolic interactionism and other scholars of the Chicago School. Thus, the thinker states that structural definitions influence, but do not determine, individual action. He remains faithful to the interactionist assumption that behavior is the result of active and reflective processes.

Stryker (1980) maintains that different structures impose different limits on the possibilities of interaction, so that the degree of role-setting of the social structures' characteristics that frame the interaction situations. These limits can change over time, since the individual action is not only influenced, but can also change roles and structure. This can occur when individuals or groups use their reflexivity to break the structure and act outside the patterns of interaction, thus creating new patterns and roles. In summary, it can be said that Stryker (1980) seeks, through his structural symbolic interactionism, to study the integration and interdependence between the micro and macro-levels of social interaction.

Conceptually, Stryker (1980) uses some terms derived from the theory of roles, such as "role conflict," which refers to conflicting expectations from others or individuals about the action, and "role tension," which alludes to situations in which an individual's obligations and demands exceed his ability to meet them properly. The concepts of "role" and the interactionist notions of "structure," "interaction" and "self" are the basic elements used by Stryker (1980) for proposing the concepts of "identity salience" and "role commitment." By "identity salience," we mean the prevalence of one of the several hierarchically organized identities owned by an individual. "Role commitment" refers to the importance that a person attaches to a satisfactory performance in a given role. The greater the "salience of identity" and the "role commitment," the greater the chance that the person will adopt the behaviors associated with a given role.

In summary, it can be said that Stryker (1980) seeks, through its structural symbolic interactionism, to study the integration and interdependence between the micro and macro-levels of social interaction.

5.3 The Companies "Modelo" and "Capixaba"

The "Modelo" Company

At the beginning of the twentieth century, Brazil became an important destination for families seeking to flee their countries, which were involved in wars. Thus, onwards, a new large flow of immigrants arrived in Espírito Santo, which further warmed up the production and consumption of goods in the region (Oliveira, 1975).

The different Europeans immigrants who landed in Espírito Santo during the twentieth century include Wilhelm (fictitious name), a German businessman who, after observing the Brazilian scenario, conducive to the production and commercialization of consumer goods with which he dealt before the war, decides to create a company in Brazil to continue the business. The activities of the newly founded company—called Wilhelm S/A (fictitious name)—start in a densely populated region of the Litoral (fictitious name) city, located in the coastal area of Espírito Santo.

Between the 30s and 50s, the neighborhood where the second headquarters of Wilhelm S/A was established begins to be populated due to the company's growth. The job opportunities brought by Wilhelm S/A attract people from different places, who start to form a larger community of residents around the company. In this framework, Wilhelm starts to represent an icon for the community which incorporates the figure of the authoritarian and loving father that was previously conveyed to the *Senhor de Engenho* (owner of the sugarcane plantation and sugarmill) and, later, to the large landowner.

Labor relations in the colonial period in Espírito Santo were characterized by the economic dependence on the *Senhor do Engenho.* He managed his production unit and the family unit concurrently, without clear boundaries between both roles. Just like in other parts of the Brazilian territory (Davel & Vasconcelos, 1997), his relationship with employees was not just that of an exploiter. *Senhor do Engenho* was above all a reference for the slaves, who counted on his support to satisfy their needs. Thus, the colonial community in this region was permeated by relationships of affection and submission between the employer, the employee and their families; the *Senhor do Engenho*was the paternal reference in this ethos. The actors change with time, but the relationships of economic dependence, uncritical submission and affectivity remain. These are characteristic of workers' relationship with the people who occupied positions of hierarchical superiority in the formation of Espírito Santo and Brazil (Oliveira, 1975).

After a financial crisis in the 60s, Wilhelm invited a new partner to share with him the leadership of the company, whom we will call Anton. At that time, the company's name is changed to Modelo S/A (fictitious name). Both the company's new name and logo refer to the people in the community who informally marketed the company's products. Anton's entrepreneurial vision lead the company to adopt a growth strategy that resulted in national projection in the 1960s. In parallel to this process, the community around the company grew more and more, enhancing the dependence and gratitude relationship of the community in relation to the company. In the following decade, the descendants of Wilhelm and Anton reach an agreement to put the company up for sale. The consensual positioning of all heirs in favor of negotiating the company reassures some residents, who realize that the sale is a necessary evil. However, part of the community, fearing that the sale of the company shall mean the extinction of the brand or the end of the company's operations in the city of Litoral, starts to speak out against the operation. In an operation that split the community members opinion, in 2002, the company Modelo was sold to the multinational Mundial S/A. However, the company continues to operate under the current company's name Modelo.

The "Capixaba" Company

The coffee crisis that occurred in the 1960s contributed to the acceleration of the industrial growth in Espírito Santo. The crisis spurred the development of an economic growth plan that led to the intention of replacing the agricultural economic matrix with an industrial matrix (Bueno, 1999).

In the 60s and 70s, implementation of the region's recovery policies began. The following years witnessed the set up of large industrial plants to mainly supply the foreign market. Companies such as Vale, CST, Samarco and Aracruz Celulose are a few examples of companies that got established with this purpose. At that time, the large plants that were set up in the industrial sector in Espírito Santo include the company Capixaba, a large corporation with international operations (Alves Filho, 2000).

The Capixaba company originated from a railway transport company founded in the early twentieth century. In the 1940s, the company started to transport commodities. In the 1960s, Capixaba's first subsidiary for the production of commodities was created. The 1970s and 1980s were marked by the international expansion of the company's shares. In the 2000s, the company further expanded its operations with the construction of a production plant in the interior of Espírito Santo (Oliveira, 1975).

Capixaba's relationship with the Litoral community is characterized by:

> Social and environmental responsibility actions to help minimize the impact of pollution brought to the surroundings. There's no way, their productive activity (...) is polluting. There is no way not to pollute. it is a company distanced from the community, like nobody knows the name of anyone who works there in Capixaba. The majority of the people who work there came from Rio, São Paulo, Minas. So, it is something more distant, inaccessible. The actions they take do not have the affection that they had in Modelo's history. They are aloof. It's a different relationship. Modelo was a "father" to the city of Litoral, Capixabadoes not have that position (resident of the Litoral community's comment).

This testimony reveals the contrast between the position that the companies Capixaba and Modelo occupy in the context of Litoral city. While Modelo was created with the participation of the community, which is reflected in the actual company's name, and was marked by a paternal relationship with the community, the Capixaba company, on the other hand, is characterized as a large multinational corporation seen by the community as something "more distant" and "inaccessible."

It was in this scenario of contrasting historical relations between the two companies that the survey was conducted and a theory was built from the perspective of Striker's symbolic interactionism, which aims to explain the relationship between companies and communities located in their geographical surroundings.

5.4 Theory Presentation

The theory developed from the perception of 24 residents in communities located in the geographical surroundings of the Modelo or the Capixaba company, in the city of Litoral, comprises the following categories of elements: dignity objects, dignity symbols, business conduct toward objects dignity, organizational tangibility, critical situations and community expectations (Fig. 5.1).

5.4.1 *Objects of Dignity*

Dignity objects represent, using Jacobson's (2009) terminology, the dignity of the community's self. The locus of the phenomenon in this category is the community. However, our study objective was focused on the relationship between companies and the community assessed. Based on Jacobson's taxonomy (2009), we could say that the phenomenon of interest in this study is found in the relational dignity between community and companies. When focusing our interest in the interaction between community and companies, we ought to understand the symbolic actions existing in the relationship between both social actors. Which are the symbols agreed to

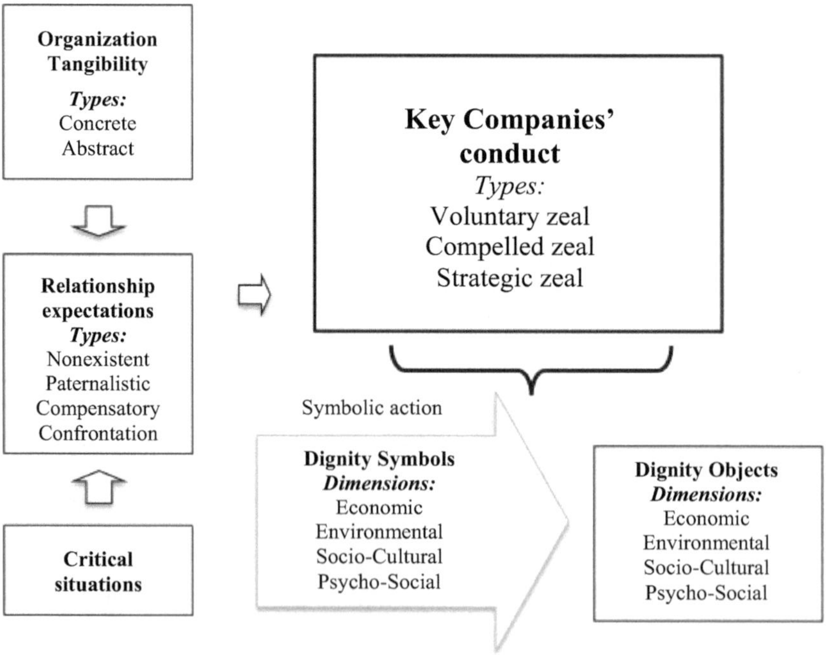

Fig. 5.1 Theoretical model built in the research

represent a dignified/unworthy relationship between companies and the community? Understanding these potential symbols would be useful to us, since the meaning of a significant symbol does not lie in the reaction of the recipient, but in the joint response between the emitter of the gesture and the recipient (MEAD, 1972). From this reflection, we began to explore in the interviews the community's understanding regarding the elements that could symbolize a relationship of dignity or indignity.

Based on the survey respondents' reports on the experiences they had with Modelo, it was possible to encode different meanings for dignity. These meanings reflect four different dimensions of dignity: economic, environmental, socio-cultural and psycho-social. Among the "objects of economic dignity," we highlight "employment." The meaning attributed to this object is that of subsistence. We mention as examples of "socio-cultural objects of dignity," the "city squares" and "beaches" located in the community, which are interpreted with the meaning of social interaction and cultural expression. Among the "objects of environmental dignity," we can mention the "air" and the "beaches" of the region, and their meanings refer to the health and environmental sustainability of the community. Among the "objects of psycho-social dignity," we find the "Christian Monument" (fictitious name for a monument of religious worship located in the region of Litoral) and the "Modelo company" itself, to which an attributed meaning of pride was identified.

5.4.2 Symbols of (in)dignity: Understanding the Action Against Objects of Dignity

The (in)dignity symbols found were initially coded, and the resulting codes went through a focused coding process. This process resulted in four categories of (in) dignity symbols, which reflect the same dimensional structure found in objects of dignity.

Among the "symbols of dignity" classified in the economic dimension," the Litoral Fashion Pole and Modelo company stand out, because they symbolize the dignity interpreted in the community's livelihood. When shown a picture of the company Litoral Fashion Pole taken by a participant who was asked to photograph something that symbolized a worthy relationship between the company and the community, one interviewee stated that:

> The dignity in this [photo] is in the factory, isn't it? Everyone, when they think of Litoral thinks of Modelo; we really need it to support our children. It all started with them. I like to say that every child who was born here, in one way or another, drank the milk from there (Symbol of dignity - economic dimension).

Among the symbols of (in) dignity classified in the environmental dimension, we identified the "Porto on our horizon" (in reference to the port where industries are located and which is within reach of the viewers of one of the beaches in the region), "*Pó preto*" (Black dust) (a common expression in the community to designate air pollution) and "empty beach on a warm day." For the interviewees, these elements symbolize the Capixaba company's indignity relations with the community, in a reference to the beach and air pollution attributed to the company's operations. One of the interviewees who received a camera and a request to photograph some element that symbolized a relationship of (in) dignity with the companies in the region photographed a car covered with a black dust and the empty beach in the background, on a sunny day.

The "socio-cultural events" were identified as symbols of dignity in the socio-cultural dimension, while the "Modelo products around the world," the "Modelo logo" (in reference to the fact that the company Modelo has a logo that makes a metaphorical allusion to its history with the city of Litoral and that such products are traded internationally) were classified in the psycho-social dimension.

In addressing this category, we started to direct the analysis of the community's dignity toward the interaction between the community and the companies. In the presentation of the next category that makes up the theory, we analyze how the community interprets the symbolic behaviors and actions of organizations in relation to objects of dignity.

5.4.3 Business Conduct Toward Objects of Dignity

Adopting an interactionist perspective, we cannot say that, by acting toward these elements that represent the dignity of the community, companies are producing a "good" or "malicious" action or whether their justifications for actions of this kind are true or false. An interactionist investigation should not speculate on the truth or lie of the motives presented by social actors. However, it is coherent, from an interactionist point of view, to be interested in identifying the vocabulary of gestures used by the actors to justify their actions or the interpretations that social actors make of the intentions of others. As the motive is seen here not as anteceding the action, but built on it (Mills, 1940; Albas & Albas, 2003), we are not interested in seeking to access the "truth" about the motives of organizations when acting toward objects of dignity. Our interest, however, lies in the assessments that community members make regarding the organizations' conduct. In this category, we seek to understand and conceptualize the social meaning of the words used by the community's members to assess the conduct and intentions of business organizations in relation to objects of dignity.

Based on the interviewees' reports, some key behaviors of the companies were identified. We call "key business conduct" the interpretations made by community members regarding the patterns of actions taken by companies with respect to objects of dignity. Three types of key conduct were identified, voluntary zeal, compelled zeal and strategic zeal.

The voluntary zeal refers to the care that companies show on their own initiative regarding the objects of dignity in the community. This interpretation refers to situations in which the community understands that, even without being charged by the government or by the residents, some companies will volunteer actions that appear to be a feeling of care for the community's dignity symbols. Some respondents when asked how they saw the way companies in the region dealt with the dignity objects indicated by them, replied that the company Modelo "takes care of us," "saves this city," referring to care initiatives that the company had no obligation to take, such as renovating city squares, promoting sporting events and beach parties. Respondents revealed that they perceived the company Modelo assuming public interest achievements that would be the government's obligation, as they were interested in caring for the community.

A second key conduct identified as a recurring interpretation in the community was what we call compelled zeal. Compelled zeal refers to the care companies show regarding objects of dignity due to legal motivation or social pressure, and not voluntary motivation. A third type of zeal, interpreted as instrumental, was categorized as "strategic zeal," which we define as the care that companies give to objects of dignity and that is interpreted by the community as instrumentally motivated. To this type of conduct classification, community members link companies that strategically seek to transmit a characteristic image of voluntary zeal.

5.4.4 Community Expectations Regarding the Relationship with Companies

The organizations' conduct has no intrinsic meaning; it is interpreted in different ways by members of the community. In this category, we seek to answer the following question: what precedes the different interpretations of zeal?

To try to understand this process, we asked the interviewees, how they interpreted the behavior of companies toward objects of dignity and, based on the responses received, we asked why they think that way. The responses pointed to the fact that people interpret symbolic organizational actions based on their expectations about these actions.

Some interviewees stated that they did not know the companies in the region and that, for this reason, they were not able to interpret the organizations' key behaviors or even tell what expectations they had regarding them. Such data led to the construction of the "non-existent" expectation category. We classified as "paternalistic expectations" statements that revealed the perception of a community with no assistance from the government and dependent on companies' initiatives for its dignity to be promoted. A third type of expectation found was what we call "compensation expectation." The fragments gathered under this category portrayed a view that companies have the right to exploit community resources. However, they must compensate for this exploitation with actions that satisfy the needs of the community that represent their dignity. This is not an expectation for paternalistic actions, but a simple trade-off relationship between the community and the companies.

Some interviewees expressed a critical view regarding the performance of companies and their relationship with the community. For these people, the relationship is seen as predatory. This view is based on the assumption that companies seek to abuse the possibility of exploiting community resources and do the least possible in terms of compensation. This expectation is associated with the idea that the relationship between companies and the community must be guided by actions of community resistance. Thus, the relationship is seen as inevitably characterized by the confrontation of interests and disputes over the goals of each actor involved.

5.4.5 Organizational Tangibility: Understanding Expectations About Companies

We call organizational tangibility the set of characteristics that some companies have and that make them more frequently remembered by the community. More tangible companies jump more into the minds of community members, which enhances the community's expectations in their regard. Thus, people who have paternalistic expectations in relation to certain companies tend to expect more paternalistic actions than those that are more tangible, that is, that are more frequently remembered by the community. During the analysis, we found two properties of organizational tangibility, which we call concrete and abstract tangibility.

Concrete tangibility refers to the memory that a company brings to mind in a community due to the interaction that residents have with the company's physical image. On the other hand, the abstract tangibility refers to the memory that a company evokes in a community due to the interaction that the residents of the region have with the brand, the affectionate relationship with the company and its exposure in the media. In this case, the characteristics of the business of the company in question, the history of interactions with the community and the interference of the media are all elements that contribute for a company to be more or less remembered by the community.

5.4.6 Critical Situations and Changes in Community Expectations

The organizational tangibility concept helped us to identify changes in the degree in which the community expectations—be they paternalistic, compensatory or confrontational—are manifested. However, another question regarding the changing expectations of the community was present: do people change their expectations over time? If so, under what conditions are those expectations changed? Are there cases of people with paternalistic expectations, for example, who switch and expect a compensation relationship?

The reports obtained suggest that this type of expectations change occurs especially when the community experiences periods of crisis in which certain objects of dignity—in this community assessed, the health, employment and economic sustainability of the region—are endangered. We call these circumstances "critical situations."

The development of the categories presented allowed the construction of the theoretical research model, which is shown in Fig. 5.1.

5.4.7 Discussion of the Theoretical Model Constructed in the Research

Based on Stryker's symbolic interactionist perspective (1980), the data showed that community members classify and name the elements that represent their dignity (objects of dignity). They do not respond to a world with inherent meanings, but to a categorized world, which is the object of classification (Mead, 1972). Expressions that conveyed the concern for a "more dignified life" were recurrent in the data and were used by the interviewees to portray the needs that, when satisfied, bring dignity to their lives. These needs referred to physical aspects—such as the beach and the air—and social aspects, such as the feeling of pride and social interaction.

The social, physical and biological environment that forms a community is symbolic. The behavior of community members is not fragmented and produced according to individual judgments in each situation. There are symbols present in the environment that guide and organize the collective behavior of the community. The symbols of (in)dignity, another concept built on the theory that we approach here, present agreed and shared definitions.

These definitions of dignity shared by the community are available for use in routine situations. However, some people may not be aware of the cultural definitions of dignity in a certain context in a community, such as a newcomer or a child growing up in that environment. In such cases, people generally learn the agreed definitions of dignity through interaction situations. However, in times of social changes, some definitions of dignity shared in the community can be challenged in the face of new experiences. These definitions can be revised and reformulated during times of crisis, which we call "critical situations." When community members felt their dignity threatened, they had to reconstruct their definitions of what their dignity represents, since the context in which the symbols were formed was no longer the same.

Roles represent expectations linked to positions (Stryker, 1980). We identified in the category "expectations regarding the relationship" that there are in the community, different roles attributed to organizations: that of caring as a father (paternalistic expectation), that of compensating the exploitation of resources with acts that satisfy community needs (expectation of compensation) and to seek, in an abusive way, to exploit community resources (expectation of confrontation). These roles that community members assign to companies in the region are social and symbolic. They are relatively stable positions, characterized as morphological components of the social structure and allow the community to recognize themselves and the companies as occupants of positions in the context of interaction.

"Organizational tangibility" proved to be one of the factors that influence the construction of different expectations and roles. Companies that are most often remembered by community members are more tangible, which enhances the community's expectations about them.

Thus, it can be said that the meanings of dignity in the context of the relationship between the social actors of interest in this research are constructed by the community according to the way its members interpret and evaluate the zeal present in business conduct in connection with the objects of dignity.

5.5 Implications for Management

The experiences reported by community members and the other data we obtained during the survey suggest that dignity within the scope of the relationship between companies and the community is not interpreted by its members in an absolute way, but according to the significance of dignity for each one of them. Dignity does not have an inherent meaning. In an interactionist perspective, it is not possible to identify what the dignity of a community represents in an absolute sense, nor to issue a judgment of an inherently dignified or unworthy relationship between social actors.

The perspective presented, that is, dignity as a social construction, differs from the understanding in the literature that the relationship of dignity depends primarily on the search for power symmetry by the social actors involved (Jacobson, 2009; Salzmann, 2006). Although this search may exist, the relationship of dignity was seen here as dependent on the interpretations that community members make of business conducts, confronting them with the expectations they have regarding these relationships. Applying Thomas's maxim (1937) in connection with this investigation, we can say that if the members of a community define their relationship with a company as being (un)worthy, they experience the consequences of a (un) worthy relationship.

It is important to underscore that the theory proposed for being based on the interactionist perspective may or may not be valid for other realities. However, it draws attention to the importance of companies seeking to know what a dignified relationship between them and the surrounding communities means. In order to understand the socially constructed concepts of dignity in a community, we ought to understand what its residents consider to be a representative of their dignity. We believe that the concept of dignity objects and their environmental, economic, psycho-social and socio-cultural dimensions, which emerged during the construction of the theory, can be useful to facilitate the understanding of dignity relationships between companies and the community. The central category "zeal" shows itself as a promising category to guide this relationship, as well as the categories that make up the proposed theoretical model.

5.6 Final Remarks

The objective of this chapter was to present the organizational dignity from an interactionist perspective and propose a theory that would allow explaining the relationship between companies and the communities located in the companies' geographic surroundings. To this end, the investigation was carried out with the participation of residents of a community called fictitiously "Litoral," in which two companies are located. A national company founded by a German immigrant in the first half of the last century that in this work was named the company "Modelo" and a multinational company (called Capixaba) that settled in the community in the second half of the twentieth century.

The residents' expectations in relation to the company's eager interest for the community of its geographic surroundings and the way it responds was at the central core of the proposed theory. The expectations of the community are shaped and reformatted in a dynamic relationship with the concrete or abstract tangibility of the company, the critical situations experienced and the business actions in response to these situations. The company's zeal for the community is represented by symbols of dignity and objects of economic, environmental, socio-cultural or psycho-social dignity.

Because the theory proposed was built from data originating from a specific community, other studies should be developed in order to test the theory structure in other contexts. The enlargement of studies will make possible the generation of new knowledge about the dignity relationships between companies and communities located in their geographic surroundings and consequently contribute to a more dignified management of these relationships.

References

Albas, C. A., & Albas, D. C. (2003). Motives. In L. T. Reynolds & N. J. Herman-Kinney (Eds.), *Handbook of symbolic interactionism* (pp. 349–366). Oxford: Altamira.

Alves Filho, I. (2000). *História dos Estados Brasileiros*. Rio de Janeiro: Revan.

Beyleveld, D., & Brownsword, R. (2001). *Human dignity in bioethics and biolaw*. Oxford: Oxford University Press.

Bueno, E. (1999). *Capitães do Brasil:A saga dos primeiros colonizadores A saga dos primeiros colonizadores*. Rio de Janeiro: Objetiva.

Cohen, J. (1960). A coefficient of agreement for nominal scales. *Educational and Psychological Measurement, 20,* 37–46.

Davel, E., & Vasconcelos, J. (1997). Gerência e autoridade nas empresas brasileiras: uma reflexão histórica e empírica sobre a dimensão paterna nas relações de trabalho. In F. P. Motta & M. Caldas (Eds.), *Cultura organizacional e cultura brasileira*. São Paulo, Atlas.

Jacobson, N. (2009). A taxonomy of dignity: a grounded theory study. *BMC International Health and Human Rights*, v. 9.

King, B. G., Felin, T., & Whetten, D. A. (2009). Finding the organization in organization theory: A meta-theory of the organization as a social actor. Organization Science, *Articles in Advance,* pp. 1–16.

Mead, G. H. (1972). *Mind, self and society*. Chicago: University of Chicago Press.
Mills, C. W. (1940). Situated actions and vocabularies of motive. *American Sociological Review, 5*, 904–913.
Oliveira, J. T. (1975). *História do Estado do Espírito Santo* (2ª ed.). Vitória: Fundação Cultural do Espírito Santo
Pullman, D. (2001). Universalism, particularism and the ethics of dignity. *Christian Bioethics, 7*(3), 333–358.
Salzmann, O., & Prinzhorn, J. (2006). Cities and communities: Local actors in corporate sustainability. In U. STEGER (Ed.), *Inside the mind of the stakeholder*: The hype behind stakeholder pressure (pp. 157–172.). New York: Palgrave Macmillan.
Salzmann, O. (2006). Companies and their stakeholders: Recent trends in their interaction. In U. Steger (Ed.), *Inside the mind of the stakeholder:* The hype behind stakeholder pressure (pp. 19–29). New York: Palgrave Macmillan.
Santos, M. A. C. (2004). Responsabilidade penal das pessoas jurídicas de direito público por dano ambiental: uma análise crítica. *Jus Navigandi,* v. 8, n. 199.
Sarlet, I. W. (2001). *A eficácia dos direitos*. Porto Alegre: Livraria do Advogado.
Stryker, S. (1980). *Symbolic Interactionism:* A social structural approach. California: The Benjamin/Cummings.
Thomas, W. I. (1937). *Primitive behaviour.* New York: McGraw-Hill.

Chapter 6
Dignity Under the Phenomenological Perspective

Claudia Segadilha Adler

Abstract The main objective of this chapter is to bring a phenomenological perspective to dignity at work. First, it explains the main human process to phenomenology, i.e., the process of becoming, and how it relates to dignity. The process of becoming is dynamic and intersubjective. It occurs in all dimensions of human life, including work. Here are used the classic authors from phenomenology and social phenomenology, Kierkegaard and Buber, and Rogers, the main author from humanistic existential psychology to explain such a relation between work and becoming. The chapter shows a method to investigate that phenomenon, respecting the phenomenological epistemological position, and scientific criteria. This method was applied in a research with Brazilian professors, which brings evidence about the process of living dignity at work as a part of the process of becoming. This evidence shows a deep relationship between living dignity and being yourself. Their work brings a complex sense of achievement, connected to their essence, which is the core idea in connecting dignity to the process of becoming. Therefore, the major contribution of the chapter is to offer a humanistic, positive discussion about dignity at work, pointing out possible management strategies to promote such dignifying workplaces.

Keywords Human dignity · Dignity at work · Phenomenology

6.1 Introduction

This chapter is a reflection about dignity as part of the process of being theorized by phenomenology and core a concept to humanistic psychology. This paper discusses how a person who can live as their own self reaches not only self-actualization, but also dignity.

Claudia Segadilha Adler: In memoriam.

C. S. Adler (✉)
Rio de Janeiro, Brazil
e-mail: claudiaadler@globo.com

M. L. Mendes Teixeira and L. M. B. de Oliveira (eds.), *Organizational Dignity and Evidence-Based Management*, https://doi.org/10.1007/978-3-030-68560-7_6

Many articles discuss aspects about law and human rights, pointing out important aspects to build worthy workplaces. Others shed light on disrespect, exclusion, and even violence (symbolic or otherwise). All these are very relevant aspects about organizational dignity, but focused on negative aspects to be avoided, and on how to prevent them. This debate intends to focus on positive aspects that allow people to feel dignity as part not only of their lives, but of who they are. Despite race, gender or any other specific trait, anyone who can live the continuous process of becoming free, which comprises all such traits, actually being who they are, can live[1] dignity, not as isolated blocks or terms, but as a complex set of elements that are part of who they are. This process allows not only proper conditions for organizational dignity, but also for living dignity.

Therefore, the main objective of this chapter is to bring a phenomenological perspective to dignity at work. The first objective is to explain the main human process to phenomenology, i.e., the process of becoming, and how it relates to dignity. The second objective intends to show a method to investigate that phenomenon, respecting the phenomenological epistemological position, and scientific criteria. The third objective brings evidence about the process explained in the first objective, specifically related to work. Therefore, the main contribution of the chapter is to offer a humanistic, positive discussion about dignity at work.

6.2 Phenomenological Influence in the Light of Human Life and Dignity

Phenomenological contribution appears in the work by many authors. Here, one specific author plays an important role. Rogers (1961), a psychologist deeply influenced by Kierkegaard (1941 [1849]) and Buber (1974), presents a phenomenological interpretation to Dignity. It is an important part of human life. Actually, it is crucial. The essential human process, the process of **becoming**, reaches for worth and dignity: "Man as a process of becoming; as a process of **achieving worth** and **dignity** through the development of his potentialities;" (Rogers, 1961, p. 395, emphasis added).

In this perspective, man is understood as a fluid process, continuously changing, evolving, always seeking to fulfill the whole set of his capacities. This set exists in every person and will be expressed whenever possible. However, it is important to understand how Rogers created this existentialist explanation from Kierkegaard and Buber.

Kierkegaard (1941 [1849]) states that human despair has two aspects. On the one hand, man has "that of not willing to be one's own self, of willing to get rid of oneself," on the other hand, stands its opposite "despair at willing to be one's own self" (p. 10). Despair to become is an important contribution to this discussion. Not being the self is uncomfortable, unpleasant to the person. Kierkegaard (1941 [1849],

[1] In phenomenology, living and experiencing have different meanings. Experience is punctual, ephemeral, while live is continuous.

p. 29) states, “In so far as the self does not become itself, it is not its own self; but not to be one’s own self is despair.”

This evidences a discomfort for those who do not partake the process of becoming. Nonetheless, this is an important element to promote a continuous movement to the process: “despair in this case is not merely passive suffering, but action.” (Kierkegaard, 1941 [1849]) p. 70). It also points out to the human nonconformism. Man does not simply accept what is given. He is constantly trying to build himself. “The formula constantly is: in despair to will to be oneself.” (p. 78) This is inherent and positive “despair does not come from without but from within. And in the same degree despair is more and more positive” (p. 114).

Rogers adds the notion of “good life” to Kierkegaard’s concept of the process of becoming: “It involves the stretching and growing of becoming more and more of one’s potentialities. It involves the courage to be. … when the individual is inwardly free, he chooses **as the good life this process of becoming**” (Rogers, 1961, p. 196, emphasis added). This “good life” is also a worthy, dignifying life. In this situation, the person lives in a dynamic balance in which the process of becoming happens; thus, the person can develop their potentials and live dignity.

Buber (1958) influences Rogers’ work in a different aspect. He brings the idea of relations. A phenomenology of relations. He states that “**To man the world is** twofold, in accordance with his twofold attitude” (Buber, 1958, p. 3, emphasis added). This is because there are two primary words: **I-Thou** and **I-It**. They are combined, not isolated. And the **I** from each primary word is different; it is also twofold. These primary words call up relations.

> Primary words do not describe something that might exist independently of them but being spoken they bring about existence. Primary words are spoken from the being. (Buber, 1958, p. 3).

The realms of **It** and **Thou** have different basis. The second primary word exists in experience, but the first only exists in relation “When **Thou** is spoken, the speaker has no **thing**; he has indeed nothing. But he takes his stand in relation.” (Buber, 1958, p. 4, emphasis added).

“**The man who experiences** has not part in the world. For it is ‘in him’ and not between him and the world that the experience arises.” (Buber, 1958, p. 5, emphasis added) Here, he separates the world of experience from the world of relation. There are three spheres in the world of relation: Life with nature, life with men, and life with spiritual beings.

Buber (1958) claims that in life with men, “the relation is open.” Here, “we can give and accept the **thou**” (p. 6, emphasis added). In other words, a person cannot experience the other, because that would turn them into an object. People live relations with each other.

> I do not experience the man to whom I say **Thou**. But I take my stand in relation to him, in the sanctity of the primary word. Only when I step out of it do I experience him once more. In the act of experience, **Thou** is far away. (Buber, 1958, p. 9, emphasis added).

Hence, relation is mutual and does not objectify. In the author’s concept, there is no **Thou** without **I**. “The **Thou** meets me. But I step into direct relation with it.”

(p. 11, emphasis added) And the primary word is also a primary act: "my speaking of the primary word to it is an act of my being, is indeed **the** act of my being." (p. 11, emphasis added) Consequently, the process of becoming happens in relation "I become through my relation to the **thou**; as I become **I**, I say **Thou**." (p. 11, emphasis added).

For Buber (1958, p. 11), meeting is an essential part of becoming "All real living is meeting." Rogers uses this specific essential relation to explain human growth in any part of life:

> If I can provide **a certain type of relationship**, the other person will discover within himself the capacity to use that relationship for growth and change and personal development will occur. (Rogers, 1961, p. 33, emphasis added).

Rogers explains reality as a first condition for relationship: "It is only by providing the **genuine reality** which is **in me**, that the other person can successfully seek for the **reality in him**." (p. 33, emphasis added) A clear link to Buber's essential meeting. It is not any kind of encounter. I must be truthful to myself, and show it allows the other person to do the same.

Two other conditions are part of Rogers' constructive relationship: Acceptance and liking; and a continuing desire to understand. By acceptance, he means an appreciation for every aspect of a person, either positive or negative. "This acceptance of each fluctuating aspect of this other person makes it for him a relationship of warmth and safety, and the safety of being liked and prized as a person seems a highly important element in a helping relationship." (p. 34).

The desire to understand is a "sensitive empathy" (p. 34) indispensable for acceptance to actually mean something:

> It is only as I **understand** the feelings and thoughts which seem so horrible to you, or so weak, or so sentimental, or so bizarre – it is only as **I see them as you see** them **and accept them and you**, that you feel really free to explore all the hidden nooks and frightening crannies of your inner and often buried experience. (Rogers, 1961, p. 34, emphasis added).

Therefore, a constructive, helpful relationship is transparent, deeply empathetic and accepts both people as they are, one trying to see the other through **his/her own eyes**. Here, we can see a deep phenomenological influence, which points out the necessity of a phenomenological method to understand how man live dignity. But not any phenomenological method; it must also address relations. That is why social phenomenology was chosen to understand how people can live dignity i n their work.

6.3 A Social Phenomenological Approach to Research

The aim of phenomenology is to study human phenomena, such as making sense of things as they are experienced in consciousness, regardless of causality or other aspects of natural sciences. It seeks the essence of such phenomena as it is presented from and by the subject of research.

Social phenomenology understands that people do not construct meaning individually, but in their relations with others. Not only with, but through others, as explained above. So, the essences found in social phenomenological research are considered to be constructed in an intersubjective way. Alfred Schutz developed a social phenomenological method.

Schutz's methodological position (Wilson, 2002) comes from Weber and Husserl. Weber introduces the concept of "ideal types," and Husserl adds the comprehension of the process of typification as crucial to understanding how people make sense of the world. Hence, Schutz creates a method for scientific typification, which also intends to make sense of the world, but considering structures of relevance and research objectives. This typification follows three general postulates: of logical consistency; of subjective interpretation; and of adequacy. Together, these postulates are a criteria to identify, classify, and compare forms of social action and interaction, into types (Wilson, 2002).

The first postulate sets the scientist apart from the ordinary person. Scientific constructs have objective validity. The second one anchors the research in the core phenomenological attitude to look at a phenomenon as the subject tells you, respecting their subjective interpretation. The third postulate ensures that constructs created by the scientist are understandable to the social actor, because they are consistent with the common-sense experience.

This method implies that these types emerge from data collected. Accordingly, relations between these types create synthesis and themes, all emerging from data, always being trustworthy to the interpretations by those who were part of the study.

6.4 Evidencing Dignity at Work as Part of the Process of Becoming

Assuming dignity as a goal to the process of becoming, and as an interpersonal process, data collected from 20 college professors were used to develop a social phenomenological study about dignity at work. Professors were interviewed at their workplaces. From their speech emerged the typification, themes, and syntheses, in which one can perceive a central theme to which others connect.

6.4.1 Personal Types

Data showed that professors created "personal types." This typification corresponds to their interpretation about their selves and about others. However, this interpretation is not only about how they are and act, but also about what they seek, what is meaningful to their lives. It is also about their purpose in life. Seven personal types were found:

- **Competitive type**
  This type values challenge. It is considered motivator, something that makes them "feel alive." Overcoming obstacles is considered an achievement that leads these people to act toward achieving these goals. It also comprises the possibility of personal recognition and fame.

- **Pioneer Type**
  This type describes curious people who seek out discovery and new things. They are continuously interested in learning more, exchange ideas with others, and develop more knowledge. They also enjoy innovation.

- **Serious/correct type**
  This type is concerned with doing the right thing, following rules, deadlines, and laws. They understand this as the "right" way of being. They are dedicated, disciplined, and have a "sense of justice," clearly knowing the difference between right and wrong, and enjoying to choose the right. They also feel deeply upset when misinterpreted.

- **Affectionate type**
  This type cares about being accepted, loved. They try to please other people and feel rewarded by responses of appreciation such as gratitude, tributes, signs of affection, and appreciation. Honors in ceremonies are considered evidence of recognition and gratitude. These are important positive and valuable elements to this type. These honors are described as "comforting," because they reassure that the professor "made a difference in their lives."

- **Emotional type**
  This type shares with the affectionate type the trait of evidencing sentimental aspects of the subject. However, the emotional type is impulsive. They are driven by emotions and feelings, they have emotional bursts, "lose their minds," And they also choose their careers emotionally, because they like it, despite financial or social status. These feelings are considered crucial for the profession.

- **Multiple type**
  This type appreciates the capacity of doing many activities at the same time. They teach, research, and also perform managerial activities in their institutions. They cherish that capacity. It gives them a sense of "fulfillment" because doing many things is rewarding, rather than because other people recognize their work. But that does not mean they do not like appreciation. Appreciation is considered a consequence of their work, not the reason for doing so many things.
  This type has difficulties to being different. Even if the multiple activities cause overload or diseasing, they find difficult doing away with some of them.

- **Artistic type**
  This type values the use of imagination, creativeness. They consider their work as an artistic expression, because designing the material for a class involves a creative process. So it demands an artistic sensibility, and they can express it.

Personal types are neither mutually exclusive, nor have any kind of hierarchy. A professor can be competitive and artistic, pioneer and emotional. Personal types, however, influence the objectives of life. The way someone perceives the self, and what they value are drivers of the goals they pursue. Therefore, the personal types influence the individuals' purposes in life.

6.4.2 Objectives of Life

Professors expressed their "objectives of life" in a myriad of ways. In the same way explained by Rogers (1961), each objective appeared in the speech connected to self-fulfillment. On this part of data collection, when professors were talking about their objectives of life related to the work they perform, dignity emerged in phrases such as "I believe that what I do is dignifying." They perceive their work as something that makes them worthy. However, there were four different possibilities to these objectives that, similarly to the personal types, are neither exclusive nor hierarchical. Since they were recurrent, they can also be treated as a form of typification. The types of objectives of life found were: perpetuity, triumph, usefulness, and transformation.

- **Perpetuity**
  This objective of life seeks to overcome death and human finitude. Perpetuity is possible thanks to the legacy left by the professor. This legacy can be something produced (scientific development, contribution to community) or the influence they have on their students. They are not forgotten after death, because their product will survive, they will be part of history, and students will remember them. What students learn in their classes is also part of their legacy. It is the same principle as reproduction, but here heritage is not biological or financial, it is a professional heritage. Students become professionals that perpetuate in the way they work what they learned from the professor. In other words, legacy is part of their professional training. So, perpetuity is achieved through someone else.
- **Triumph**
  This objective is driven by achievement, challenge the constant search for triumph is a part of it. In it, having success is not paramount, but being successful in something difficult, effort intensive. These professors value overcoming though situations. They are inspired by challenge. It makes them "feel alive." They enjoy it because it gives them a sense of victory and power ("I can handle it," "Few can do what I do"). Each example of overcoming is a victory, a moment of glory and self-achievement.
- **Usefulness**
  This objective emerged in speeches about helping others, making some kind of contribution to the other. The possibility to help is important. They cherish the idea that they can help students to become competent professionals and contribute to their development through the content delivered. These professors like interacting with students, it is pleasant for them. They also enjoy going beyond the content

of the class and being able to help students in other aspects of their future career. They feel frustrated and unworthy if they are forced to teach something useless, because it will not help students to be successful professionals.

In this objective of life, the I-Thou relation of Buber (1958), as discussed in the essential meeting from Rogers (1961), can be observed. The professor is in an essential encounter with the student because he/she is there for that student: open to him/her in order to help him/her. It is not an objectified, instrumental relation. The professor does not "own" knowledge and "gives" it. He/she is genuinely there to assist the student to build that knowledge. The student is perceived as an autonomous person, who learns new concepts and ideas enabled by the professor. Learning occurs through this encounter. It is a "connection," a situation of "sharing lives." The professor seeks to understand and value students.

Usefulness also applies to other aspects of a professor's work, for example, helping their institution, and somehow contributing to science. One can to do a lot for an institution by holding a position of coordination, helping to solve daily and unexpected issues. Being useful to science means expanding current knowledge. One professor explains this objective as a core aspect of her life that sets "her place in the world."

6.4.3 The Place in the World

- **Transformation**

  This objective relates to making a meaningful change in the *status quo*. These professors seek to cause transformation of something (knowledge, science) or someone, regardless if in small scale (one person) or large scale (society). Relevance lies in significance and depth. It is also a form of empowerment: they are agents who interfere in the course of life, rather than mere passive spectators. They can "make a difference." And they feel rewarded and stirred when someone tells them "you changed my life." It is comforting, a sense of mission accomplished.

  Once again, it should be noted that these objectives do not exclude each other. A professor may long for perpetuity and transformation. But all of them presented objectives. Some shared with a group, others not. However, objectives were always attached to the person each one of them is. Therefore, their behavior as professors, the way they perform their activities is also a manifestation of who they are. A feeling of honesty, of "acting as myself." This was a theme that emerged frequently. Hence, it deserves attention.

- **Acting as myself**

  In the speeches of the respondents, when discussing their experiences as professors, it could be observed that people reconciled their view of themselves with the way they act in the activity of teaching. They could make the class their own, giving a personal touch to it. The point was not specifically what they did, but the common aspect that any of them could be genuine as a person when they were acting in class. They could identify their selves, "this is me." This way, being a professor consorts with the process of becoming. It is not simply an occupation; it is a part of this person.

The classroom is customized. They can be spontaneous, natural. A humorous person can be playful, for example. This freedom of being true to their selves appeared in all interviews. However, the actions were not so free. There were many ways of translating this theme into practice.

Another aspect that came out from this specific way of working was the possibility of being authentic to personal values and principles. This aspect was considered very important, because professors can guide their behavior at work based on their beliefs of right and wrong, good or bad. And they also perceive a freedom of choice about their work (disciplines to teach, research to conduct), enabling to opt for activities with which they identify.

So, "acting as myself" shows up this idea that working as a professor lines up with the person he/she is. It "fits," "matches," "aligns" with interests and values. It is a part of life. Two matters constantly repeated as part of this construct were freedom and pleasure.

Freedom was mentioned both directly "I have freedom," and indirectly "I can speak." It is a chance for being authentic, not a space for impunity or violence. It is a responsible freedom, limited by the respect for others and obedience to rules. They are completely aware that actions have consequences. And that such freedom may not happen. Some institutions are pretty restrictive. As one of the professors said in an interview, some institutions do not accept suggestions and do not permit customization of classes. There are strict patterns to follow, which she called "being in hell." This specific person lived both alternatives of workplaces: one in which she could only follow patterns previously stated, and another where she could enjoy freedom to be herself. Then she declared, "I had contact with heaven and hell. … I had contact with dignity and the lack of dignity." This points out that freedom can be restricted at the workplace. So, it is perceived as a possibility to be cherished, not a mandatory requisite.

The professors interviewed repeated they "like" their work, it "amuses" them, is a "pleasure." These descriptions show a positive relationship with their activities as professors in workplaces that allow them to be their selves. They can create a classroom space that is personal, make them feel as their own classroom. Not because they are careless or irresponsible, and do not want to follow rules. It is the opposite. They love what they do, are deeply connected to it as subjects, and want to do their best. But this best is singular. The best of A is not the same as the best of B.

That is why choice means so much, i.e., create their own path to contribute to science, students, and the institution they work at. Being a professor like that means to be able to live the process of becoming as a professor. It is a life choice that lets "acting as myself" occur in order to fulfill the objectives of life. It is possible to be yourself (personal type) at work, develop yourself as a person and a professional there. Thus, two syntheses are found: living as a professor, and being myself as a professor.

- **Living as a professor**
  As mentioned before, the work configuration of these professors has room enough for customization, a "personal touch" to their classrooms, and orientation activities. In a certain way, it turns them into "my classroom" and enables "being myself as a professor." This means a singular construction, according with the personal types. At this point, the different possibilities and alternatives of career disclosed another typification: there are types of professors. Professors more engaged in research, professors more dedicated to teaching, professors dedicated to administrative activities at the university, and professors that try to balance different activities equally.

The synthesis "being myself as a professor" recaptures the feeling of honesty, authenticity and freedom mentioned in "acting as myself." It presents how these professors built this way of working that is personal and genuine, explaining methodological choices, conducts considered correct, and behaviors adopted. Therefore, descriptions shared the same dynamic involved in creation, but not the same configuration.

All these elements allowed understanding what these professors mean when they talk about realization. They described their selves (personal types), what they want in life (objectives of life), and how they achieve it through their activities (being myself as a professor, in the type of professor I work as), which allow them to be authentic to who they are (acting as myself). The dynamic process happening between this set of related elements is the professors' interpretation of what they understand as "living as a professor."

Their understanding of fulfillment goes back to the process of becoming, as explained by Rogers (1961, p. 35), which has a tendency toward self-actualization:

> [...] the directional trend which is evident in all organic and human life-the urge to expand, extend, develop, mature-the tendency to express and activate all the capacities of the organism, to the extent that such activation enhances the organism or the self.

Here comes up a central theme that connects all the other elements. This central theme is the experience of being accomplished, achieving realization due to working (and living) as professor. In other words, living realization through being a professor. Not any kind of professor, but being a professor in their specific and personal way. Nevertheless, it is necessary to point out that these are professors who feel deeply connected to their profession.

Living realization through being a professor appeared connected to multiple positive feelings: being victorious, happy, pleased, satisfied, joyful, and gratified. They also have an emotional link with the profession: they like to be professors. These elements feed a virtuous cycle: I am accomplished because I do something I like; I like what I do because it makes me accomplished. In other words, the sense of achieving is attached to positive feelings, and these feelings enhance the sense of realization. That does not mean these professors do not face difficulties, setbacks, frustration, loss, and disappointment. They do. But the gains involved in living realization through being a professor provide them with a balance in professional life that helps them cope with problems, negative feelings, and situations that may come about.

However, it is not a causality relation in strict sense. It is possible to identify the motives that drove the choices of these professors, and understand that specific selection. This, however, is not supposed to create generalization on a large scale, because a different social scenario could bring different interpretations about this profession. The point is the dynamic process involved.

Such a realization also enabled them to live dignity, because it is connected to them. In other words, their process of becoming happens when they are working. They can be themselves, develop their capacities, and evolve there. They do not just fulfill a task, they reach self-actualization. It is a process of living dignity as professors.

Put differently, they can reach self-actualization as individuals through their work as professors. When performing their activities, they achieve their objectives of life, what gives them a sense of realization. Yet, they can perform it honestly, being authentic. So, it is also realization to the self. That is why it is also a sense of living dignity. There is no need to play a part, to wear a mask. They are true to their personal types, ideas, and values. Relations with students can be essential meetings, instead of fake relations. There is no sham. Respondents presented this idea in their speeches: "I found myself in teaching," "I only fit in teaching," "I don't see myself doing anything else," "Here, in academic environment, I can explore my potential and interests to the maximum, hence, I feel closer to, I don't know, something that is me."

However, in this process of accomplishment, both personal and professional at work, there are some conditioning points which facilitate or hinder such an experience of accomplishment through work. Most of them are external, a matter of context: people they work with, specific characteristics from organization and students. These are not elements of the process of becoming per se, but once they are interpreted by the subjects, they gain meaning and become part of the process. However, one of them deserves special attention, not only because it is an important part of experience, but also because it appeared in every speech with the same meaning. It is the respect, which appears as an imperative condition to this relationship between experiencing accomplishment through work and living dignity. If there is no respect, all the positive aspects and experiences mentioned are threatened. So, respect is a starting point, which should not be missing if dignity at work is being discussed.

6.5 Implications for Management

The evidence brought by studying professors indicates a deep relationship between living dignity and being yourself even when other conditions where poor, such as old computers and low budgets, freedom to do what is meaningful to them, a work that provides a path to fulfill their process of becoming was enough to allow living dignity. They do complain about workplace conditions such as old computers and low budgets, but freedom to be their selves as professors overcomes difficulties.

These were professors from different universities, states, work regimes, ages, and many other aspects. Some have modern workplaces and high salaries. Others do not. But they are all proud to be professors because it is fulfilling to them as human beings. It brings a complex sense of achievement, connected to their essence, which is the core idea in connecting dignity and the process of becoming. They can work, succeed, and be their own selves.

This dynamic, exposed in the example, can be extrapolated to other professions and workplaces. If we look from the organizational point of view, some organizational processes from human resources gain new perspectives. Selection process must not only worry about the content in the *resumé*, but with the connection and expectations, this professional has with his/her career. Organizational and personal values must also be consistent. The internal policies and rules should provide enough freedom for them to turn their work "their own" and feel confident to express ideas. It is also important to create coaching plans that unite their objectives of life with the organizations' necessities and goals.

In practical terms, it means a great investment in management. From the highest CEO to the humblest worker, people must respect each other. There must be freedom, room for difference, but never to disrespect. There also must have a deep and genuine effort to show the values and goals of the company to all employees, so that people can know where they are and make it their own. It is necessary to constantly improve communication: actually, get to know and listen to people. Prepare managers to really look at and listen to their teams. In the same way, technology and economy are dynamic, so is the process of becoming. Even more so. Thus, dialog is absolutely necessary and thrust is a key element to a successful humanistic, "phenomenologically" based management. These people will be confident to share their hopes, dreams, and fears, showing managers their difficulties and aspirations, hence allowing meaningful career building. It is the I-Thou relationship happening in the workplace.

When people feel free to be their selves and turn their work into "their own," they can reach their life objectives through work and live dignity. Work is not an external imposition or obligation; it is part of the process of becoming.

6.6 Final Remarks

This chapter hopes to offer an understanding of dignity as part of the human process of becoming, a dynamic and intersubjective process, which occurs in all parts of human life. Hence, it is possible to comprehend work as a part of this intersubjective process; therefore, one can live dignity at work. To show this specific link, a small study, with one specific group of professionals, is presented. Nonetheless, such research follows carefully a social phenomenological method and has no pretension for more than offer a first glimpse of this approach to organizational dignity.

Although these findings are restricted to a group of professors, and a deeper investigation is necessary, it points out that the phenomenological process of becoming is linked to materializing the objectives of life by being their selves as professionals. There are many ways to live the process of becoming, and work is one of them. Feeling as a worthy professional, being yourself, helps to feel as a worthy person.

Following this line of thought, managers can choose the phenomenological approach to dignity as a path to promote dignity at work. It is not a simplistic choice. However, once the managers understand how work and workplace can contribute to their employee's process of becoming, they can realize the central role work plays in these employees' lives. It is not just an occupation: it is an essential part of their selves. Their process of becoming is happening as they are working. Human resources management no longer applies. It must turn into a human management: with people to people. Human beings can no longer be objectified as means to an end. Employees are, indeed, stakeholders. Perhaps, very important ones. Hence, companies can create a virtuous cycle: they contribute with the process of becoming of their employees, by allowing them to reach their objectives of life being their selves, and by developing their potential through work; and these workers deliver their very best to the company, because it enables them to feel worthy and happy as their own selves.

Understanding dignity at work throughout a phenomenological perspective shows it as core concept in the process of becoming. People strive to become worthy professionals, because this is part of who they are. When someone introduces him/herself as a professor, and the phrase is built as "I **am** a professor," this idea of a deep connection between work and self-perception emerges. The data showed that the interviewed professors had such a connection. "I am a professor" also meant "I become by being a professor, because I found my place as a worthy person in the world."

As a conclusion, it is possible to interpret that organizations that respect their employees as human beings, allowing them to live their process of becoming in and through their work also allows them to live dignity. This is positive for both sides: on the one hand, the organization will have satisfied, motivated employees, which have better performances; on the other hand, workers will feel good about their selves, seek an achievement that is meaningful to them and live dignity.

References

Buber, M. (1958). *I and Thou* (2a ed.). Translated into Portuguese by Ronald Gregor Smith. New York: The Scribner Library.

Kierkegaard, S. (1941 [1849]). *The sickness unto death*. Princeton, NJ: Princeton University.

Rogers, C. R. (1961). *On becoming a person*. Boston: Sentry Edition, Houghton Mifflin Company.

Wilson, T. D. (2002) . Alfred Schutz phenomenology and research methodology for information behavior research. In*ISIC4 – Fourth International Conference on Information Seeking in Context,* Universidade Lusiada, Lisbon, Portugal, September 11 to 13, 2002. Available at www.comminfo.rutgers.edu/~belkin/612-05/wilson-schutz.pdf. Accessed on December 10, 2019.

Part II
Organizational Dignity in Employee Perception

Chapter 7
Organizational Dignity in the Perspective of Brazilian, Portuguese and Mozambican Employees

Maria Luisa Mendes Teixeira, Silvia Marcia Russi De Domenico, and Lucia Maria Barbosa de Oliveira

Abstract The aim of this chapter was to compare organizational dignity evaluated by employees of three countries: Brazil, Portugal, and Mozambique. These countries have some cultural aspects in common as Brazil and Mozambique were colonized by Portugal. Could the organizational dignity perceived by employees be the same? In order to achieve the objective of evaluating practices of organizational dignity perceived by Brazilian, Portuguese and Mozambican employees and answer the question, an organizational dignity taxonomy is proposed. The characteristics of a dignified organization were identified, and the EPRA-DO scale to measure organizational dignity practices was refined. The results showed that Brazilians, Portuguese, and Mozambican employees evaluate organizational dignity of the companies they worked for differently. The factor of organizational dignity Practices of Promotion of Employees impact Brazilian employees' satisfaction almost twice as much as Portuguese and Mozambican. These results are important and call attention for management. In spite of the fact that the companies are in countries that have the same cultural root does not mean the employees evaluate the organizational dignity in the same way. These findings are especially important as organizational dignity influences the employee's satisfaction with company.

Keywords Worthy organization characteristics · Organizational dignity measurement · Employees

7.1 Introduction

Some studies have been developed reviewing the practices of organizational dignity in the relationship between corporations and several stakeholders. Araújo (2013), for example, reviewed the practices of dignity between corporation and community;

M. L. M. Teixeira (✉) · S. M. R. De Domenico · L. M. B. de Oliveira
São Paulo, Brazil
e-mail: marialuisa.teixeira@mackenzie.br; malluluisa@gmail.com

L. M. B. de Oliveira
e-mail: lmbdo@terra.com.br

M. L. Mendes Teixeira and L. M. B. de Oliveira (eds.), *Organizational Dignity and Evidence-Based Management*, https://doi.org/10.1007/978-3-030-68560-7_7

Louback (2012) investigated the practices of dignity between call center companies and customers. Ferreira (2017) examined the relationship between practices of dignity perceived by customers and organizational values. Kosmann (2018) studied dignity in the B2B relations, to mention just a few.

Some studies intend to analyze the evaluation of employees about the dignity of the company in which they work. Santana (2011) developed that kind of study in a private financial organization, and Valença (2014) performed another study in a public financial institution. Teixeira et al. (2014) reviewed the organizational dignity perceived by Brazilian employees from different geographic regions of Brazil. Mendes et al. (2018) investigated the perception of managers and non-managers about the dignity of their companies.

Studies with employees typically apply the EPRA-DO scale developed by Teixeira et al. (2011). The scale proved to be reliable and valid in several samples from different geographic regions of Brazil. However, would the EPRA-DO scale be reliable and valid when applied to employees in other countries? This question fostered us to, in a first stage, apply the scale to countries sharing similar cultural matrix, as is the case to Brazil, Portugal, and Mozambique.

We took the opportunity to refine the EPRA-DO scale to make it more parsimonious and rule out the instability of some few items.

The refined EPRA-DO scale resulted in 24 items, with reliability above 0.7 (Bido, 2012), convergent validity following the AVE criteria (Fornell & Larcker, 1981), and discriminant validity following the criteria of square root of AVE of each latent variable (Chin & Newsted, 1999).

The scale proved to be valid for the three samplings. The organizational dignity evaluations were compared among employees in the three countries. Moreover, the influence of organizational dignity on the satisfaction with the company and the possibilities for management-based interventions aimed to increase the employees' satisfaction were analyzed.

7.2 Organizational Dignity: A Taxonomy

Teixeira et al. (2010) turn to King et al. (2010) to advocate for the organization as a social actor, investigating the concept of worthy company in the perception of the Brazilian workers. Other authors also join this squad, like Ahmed and Machold (2004), who support that additionally to economic agency, organizations are also an agency as corporate citizen that concerns actions in both the community and the society that host them. The idea of organization as social actor is not new, dating back to Selznick (1949) who acknowledged the individual and exclusive character of the organization as a social actor. That said, it would be appropriate labeling the term 'organizational' with the adjective 'dignity,' in agreement with the authors that advocate for the agency of organizations. The concept of dignity gives rise to heated debates involving different concepts: one that supports the universal concepts of dignity, and other that claims the impossibility of establishing one single concept detached from time and space. This polarity is rooted in history and drags on since the ancient Rome times (Riley, 2010).

The Eastern world has associated dignity to time and space, and to the distinction of the individual in the society they live, via distinguished social status or legal differentiation, where some category of human beings are deprived from dignity, as happens with slaves (Riley, 2010). This differentiation is of cultural nature, socially assigned, and can take on different shapes like social conformity, for example (Kohen & Leung, 2008).

As a universal and normative concept, dignity is rooted in Christianity, in the Enlightenment concept of world, and in post-war human rights in the second half of the twentieth century. The Christian world is the cradle of the idea of creation of human beings in God's image, superior to the other beings, having the right to governing nature (Kristellar, 1979). Kant's concept of valuation of reason stands out in the Enlightenment (Kant, 2005). This concept still influences the concept of dignity in the western world (Gosdal, 2007), similarly to the concept of universal rights in the Declaration of Human Rights enacted by the United Nations Organization in 1948.

Apart from the concept of dignity as assigned dignity (distinction) or inherent to the human being, either influenced by Christianity or by the human rational nature (universal), there are other opposing concepts, like that of social construction (Jacobson, 2007). In this sense, dignity is built in the interactions between people, constituted in encounters that either promote or violate dignity.

Teixeira et al. (2014), debating on the possibility of building a theory of organizational dignity, propose a taxonomy of dignity that is classified according to scope and materiality. With regard to the scope, organizational dignity is classified in 'private dignity' corresponding to 'distinction' and 'social construction,' and 'universal dignity' which is subdivided into 'moral' and 'rights.' Regarding materiality, dignity may be classified as abstract (moral, distinction, rights) or concrete when it refers to organizational practices that underpin the relationships with stakeholders, whether they are employees, customers, vendors, or even the society and the environment.

The multifaceted and multidimensional nature of the concept lead to deeper discussions about the practices of organizational dignity to be evaluated by stakeholders, since stakeholders evaluate organizational dignity considering not only themselves as deserver of worthy relations, but also considering how they perceive worthy relations regarding the others.

7.3 Characteristics of a Worthy Company

The characteristics of a worthy company were identified based on a survey comprising 200 participants. An online questionnaire was sent to participants containing one single question: what words or expressions would describe a worthy company? Participants belong to the networking to the research group, who indicated other individuals, and so on. Of the 200 respondents, 197 informed their sexual gender, resulting in 105 men (53.3%) and 92 women (46.7%). The average age of respondents is 39.95 years, in a range from 20 to 69 years old holding higher education degree (99.5%). Altogether, 551 responses were submitted and analyzed through content analysis.

Of the responses submitted, 54.4% were classified as values; 34.7% concerned relationship with stakeholders; 4.0% concerned results for stakeholders; 0.4% concerned the attributes of the companies' employees; and 6.5% concerned corporate attributes.

Responses were assigned to the category of values based on the categories of terminal and instrumental values. Terminal values concern final stages of life, while instrumental values concern how these stages are reached (Rokeach, 1973). The following values were identified in the responses: honesty, justice, respect, transparency/truth/sincerity, responsibility, seriousness, confidence and recognition, leadership, loyalty, solidarity.

The responses classified as 'environmental responsibility,' 'social responsibility,' 'relationships with employees,' 'relationships with customers,' and 'relationships with the government' were considered as 'relationships with stakeholders'; Considering that, despite the multitude of concepts about the meaning of stakeholders, all concepts share a common point: groups of interest that are somehow connected to the organizations, as suggested by Starik (1994). Considering the environment as a stakeholder may seem odd, but Starik (1994) himself, when discussing the criteria to consider what entities should be included in the concept of stakeholders, points out that the nature of stakeholders should not be restrained to human beings. According to the author, at least earth's atmosphere, hydrosphere, lithosphere, and biosphere should be regarded as stakeholders of human organizations.

The category 'relationships with employees' ranked 1st in the references by respondents, summing 81 statements that accounted for 42.4% of the total references concerning relationships with stakeholders. Actions related to 'social responsibility' (20.1%) ranked 2nd followed by 'relationships with clients' (16.2%) ranked in 3rd, 'environmental responsibility' (13.8%) in 4th, and 'relationships with government' (7.3%) in 5th.

Most statements concerning relationships with employees bear upon respect to the employee, fair labor relations, and valuation of the employee (60.5%). These categories were pooled into a broader category named 'ethics toward employees' in the sense of morality. The second pool of categories was named 'hygienic factors' and gathered elements of 'safety' and 'healthy and welcoming environment,' assembling 21% of the mentions. Finally, the pool of categories named 'opportunities for growth' came next, involving 'motivation for development' and 'challenging job' (18.5%).

The frequency and classification of responses concerning relationships with employees suggest that employees perceive that organizations still have a great deal to do regarding basic aspects such as treating employees following a moral of respect and consideration. The same is true for basic hygienic aspects related to service contract, wage, and healthy workplace.

The 'social responsibility' category, ranked 2nd, was mentioned 40 times, mostly corresponding to the statement-answer 'social responsibility,' or with the same meaning as, for example, the expression 'socially engaged' or 'social commitment.'

The expression 'social responsibility' has been largely used by the media to refer to a wide range of social actions developed by companies, mainly those of welfare nature. Here, the expression was reflected in the results found, accounting for 80% of the statements related to the category. This result suggests that respondents believe that, to be worthy in the light of social responsibility, companies should focus their actions mainly on welfare-centered activities.

Customers were the third stakeholder mentioned more frequently by respondents, with 31 quotations split among statements related to products, services, and care, added with others related to respect and transparency.

Answers related to 'environmental responsibility,' ranked 4th, similarly to the responses related to 'social responsibility' are gathered under the broader expression 'environmental responsibility' and account for 64% of the statements. This expression is also very frequent in the media. As it is a very comprehensive expression, it does not allow the effective identification of what respondents do think. Concretely, it does not make clear what practices of environmental responsibility are expected to be developed to consider a company as worthy in this light. On the other hand, despite the frequent discussions about environmental responsibility in the media, this category was not among the categories most mentioned by respondents. These results are coherent with Matsushita (2004), who found in the results of his work that environment is one of the stakeholders less appraised.

Government **was the fifth** stakeholder, mentioned by respondents in 14 statements approaching compliance with fiscal, tax, labor laws, and other obligations of legal and civil nature.

Relationships with shareholders were not explicitly mentioned. However, they could be inferred from the corporate features that, in addition to clear reference to profitability and competitiveness, refer to other associated features such as competence, flexibility, entrepreneurship, openness to change, among others. This category accounts for 6.5%, with more references than environmental responsibility, for example.

The categories identified through the classification of statements provided by respondents as responses may be classified considering the achievement of the concept, i.e., the cognitive representation of what a worthy company should be. In this sense, categories could be arranged in three sets: (a) set of antecedents; (b) set of attributes; (c) set of consequents.

The set of antecedents is represented by one single category: 'characteristics of leaders,' while the set of categories of consequents is represented by the category 'results for stakeholders.' The set of attributes is represented by the following categories: 'values,' 'relationships with employees,' 'relationships with customers,' 'relationships with government,' 'social responsibility,' 'environmental responsibility,' 'corporate characteristics' (Fig. 7.1).

The results found revealed that suppliers as a category of stakeholders do not deserve the respondents' attention regarding attitudes to be taken by corporations to be considered as worthy. The reason why this category was not considered should be further investigated.

'Values' came up as the main category for companies to be considered as worthy, including transparency, sincerity, and truth. This supports the concept of organizational dignity proposed by Teixeira et al. (2008), but does not exhaust it. In other words, as mentioned in the theoretical framework, communication actions are not enough for considering a company as worthy.

Apart from other values than transparency, results point out sets of actions aimed at stakeholders, as well as corporate characteristics. Results show that in their concept of a worthy company, respondents do not rule out profitability or satisfaction of shareholders, provided these are considered simultaneously with the satisfaction of other stakeholders. However, the perception of respondents about these actions deserves some remarks.

Respondents seem to miss a clear idea about the society-oriented actions that companies are expected to develop in order to be socially responsible. Or, maybe, they do not hold an accurate critical posture on this matter, since most responses related to this category consisted in the expression 'social responsibility,' that is frequently used by the media and may comprise a wide range of actions toward welfare. The same lack of precision comes up when they approach environmental responsibility. The environmental responsibility so discussed in the media was not included among the main categories of attributes related to a worthy company, lagging behind other stakeholders such as employees and customers.

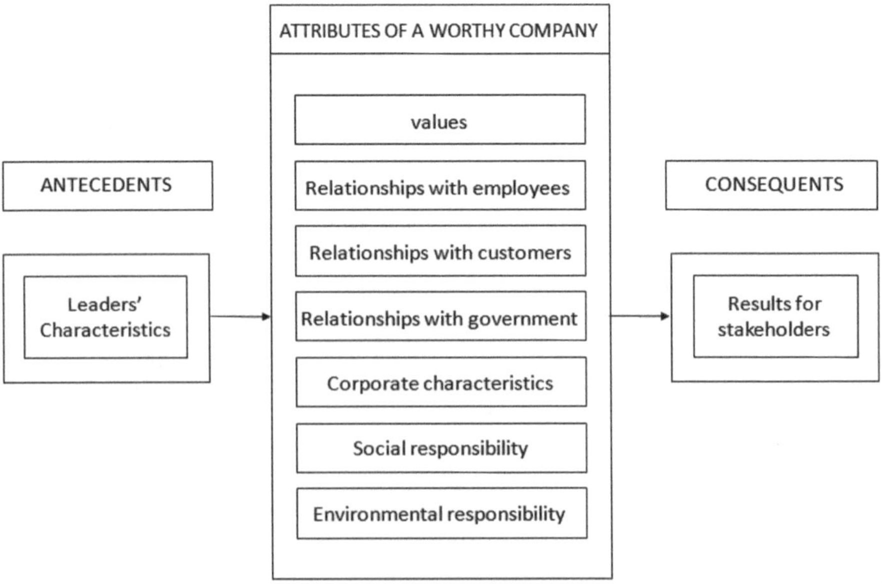

Fig. 7.1 Conceptual model of a worthy company in the perspective of the Brazilian employees

The emergence of 'values,' such as 'relationships with employees' and 'social responsibilities' as main categories, added to the fact that most statements in the employee-related category referred to basic aspects such as respect to employees, justice, appraisal, hygienic factors; because of this it is clear that in the perception of respondents the companies have yet a lot to do before becoming worthy. This perception suggests that companies are in those audiences' debt.

7.4 How Dignity of an Organization Should Be Assessed in the Perspective of Employees

The first version of the EPRA-DO scale aimed at assessing the dignity of an organization, i.e., organizational dignity, was developed by Teixeira et al. (2011). The five-point scale, ranging from 'absolutely disagree' to 'absolutely agree' comprised 31 items spread over five factors, namely: F1-Practices of Promotion of Employees, F2-Practices of Social Responsibility, F3-Practices of Respect to the Rights of Employees, F4-Practices of Offer of Quality Products and Services, F5-Non-misleading Practices (Transparency).

This scale had been previously applied to many studies, retaining these five factors with some changes to their structure, where one or another item was displaced from a factor to another. The instability of some items could affect the comparative evaluation of the practices of organizational dignity perceived by employees, along with the study of their antecedents and consequents. Because of that, it was necessary to refine the EPRA-DO scale. To refine the scale, it was applied to a sampling of 407 employees in the State of Sao Paulo (51%), of which 51.2% were male and 48.8% female, 50% aged from 18 to 31 years, 75% from 18 and 42 years, holding undergraduate or graduate degree (80%).

In order to reduce the number of items and produce better balance between items by factor, the first procedure was to rotate the exploratory factor analysis (EFA) through the extraction of main components and varimax rotation. The EFA resulted in KMO = 0.946, five factors, explained variance = 63.54%, and Cronbach's alphas above 0.8. The analysis of the rotated matrix and of the contribution of each item to the reliability of factors did not allow the identification of opportunities for reduction. Therefore, the correlational analysis by factor was selected. It considered the intensity of correlation and number of pairs with the highest or lowest correlations comparatively to the items within the factor.

For Factor A, the highest correlations are above 0.6, and this cutoff was elected to select the variables to be included in the new short scale, according to the number of pairs of correlations to which they belonged. Factor B relied only on four variables, which is the minimum number of items required to minimize the bias of measurement models (Chin & Newsted, 1999). In the five-variable Factor C, one of the variables recorded four correlations below 4.0, behaving differently from the others that recorded higher correlations and, therefore, was ruled out. No variable in Factor

D presented a number of correlations in the correlation index capable of differentiating them from the others. The same happened with Factor E. These procedures resulted in the reduction of seven items. The remaining 24 items were subjected to EFA with Promax rotation, and axis factoring extraction method, resulting in KMO = 0.946, five factors, and explained variation = 58.66%. The quantity of items and Cronbach's alphas of each factor were as follows: (a) F1-Practices of Promotion of Employees—seven items and 0.926; (b) F2-Practices of Social Responsibility—five items and 0.856; (c) F3-Practices of Respect to the Rights of Employees—four items and 0.805; (d) F4-Practices of Offer of Quality Products and Services—four items and 0.837; (e) F5-Non-misleading Practices (Transparency)—four items and 0.761.

The convergent and discriminant validities were assessed applying the 24-item EPRA-DO scale through an electronic form to a sampling of 199 professors of universities from the northeast and southeast regions of Brazil, with age up to 40 years, mostly men (61%), of whom 20% held managerial positions. Data were subjected to confirmatory factor analysis (CFA) through partial least squares—path modeling (PLS-PM). The application of the PLS-PM as measurement model requires meeting some criteria do increase the accuracy of the model. These criteria include, among others: Sampling size—ten times the number of indicators of the latent variable with the highest number of indicators; number of indicators of each latent variable, at least four (Chin & Newsted, 1999); latent variable reliability higher than 0.9, preferably 0.95 when important decisions will be made based on the tests results, and 0.7 at early stages of the construct validity (Nunnally & Bernstein, 1994).

The PLS-PM measurement model implies assessing the construct validity, through the assessment of convergent and discriminant validities. The convergent validity is assessed through the average variance extracted (AVE) that must be equal to or higher than 0.5 (Fornell & Larcker, 1981); composite reliability equal to or higher than 0.7 (BIDO, 2012); and t value between each indicator and related latent variable at a minimum level of 0.5 (Gefen & Straub, 2005). The discriminant validity, in turn, is assessed by means of the analysis of the factor loading of each factor, which must be higher in the latent variable to which it belongs, and lower in the other variables. Gefen and Straub (2005) mention, for illustration purposes, that if the load of an item is 0.7 in the expected variable, it should not exceed 0.6 in the remaining variables. Another analysis is performed through the square root of AVE of each latent variable, which must be higher than the correlation between the latent variables (Chin, 1998). Gefen and Straub (2005) refer to the non-existence of any standard regarding the amplitude of that difference.

The short EPRA-DO scale (24 items) proved to have proper psychometric properties to assess organizational dignity in the perspective of employees, considering that it meets the criteria of convergent and discriminant validities: (a) AVE of each latent variable ranging from 0.608 to 0.618; (b) composite reliability ranging from 0.861 to 0.917; (c) Cronbach's Alpha between 0.784 and 0.893; square root of AVE higher than the correlation between the LVs; (d) the factor loading of each item higher in the expected LV higher than the factor loading of the other variables.

7.5 Organizational Dignity in the Perspective of the Brazilian Employees

The study comprised 2509 employees distributed over the southeast (42%) and north-east (58%) regions of Brazil. These regions were selected due to research group's local networking. Gender distribution was well-balanced, with a slight difference in favor of women (51%). Most respondents were aged up to 45 years (70%) and held undergraduate and graduate degree (70%).

The first procedure to assess the practices of organizational dignity perceived by employees was to verify if the measurement model was valid for the sampling data, otherwise the assessment with the proposed LVs would be derailed. The results found confirmed the convergent validity and met the criteria proposed by Fornell and Larcker (1981), Bido (2012), as much as the t test criterion proposed by Gefen and Straub (2005). The discriminant validity was also confirmed following the criteria of Chin (1998) and Gefen and Straub (2005).

Factor F5-Non-misleading Practices (Transparency) reached the highest mean value (4.38), followed by F3-Practices of Respect to the Rights of Employees (4.03), F4-Practices of Offer of Quality Products and Services (3.51), F2-Practices of Social Responsibility (2.95), F1-Practices of Promotion of Employees (2.85). In order to verify the significance of the difference between means, the Paired Samples t Test was calculated, considering a significance level = 0.5. Results show that the factors' means differ from each other.

7.6 Organizational Dignity in the Perspectives of Portuguese and Mozambican Employees

The Scale of Practices of Dignity was adapted to the European Portuguese and applied in both countries, Portugal and Mozambique. The studies developed in both countries are presented below.

7.6.1 Organizational Dignity in the Perspective of Portuguese Employees

The sampling of Portuguese managers and employees comprised 197 subjects in the age group of 20 to 60 years old, with approximately 60% of respondents holding undergraduate or graduate degree, and 63% of male respondents. In this sampling, the convergent analysis of the EPRA-DO scale led to the exclusion of one variable. The convergent and discriminant validities of the results of the scale without that item, therefore with 23 items, were confirmed. The convergent validity was confirmed according to the loading factor and AVE, while the discriminant validity was confirmed through both criteria of crossed-loading, and of square root of AVE. Cronbach's alphas and composite reliability certified the scale reliability for the sample.

Factor F3-Practices of Respect to the Rights of Employees achieved the highest mean in the sampling of Portuguese employees (4.46), followed by factor F5-Non-misleading Practices (Transparency) with mean = 4.39, F2-Practices of Social Responsibility (4.07), F4-Practices of Offer of Quality Products and Services (3.60), and F1-Practices of Promotion of Employees (3.27). The Paired Samples t Test showed no statistical difference between Factors F3 and F5. Both factors are ranked first in the evaluation of practices of organizational dignity.

Results for the Portuguese sample were slightly different from those for the Brazilian sample. While the Brazilian employees better evaluated factor F5-Non-misleading Practices (Transparency), the Portuguese employees better evaluated F3-Practices of Respect to the Rights of Employees. It suggests that the Portuguese's evaluation of respect to the rights of employees as a factor that translated the organizational dignity of their companies was even better than that of the Brazilians.

7.6.2 Organizational Dignity in the Perspective of Mozambican Employees

The study comprised 201 Mozambican managers and employees in the age group of 20 to 40 years, of which 60% concluded primary or secondary school, and 60% were men. The validity of EPRA-DO construct was confirmed by the results that certified the convergent and the discriminant validities based on the factor loading and AVE criteria, respectively; the crossed-loading and square root of AVE were higher than the correlation between latent variables. Cronbach's alphas also certify the reliability of all factors.

The factor F3-Practices of Respect to the Rights of Employees reached the highest mean (4.34), followed by factor F5-Non-misleading Practices (Transparency) (4.11), and of factors F2-Practices of Social Responsibility with means of 3.63 and 3.64, respectively. Factor F4-Practices of Offer of Quality Products and Services recorded the lowest mean. The Paired Sample t Test showed that means of factors F1 and F2 had no statistically significant difference.

7.7 Comparison of the Evaluations of Practices of Organizational Dignity

The best evaluated practices of organizational dignity evaluated by the employees from the three countries participating in the survey were F5-Non-misleading Practices (Transparency) and F3-Practices of Respect to the Rights of Employees. Both practices ranked first for the Portuguese employees (Fig. 7.2).

Despite the favorable evaluation of factor F5, the ANOVA and Scheffé tests revealed differences between the three countries (Figs. 7.2 and 7.3). Transparency practices were better evaluated in Portugal, while the results of the Brazilian and Mozambican samples were similar. Likewise, the three countries showed significant statistical difference for Factor F3. Brazil was the country that best rated the Practices of Respect to the Rights of Employees.

F1-Practices of Promotion of Employees was the worst-rated factor for Brazilian and Portuguese employees, while in Mozambique, it ranked first. Considering the statistically significant differences (ANOVA and Scheffé), the Portuguese employees were more skeptical in relation to the Practices of Promotion of Employees.

Factor F5 gathers practices such as 'try to deceive the customer,' 'try to deceive the employee,' 'exploitation of employees,' and 'evade taxes' with reverse direction. This factor belongs to the category of organizational dignity materiality in the abstract, moral, and universal scope modality. Results for the three samplings are intriguing if compared to the results of factor F1-Practices of Promotion of Employees, since it was one of the worst-rated factors.

The positioning of F5 in the three samplings ranging from 'agree a lot' to 'completely agree,' with most responses of 'completely agree,' seems quite strange.

Ranking	Brazil	Portugal	Mozambique
1st.	F5-Non-misleading Practices (Transparency)	F3-Practices of Respect to the Rights of Employees reached the highest mean in the sampling of Portuguese employees F5-Non-misleading Practices (Transparency)	F3-Practices of Respect to the Rights of Employees
2nd.	F3-Practices of Respect to the Rights of Employees	F2-Practices of Social Responsibility	F5-Non-misleading Practices (Transparency).
3rd.	F4-Practices of Offer of Quality Products and Services	F4-Practices of Offer of Quality Products and Services	F1-Practices of Promotion of Employees, F2-Practices of Social Responsibility
4th.	F2-Practices of Social Responsibility	F1-Practices of Promotion of Employees.	F4-Practices of Offer of Quality Products and Services
5th.	F1-Practices of Promotion of Employees		

Fig. 7.2 Different rankings of factors in the three countries

F1-Practices of Promotion of Employees,
Brazil (3.49) ≠ Portugal (3.27) ≠ Mozambique (3.63)

F2-Practices of Social Responsibility
Portugal (4.07) ≠ Mozambique (3.64) ≠ Brazil (4.02)

F3-Practices of Respect to the Rights of Employees
Portugal (4.46) ≠ Brazil (4.62) ≠ Mozambique 4.34

F4-Practices of Offer of Quality Products and Services
Brazil (3.55) ≠ Mozambique (2.80) ≠ Portugal (3.60)

F5 Non-misleading Practices (Transparency)
Brazil (4.18) ≠ Portugal (4.39) ≠ Mozambique (4.11)

Fig. 7.3 Difference of factors' means in the three countries

Would there be a mirror effect, so that when answering about moral actions of the organization toward stakeholders, employees would perceive themselves as part of those actions? Or, otherwise, would they perceive that their organizations comply with labor laws (Factor F3), which is part of the concrete and universal dignity, be enough for them to abstract a favorable evaluation of the abstract moral universal organizational dignity in the relationship with their selves and the other stakeholders? These issues deserve to be deepened in further studies. Regrettably, the dignity of relationships with employees seems to be all about complying with labor laws.

The fact that Mozambican employees were less skeptical in relation to Practices of Promotion of Employees, while Portuguese employees were the most skeptical, also raises some questions. Would the Mozambican employees be less skeptical because they face more difficulties for surviving than the Brazilian and Portuguese employees? Would the Portuguese employees be more skeptical because they experience better living conditions than the Brazilian and Mozambican employees? Would living conditions affect the perception of organizational dignity? This is yet another issue that deserves attention to continue with studies about organizational dignity.

Another result that deserves attention is the Practices of Social Responsibility factor F2, which is also a factor of moral, abstract, and universal dignity. In Mozambique, it got the third lowest mean, suggesting that worthy relationships with the society are not yet part of the reality of the organizational schedule, and that the discourse on social responsibility is away from the practice.

The Practices of Offer of Quality Products and Services recorded an intermediary evaluation, except for the Mozambicans that made the worst evaluation either compared to the other factors or compared to the other two countries.

7.8 Implications for Management

The multiple regression analysis with sample-to-sample data was performed to ponder over the implications of organizational dignity on management, in an attempt to identify the influence of those practices on the satisfaction with the company. For the three samples, the factor F1-Practices of Promotion of Employees was the most influent factor on the satisfaction with the company. In Brazil, this factor explained 41.2% of the satisfaction of employees with their companies, in Portugal 29.7%, and in Mozambique 29.9%. The factor F2-Practices of Social Responsibility in Portugal accounted for 2.3%, in Mozambique for 1.5%, and in Brazil for 2.0%. The other factors do not influence the satisfaction with the company neither for the Portuguese nor for the Mozambican employees. For Brazilians, the factor F5-Non-misleading Practices (Transparency) accounted for 6.4%. The factors F3-Practices of Respect to the Rights of Employees, F4-Practices of Offer of Quality Products and Services did not influence the satisfaction of employees with their companies in any of the samples.

Therefore, the Practices of Promotion of Employees hosts the opportunity for managers to influence the satisfaction of employees with the company. To know what Practices of Promotion of Employees influence more the satisfaction of employees with their companies, the multiple regression was calculated considering the satisfaction with the company as the dependent variable, and the variables included in factor F1-Practices of Promotion of Employees as independent variables. Regarding the Brazilian sampling, the variables that more influenced satisfaction with the company were as follows: acknowledge the value of the employee; offer opportunities to employees; promote based on merit; enable the participation of employees in the processes of promotion. For the Portuguese sampling, the most influent variants were: offer conditions for the professional development; offer opportunities to employees; and promote based on merit. For the Mozambican sampling, in turn, the most influent variables were: offer conditions for the professional development, offer opportunities to employees, and acknowledge the value of employees. The common variable for the three countries was offer opportunities to employees. Therefore, these are variables that should be continuously monitored, considering their influence on the evaluation of organizational dignity perceived by employees.

7.9 Final Remarks

The objective proposed to this survey was to evaluate practices of organizational dignity perceived by Brazilian, Portuguese and Mozambican employees, considering them as interconnected in a networked relationship involving employees, customers and society. To that, the EPRA-DO scale firstly developed by Teixeira et al. (2011) was refined.

Results showed that employees give favorable evaluation about the relationships of dignity of their organizations, tending to disagree that relationships are driven by deceitful practices. It raises the hypothesis that when employees evaluate the organization, they see their own image reflected on it and, therefore, respond in a way to prevent cognitive dissonance. This topic demands further studies to elucidate this issue.

The dignity of relationships between organizations and employees is virtually restricted to complying with the labor laws. The practices of promotion of the development of employees are the less perceived by the employees. As these are practices of dignity of private and concrete scope—distinction, it is observed that employees tend to feel underestimated by the companies. It could be said that dignity is being recognized only as compliance with labor rights. This factor and the offer of quality products and services to customers seem to explain the main influence on organizational dignity evalution.

The Portuguese employees were the most skeptical about the evaluation of Practices of Promotion of Employees, and the ones that best rated the Non-misleading Practices. Mozambican employees recorded the worst evaluations of Practices of Social Responsibility, and Practices of Offer of Quality Products and Services.

The Practices of Promotion of Employees were the ones that most influenced the satisfaction with the company in the samplings of employees from the three countries. However, in order to enable managers to identify what indicator of these practices deserves more attention, the intensity of influence of all indicators should be verified in each company to select those providing stronger leverage.

The practices of organizational dignity, notably those related to the Promotion of Employees, proved their relevant potential to promote the satisfaction of employees with their companies.

References

Ahmed, P. K., & Machold, S. (2004). The quality and ethics connection: Toward virtuous organizations. *Total Quality Management, 15*(4), 527–545. https://doi.org/10.1080/1478336042000183604.

Araújo, B. F. B. A. (2013). Construção dos Significados de Dignidade no âmbito da relação entre Empresas e Comunidade. In Annals of the *XXXVII ENANPAD*, Rio de Janeiro, RJ.

Bido, D. S. (2012). *Modelagem de Equações estruturais com estimação PLS*. ANPAD.

Chin, W. W. (1998). The partial least squares approach for structural equation modeling. In G. A. Marcoulides (Ed.), *Methodology for business and management. Modern methods for business research* (p. 295–336). Lawrence Erlbaum Associates Publishers.

Chin, W., & Newsted, P. (1999). Structural equation modeling analysis with small samples using partial least squares. In R. Hoyle (Ed.). *Statistical strategies for small sample research* (pp. 307–341). Sage Publications.

Ferreira, M. S. (2017). Dignidade e Valores Organizacionais sob o olhas do cliente. IV Congresso Lusófono em Comportamento Organizacional e Gestão. São Paulo. SP. Brasil, 23 e 24. Retrieved November, 10, 2020 from https://fdocumentos.tips/document/iv-congresso-lusfono-de-comportamento-organizacional-e-condies-para-que-se.html.

Fornell, C., & Larcker, D. F. (1981). Evaluating structural equation models with unobservable variables and measurement error. *Journal of Marketing Research, 18*(1), 39–50. https://doi.org/10.1177/002224378101800104.

Gefen, D., & Straub, D. (2005). A practical guide to factorial validity using PLS-graph: Tutorial and annotated example. *Communications of the Association for Information Systems*, 16. https://doi.org/10.17705/1CAIS.01605.

Gosdal, T. C. (2007). *Dignidade do Trabalhador:um conceito construído sob o paradigma do trabalho decente e da honra.* LTr.

Jacobson, N. (2007). Dignity and health: A review. *Social Science & Medicine, 64,* 292–302. https://doi.org/10.1016/j.socscimed.2006.08.039.

Kant, I. (2005). Fundamentação da metafísica dos costumes. Tradução Paulo Quintela. Lisboa: Edições 70.

King, B. G., Felin, T., & Whetten, D. A. (2010). Finding the organization in organizational theory: A meta-theory of the organization as a social actor. *Organization Science, 21*(1), 290–305. https://doi.org/10.1287/orsc.1090.0443.

Kohen, D., & Leung, A. (2008). Dignity in western versus in Chinese cultures: Theoretical overview and practical illustrations. *Business and Society Review, 113*(4). https://doi.org/10.1111/j.1467-8594.2008.00329.x.

Kosmann, G. (2018). *Dignidade Organizacional na Relação Entre Fornecedor e Cliente, em Contexto Business to Business.* Dissertação de mestrado. Programa de Administração de Empresas: Universidade Presbiteriana Mackenzie.

Kristellar, P. O. (1979). *Renaissance thought and its sources.* Colombia University Press.

Louback, J. C. (2012). *Dignidade e relações de poder: um estudo em um call center à luz de Foucault.* Doctorate thesis in Business Administration, Mackenzie Presbyterian University (UPM), Sao Paulo, SP, Brazil. Retrieved from https://tede.mackenzie.br/jspui/handle/tede/790.

Matsushita, M. (2004). A Influência dos Valores dos Gestores no Papel de Recursos Humanos. 2004. 0 f. Dissertação (Mestrado em Administração de Empresas) - Universidade Presbiteriana Mackenzie.

Mendes, L. H. L., Oliveira, M. L. B., Teixeira, M.L.M. & Lucian, R. (2018). Espiritualidade *versus* Dignidade nas Organizações: estudo com gestores e não-gestores. XXI SEMEAD Seminários em Administração, FEA-UPS, São Paulo, novembro de 2018 ISSN 2177-3866

Nunnally, J. C., & Bernstein, I. H. (1994). *Psychometric theory* (3rd ed.). New York, NY: McGraw-Hill Inc.

Riley, S. (2010). Human dignity: Comparative and conceptual debates. *International Journal of Law in Context, 6*(2), 117–138. https://doi.org/10.1017/S1744552310000030.

Rokeach, M. (1973). *The nature of human values.* New York, NY: Free Press.

Santana, M. M. (2011). *Dignidade Organizacional: um estudo em uma organização financeira* (Master's degree dissertation). Mackenzie Presbyterian University, Sao Paulo, Brazil.

Selznick, P. (1949). *TVA and the grass roots: A Study in the sociology offormal organization.* Harper and Row.

Starik, M. (1994). Essay by Mark Starik. pp. 89–95 of The Toronto conference: Reflections on stakeholder theory. *Business & Society*, (33), 82–131.

Teixeira, M. L. M. et al. (2008). Dignidade Organizacional: valores e relações com stakeholders. In M. L. M. Teixeira (Org.). *Valores humanos & gestão: novas perspectivas*, Senac.

Teixeira, M. L. M., Dias, S. M. R. C., Araujo, B. F. B., Paz, M. G. T., & Oliveira, L. M. B. (2010). O conceito de empresa digna na percepção de trabalhadores brasileiros. In Anais do Congreso de la asociación latinoamericana de sociología del trabajo, Anais ALAST, Ciudad do México, México.

Teixeira, M. L. M., Domenico, S. M. R., & Dias, S. M. R. C. (2011) Proposta e validação de um modelo de Dignidade Organizacioanal. *Relatório parcial de pesquisa* (Tech. Rep.). Mackenzie Presbyterian University.

Teixeira, M. L. M., Domenico, S. M. R., Dias, S. M. R. C., & Mendes, L. H. L. (2014). *Práticas de Dignidade Organizacional Percebidas por Trabalhadores na Relação entre Organizações e Stakeholders*. Rio de Janeiro/RJ: XXXVIII ENANPAD.

Valença, J. B. M. (2014) Mentoria na Relação entre Estresse e Dignidade Organizacional em uma Instituição Financeira. Dissertação de mestrado. Mestrado Profissional em Gestão Empresarial. Centro de Pesquisa e Pós-Graduação em Administração. Faculdade Boa Viagem – DeVry Brasil.

Chapter 8
Perception of Deaf People on Dignity in Organizations

Rosana Juçara de Souza Reis, Michel Mott Machado, Hajnalka Halász Gati, and James Anthony Falk

Abstract The aim is to comprehend how organizational dignity is perceived by the deaf in their interactions with colleagues, bosses, and the organization itself. Organizational dignity is being studied, today, under several aspects. However, research is scarce on the relationship between dignity and organizational inclusion, focusing specifically on the deaf. A qualitative study was performed with interviews from 13 oral and non-oral deaf persons, employees in different segments. Most parts of deaf employees felt socially isolated, unconsidered in human resource practices as a target for organizational opportunities. Lack of oral language was the main difficulty for communication within the organization, although the maintenance of an interpreter is supported by law. Dignity for the deaf was based on the elements of valorizations, respect, and equality. The data suggest that the more intense the experience with the violation of dignity, the less the feeling of inclusion and the greater risk of social isolation of the deaf. It is believed that, among other aspects, an organizational position aimed at reciprocal recognition and mutual cultural enrichment will contribute to the improvement of the quality of relationships between the deaf and the hearing.

Keywords Deaf people · Human dignity · Violation of dignity

8.1 Introduction

Dignity is a recurring issue in human history. Within the field of administration, it is noted that the majority of the studies directed to the theme are focused on the dignity of the worker (Teixeira et al., 2014). In fact, regarding this field called 'dignity in the workplace,' it appears that people with disabilities (PwD) have not been sufficiently contemplated, especially deaf people.

Hajnalka Halász Gati: In memoriam.

R. J. de Souza Reis (✉) · M. M. Machado · H. H. Gati · J. A. Falk
São Paulo, Brazil
e-mail: rosanareis22@gmail.com

M. L. Mendes Teixeira and L. M. B. de Oliveira (eds.), *Organizational Dignity and Evidence-Based Management*, https://doi.org/10.1007/978-3-030-68560-7_8

On the other hand, it appears that there are several studies that focus on PwD, mainly from a framework in the discussion of diversity and inclusion (Torres & Perez-Nebra, 2014; Stolarczyk, 2016). Concomitantly, there is also a gap in the production of knowledge focused on the relationship between dignity and the management of diversity and inclusion, including with regard to the reality of deaf people.

Taking the Brazilian context as a reference, according to the census of the Brazilian Institute of Geography and Statistics, the number of deaf people almost doubled between 2000 and 2010 (about 9.7 million), of which, around 3 million are in the age group of 20 to 54 years of age (Brazil, 2010), which represents an economically active portion of this population. Law No. 8213/91 (Brazil, 1991), the Law of Quotas, guarantees basic rights to PwD, among which is the establishment of percentages of employment opportunities for purposes of insertion in the labor market.

Undoubtedly, this law brought a possibility of social advancement, as well as increasing the challenges to the management and inclusion of diversity in organizations. In this sense, it is relevant to add dignity to the management of diversity and inclusion in organizations, having the discussion on the radar about the extent to which policies have been developed that promote an effective inclusion of deaf people in organizations (Torres & Pérez-Nebra, 2014) through a decent organizational action in relation to these people (Teixeira, 2008; Teixeira et al., 2014). This being given, the objective of this chapter is to discuss the vision of dignity from the point of view of deaf people in organizations.

To achieve this objective, a qualitative, descriptive, bibliographic, and field investigation was carried out, conducted in companies located in the Metropolitan Region of Recife, state of Pernambuco, in northeastern Brazil. In a conversational way, semi-structured interviews were carried out with 13 deaf people, between oralized (9) and non-oralized (4) employees. The elaboration of the interview script and the subsequent interpretation of the data/discussion of the results were based on the elements of promotion/violation of dignity and from the perspective of the concepts of 'self-dignity' and 'social dignity' (Jacobson, 2009).

In addition to this introduction, this chapter has been structured in four parts. In the first part, the concepts of dignity and its study from an organizational point of view are presented. This is accompanied by the analysis of diversity and inclusion of PwD in organizations and followed by the issue of deaf people and communication. Furthermore, some experiences of promoting/violating the dignity of deaf people in the workplace are presented in this third section. Finally, in the last part, some managerial implications are pointed out and some final considerations are presented.

8.2 Conceptions of Dignity and the Study in an Organizational Perspective

In Ancient Greece, dignity was not considered a full human characteristic, nor was it an absolute or sacred value. Instead, it was an attribute only of free men (Riley, 2010). The Judeo-Christian perspective was fundamental to the process of disseminating dignity as intrinsic to the human being, a tradition that influenced the conception that man would be inherently good, once considered the image of God (Koehn & Leung, 2008). Tomas de Aquino affirmed the universality of human dignity influenced by the vision of dignity coming from God, as well as by his rationality (Nicolas, 2003), which would give him a dignity due to his condition as a human being (Aquino, 2008).

In the Middle Ages, dignity would also be associated with social groups/individuals, depending on social status, which would bring the notion of dignity conceived as a distinction (Gosdal, 2007). In addition, the Renaissance period challenged the understanding of dignity by integrating a positive view of man as a being endowed with reason given by the Creator, possessing his own dignity and capable of making personal moral choices. As such, dignity was something inherent to man himself, as well as what his action produces (Riley, 2010). In addition, there is the idea of the dignity of man as associated with his freedom granted by God (Mirandola, 1988).

The Kantian idea that the essentiality of man's dignity is found in his humanity, that is, an intrinsic value of human beings, can be considered as basic to the development of the modern concept of dignity (Riley, 2010). In the Foundations of Metaphysics of Customs, there is an enlightenment influence on his conception of dignity, which brings with it the dimension of the moral value emanating from humanity itself (Kant, 2005). Such a view undoubtedly shaped the modern understanding of the term, at least in the West, providing the basis for some legal approaches, such as the understanding of human rights in a universalist perspective (Riley, 2010; Sarlet, 2008).

Taken from a sociopolitical perspective, dignity can be seen as something to be preserved and guaranteed by universal law, as well as through the clash of social and political forces within the state (Medeiros & Teixeira, 2017). There is also the conception of dignity as activated through civil society and the democratic process, based on communicative action and popular participation (Habermas, 2010).

A vision that aims to overcome the sociopolitical conception is one that denounces the colonization of human rights by a modern rationality, which brings to light the need to decolonize the concepts of humanity and that of being human (Mignolo, 2013), similarly with respect to the difference in conceptions of human dignity (Santos & Nunes, 2010). Medeiros and Teixeira (2017) admit the need to establish an intercultural dialogue on human dignity in order to have a mixed understanding of human rights, a view that opens the possibility for a postmodern and critical approach to dignity (Machado & Teixeira, 2017).

There is also the understanding of dignity in the human and social dimensions (Jacobson, 2007, 2009), the first being inherent to individuals and the second classified in two categories: self-dignity (in relation to oneself) and dignity in the relationship (in an individual's interactions) with other individuals and in society. This approach, in turn, presents elements that promote and violate dignity, as shown in Fig. 8.1.

Within the field of studies called 'workplace dignity,' many research issues have been contemplated, such as: dignity at work/of the worker (Hodson, 2001; Hodson

PROMOTION OF DIGNITYy		VIOLATION OF DIGNITY	
Estime, attention, courtesy	**Respect**	**Disrespect**	Retaliation or generalized disrespe3ct
Identification with the other	**Empathize**	**Ignore**	Lack of consideration, attention or care
Assume the weight of a situation	**Control**	**Condesention**	Give in to the sentiments or wishes of someone
Raise capacity or competency / autonomy	**Empower**	**Diminish**	Make someone feel diminished or less
Encourage others in difficult situations	**Presence**	**Indiference**	Consider na individual invisible or without voice
Be autosufficient	**Independence**	**Dependency**	Force dependency on others for basic necessities
Dignity of others	**Resistence**	**Contempt**	Treat people as if they have no value
Recognize the humanity in others, show apreciation	**Recognition**	**Branding**	Brand with the connotation of moral deficiency or social infiriority
Demonstrate respect	**Cortesy**	**Difamation**	Make na individual seem threatening or dangerous
Minimize differences, asymmetry	**Equalizing**	**Objetification**	Treating someone as a thing, not a person
"Only survive" in difficult circumstance or "do the best possible"	**Perseverance**	**Discrimination**	Treat someone bad based on their status reached
Recognize the value of others	**Elevate**	**Exploration**	Use or see someone only as a means to reach the objective
Fortify oneself	**Encourage**	**Grouping**	See someone as unique, but only as a vember of a colectivity
Rise up in favor of the oppresed	**Defend**	**Repulse**	Treat others as if they were contaminated
Fortify oneself against dignity violations	**Prepare**	**Suspect**	Distrust/treat some as commiting wrong doings
Not judge differences	**Acceptance**	**Exclusion**	Make someone feel undiserable
Honor os estime others	**Love**	***Bullying* – moral molestation**	Threaten ou intimidade na individual

Fig. 8.1 Elements of the promotion and violation of dignity. *Source* based on Jacobson (2009)

& Roscino, 2004), wages and decent life (Rayman & Reynolds, 2001), gender and dignity at work (Crowley, 2013), meaning and alienation of work and its reflexes on the worker's life (Hodson & Roscigno, 2004), market demands, competition, productivity and dignity (Shahinpoor & Matt, 2006), lack of respect at work (Sayer, 2007), the importance of dignity at work (Bolton, 2007), LGBTQ experiences and dignity at work (Baker & Lucas, 2017), dignity and work behavior of employees (Lucas et al., 2017), dignity in the workplace, and the strength of migrant work (Lucas et al., 2012), among other issues.

Another current stream of study is that dedicated to discussing aspects related to responsible management and human dignity (Davila-Gomez & Crowther, 2012). There is also the humanistic management approach (Pirson, 2017), which addresses, for example, leadership and the establishment of a culture of dignity (Hicks, 2016), dignity in human resource management, and the role of democracy in the workplace (Bal et al., 2017), among other topics.

Still in the field of organizational management and dignity, when observing that a worker may remain isolated in relationship with the organization and the other social segments, Teixeira (2008) critically approached the concept of organizational dignity

(DO) proposed by Margolis in (1997). He suggests the construction of organizational actions based on trust and reciprocity, as presuppositions for the understanding of a dignified organization. In this direction, Teixeira et al. (2014) analyzed the DO practices perceived by workers in the relationship between stakeholder organizations.

Yet, there are still efforts toward another theoretical proposition of DO, which would be linked to practices and shared values within the organization, which could also be experienced by stakeholders in interaction with the organization (Teixeira & Bilsky, 2015). One step further was the identification of four facets of the DO construct: cultural elements; ethical guidance; focus (more oriented toward the personal or social aspect); and classifying the DO, from top to bottom, as moral, legal, or pragmatic (Teixeira, 2016).

8.3 PwD Diversity and Inclusion in Organizations

When considering the Brazilian context, it is known that, historically, PwD were placed on the margins of employability (Snell & Bohlander, 2015), making the possibility of self-support very difficult while stretching the laws of labor rights (Lima, 2012).

Despite recognizing social progress with the aforementioned quota law, one should at least suspect that it, by itself, is not able to guarantee that PwD are treated fairly, and that they feel included in work organizations, have equal opportunities and are represented in all functions and organizational levels. These are all aspects that have the meaning of an effective inclusion (Torres & Pérez-Nebra, 2014).

By inclusion, the idea of a perception of people's acceptance is assumed here, this linked to a feeling of being welcomed and valued as a member of a certain organization, at its different levels (Hayes, 2002). Otherwise, it would be from the perception of individuals in relation to their acceptance, respect, and appreciation, in view of their group and individual identity, which would consist of the person actually feeling included (Torres & Pérez-Nebra, 2014). Thus, coherently with such perspectives, the experience of inclusion depends on an inclusive behavior, in order to promote an inclusive climate (Torres & Pérez-Nebra, 2014).

When analyzing studies aimed at the inclusion of PwD, it may be noted that they usually portray some of the difficulties that these individuals face within the walls of the organization. Some examples are: characteristics of work environments, hiring, and reception (Gilbrid et al., 2003); accessibility in leisure, work, and education (Sassaki, 2009); deafness and prejudice (Witkoski, 2015); the importance of the work of the disabled person (Ragazzi, 2010); diversity policy and work relations (Irigaray & Vergara, 2011); public policies and organizational practices in the insertion of the deaf (Irigaray & Vergara, 2012); the fundamental right to social inclusion (Lima, 2012); and the meaning of work (Lima et al., 2013).

On the other hand, Thompson (2010; Torres & Pérez-Nebra, 2014), instead of looking at the PwD, analyzed the difficulties that recruitment and selection professionals themselves often face with government programs and the lack of interest of some PwD groups in working.

In general, what can be seen in most studies is the need to promote awareness in dealing with issues relevant to PwD in order to provide the effective inclusion of these people in organizations. In the case of the deaf, in particular, listeners may not know how to approach them, how to treat them or behave in front of them, as personal contact can cause strangeness right from the start (Ragazzi, 2010; Silva, 2006). This type of attitude/ strangeness behavior toward the other can be derived from stereotype, prejudice, and discrimination (Torre & Pérez-Nebra, 2014).

When referring to paradigmatic aspects of research on diversity and inclusion, Torres and Pérez-Nebra (2014) suggest three positions: (1) discrimination and justice; (2) access and legitimacy; and 3. learning and effectiveness. The first assumes that 'we are all equal' or 'we want to be all equal,' with assimilation being the central idea. The second is based on the idea of accepting differences, with differentiation as the main idea. The third is represented by the main idea of integration/inclusion, whose focus would be on the admission of a single team with their differences.

All of these issues related to diversity and inclusion in organizations, no doubt, evoke the need for the idea of inclusive diversity management (Hanashiro, 2008). However, despite the need to establish/mature such a management perspective, in practice, it is recognized that a feeling of devaluation that involves the PwD is common in organizations, possibly because they feel excluded, despite being inserted. It has been suggested that this question may arise (Jacobson, 2009), due to the various forms of violation of dignity within relationships which may result in a more or less serious process of social isolation of PwD (Cacioppo et al., 2008), with all the risks that this phenomenon can bring to people's psychological and physical integrity (Cacioppo & Cacioppo, 2013).

Social isolation comprises a continuous process that can even occur with high levels of absence of social contact. Physical isolation can contribute to loneliness, the latter understood as a pain that is felt when the need for connection is not met, and can be felt anywhere, even when surrounded by family and friends (Cacioppo & Cacioppo, 2013).

Cacioppo et al. (2008), likewise, suggest that the quality of social relationships, more than their quantity, is an essential part of what is necessary for a healthy and happy life. In this sense, it is thought that actions that promote dignity should be more frequent in organizations in order to develop better-quality social relationships.

In relation to deaf people, there is a static process and limited phenomenon called the *glass ceiling*, when they assume certain roles in organizations, only as determined by the law (Irigaray & Vergara, 2011). If so, it is thought that such an insertion, more than the desirable feeling of 'being part of,' may actually trigger a process of social isolation, in addition to a possible feeling of loneliness, which should, in fact, lead to a reflection on how to mitigate such a problematic situation (Cacioppo & Cacioppo, 2013).

In order to broaden the knowledge about the life experiences of deaf people, whether in the family, in work organizations or in the wider society, research efforts are underway (Reis et al., 2019) especially with regard to their feeling of inclusion, their more or less intense situation of social isolation, their feeling of loneliness, as well as the protection/violation of dignity in the relationship.

8.4 Deaf People and Communication: Listening Eyes and Hands that Break the Silence

Language, in the strict sense of the word, can mean 'the faculty of speaking (potential speech) or the totality of human languages' (Comte-Sponville, 2003, p. 352), being also a means for human beings to build their world, within a universe of words (Chanlat & Bédard, 1996). Language makes thinking real (Leal, 2007), so that speech would be for the constitution of the individual, as well as language for the definition of the human species, an essential element for the construction of personal existence (Chanlat & Bédard, 1996).

According to Comte-Sponville (2003, p. 236), speech would be the 'creation of a discourse by means of the updating of a language (as a faculty), through a language (as a conventional and historical system),' the latter being '[...] a set of conventional signs, articulated [...] and submitted to a number of structures [...]' (Comte-Sponville, 2003, p. 236). Furthermore, it is thought that 'when a speaker finds himself in the same conditions as all the other members of the group, there we find a norm, on the basis of which we can evaluate his characteristics of individual expression' (Chanlat & Bédard, 1996, p. 131).

That said, it is admitted that the type of reality we apprehend can be considered an implication of the language by means of which human beings express themselves (Chanlat & Bédard, 1996), being reasonable to consider, therefore, that in the case of deaf people, speakers of a particular language, there can be different meanings for a given signifier.

In this sense, communication would not only be possible through verbalized speech, since deaf people usually communicate without using verbalized words, using a peculiar and structured language, which in Brazil is called Libras—Brazilian Sign Language (Segala & Kojima, 2012), being considered their mother tongue (Law 10.436/2002). The hands take the place of the spoken words and give 'body' to the thought.

Thus, sign language uses hands, arms, and eyes and makes use of facial expressions, which are intonation mechanisms, such as facial and/or body expressions being responsible for expressing emotion, transmitting attitudes and communicating personality traits, and fundamental elements in nonverbal communication (Segala & Kojima, 2012). In the view of the oralists, the deaf persons who communicate with their hands are the ones who are classified in a subgroup outside the ability of the oralized person, the latter being close to the listener as a sign of superiority (Witkoski, 2015).

Aware of some of the barriers encountered by deaf people, one of the most relevant is that of communication. In order to meet the demands of the deaf to materialize their communication with the listeners, the Brazilian state instituted Law No. 12319/10 (Brazil, 2010), which regulates the exercise of Libras interpreters, and where public and private institutions are obliged to maintain an interpreter to assist the deaf citizen and guarantee their right to communication (Decree Nº 5626/05).

It should be recognized that such legal provisions signal for a dignified act in the relationship with deaf people. However meritorious they may be, it may still not be enough to carry out a process of inclusion and protection of dignity in organizations. It is known that the process of cultural adjustment in a foreign culture involves the question of language (Kelman, 2010). That being so, the deaf who dominate Portuguese can adapt more easily, with their inclusion process being less painful. However, it is believed that there may be a more democratic and dignified perspective, that of an intercultural adaptation. In this case, the actors recognize each other and are willing to submit to a mutual cultural enrichment in a given cultural space (Machado & Teixeira, 2017).

8.5 Experiences of Promoting/Violating the Dignity of Deaf People in the Workplace

As an initial recognition, it is clear that there is understanding on the part of the deaf that relationships are essential to the inclusion of PwD, and that this should be the responsibility of everyone involved. What is expected is that good-quality relationships are established through which PwD feel accepted, respected, and valued, considering their group and individual identity (Torres & Pérez-Nebra, 2014). In addition, the ideal considered would be that for relationships to be based on a dignified act (Machado & Teixeira, 2017; Teixeira, 2008).

In general, 'the help of the other' to learn the job, and consequently, to perform their professional role well, suggests that good-quality relationships have potential for the 'sense of team,' as well as the generation of a 'favorable environment to learning,' which is shown to be favorable to the promotion/protection of dignity. According to Jacobson (2009), this approaches the perspectives of' empowerment 'and respect.' Thus, it can be said that the sense of dignity as being promoted/protected tends to be perceived by the deaf in these situations of 'solidarity,' in 'helping others,' and in 'teamwork,' as can be seen from the following statement collected in a interview: 'A lot of people helped me, and I felt important.'

In the experience of deaf people, the fact of feeling 'respected' seems to have positive implications for the feeling of 'security' and 'well-being,' which can be provided with the collaboration/help of everyone in the organization. This is apparent whether in the situation of work or not, and brings up a feeling of 'belonging,' experienced by the deaf as they perceive that they are well received by the listeners, as well as accepted in their deaf condition.

The result of good interaction can result in increased self-esteem (Lima, 2012) and the 'strengthening of yourself' (Jacobson, 2009). Regarding this potential for learning, the establishment of productive relationships, as in the cases presented above, tends to undermine social isolation.

Not only is the relationship with co-workers relevant to the deaf, a good relationship with their boss is essential for them to feel part of the whole. This fact can be observed in the following statement, when one of the deaf refers to 'help from the boss': 'In this company I now have a lot of help.'

The support of bosses is essential in the process of feeling as belonging, recognized as a sign both of 'appreciation' and of 'potential growth in the organization.' In this last aspect, in particular, the correct conduct of hierarchical superiors is probably not enough, since it is necessary to define specific organizational policies in order to promote inclusive diversity management and avoid the glass ceiling syndrome (Hanashiro, 2008; Irigaray & Vergara, 2011; Torres & Pérez-Nebra, 2014).

It has also been recognized that this insertion in organizations may have brought to the deaf expectations of growth, appreciation, a certain sense of being equal to the listener, in addition to a potential increase in self-esteem. However, when it comes to the feeling of being equal, it seems that it stems from assumptions based on a position of discrimination and justice, so that it does not escape the limitations of the adage of 'we all want to be equal' (Torres & Pérez-Nebra, 2014).

On the other hand, in their organizational experiences, several deaf people reported flagrant negative experiences. The 'contempt' for being deficient and the 'devaluation' for being different caused the segregation imposed by some listeners. The presence of prejudice and discrimination in relation to the deaf can be considered a fact in the experiences of most of them. Furthermore, the reported experiences of contempt and segregation certainly do not contribute to their inclusion in organizations; on the contrary, it makes it difficult or even impossible. Here is an excerpt considered as representative of the social isolation imposed on the deaf by listeners:

> [...] this relationship issue is more difficult because I joined just recently. I'm a little separated. I'm alone because I can't communicate with people. I feel like I need a lot of help to feel safe, and I still haven't achieved that level of relationship.

Several aspects that corroborate the pain suffered by the deaf can be established by this speech. One notices, for example, a certain 'blaming herself' for having entered recently, for being a little separated or even because 'she cannot communicate with people.' In addition to the lack of diversity and inclusion policies, a culture of inclusion, and consequent inclusive behaviors, there is a certain convenience in allowing the deaf to blame themselves for not being able to communicate. In fact, certain elements of dignity violation are recognized, such as ignore, indifference, contempt, discrimination, disgust, and exclusion (Jacobson, 2009). When they feel disrespected as people and treated as a 'thing,' there is also the element of objectification (Jacobson, 2009).

An organization that allows itself to deal with its internal stakeholders in this manner behaves against a dignified organizational action (Teixeira, 2008), and these experiences of violation of social dignity in the relationship seem to be related to a process of social isolation which, as is already known, can bring serious risks to people's mental and physical health (Cacioppo & Cacioppo, 2013).

Silva (2006) relates prejudice to a defense mechanism for something that represents a threat, a risk of imminent social denial, assuming that the relationship or approximation with the deaf can become a threat of rejection by society. The role of stigmatization (Torres & Pérez-Nebra, 2014) of PwD, and those who relate to them, reaches back into the marginal inclusion process of the deaf (Lima, 2012). This does not mean that the stigma has decreased, however, based solely on the fact of the PwD being inserted in organizations, since what seemingly exists is only a tolerance on the part of colleagues and managers due to legal impositions (Irigaray & Vergara, 2011).

It seems obvious that the deaf are victims of discrimination in organizations, which is evident even within the process of hiring, as can be seen in the following testimony: 'It [the company] hires the deaf to work anywhere or on anything, […] I think the company only hires the deaf because of the law. They don't respect people.'

The way in which a good part of the hiring takes place does not promote the dignity of the deaf; on the contrary, it could be seen as an 'exploitation' (Jacobson, 2009).

When focusing on the period of permanence of deaf employees in organizations, complaints related to the 'lack of opportunity' are evidenced, also represented by the notion of 'lack of appreciation/recognition,' since the individuals in this group tend to remain in the same positions for a long period of time, which suggests that deaf people are not normally considered targets of opportunities for career development. This factor effectively does not contribute to inclusion in organizations. The following are excerpts from two statements that corroborate this interpretation: 'It [the company] does not give the disabled a chance.' and 'I have a deaf colleague who was promoted, but this is not common. It is very difficult for the deaf to grow in the company.'

Although many deaf people are able to perform more demanding and competitive functions, they usually occupy low-paid positions (Ciszewski, 2005). In practice, they are almost always directed to general services, cleaning, warehouses, or areas with little chance of ascendancy, and they are hostages to the glass ceiling syndrome (Irigaray & Vergara, 2011; Torres & Pérez-Nebra, 2014).

Communication is another aspect to be analyzed. In this item, there is a conglomeration of manifested feelings, such as apprehension, nervousness, restlessness, anxiety, etc., so that even for the oralized deaf the 'communication barrier' persists as a hindrance to a good quality living together in the workplace. These problematic experiences can be corroborated by the visible difficulties in communication observed in organizations with PwD, generally more unfavorable to the deaf (Witkoski, 2011).

Still in the communication process, there were situations of hostility in some organizations studied, which sometimes generated expressions of indignation, discomfort, and anger on the part of the deaf. This situation is represented by the following statement: 'They call me a jackass; it was just like that little story of the monkey who doesn't want to hear. Why do they call me that? I'm just like them, I work, I'm smart, I'm capable!'

Through this and other unpleasant experiences lived by the deaf, it is possible to indicate several elements of violation of their dignity: 'disrespect,' 'diminution of the other,' 'contempt,' 'labeling,' 'objectification,' 'exclusion,' ' bullying ' (Jacobson, 2009).

Communication shows itself as a sensitive point for deaf people. According to a utopian-realistic view of a possible emancipatory dignity, the ideal would be a posture of reciprocal recognition and mutual cultural enrichment in organizations (Machado & Teixeira, 2017) which could come to contribute to improving the quality of relationships, essential to health and happiness (Cacioppo et al., 2008).

When focusing on the deaf in organizations, it is noticeable that prejudice and discrimination tend to weaken their inclusion. They expose them to a persistent process of violation of dignity, in both human and social dimensions (self-dignity and dignity in the relationship), which can lead them to a dangerous situation of social isolation.

From what has been present, several elements can be established as contributing to the undesirable condition of social isolation of the deaf in organizations. This can happen, for example, through 'bullying,' 'invisibility,' 'non-respect for their identity and culture' and 'lack of communication,' among other undesirable behaviors.

8.6 Implications for Management

With reference to the paradigms of inclusive diversity in organizations, based on the companies studied, it can be said that what was perceived was the predominance of the 'discrimination and justice' position, bringing with it the idea of similarity (Torres & Pérez-Nebra, 2014), which, in a way, can contribute to mask processes of subordination of the other, the different, the minority. This position, it is defended here, can feed or renew processes of exclusion and social isolation of PwD, as it tends not to sufficiently consider—or even to disregard—the complexity of the situation, as well as possible organizational and managerial problems that may arise from it, such as the deterioration of the organizational climate, for example. It is widely known that a deteriorated organizational climate tends to have dysfunctional impacts on the organization's performance and management (Robbins, 2005).

A sensitive point that was verified in the present study has to do with the communicative difficulties to the inclusion in the organizations. In this regard, in particular, it is recommended to adopt an organizational posture aimed at reciprocal recognition and mutual cultural enrichment, qualitatively superior to the simple idea of tolerance. In practical terms, it is thought that the hiring of sign language interpreters could be welcome, both to facilitate communication in more immediate work situations and for a broader educational process in the organizational sphere.

In addition, to avoid and/or correct undesirable situations of discrimination in the organizational sphere, with a view to creating and guaranteeing a healthy and productive work environment, where dignity is protected and well-being promoted (Pirson, 2017), it is understood that organizational management would need to consider a tripod of generic lines of action: (i) educational/training action; (ii) coercive/punitive action; and (iii) wide communication action. This tripod, supposedly, if carried out and managed systematically, can come to influence certain elements of a given organizational culture, in the sense intended here, among other aspects.

Finally, in order to maximize the advantages of diversity in organizations, as well as minimize its disadvantages, it is understood that competent inclusive diversity management is necessary.

8.7 Final Remarks

The objective of this chapter was to reflect on the vision of dignity from the point of view of deaf people in organizations. Although the word 'dignity' was not mentioned by the research participants, they used other words to designate what they wanted to be understood. Therefore, the senses of dignity attributed by the deaf were based on the notions of 'appreciation,' 'respect,' and 'equality' in relation to the listener. It is noteworthy that during the coexistence between co-workers and bosses, the presence of the elements of appreciation, respect and equality, was not the rule; on the contrary, the experience with elements of violation of dignity in the relationship was present in everyday life.

From the point of view of the diversity and inclusion paradigms in organizations, the reports indicate a predominance in assumptions of the 'discrimination and justice' position, which tends to highlight 'we are all equal' or 'we want to be all equal,' having assimilation as its central idea.

It was found that most deaf people had extensive experiences with elements that violate dignity, and only a few with promoting or protective components. The predominance of the former situation over the latter generated a feeling of 'non-acceptance,' of 'non-inclusion,' of 'not belonging,' which almost always seems to lead to a situation of social isolation.

Based on these experiences, the following hypotheses can be inferred: (i) The more intense the experience of the deaf with elements that promote dignity, the greater the propensity of the individual to feel included and, consequently, the lower the risk of social isolation; (ii) conversely, the more intense the experience with elements that violate dignity, the lower the feeling of inclusion and, therefore, the greater the risk of social isolation.

Regarding the communicative difficulties of inclusion in organizations, it is considered advisable to adopt an organizational posture aimed at reciprocal recognition and mutual cultural enrichment. This action could contribute to improving the quality of relationships, something important for a healthy and happy work life.

It is believed that the inference and recommendation now proposed bring new perspectives to the reflections on the behavior of individuals and group interactions in organizations. In this sense, this chapter sought to contribute to studies on human and social management in organizations, based on an observation of dignity in organizations linked to the inclusive management of diversity, and the risk of social isolation, focusing on PwD, in general, and deaf people in particular.

As a suggestion for future research, it is understood that the confirmation or refutation of the proposed hypothesis, with other types of PwD in mind, would be pertinent and timely, as well as the deepening of theoretical reflection on the possible relationships between dignity, diversity management and inclusion and social isolation in organizations.

References

Aquino, T. (2008). O ente e a essência. Portugal: Luso Sophia.

Bal, P. M., & De Jong, S. B. (2017). From human resource management to human dignity development: A dignity perspective on HRM and the role of workplace democracy. In M. Kostera & M. Pirson (Eds.), *Dignity and organizations*. London: Palgrave Macmillan.

Baker, S. J., & Lucas, K. (2017). Is it safe to bring myself to work? Understanding LGBTQ experiences of workplace dignity. *Canadian Journal of Administrative Sciences, 34,* 133–148.

Bolton, S. C. (2007). Dignity *in* and *at* work: Why it matters? In S. C. Bolton (Ed.), *Dimensions of dignity at work*. New York, NY: Routledge.

Brasil. *Decreto n. 5.626, de 22 de dezembro de 2005.* Regulamenta a Lei no 10.436, de 24 de abril de 2002, que dispõe sobre a Língua Brasileira de Sinais - Libras, e o art. 18 da Lei no 10.098, de 19 de dezembro de 2000. Brasilia, DF. Disponível em: https://www.planalto.gov.br/ccivil_03/_ato2004-2006/2005/decreto/d5626.htm

Brasil . *Instituto Brasileiro De Geografia E Estatística -IBGE.* Censo demográfico de 2010. Disponível em: https://www.ibge.gov.br/home/estatistica/populacao/censo2010/

Brasil. *Lei n. 8,213, de 24 de julho de 1991.* Dispõe sobre os Planos de Benefícios da Previdência Social e dá outras providências. Seção VI, Dos Serviços. Subseção II, Da Habilitação e da Reabilitação Profissional. Artigo 93°. Brasília, DF. Disponível em: https://www.planalto.gov.br/CCIVIL_03/leis/L8213cons.htm.

Brasil . *Lei n. 10.436, de 24 de abril de 2002.* Dispõe sobre a Língua Brasileira de Sinais – Libras. Brasília, DF. Disponível em: https://www.planalto.gov.br/ccivil_03/leis/2002/l10436.htm.

Brasil . *Lei n. 12.319, de 1 de setembro de 2010.* Regulamenta a profissão de Tradutor e Intérprete da Língua Brasileira de Sinais - LIBRAS. Brasília, DF. Disponível em: https://www.planalto.gov.br/ccivil_03/_Ato2007-2010/2010/Lei/L12319.htm.

Cacioppo, J. T., Hawkley, L. C., Kalil, A., Hughes, M. E., Waite, L. J., Thisted, R. A., et al. (2008). Happiness and the invisible threads of social connection: The Chicago health, aging, and social relations study. In M. Eid & R. Larson (Eds.), *The science of well-being* (pp. 195–219). New York: Guilford.

Cacioppo, J. T., & Cacioppo, S. (2013). *Social isolation.* In XXXIV Interamerican Congress of Psychology – Knowledge, Diversity and Integration, Brasília – DF.

Chanlat, A., & Bédard, R. (1996). Palavras: a ferramenta do executivo. In J. F. Chanlat (Coord.). *O indivíduo na organização: dimensões esquecidas.* (v. I). (pp. 125–148) São Paulo: Atlas.

Ciszewski, A. C. V. (2005). *O trabalho da pessoa portadora de deficiência.* São Paulo: LTr.

Comte-Sponville, A. (2003). *Dicionário filosófico.* São Paulo: Martins Fontes.

Crowley, M. (2013). Gender, the labor process and dignity at work. *Social Forces, 91*(4), 1209–1238.

Davila-Gomez, A. M., & Crowther, D. (2012). Managerial responsibility for human dignity. In A. M. Davila-Gomez & D. Crowther (Eds.), *Human dignity and managerial responsibility: Diversity, rights, and sustainability*. Surrey; Burlington, USA: Gower Publishing Company.

Gilbrid, D., Stensrud, R., Vandergoot, D., & Golden, K. (2003). Identification of the characteristics of work environments and employers open to hiring and accommodation people with disabilities. *Rehabilitation Counseling Bulletin, 46*(3), 130–138.

Gosdal, T. C. (2007). *Dignidade do trabalhador: Um conceito construído sob o paradigma do trabalho decente e da honra*. São Paulo: LTr.

Habermas, J. (2010). *Teoria de la acción comunicativa: Racionalidade de la cción y racionalización social*. Madri: Taurus.

Hanashiro, D. M. M. (2008). Convivendo com a diversidade cultural. In D. M. M. Hanashiro, M. L. M. Teixeira & L. M. Zacarelli (Orgs.). *Gestão do fator humano: uma visão baseada em stakeholders* (2nd ed.). (pp. 45–76) São Paulo: Saraiva.

Hayes, B. C. (2002). *Creating inclusive organizations: its meaning and measurement*. Dissertation (Ph.D. in Philosophy), Old Dominion University, Norfolk.

Hicks, D. (2016). A culture of indignity and the failure of leadership. *Humanistic Management Journal, 1*, 113–126.

Hodson, R., & Roscigno, V. J. (2004). Organizational success and worker dignity: Complementary or contradictory? *American Journal of Sociology, 110*(3), 672–708.

Hodson, R. (2001). *Dignity at work*. New York, NY: Cambridge University Press.

Irigaray, H. A. R., & Vergara, S. C. (2011). O tempo como dimensão de pesquisa sobre uma política de diversidade e relações no trabalho. *Cadernos EBAPE.BR, 9*(4), 1085–1098.

Irigaray, H. A. R., & Viana, A. (2012). A Inserção dos Surdos no Mercado de Trabalho: políticas públicas, práticas. *XXXVI Encontro da Associação Nacional de Pós-Graduação e Pesquisa em Administração – EnANPAD*, Rio de Janeiro, RJ.

Jacobson, N. (2007). Dignity and health: A review. *Social Science & Medicine, 64*, 292–302.

Jacobson, N. (2009). A taxonomy of dignity: A grounded theory study. *Social Science & Medicine, 64*, 292–307.

Kant, I. (2005). *Fundamentação da metafísica dos costumes e outros escritos*. São Paulo: Martins Claret.

Kelman, C. A. (2010). Multiculturalismo e surdez: uma questão de respeito às culturas minoritárias. In E. Fernandes (org.). *Surdez e bilinguismo* (3. ed., pp. 87–103). Porto Alegre: Mediação.

Koehn, D., & Leung, A. (2008). Dignity in Western versus in Chinese Culture: Theoretical overview and practical illustrations. *Business & Society Review, 113*(4), 477–504.

Leal, M. M. (2007). Aplicação dos princípios da dignidade da pessoa humana e boa-fé nas relações de trabalho – as interfaces entre a tutela geral das relações de trabalho e os direitos subjetivos individuais dos trabalhadores. *Revista Jurídica, 8*(82), 84–99.

Lima, J. N. (2012). *Direito Fundamental à inclusão social: Eficácia prestacional nas relações privadas*. Curitiba: Juruá.

Lima, M. P., Tavares, N. V., Brito, M. J., & Cappelle, M. C. A. (2013). O sentido do trabalho para pessoas com deficiência. *Revista De Administração Mackenzie, 14*(2), 42–68.

Lucas, K., Kang, D., & Li, Z. (2012). Workplace dignity in a total institution: Examining the experiences of Foxconn's migrant eorkers. *Journal of Business Ethics*, 1–16.

Lucas, K., Manikas, A. S., Mattingly, E. S., & Crider, C. J. (2017). Engaging and misbehaving: How dignity affects employee work behaviors. *Organization Studies*, 1–23.

Margolis, J. D. (1997). *Dignity in the balance: Philosophical and practical dimensions of promoting ethics in organizations*. (Ph.D. dissertation), Harvard University, Cambridge.

Machado, M. M., & Teixeira, M. L. M. (2017). Dignity in the context of organizations: A look beyond modernity. *Mackenzie Management Review, 18*(2), 80–103.

Medeiros, A. L., & Teixeira, M. L. M. (2017). Limites da dignidade dos docentes nas práticas de gestão em universidades brasileiras. *Revista GUAL, 10*(1), 134–154.

Mignolo, W. (2013). Decolonialidade como caminho para a cooperação. Entrevista. *Revista do Instituto Humanitas Unisinos – IHU On-line*, 431(XIII). Disponível em: https://www.ihuonline.unisinos.br/index.php?option=com_content&view=article&id=5253&secao=431.

Mirandola, G. P. D. (1988). *A dignidade do homem*. São Paulo: GRD.

Nicolas, M. J. (2003). Introdução à Suma Teológica. In *Suma Teológica* [1265–1274]. São Paulo: Edições Loyola.

Pirson, M. (2017). *Humanistic management: Protecting dignity and promoting well-being*. New York, NY: Cambridge University Press.

Ragazzi, I. A. G. (2010). *Inclusão social: A importância do trabalho da pessoa portadora de deficiência*. São Paulo: LTr.

Rayman, P., & Reynolds, J. (2001). *Beyond the bottom line: The search for dignity at work*. New York: Palgrave.

Reis, R. J. S, Gati, H. H., & Machado, M. M. (2019). Isolamento social dos surdos em organizações. *XXII SemeAd – Seminários em Administração FEAUSP*.

Riley, S. (2010). Human dignity: Comparative and conceptual debates. *International Journal of Law in Context, 6*(2), 117–138.

Robbins, S. P. (2005). *Comportamento organizacional*. São Paulo: Pearson Prentice Hall.

Santos, B. S., & Nunes, J. A. (2010). Introdução: para ampliar o cânone do reconhecimento, da diferença e da igualdade. In B. S. Santos (Org.). *Reconhecer para libertar: os caminhos do cosmopolitismo multicultural*. Rio de Janeiro: Civilização Brasileira.

Sarlet, I. W. (2008). *Dignidade da pessoa humana e os direitos fundamentais na Constituição Federal de 1988*. Porto Alegre: Livraria do Advogado Editora.

Sassaki, R. K. (2009). Inclusão: acessibilidade no lazer, trabalho e educação. *Revista Nacional de Reabilitação (*Reação).

Sayer, A. (2007). Dignity at work: Broadening the agenda. *Organization, 14*(4), 565–658.

Segala, S. R., & Kojima, C. K. (2012). *A imagem do pensamento: Libras – língua brasileira de sinais*. São Paulo: Escola Educacional.

Shahinpoor, N., & Matt, B. F. (2006). The power of one: Dissent and organizational life. *Journal of Business Ethics, 34*(4), 663–683.

Silva, L. M. (2006). O estranhamento causado pela deficiência: Preconceito e experiência. *Revista Brasileira De Educação, 11*(33), 424–561.

Snell, S., & Bohlander, G. A. (2015). *Administração de recursos humanos*. São Paulo: Cengage Learning.

Stolarczyk, P. (2016). Equality of chances for people with disabilities in the labor market. Acta Sci. Pol., *Oeconomia, 15* (2), 139–149.

Teixeira, M. L. M. (2008). Dignidade organizacional: valores e relações com stakeholders. In M. L. M. Teixeira (Org.). *Valores humanos e gestão*: novas perspectivas. São Paulo: Editora Senac.

Teixeira, M. L. M., De Domenico, S. M. R., Dias, S. M. R. C., & Mendes, L. H. L. (2014). Práticas de dignidade organizacional percebidas por trabalhadores na relação entre organização e*stakeholders.XXXVIII Encontro da Associação Nacional de Pós-Graduação emAdministração* – EnANPAD, Rio de Janeiro.

Teixeira, M. L. M., & Bilsky, W. (2015). Faceting organizational theory. In *15th Facet theory conference*. Nova York.

Teixeira, M. L. M. (2016). Organizational dignity theory: a proposal. *XIX SemeAd – Seminários em Administração FEA-USP*, São Paulo-SP.

Torres, C. V., & Pérez-Nebra, R. (2014). Diversidade e inclusão nas organizações. In J. C. Zanelli, J. E. Borges-Andrade & A. V. B. Bastos (Orgs.). *Psicologia, organizações e trabalho no Brasil* (2nd ed., pp. 526–546) Porto Alegre: Artmed.

Witkoski, S.A. (2011). Educação de surdos e preconceito: bilinguismo na vitrine e bimodalismo precário no estoque. (Tese de doutorado). Universidade Federal do Paraná, Curitiba.

Witkoski, S. A. (2015). Surdez e preconceito: A norma da fala e o mito da leitura da palavra falada. *Revista Brasileira De Educação, 14*(42), 565–606.

Chapter 9
Dignity in the Relationship Between the Brazilian and Other Latin American Workers

Michel Mott Machado

Abstract The purpose of this chapter was to discuss the projection and symbolization of the dignity of Latin American expatriates in Brazil. It is argued that the cultural adjustment of expatriates tends to suspend their cultural base producing vulnerability and promoting the violation of dignity. From a critical postmodern approach, it conducted ten face-to-face semi-structured interviews with expatriate executives from four South American countries, with symbolic cartography being the method of analysis adopted. It was found that the omission and neglect in organizational management tend to reproduce the projection of the dignity of the Latin American expatriate to the periphery of organizations. For practical applications to organizational management, it is recommended of a critical reflection on the expatriation process in organizations, from the top of organizations and based on an intercultural perspective, besides strategies aimed at building an organizational environment that values diversity, protecting dignity, and promoting well-being.

Keywords Expatriation · Latin Americans · Symbolization of the dignity

9.1 Introduction

The end of the twentieth century and the beginning of the twenty-first brought profound implications for the mobility of capital and people in different parts of the globe (Sassen, 1988), redesigning countries in migratory spaces in the international division of labor (De Hass, 2010; Baeninger, 2018). Besides, conflicts and persecutions have also been pointed out as reasons for the considerable increase in forced displacements in 2015, having reached the highest level ever recorded (Edwards, 2016). This, by the way, can be just a glimpse of what is to come, considering the close relationship between climate change and migration (Klein, 2017).

Rosana Baeninger, in an interview to the *Pesquisa* FAPESP (Fioravanti, 2015), pointed that there has been, in Brazil, what she called distancing from the other,

M. M. Machado (✉)
São Paulo, Brazil
e-mail: michelmottmachado@gmail.com

M. L. Mendes Teixeira and L. M. B. de Oliveira (eds.), *Organizational Dignity and Evidence-Based Management*, https://doi.org/10.1007/978-3-030-68560-7_9

including hostile manifestations. This would result from the distancing from the European white historical pattern, the absence of explicit demand by the hand of foreign workers, in addition to the scarcity of public policies aimed at promoting the social interaction of twenty-first-century immigrants. In line with this concern, the formulation and analysis of public policies aimed at human nurturing to protect the dignity and promote well-being have been defended, considering migratory flows and ethnic–social minorities (Machado et al., 2019).

Given this scenario, disregarding the organizational strategies aimed at the effects of globalization (Santiago & Machado, 2015) is unreasonable because, in addition to mobility being considered a symbolic capital in the organizational world (Freitas, 2009), multinationality is a characteristic of organizations operating in the global context (Teixeira et al., 2017). This brings up the need for a discussion on intercultural management (Davel et al., 2008; Freitas, 2009), in addition to policies for the international management of people/international mobility of people (McNulty & Selmer, 2017).

Although expatriation is contemplated by academic interest (Mott et al., 2012; McNulty & Selmer, 2017), it is noted that studies focused on 'cultural adaptation' have failed to consider interculturality in its core. In this direction, it is proposed to address this issue, to look at dignity in organizations from a postmodern and critical perspective (Machado & Teixeira, 2017), as well as a possible intercultural adaptation (Machado & Teixeira, 2015a, 2015b).

The purpose of this chapter was to discuss dignity in the relationship between the Brazilian workers and other Latin Americans, having the vision of the latter as the focal point. It was assumed that cultural adaptation of expatriates presupposes suspending their cultural base. This perspective generates vulnerability in relationships; therefore, it is a perspective of violation of dignity. To this end, a qualitative, exploratory-descriptive, bibliographic, and field investigation was conducted, with semi-structured interviews being conducted with 10 Latin American expatriates in Brazil, adopting the symbolic cartography as method of interpretation (Machado, 2015).

The chapter is structured in four parts. The first one addresses central ideas of the Portuguese sociologist Boaventura de Sousa Santos, the search for new perspectives on the cultural adaptation of expatriates, and the dignity in organizations. Then, the results of the symbolic cartography are presented. The fourth part addresses some managerial implications. Finally, some considerations are made.

9.2 An Approach to the Thought of Boaventura de Sousa Santos

First of all, it is important to understand that the Portuguese sociologist, Boaventura de Sousa Santos, has an intellectual production and political posture aimed at reinventing social emancipation from the perspective of a new political culture, a new democratic theory (Santos, 2007, 2010a, 2010b).

To this end, an important milestone was the publication of the book 'A speech on the sciences,' in 1987, in which the author adopts an anti-positivist position (Santos, 2010c). This vision is deepened in 1989 with the work 'Introduction to a postmodern science,' where he discusses the profound crisis of modern science (Santos, 1989). A development of this path was the advent of a new emerging paradigm, called 'critical postmodernity' (Santos, 2010c), or 'prudent knowledge for a decent life' (Santos, 2006a, 2011).

With a view to the social and political in postmodernity (Santos, 2010b), the author sought to propose a new political culture (Santos, 2010a), with social emancipation being understood as transformation of unequal power relationships into shared authority relationships (Santos, 2010a). What is proposed is a global politicization of social practice (Santos, 2010b), an emancipatory process based on the principles of equality, and the recognition of difference (Santos, 2010a).

A step further along this path was the reinvention of social emancipation by learning from the South, which presupposes admitting the violence of colonialism, and the recognition of social groups that suffered/suffer from the epistemological exclusivity of modernity, and the reduction of emancipatory possibilities (Santos, 2010a), hence a move toward a critical post-colonial theory (Santos, 2010a). This view would give rise to the production of a cosmopolitan reason that would be provided by the conjunction of the work of translation, and the sociology of absences and emergencies (Santos, 2010a).

The sociology of absences, in turn, would be the approach that seeks to elucidate the mechanisms of concealment/discrimination of the diversity of experiences/existences in the world, while denouncing the processes of social disqualification (Santos, 2010a). In this view, the modes of production of absence are identified (monoculture of knowledge and scientific rigor; monoculture of linear time; monoculture of the naturalization of differences; the logic of the dominant scale; monoculture of capitalist productivity criteria), and respective *modus operandi* of forms of social disqualification (Santos, 2010a). On the other hand, the sociology of emergencies is the approach that analyzes what exists as a future tendency or possibility in a practice, experience, or way of knowing (Santos, 2010a). Also, the close relationship between the sociology of absences and of emergencies extends the present and contracts the future, to expand the diversity of knowledge/experiences that can be made intelligible via the translation work (Santos, 2010a). Monocultures that produce absences are replaced by an ecology of knowledge, which is based on the idea of epistemological diversity (Santos, 2010a), or still, an epistemology of the fight against cognitive injustice (Santos et al., 2005).

To expand the canon of recognition of difference and equality, words such as multiculturalism, multicultural justice, collective rights, and plural citizenships are considered, driving the tensions between difference and equality, which are at the center of the struggles of emancipatory movements, with an alternative or non-hegemonic understanding of human dignity (Santos & Nunes, 2010). With this approach, we allude to the controversial and tensioned aspect posed by the concept of multiculturalism (Santos & Nunes, 2010), in addition to recognizing that it is a concept that assumes a dominant culture that tolerates the existence of other cultures (Santos &

Meneses, 2010). Instead, the idea of interculturalism is reinstated, which presupposes reciprocal recognition and availability for mutual cultural enrichment (Santos & Meneses, 2010), a concept that transcends that of multiculturalism, since it aims to overcome the relationship between a dominant culture and a dominated culture.

9.3 Cultural Adaptation of Expatriates or in Search of New Perspectives?

In the field of expatriation studies, it is possible to find the strategic, power, psychodynamic, and culturalist currents (Nunes et al., 2008). As we are seeking to transcend the concept of 'cultural adaptation,' attention will turn exclusively to the latest trend.

In the culturalist current, the central element of studies is found in the cultural adaptation as a determinant component for the success of expatriation (Nunes et al., 2008). In this direction, studies have focused on several themes, for example, the cultural adaptation of expatriates (Cole & McNulty, 2011), the cultural adaptation of the family (Lazarova et al., 2010; Freitas, 2010), the definition of profiles of personality and influence on the cultural adaptation process (Kittler et al., 2011), the high-quality intercultural relationship between expatriates and their local hosts (Van Bakel et al., 2015), among other subjects.

In this field of research, one of the main theoretical approaches is the model related to cultural adjustment of expatriates (Black et al., 1991), which advocates that there may be a reduction in uncertainty in the cultural adjustment process if there are greater knowledge and understanding of the host country's culture. Another influential perspective is the one that assumes cultural adaptation to the destination country as the main factor of success in expatriation (D'Iribarne, 1993), besides the approach of cultural differences when comparing different national cultures (Hofstede, 2003).

An issue that draws attention is that studies relating to cultural adaptation/adjustment disregard the concept of interculturalism, as assumed in this study. The term 'intercultural adjustment,' to say the truth, has even been used, being admitted as the intensity by which individuals feel psychologically comfortable living outside their country of origin (Caligiuri, 2000). This, however, does not seem to come closer to the emancipatory idea of interculturalism (Santos & Meneses, 2010). In a context of global mobility, approaches to the idea of interculturality can contribute to better-quality coexistence between 'host–host' (Freitas, 2008); however, certain doubts in the use of the terms 'multicultural' and 'intercultural' should not be neglected (Machado & Teixeira, 2019). Therefore, reflections on 'intercultural adaptation' are needed from epistemological perspectives external to the mainstream, for example, by adopting the critical postmodern approach (Machado & Teixeira, 2015; 2015a).

Thus, based on the idea of shared authority relationships (Santos, 2010), as well as interculturalism (Santos & Meneses, 2010), the intercultural adaptation advocated here should be based on the pillars of equality and difference, based on mutual recognition and availability for mutual enrichment between various cultures that share a given cultural space, that is, a relationship embodied in the ecology of knowledge. This proposition is consistent with the understanding of dignity beyond the modern (Machado & Teixeira, 2017).

9.4 Dignity in Organizations: A Look Beyond Modernity

When looking for an approximation of the theme 'dignity' with the 'organizations' and their 'management,' the most influential line of studies is the so-called workplace dignity. This makes sense since the issue of work can be considered essential to dignity (Hodson, 2001). In this current of research, studies have been directed to several themes, such as: dignity at work and law (Brodie, 2004); relationships between the formal structure of work and dignity (Greenspan, 2002); positive/significant participatory experiences related to work organizations (Hodson, 1996); meaning and alienation of work and its impacts on the worker's life (Hodson & Roscigno, 2004); job security, salary, and dignified life (Rayman & Reynolds, 2001); relationships between managers and employees (Sayer, 2007); gender and dignity at work (Crowley, 2013); importance of dignity at work (Bolton, 2007); LGBTQ experiences and dignity at work (Baker & Lucas, 2017); employees' dignity and work behaviors (Lucas et al., 2017); dignity in the workplace and migrant workforce (Lucas et al., 2012); tensions between productivity and dignity (Auerbach, 1988; Shahinpoor & Matt, 2006); dignity and content of work in different professional fields (Chiappetta-Swanson, 2005; Lawless & Moss, 2007); lack of respect for dignity at work (Heloani, 2004; Sayer, 2007; McMullen, 2011), among other issues.

In the approach based on the concept of 'organizational dignity,' initially proposed by Margolis (1997), one identifies the path that has been supported by the Habermasian communicative perspective (Teixeira, 2008), in the approach of stakeholders (Teixeira et al., 2014), and on the theory of facets (Teixeira & Bilsky, 2015; Teixeira, 2016). However, despite the significant advances in the field of study, it is understood that dignity in/of organizations could comprise the ideas of shared authority (Santos, 2010a), ecology of knowledge (Santos, 2010a), and interculturalism (Santos & Meneses, 2010). Therefore, it is proposed that:

There would be dignity in organizations when relations were embodied in three pillars: (i) in the transformation of unequal power relations into relations of shared authority, which would give rise to respect for the principles of equality and difference, (ii) to the ecology of knowledge (of different knowledge), (iii) to the mutual recognition and availability for mutual enrichment between various cultures that share a given cultural space (Machado & Teixeira, 2017).

9.5 Symbolic Cartography of the Dignity of Latin American Expatriates in Their Experiences in Brazil

To operationalize the symbolic cartography, it was decided to analyze the subjects' formal/informal relationships in the organizational scope (large scale), as well as the organizational policies focused on the expatriation process (medium scale), and other relationships not experienced exclusively in the organizational space (small scale) (Machado, 2015). Based on the identification of 'absences' / 'emergencies,' the center/periphery projection of dignity was carried out, followed by symbolization using the mythological figures Athena (emergence of dignity) and Ares (absence of dignity) (Machado, 2015). Projections were construed based on the theory of the sociology of absences and emergencies (Santos, 2010; 2011), in addition to the concept of dignity in organizations (Machado & Teixeira, 2017).

9.5.1 Absences and Emergencies

In the production of absences in the BRA → LAE relationship (where BRA means 'Brazilians,' and LAE 'Latin American expatriates'), there is ample evidence of violation of the dignity promoted by the former, according to the LAE's view.

Thus, taking the large and small scale as a reference, the following absences are highlighted: 'low receptivity/superficial hospitality,' 'non-recognition of knowledge (ignorant),' 'non-recognition based on the criteria of capitalist productivity (unproductive/disqualified),' 'naturalization of difference (sending signals of inferiority),' 'low reciprocal recognition and availability for mutual enrichment (difficulty in understanding cultural differences),' 'pressure for linguistic and cultural adjustment.' Here are some testimonial representatives of absences (BRA → LAE):

> We arrived and received 500,000 invitations to eat pizza. I was waiting. Wow … no calls! Another weekend, none! […], then the dark side of the moon started to happen […]. So, we started to feel very sad, because had no relationships. But they were all very pleasant, very polite.
>
> When I gave ideas, people disqualified. Did you understand?! They disqualified, […], in the meeting with the boss and such, then the attitude was always to question […].
>
> […] if the person who is in positions above or are your peers are Europeans, I don't know if Americans, but being Europeans, I think they have a greater professional respect than if they are Latinos.
>
> Latin America does not exist! […], they look more outward, more towards Europe […]. But the countries around them, they don't even notice […].
>
> I think Brazilians think or feel they are not part of the Latin American people.
>
> […] sometimes Brazilians think they are the best […]. In the beginning, it is, wow, there comes a time when you feel inferior.
>
> […] I feel that they feel a little superior. I never felt inferior!.
>
> You have to speak Portuguese man! You are in Brazil, speak Portuguese!.

In the LAE → BRA relationship (small scale), thus according to LAE's perspective, the following absences were found: 'low reciprocal recognition and availability for mutual enrichment (difficulty to understand cultural traits/difficulty to appreciate BRA),' and 'reinforcement of negative stereotypes.'

Regarding absences (small scale) based on the LAE → LAE relationship, the following stands out: 'prejudice/discrimination by appearance,' 'use of elements of cultural/national identity only in the sphere of the home,' and 'appreciation for what comes from outside (foreignism).' As a representation of this last absence, an excerpt from an interview is found below:

> [...] the Colombian who hasn't been to Brazil yet, sees Brazil as something bigger, something like...wow, it's Brazil! I think the Colombian has that ... Outside everything is better.

Regarding absences (small scale) in the BRA–BRA relationship, always from the perspective of LAE, it was found: 'lack of self-esteem (low self-esteem)' and 'non-identification with what one is (Latin American).' Concerning absences on a medium scale (organizational policies aimed at the expatriation process), some forms were also identified: 'precarious employment relationship for cost reduction,' 'deficient support of the company concerning organizational and bureaucratic procedures,' 'non-observance of laws, rules, norms, and procedures,' and 'absence of human resources policies with a focus on interculturality.'

About emergencies (small and large scale), in the BRA → LAE relationship, it was identified: 'demonstrations of interest in the culture of the other' (small scale), 'Brazilian cultural characteristics that generate well-being for the other' (small scale), 'appreciation of difference' (large scale), 'recognition of knowledge—respect/consideration/appreciation' (large scale). The testimonial below represents some of the emerging practices:

> There was a group of super open managers... The staff valued the difference [company 1]. Now I am working in a project company, in a multicultural environment, there are many people from all over Brazil, [...], always with very positive feedback, the staff came up, tried to help, you feel they valued the work [company 2].

When considering the LAE → BRA relationship (small scale), it was identified: 'interest in the Brazilian culture/history,' 'sense of equality—not feeling inferior,' 'self-worth stance—the pride of national origin,' ' mutual support, friendship, and love within the family (a process of affective independence about Brazilians),' 'appreciation and reaffirmation of cultural/national identity (pride of national origin/use of cultural/national identity symbols),' 'proactivity in building more long-lasting relationships with Brazilians.' On a large scale, it was observed: 'sense of equality—not feeling inferior,' 'knowing and relating to others,' 'returning to their cultural roots (back to the basis),' 'valuing and reaffirming cultural/national identity (pride of national origin/use of cultural/national identity symbols,' 'transforming difficulties into opportunities for personal development').'

Regarding emergencies in the LAE → LAE relationship, it was identified: 'feeling of self-worth—the pride of national origin (small scale),' 'appreciation and reaffirmation of cultural/national identity—use of cultural/national identity symbols (small and large scales),' 'return to its cultural roots—back to the basis (large scale).' Regarding the BRA → BRA relationship, always according to the expatriates' view, no evidence of emerging practices was identified.

Regarding emergencies (medium scale), it was a matter of analyzing how organizational policies work in the expatriation process. In this category, there were 'organizational and bureaucratic procedures' that facilitated/helped the expatriation process, especially those related to documentary, legal, and logistical issues. In the LAE → BRA relationship—on the same scale—there was a 'distinction without discrimination—appreciation of cultural/national identity,' as well as a 'disposition to say no.'

9.5.2 Projections (Center/periphery)

In the so-called microspace of broad sociocultural relations (small scale), the focus was on the subjects' general experience with the Brazilian culture, with the super fact of dignity being the recognition of LAE's knowledge. Thus, the following emphatic projections to the periphery were identified: 'non-recognition of knowledge—ignorant,' 'non-recognition based on the criteria of capitalist productivity—unproductive, disqualified,' 'naturalization of difference—sending signals of inferiority,' 'low reciprocal recognition and availability for mutual enrichment,' 'pressure for linguistic and cultural adjustment.' Furthermore, whenever the BRA referred to Latin Americans or Latin American countries, as 'backward' and / or 'underdeveloped,' what was being done was the projection of dignity to the periphery, the basis of which was the absence called 'linear temporality' (see Santos, 2010a).

Regarding the projections to the periphery in the LAE → LAE relationship (microspace of broad sociocultural relations), whose super fact of dignity was the recognition of their knowledge, three projections were identified: 'prejudice and discrimination by appearance,' 'use of elements of cultural–national identity only in the sphere of the home,' 'appreciation for what comes from outside—foreignism.' According to the LAE → BRA relations (small scale), the super fact of dignity was adjusted for the recognition of the knowledge of the BRA by the LAE, with the following projections emerging to the periphery: 'reinforcement of negative stereotypes,' 'low reciprocal recognition and availability for mutual enrichment.'

In the BRA → BRA relations, on a small scale (microspace of broad sociocultural relations), the super fact of dignity was the 'recognition of their knowledge,' resulting in projections to the periphery: 'lack of self-esteem—low self-esteem' and 'not identifying with what you are.' It is assumed that the Brazilian cultural trait of foreignism contributes to this process of 'not recognizing oneself,' which makes it difficult to identify as a Latin American (Machado & Teixeira, 2019b).

In the micro-organizational space (large scale), when subjects realized their knowledge was recognized by Brazilian co-workers (the super fact that founders of dignity), it can be said that dignity in relationships was designed for the center of the organizational space. In the same way, considering only the microspace of broad sociocultural relations (small scale), the projection of dignity at the center was noticed when subjects understood that their knowledge was recognized by the Brazilians; on a medium scale, the projection of dignity toward the center was perceived when and if the organization adopted any appropriate approach about interculturality, the super fact of dignity.

Thus, having BRA → ELA relationships (micro-organizational space—large scale) as a reference, an emphatic projection to the center was perceived through the 'presence of appreciation of difference,' although it was not very frequent. Even so, the potential of this emergency has to do with a logic of opposition to the monoculture of naturalization of differences, which would facilitate inter-knowledge (Santos, 2010a). Other projections to the center in the microspace were the following: 'respect, consideration and appreciation' (not emphatic), and 'good receptivity' (not emphatic). On a medium scale of the organization's microspace, no projections to the center were identified, that is, intentional actions aimed at interculturality at the organizational level. As for the projections of dignity in the microspace of broad sociocultural relations (small scale), whose super fact was the recognition of LAE knowledge by BRA, there are two weak emergencies: 'demonstrations of interest in the culture of the other' and 'cultural characteristics that generate well-being for the other.'

9.5.3 *Symbolization*

Symbolization is understood as the visible face of the representation of reality (Santos, 2011). For this, we used the mythical figures of Athena (representation of emergencies) and Ares (representation of absences).

When considering the abundant projections of dignity to the periphery in BRA → LAE relations, the applicable symbolization is that of Ares. What was seen was the predominance of the non-recognition of the other's knowledge, as well as the lack of respect for difference, and little or no emphasis is given to interculturality. The reasons why the Brazilians violated the dignity of other Latin Americans may be related to some promotions of absences about themselves, such as the 'lack of self-esteem—low self-esteem' and the 'non-identification with what is happening,' which may be based on foreignism (Calás & Arias, 2007; Machado & Teixeira, 2019b), on the mirror-effect (Irigaray & Vergara, 2010), on the inferiority complex (Calligaris, 1993), as well as on the Gulliver (Araújo et al., 2013).

In the LAE → BRA relations, the figure of Ares was also present, especially due to the following projections to the periphery: 'reinforcement of negative stereotypes' and 'low reciprocal recognition.' A cultural trait apparently common among former Latin American colonies, the foreignism (Calás & Arias, 2007) may be one of the possible reasons for this projection of dignity to the periphery. Also, in the projection to both the BRA → BRA and LAE → LAE peripheries, invisibility or absence was perceived. In this sense, the figure of Ares was present again.

When looking at the BRA → LAE relations, considering the organizational microspace (large and medium scale), and the microspace of broad sociocultural relationships (small scale), there was also evidence of emergencies, consequently of projections to the center. If so, it was understood that the relevant symbolization would be that of Athena, since one could perceive the predominance of elements that reflected the recognition of the other's knowledge. In the organizational scope (medium scale), however, there was a lack of 'Apollonian' actions, in the sense of emphasizing intentional actions that developed a sense of interculturality.

Regarding the LAE → BRA relationship (large, medium, and small scale), the projections of dignity to the center of microspaces were as follows: 'self-worthy attitude,' 'opening up to the other, but without losing the essence,' 'interest and/or appreciation for the Brazilian culture,' 'interest in the history of Brazil and its future,' 'knowing and relating to the other,' 'returning to your cultural roots,' 'proactivity in building more long-lasting relationships,' 'disposition to say no,' 'distinction without discrimination.' Thus, it was understood that Athena would represent these emergencies of dignity, evidencing elements that reflected the recognition of knowledge and the availability to mutual cultural enrichment, assumptions of inter-knowledge. Regarding the BRA → BRA relationship, there was an absence of projections of dignity to the center, so that the figure of Ares completely predominated. It is believed that this self-peripheralization' may be associated with a possible 'lack of self-esteem—low self-esteem,' as well as 'non-identification with what one is.'

By observing the quantity and intensity (emphatic/non-emphatic) of projections to the periphery from the relations between Brazilians and other Latin Americans, compared to the projections at the center considering the same relationships, using the mythological metaphor, one can say that the presence of Ares (violence/injustice) was much more frequent than that of Athena (knowledge/justice).

9.6 Implications for Management

The unfavorable results for Latin American expatriates in their relations with Brazilians in Brazil certainly bring challenges to organizational management, especially if we consider the cultural and behavioral obstacles to the construction of inter-knowledge/interculturality.

Taking a managerial point of view as a reference when focusing on the search for maximizing the advantages linked to international people management policies, or even to the strategic perspectives of international mobility, such as organizational expatriation, for example, it is at least worrying the absence of human resources (HR) policies aimed at interculturality in the organizations studied. This is because, among other aspects, it produces a picture of wasted creative potential for an appreciation of cultural diversity in the organizational scope, not to mention, of course, the increased chance of failure of the international mobility process, from a strategic point of view.

Regarding the practical issues of the expatriation process, for example, it is understood that it would be up to the company's HR area (in the host country) to take care of expatriates, as well as of their respective families, whenever applicable, so that they would feel welcome, supported, and not deceived for any reason. In this sense, broadly speaking, it would be advisable to develop a critical reflection on the expatriation process, starting from top management.

Furthermore, the development of strategies aimed at this international mobility process could be recommended, in order to create an organizational environment that values diversity while protecting dignity and promoting well-being. In this sense, one could go beyond training focused on the expatriates to cover the development of intercultural competences of other members of the organization. Then, to maximize the advantages of diversity in organizations as well as minimize their disadvantages, it is understood that competent inclusive diversity management is necessary, including organizational expatriates and voluntary expatriates.

9.7 Final Remarks

As a theoretical contribution, we sought to bring a new look at dignity in organizations, in addition to a conceptual proposal for intercultural adaptation. It was a matter of looking for an advance in these understandings, having as central elements the ideas of knowledge recognition, ecologies of knowledge, and interculturality, elements that became central to our reflection.

Moreover, it is believed that the propositions of dignity in organizations and intercultural adaptation, now present, should be contemplated in current tensioned world, which, consequently, brings the need to consider them from a network of complex relationships and within a 'conflict' perspective in which would be an intertwining of absences and mutual emergencies and in dispute. Depending on the direction of these relations, the protection of dignity or its violation can be produced.

Foreignness can be seen as a factor of influence on how Brazilians sought non-identification with the other Latin American, or even their rejection, which invariably caused the violation of dignity (projection of dignity to the periphery) in different social and organizational spaces.

For practical applications to organizational management, it is recognized that the absence of HR policies aimed at interculturality is, at least, of concern. Therefore, the panorama glimpsed was that of organizational environments wasting creative potential arising from greater cultural diversity. In this perspective, absences in the organizational microspace tend to hinder the development of intercultural adaptation in companies and may even reinforce prejudiced and discriminatory aspects of influences arising from broad sociocultural relationships (external to the organization's internal environment), which tends to feed the process of peripheralization of dignity. This process, in turn, would reinforce the undesirable predominance of the figure of Ares over Athena in the organizational sphere.

Briefly, developing a critical reflection about the expatriation process, from the top of organizations, would be healthy. Besides, it is recommended to develop strategies aimed at this international mobility process, to create an organizational environment that values diversity, protect dignity, and promote well-being in organizations. An action in this direction, for example, would be to go beyond the most common training programs that focus on expatriates, simultaneously proposing the development of intercultural skills for those who will come to work with this foreigner.

The reflection elaborated here sought to understand the difficulties/possibilities of respectful cultural dialogue which, among other things, may prove to be an opportunity for liberation from the colonized mentality, without which we will continue to alternately reproduce the dominant arrogance and the submission of the dominated.

This discussion does not intend to be definitive on the subject, but only to open new opportunities and research fronts in the field of studies, mainly from approaches outside the mainstream. In this sense, for future investigations, it is suggested: (i) to consider the interpretation of Brazilians directly; (ii) to understand the experiences of foreigners from the Global North, in Brazil; and (iii) to focus on the dignity of Brazilian expatriates in their cultural experience abroad (Global South and Global North).

References

Araújo, B. F. V. B., Teixeira, M. L. M., & Malini, E. (2013). Estrangeirismo e complexo de Gulliver: Brasileiros na percepção de expatriados. *Organizações & Sociedade, 20*(66), 461–478.

Auerbach, J. (1988). Organized labor: Toward a new dignity in the workplace. *Journal of Career Development, 15*(1), 65–77.

Baeninger, R. (2018) Migrações transnacionais na fronteira: novos espaços da migração Sul-Sul. In R Baeninger & A Canales (Eds.), *Migrações fronteiriças* (pp. 463–472). Núcleo de Estudos de População "Elza Berquó" – Nepo/Unicamp, Campinas.

Baker, S. J., & Lucas, K. (2017). Is it safe to bring myself to work? Understanding LGBTQ experiences of workplace dignity. *Canadian Journal of Administrative Sciences, 34,* 133–148.

Black, J. S., Mendenhall, H., & Oddou, G. (1991). Toward a comprehensive model of international adjustment—An integration of multiple theoretical perspectives. *Academy of Management Review, 16*(2), 291–317.

Bolton, S. C. (2007). Dignity *in* and *at* work: Why it matters? In S. C. Bolton (Ed.), *Dimensions of dignity at work*. New York: Routledge.

Brodie, D. (2004). Protecting dignity in the workplace: The vitality of mutual trust and confidence. *Industrial Law Journal, 33*(4), 349–354.

Calás, M. B., & Arias, M. E. (2007). Compreendendo as organizações latino-americanas: Transformação ou hibridização? In F. C. P. Motta & M. P. Caldas (Eds.), *Cultura organizacional e cultura brasileira* (pp. 316–325). São Paulo: Atlas.

Calligaris, C. (1993). *Hello Brasil!: Notas de um psicanalista europeu viajando ao Brasil*. São Paulo: Escuta.

Caligiuri, P. (2000). Selecting expatriates for personality characteristics: A moderating effect of personality on the relationship between host national contact and cross-cultural adjustment. *Management International Review, 20,* 61–80.

Chiappetta-Swanson, C. (2005). Dignity and dirty work: Nurses' experiences in managing genetic termination for fetal anomaly. *Qualitative Sociology, 28*(1), 93–116.

Cole, N., & McNulty, Y. (2011). Why do female expatriates "fit-in" better then males? An analysis of self-transcendence and socio-cultural adjustment. *Cross-Cultural Management, 18*(2), 144–164.

Crowley, M. (2013). Gender, the labor process, and dignity at work. *Social Forces, 91*(4), 1209–1238.

Davel, E., Dupuis, J.-P., & Chanlat, J.-F. (2008). *Gestion em contexte interculturel: Approches, problématiques, pratiques et plongées.* Québec: Presses de l'Université Laval e Télé-Université.
De Hass, H. (2010). Migration and development: A theoretical perspective. *International Migration Review, 44*(1), 227–264.
D'Iribarne, P. (1993). *La logique de l'honneur.* Paris: Seuil.
Edwards, A. (2016). El desplazamiento forzado en el mundo bate su cifra récord. Available via *DIALOG* https://www.acnur.org/noticias/historia/2016/6/5b7e715a42/el-desplazamiento-forzado-en-el-mundo-bate-su-cifra-record.html. Accessed September 05, 2020.
Fioravanti, C. (2015). As raízes da resistência. *Pesquisa FAPESP 236.* Available via DIALOG https://revistapesquisa.fapesp.br/2015/10/13/as-raizes-da-resistencia/. Accessed September 05, 2020.
Freitas, M. E. (2008). O imperativo intercultural na vida e na gestão contemporânea. *Organização & Sociedade* – O&S *15*(46), 79–89.
Freitas, M. E. (2009). A mobilidade como novo capital simbólico nas organizações ou sejamos nômades? *Organizações & Sociedade* – O&S *16*(49), 247–264.
Freitas, M.E. (2010). Expatriação professional: o desafio interdependente para empresas e indivíduos. *GES – Revista Gestão e Sociedade 4*(9), 689–708.
Greenspan, D. S. (2002). Downsizing with dignity. *Employment Relations Today, 9*(3), 39–48.
Heloani, R. (2004). Assédio moral: um ensaio sobre a expropriação da dignidade no trabalho. RAE – *Revista de Administração de Empresas, 3*(1), 1–8.
Hodson, R. (1996). Dignity at the workplace under participative management: Alienation and freedom revisited. *American Sociological Review, 61,* 719–738.
Hodson, R. (2001). *Dignity at work.* New York: Cambridge University Press.
Hodson, R., & Roscigno, V. J. (2004). Organizational success and worker dignity: Complementary or contradictory? *American Journal of Sociology, 110*(3), 672–708.
Hofstede, G. (2003). *Culturas e organizações: Compreender a nossa programação mental: Compreender a nossa programação mental.* Lisboa: Edições Silabo.
Irigaray, H. A. R., & Vergara, S. C. (2010). Expatriados no Brasil: Diferentes nacionalidades, diferentes percepções. *Revista Gestão. Org, 8*(1), 49–60.
Kittler, M. G., Rygl, D., Mackinnon, A., & Wiedmann, K. (2011). Work role and work adjustment in emerging markets: A study of German expatriates in CEE countries and Russia. *Cross-Cultural Management, 18*(2), 165–184.
Klein, N. (2017). *Não basta dizer não: Resistir à nova política de choque e conquistar o mundo do qual precisamos: Resistir à nova política de choque e conquistar o mundo do qual precisamos.* Rio de Janeiro: Bertrand Brasil.
Lawless, J., & Moss, C. (2007). Exploring the value of dignity in the work-life of nurses. *Contemporary Nurse: A Journal for the Australian Nursing Profession, 24*(2), 225–236.
Lazarova, M., Westman, M., & Shaffer, M. A. (2010). Elucidating the positive side of the work-family interface on international assignments: A model of expatriate work and family performance. *Academy of Management Review, 35*(1), 93–117.
Lucas, K., Kang, D., & Li, Z. (2012). Workplace dignity in a total institution: Examining the experiences of Foxconn's migrant workers. *Journal of Business Ethics,* pp. 1–16.
Lucas, K., Manikas, A. S., Mattingly, E. S., & Crider, C. J. (2017). Engaging and misbehaving: How dignity affects employee work behaviors. *Organization Studies,* pp. 1–23.
Machado, M. M. (2015). *Caminhos da adaptação intercultural na expatriação: uma cartografia simbólica da dignidade de latino-americanos no Brasil.* Doctorate thesis, Universidade Presbiteriana Mackenzie.
Machado, M. M., & Teixeira, M. L. M. (2015a). *Adaptação intercultural na expatriação*: em busca de um conceito. Paper presented at the III Congresso Brasileiro de Estudos Organizacionais – CBEO, Universidade Federal do Espírito Santo, Vitória, October 28–30, 2015.
Machado, M. M., & Teixeira, M. L. M. (2015b). *Adaptação cultural ou adaptação intercultural na expatriação.* Paper presented at the XXXIX Encontro da Associação Nacional de Pós-Graduação e Pesquisa em Administração – EnANPAD, Belo Horizonte, September 13–16, 2015.

Machado, M. M., & Teixeira, M. L. M. (2017). Dignity in the context of organizations: A look beyond modernity. *Mackenzie Management Review* (Revista de Administração Mackenzie – RAM), *18*(2), 80–103. https://doi.org/10.1590/1678-69712016.
Machado, M. M., & Teixeira, M. L. M. (2019a). Em busca da diferença e da igualdade: Reflexões sobre multiculturalismo e interculturalismo. In A. P. Lombardi (Ed.), *Arqueologia das Ciências Humanas e Sociais Aplicadas 4* (pp. 73–82). Ponta Grossa: Atena.
Machado, M. M., & Teixeira, M. L. M. (2019b). Foreignism: A phenomenon contrary to the intercultural exchange between Brazilians and other Latin Americans? *Portuguese Studies Review – PSR, 27*(1), 47–65.
Machado, M. M., Prados, R. M. N., & Bonini, L. M. M. (2019). *Fluxos migratórios e minorias étnico-sociais*: Possibilidades de análise de políticas públicas voltadas à formação humana e à dignidade. In L. M. M. Bonini & R. M. N. Prados (Eds.), *Dinâmicas sociais, diversidade e cidadania* (pp. 21–48). Timburi: Editora Cia do eBook.
Margolis, J. D. (1997). *Dignity in the balance: philosophical and practical dimensions of promoting ethics in organizations*. Ph.D. dissertation, Harvard University.
McMullen, J. (2011) Balancing the right to manage with dignity at work. *Perspectives: Policy & Practice in Higher Education, 15*(1), 3–6.
McNulty, Y., & Selmer, J. (2017) Introduction: Overview of early expatriate studies, 1952 to 1979. In Y. McNulty & J. Selmer (Eds.), *Research handbook of expatriates* (pp. 3–20). Massachusetts: Edward Elgar Publishing.
Mott, M., Teixeira, M. L. M., Nakashima, C., & Araújo, G. S. (2012). Sistematização da literatura internacional sobre expatriados: Um estudo bibliométrico com destaque para metodologia empregada em anos recentes. *Revista Gestão & Tecnologia, 12*(2), 243–267.
Nunes, L. H., Vasconcelos, I. F. G., & Jaussaud, J. (2008). *Expatriação de executivos*. São Paulo: Thomson Learning.
Rayman, P., & Reynolds, J. (2001). *Beyond the bottom line: The search for dignity at work: The search for dignity at work*. New York: Palgrave.
Santiago, C., & Machado, M. M. (2015). Implicações da globalização no âmbito do saber e da prática de gestão: algumas reflexões. *REGIT – Revista de Estudos de Gestão, Informação e Tecnologia, 2*(4), 13–33.
Santos, B. S. (1989). *Introdução a uma ciência pós-moderna*. Rio de Janeiro: Graal.
Santos, B. S., Meneses, M. P., & Nunes, J. (2005). Introdução: Para ampliar o cânone da ciência: A diversidade epistemológica do mundo. In B. S. Santos (Ed.), *Semear outras soluções: Os caminhos da biodiversidade e dos conhecimentos rivais: Os caminhos da biodiversidade e dos conhecimentos rivais* (pp. 21–25). Rio de Janeiro: Civilização Brasileira.
Santos, B. S. (2006a). Introdução. In B. S. Santos (Ed.), *Conhecimento prudente para uma vida decente: Um discurso sobre as ciências revisitado: Um discurso sobre as ciências revisitado* (2nd ed., pp. 17–58). São Paulo: Cortez.
Santos, B. S. (2006b). Para uma sociologia das ausências e uma sociologia das emergências. In B. S. Santos (Ed.), *Conhecimento prudente para uma vida decente: "Um discurso sobre as ciências revisitado": "Um discurso sobre as ciências revisitado"* (2nd ed., pp. 777–821). São Paulo: Cortez.
Santos, B. S. (2007). *Renovar a teoria crítica e reinventar a emancipação social*. São Paulo: Boitempo.
Santos, B. S. (2010a). *A gramática do tempo: Para uma nova cultura política* (3rd ed.). São Paulo: Cortez.
Santos, B. S. (2010b). *Pela mão de Alice: O social e o político na pós-modernidade* (13th ed.). São Paulo: Cortez.
Santos, B. S. (2010c). *Um discurso sobre as ciências* (7th ed.). São Paulo: Cortez.
Santos, B. S., & Nunes, J. A. (2010). Introdução: Para ampliar o cânone do reconhecimento, da diferença e da igualdade. In B. S. Santos (Ed.), *Reconhecer para libertar: Os caminhos do cosmopolitismo multicultural: Os caminhos do cosmopolitismo multicultural* (2nd ed., pp. 25–68). Rio de Janeiro: Civilização Brasileira.

Santos, B. S., & Meneses, M. P. (2010). Introdução. In B. S. Santos & M. P. Meneses (Eds.), *Epistemologias do Sul* (2nd ed., pp. 9–20). Coimbra: Edições Almedina e CES.

Santos, B. S. (2011). *A crítica da razão indolente: Contra o desperdício da experiência: Contra o desperdício da experiência* (8th ed.). São Paulo: Cortez.

Sassen, S. (1988). *The mobility of labor and capital*. Cambridge, MA: Cambridge University Press.

Sayer, A. (2007). Dignity at work: Broadening the agenda. *Organization, 14*(4), 565–581.

Shahinpoor, N., & Matt, B. F. (2006). *The power of one*: Dissent and organizational life. *Journal of Business Ethics, 34*(4), 663–683.

Teixeira, M. L. M. (2008). Dignidade organizacional: Valores e relações com stakeholders. In M. L. M. Teixeira (Ed.), *Valores humanos e gestão: Novas perspectivas: Novas perspectivas* (pp. 81–92). São Paulo: Editora Senac.

Teixeira, M. L. M., De Domenico, S. M. R., Dias, S. M. R.C.,& Mendes, L. H. L. (2014). *Práticas de dignidade organizacional percebidas por trabalhadores na relação entre organização e stakeholders*. Paper presented at the XXXVIII Encontro da Associação Nacional de Pós-Graduação e Pesquisa em Administração– EnANPAD, Rio de Janeiro, September 13–17, 2014.

Teixeira, M. L. M., & Bilsky, W. (2015). *Faceting organizational theory*. Paper presented at the 15th Facet Theory Conference, New York, August 16–15, 2015.

Teixeira, M. L. M. (2016). *Organizational dignity theory: a proposal*. Paper presented at the XIX SemeAd – Seminários em Administração FEA-USP, São Paulo, November 09–11, 2016.

Teixeira, M. L. M., Paz, M. G. T., Araújo, B. F. V. B., & Machado, M. M. (2017). Expatriates: The multinationality of multinational and national firms. In E. R. Neiva, C. V. Torres, & H. Mendonça (Eds.), *Organizational psychology and evidence-based management* (pp. 267–285). Berlin: Springer International Publishing.

Van Bakel, M. S., Van Oudenhoven, J. P., & Gerritsen, M. (2015). Developing a high-quality intercultural relationship: Expatriates and their localhost. *Journal of Global Mobility, 3*(1), 25–45.

Chapter 10
Innovation in the People Agenda: A Dignity Narrative

Marcos Baptistucci

Abstract The greatest challenge of management theory has been to cope with the new demands of society. Traditional management theories have their roots in classical economy which regards the individuals as "homo economicus" who are only interested in transactional relations to fulfill their own interests. This approach to business has resulted in external negative consequences such as environment degradation, pollution and the increasing of inequalities. Humanistic is the new paradigm proposed for managerial theory putting dignity and well-being in the center. This chapter presents a narrative of an HR director who assumed the aim of moving his company toward a humanistic paradigm. In this narrative, the context is explained as the stages (archetypes) the company has been going through from economism to humanism archetype, showing that the process is not linear, but complex. Hope that this narrative can illuminate other companies to move toward the humanistic management, in spite of the difficulty of the process and the business imperatives.

Keywords HR management · Humanism · Dignity

10.1 Introduction

The greatest challenge of management theory has been to cope with the new demands of society. Scholars and practitioners are required to rethink the ways of conceiving and running business. Traditional management theories have their roots in classical economy which regards the individuals as "economicus men" who are only interested in transactional relations to fulfill their own interests (Pirson & Lawrence, 2010). This approach to business has resulted in external negative consequences (Donaldson & Walsh, 2015) such as environment degradation, pollution (Gani & Sharma, 2009), and the increasing of inequalities (Saez & Zuckman, 2014).

Anchored to authors like Mele (2003, 2009) and Pirson and Lawrence (2019) argued that the economistic paradigm has neglected ethical and social aspects of

M. Baptistucci (✉)
São Paulo, Brazil
e-mail: marcosvb@yahoo.com

M. L. Mendes Teixeira and L. M. B. de Oliveira (eds.), *Organizational Dignity and Evidence-Based Management*, https://doi.org/10.1007/978-3-030-68560-7_10

human nature, and Pirson and Lawrence (2010) considered the "economicus man" as amoral. Society needs a new management theory paradigm (Pirson & Lawrence, 2010). Companies need to change the focus from customer and owner to employees. Organizations "should primarily be employee centered" (Sikula et al., 2001, p. 3). To put people at the center is one of the principles that Jackson and Nelson (2004) proposed to run business in a new approach. These authors defend that business needs to have a purpose beyond profit.

What does it mean to put the employees into the business center management theory? What does it mean to have a purpose beyond profit? What kind of management theory is necessary to cope with the society's demands? Donaldson and Walsh (2015) proposed a new theory of business with the dignity as the cornerstone that can give (provide) answers to those questions. This theory is supported by three propositions: "P1: The purpose of business is to optimize collective value; P2: business is accountable to those who affect and are affected by its activities, those in the present, past, and future. P3: Business control must prohibit any assault on participants' dignity. P4: Optimized collective value is the mark of business success" (Donaldson & Wlash, 2015, p. 195). Business, in this proposition, means "a form of cooperation involving the production, exchange, and distribution of goods and services for the purpose of achieving collective value which provides action guidance that stretches well beyond the recognition of aggregates of individual **values**, changing the deontic status of particular actions for group members"). In turn, a participant is "someone who affects or is affected by the pursuit of collective value. Some business participants are identified through their membership in entities that affect or are affected by the pursuit of collective value," business success means "optimized Collective Value, optimized subject to clearing the Dignity Threshold. Equifinality assumed, alternative states of Business Success are possible." (Donaldson & Walsh, 2015, p. 188).

Pirson and Lawrence (2010, 2019) proposed a new paradigm for managerial theory: humanistic. This paradigm puts dignity and well-being in the center, and it is aligned with the management theory proposed by Donaldson and Walsh (2015). To move from the economic to the humanistic paradigm, organizations depend on the dignity intensity they take into account: whether the dignity is ignored, preserved, or promoted. Regarding the intensity of dignity, organizations can fit into one of these archetypes: economism, bounded economism, enlightened/masked economism (economic paradigm), paternalism/fake humanism, bounded humanism, and humanism (humanistic paradigm). Economism archetype considers individuals as resources to achieve efficiency and effectiveness and dignity is ignored. In the bounded economism, the main focus is still on wealth creation, but the preservation of dignity is taken into account. Dignity is embraced and promoted in the enlightened/masked economism, but the wealth creation continues being the main focus. The main goal of paternalism/fake humanism archetype is creation of well-being. With this mindset, organizations sometimes deprive workers of their autonomy and dignity. In turn, the main goal of bounded humanism is well-being creation and the dignity is preserved but not actively promoted. Finally, the humanism archetype embraces the dignity promotion and well-being creation as its main goals. Private companies can move from one archetype to another as they consider the dignity and welfare of society as their main goal aligned with their purpose of obtaining profits as consequence (Pirson & Lawrence, 2019).

This chapter presents a narrative of an HR director who assumes the aim of moving the Dignity Industrial Company (D.I.Co) (fictitious name) toward a humanistic paradigm. In this narrative, the context is explained as the stages (archetypes) the company has been going through. Despite Pirson and Lawrence (2019) having proposed a process to move from economism to humanism archetype, this narrative shows that the process is not linear, but complex. The companies can fit into more than one archetype during the process. We hope that this narrative can illuminate other companies to move toward the humanistic management, in spite of the difficulty of the process.

10.2 An Uncertainty Context

In the second quarter of 2020, a global pandemic suddenly covered the entire world, submitting countries, companies, cities, and their citizens to enormous crises and economic recession period never seen in the previous decades. At this time, the coronavirus was no longer just a suspicion, and it had become a tragic and tough reality which companies must deal with. As the virus runs across the continents, governments have put in place a set of initiatives in order to reduce the contamination rates and the deaths. On the other hand, those actions impacted the entire society and pushed the companies back in order to rethink their strategies for survival during that period of the history.

Despite that, the COVID-19 pandemic pushed 83,5% of the labor market in Brazil into a state of vulnerability which provoked/prompted the government to define emergency policies to support more than 26 million workers who would not have access to any income compensation under this unemployment tough scenario (Prates & Barbosa, 2020). Just like other developing countries, Brazil suffered from a state of emergency prior to the 2020 pandemic, which came from a poor recovery from the 2013–2016 economic crisis. This, and the new virus pandemic combined to create the enormous social-economic hurricane which directly impacts the entire society impacted by a competitive political war. Diving deep into the Brazilian society, the pandemic arrived with devastating effects. More than 1 million formal jobs disappeared at the start, adding those numbers to the already large line/group of 4.9 million unemployed people (McGeever, 2020; Caram & Resende, 2020). Thus, the Brazilian government decided to launch a special program, allowing companies to reduce working hours in parallel to the wages reduction which impacted 8.1 million of workers who had signed individual labor agreements. Layoffs and redesign were reduced, and a lot of jobs were protected (Ponce, 2020).

Working in a multinational company, we could follow how these impacts were approaching Latin America as the pandemic started in the other hemisphere. With more than 25 thousand employees located in 20 countries and distributed within 72 plants, this B2B company, whose main business is to offer sustainable packaging, sees its results suffer a lot in different way, such as reduced demand, lack of raw materials available, quarantine or lockdown restrictions imposed by local governments. At the same time, that it should be taking care about the anxiety, fear, and hopelessness that appeared in its labor force.

At this period of time (at this time/during this time), the future was completely unpredictable, the way it has never been before. The Acronym V.U.C.A—volatile, uncertainty, complex, and ambiguous has never fit to the history at all. Companies, governments, associations, communities, and other stakeholders put all efforts together, fighting an invisible enemy who traveled across the world and continents faster than the countries were able to deal with it. Under so much uncertainty, companies were back to the basics in order to understand what were the key elements that would support and maintain the business for the next years. Countermeasures were proposed and implemented while the society was watching one of the most devastating tragedies in the entire human history.

10.3 Aligning Business Imperative to the People Agenda: From Economism to Humanism

Founded more than 100 years ago, the Dignity Industrial Corporation (D.I.Co) is one of the most important players in its segment around the world. Based on the merger and acquisitions strategy, it has become the leader in providing a complete solution to clients, customers, and society regarding sustainable issues and protecting people and the environment. As part of the industrial revolutions across the history, during which hand production methods transited to the machine methods based on new manufacturing processes, a big portion of the company's management systems was created under the criteria in which command and control skills were the key drivers to the successful and sustainable results year by year. People were part of the asset management, integrating the whole system and moving towards better efficiency and results.

That period of the company was in line with the economic approach to management based on classic economy and scientific management. At this period, individuals were considered human machines. The main focus was on control and command (Pirson & Lawrence, 2010). This kind of management violates unconditional human dignity. Regarding the stages through which a company can evolve toward the humanistic management, we can consider that, at that time, the D.I.Co can be classified in the "economism" stage whose main feature is to ignore human dignity. Dignity is not important in the management activity (Pison, 2019).

As years went by, companies, aligned with the society changes and challenges, started to understand how important to the strategy people agenda really was. They began considering their peculiarities and their abilities to customize their processes and products to achieve an important place in the market.

The last 5 years were really important to the company. It faced big challenges in terms of people management in order to rethink its strategy and approachability. Redefining its C-levels, reducing its layers, improvising its decision-making processes, and empowering its people were the key elements that boosted the company to the new level, raising the bar internally and externally. During this period, people agenda assumed its importance inside the business and company understood that people were the fundamental element to lead that change across the world. Mission, vision, values, and behaviors were declared, integrating leaders, teams and employees, country by country, operation by operation, and connecting people to people under/within the entire system.

Health, innovation, solutions, stakeholders, and sustainability became part of its strategy which reflects directly into the values and behaviors expected. Those values and behaviors were translated from the company's mission and principles accountability combined with enterprise leadership and making sound decisions; all these have been changing the company across the world.

A new operating model was piloted during the latest/most recent years in order to simplify the matrix and reduce cost, creating a global scale and a local mindset, redefining enterprise performance management, and preserving the cultural spirit. These pillars were the fundamental units of the strategy in order to drive to effectively collaboration across functions and geographies as part of the business to business (B2B) value chain. The enterprise's strategies were based on establishing a competitive advantage by having the lowest cost of operation in the industry. Cost leadership meant low margins and fast market cycles. Under these guidelines, the company defined its roadmap unifying the business strategy with how it executes in the market, operates and organizes internally, and manages performance in order to deliver on imperatives and financial goals. At this time, people were considered the center of the entire strategy and they have represented the key element to lead the changes and overcome the new challenges.

At this point, reviewing and communicating its values broadly, human dignity entered in the D.I.Co's agenda definitely. Dignity needed to be protected, and physical, psychological or social well-being could not be harmed. Norms and HR policies were established in other to protect dignity. However, it did not mean that human dignity was promoted. This stage is named bounded humanism (Pirson & Lawrence, 2019).

10.3.1 Moving Toward Humanistic Management

In that part of the company's biography, a worldwide pandemic appeared, suddenly impacting and devastating the marketplaces across the world. These pressures came to the first levels of business agenda adding an unpredictable variable into the system and to the decision-making process: human lives. It was not about the business only; it was not only/just about the company and the costs. It was not about profits and results. In fact, it was about managing the company as part of the global society value chain. New challenges were faced and a new operating model was required. It was at that exact time that company was challenged many times and its values were judged. People asked how able the company was to move as fast as the investors expected on improving the results, managing the cost aligned to the net sales that were declining, respecting people, and preserving their current jobs.

The company readily responded to the crisis. Global guidelines were issued and communicated from corporate to the country groups in order to contain costs. Discretionary costs were reduced below the minimum levels, new hires were frozen, new investments were postponed, and job positions were discussed again with focus on efficiency (back to economism). At this time, under so many pressures, here in the South American country group, some high-position managers contested themselves in order to find different ways and approaches to get better solutions.

Since the local new C-level was created, new values became part of the business agenda. Human resources have been taking the priority items into this agenda, moving the business through people under three major pillars: efficiency, development, and engagement. The efficiency pillar was no longer dealt with by finance team only, human resource assumed a key role in the company to drive efficiency further in order to define better structures, promoting the cost-reduction mindset culture. In the last 5 years, all key indicators related to people and cost such as overhead per net sales, full time equivalent (FTEs) per tons packed have been declining tremendously. New skills have been required, creating the mindset of connectivity in order to understand beyond the numbers that drive the results. It was a tough and challenging journey, characterized by difficult conversations, management changes, and redefining of structures.

However, this first pillar was not sustained by itself. Development and engagement actions were required to support and maintain the cost-reduction mindset in the right way. Integrated development actions were put in place under a transversal approach which means that no development program was defined if it did not cover all layers in the organization. This represented a new way of training and working under squads as opposed to the hierarchy and traditional structures. People have been connected across the areas instead of within their own areas or positions. Talents and high-performance employees were recognized based on clear criteria and they competed under the equal conditions. Recognition and reward programs were rapidly implemented to guarantee that the right messages were sent to all employees at the same time. The entire company and leaders were respected the meritocracy and the years of service criteria.

From that time on, under the D.I.Co's maturity curve, the human dignity has come to be not only preserved, but also promoted. One of the most important evidences of this is the weakening of hierarchical structures. Managers, directors, and non-managers were invited to attend the same training program. Part of executives reacted to these novelties in the company. They could not imagine themselves joining the general group of employees as they did not have high hierarchical positions in the company. They were afraid of having their weak points/weaknesses exposed. All are persons, regardless of occupied position, participated in the training programs. This is the message that D.I.Co sent to everyone. Hodson (2004) called attention to the harms that managers can cause to employees when demanding overwork, limiting work autonomy, and with other dignity violations. At this stage, it is possible to say that D.I.Co company is going on with the humanistic management (Pirson & Lawrence, 2019) implementation. One could say that this is simply not true and consider this evidence totally fitting with enlightened/masked economism. However, to provoke hierarchical weakness means to provoke the weakening of managers' power upon other employees. This kind of practice means an attempt to democratize power and it has impact inside and outside company. As the premise of humanist management is the orientation to social welfare, it is possible to say that D.I.Co is moving from economic paradigm to humanistic management paradigm.

Negotiating across the value chain and its stakeholders

Let us go back to the crisis and the pandemic period of time. As mentioned before, the company was able to respond to the market and to the investors quickly, proposing tough countermeasures that impacted suppliers, employees, and customers. Worried about how these countermeasures would impact people in a short period of time, the human resources area had been challenging itself to find a new solution outside the regular basis. As human resources had assumed a relevant role within the company since 2015, it had found a breeding ground to connect other areas and experts such as legal and labor relationship departments.

In the first months under the pandemic, the federal government, with focus on preserving jobs and helping local companies, defined a provisional measure (MP) that changed a series of labor regulations. The new approach established individual agreements that considered: remote working conditions, individual and collective vacations leaving concessions, holidays anticipations, new measures for compensatory hours, postponing of payroll loans and salaries wages, suspension of regular job contracts, and salary reduction aligned with the work hours.

After putting the first wave of the discretionary countermeasures and the federal provisional measures in place, the enterprise still faced the challenge to manage its costs as the market demand had been declining. No regular measures would be enough to preserve the job positions across the operations. New and creative action would be required and it was necessary to challenge the status quo. The D.I.Co company's managers were in a particular period of time never seen in the past while HR director considered he was in the position that he always wanted to be. He could do something different. There was no way out. It would probably never happen again and he was not sure that he would face as tough a challenge. This big question appeared in his mind all the time. He must do something. Moved by those concerns, the solution come to his mind. Could it be possible to propose the salary reduction during a period of time without any work hours decrease? Why not? The government would probably not accept, the labor union would probably not sign any agreement, and it is not legal. On the other hand, the same question came again: Why not? The D.I.Co had never had to deal with this scenario and the potential answer would be "no", but he could challenge the system. Preserve the job positions was more important than any paradigm that he could have in mind. However, this was not the only thing. How would it be possible to reduce employees'salary and promote dignity following the

D.I.Co's Guide Principles of aligning business imperative to the people agenda? It would have to be a wise solution.

Starting internally, this idea was tested many times in a short period. The first reactions were not the best ones. The managing director said: "It was not feasible. Here in Brazil, we could not reduce the salary in just one direction." The local team said: "It will probably not work. It sounds a little bit crazy." But the HR director could not give up in the first round. He still continued sharing the idea across the company under transversal culture until he found a group of people who would believe that there was a minimum chance to move it forward. Members from human resource, legal, labor negotiation, occupational health joined him on this unpredictable journey, seeing the potential of preserving jobs and raising the bar in terms of people management, while the entire market was looking for reducing working hours and salaries.

The process required that main criteria and guide principles are be established. The task force team was created from members from each area mentioned above. The guide principles covered the main items aligning business imperative to the people agenda. Thus, it was not difficult to understand that the "reduction of salaries" in a period of time and the proposal of reimburse them (plus the inflation rate) in six months, along with the job stability during the same period, fitted the D.I.Co Guide Principals. This solution would have direct impact on cash instead of earnings before interest and taxes (EBIT). However, this amount of money would preserve the working in capital during the first months until the market reacted. At the end, the salaries would not be reduced, as the differences will be reimbursed in the first quarter of 2021. On the other hand, preserving jobs positions was an important issue. Frankly, the last piece of the story was the strong belief which moved the team forward without fear or excuses.

After defining the guide principles, the first draft of the negotiation contract was written. Experts from legal perspective, labor negotiation, and human resource joined with different approaches to do it. Having done that, they were ready to close the internal alignments before negotiating with the external stakeholders. Called the Wage Deferral Program, it was discussed on different layers across the organizations, covering functions and geographies. First of all, the local team would be convinced. The local steering committee was created composed of different leaderships that represented the entire organization. On this committee, they discussed the center of the negotiation, how they could protect the working capital and, at the same time, how all job positions would be preserved. From then on, the CEO and the C-level were confident and supportive, following the same direction. After removing all paradigms and concerns, it was time to elevate this conversation to regional and global areas.

The second round of negotiation considered an extensive set of steps which represented working as a team. However, they had to negotiate with different stakeholders in parallel as they did not have much time to put the plan in place. Functional leaders were informed, and they quickly understood that it represented a great opportunity for balancing the pressure that came from the pandemic, preserving the company's long-term reputation, improving the people's engagement and promoting. It meant preserving people's jobs without reducing working hours and long-term salaries, offering a period of job stability under the unemployment crisis due to the pandemic and, at the end, contributing to the preservation of the society's social welfare. From now on, it was time to move this plan externally by connecting labor union and government. Several meetings were successfully conducted with labor unions where quickly reached a great agreement, considering country inflation the fairest indicator to be used to the future reimbursements.

Finally, they were ready to put the plan in place. Even though all the team was very anxious, they could not ignore defining the individual employee agreement and the communication plan. That is the reason they redefined our action plan once more. The internal communication team was involved, and they readily defined the steps and speeches that would be covered when the leadership team would be in contact with the employees. In parallel, the legal team supported by the human resources was writing the employee contract addenda. When all this had been done, we were ready to announce the plan to all local employees.

Communication Plan, Employees Testimony and General Results

In a symphony, all orchestra musicians must work in perfect harmony. Bathed with these principles, the team had made every effort to guarantee that the actions would be put in place as planned. Faced with another challenge under the remote work, a virtual conference was set up. More than 250 employees from South America were connected at the same time. The managing director opened the meeting, explaining, and reinforcing all the tough period they were facing, how difficult it was to put all countermeasures in place and how they had been working hard to find new ways to support the business and preserve as many job positions as possible. The big stress and concerns could be noticed on the worried faces even though all of us/the employees were connected remotely. Inasmuch the conversation moved ahead. It was possible to see people sensing that, instead of bad news, a great announcement would come. The CEO closed his speech and asked for the conversation to proceed. The HR director started explaining that tough moments required creative decisions and that the D.I.Co would like to offer to everyone present a new way of taking a look at their relationship to the organization. There is not enough effort defined by the company which could recognize the high engagement levels that the company had been having in the last years. That is the reason D.I.Co would like to announce a new countermeasure where the salaries will be reduced in different ranges (from 5 to 15%) related to the layer everyone was located for the next 6 months. However, this amount would be reimbursed in the first quarter of the next year and the value would be adjusted according to the country's inflation rate. Moreover, in return for their efforts, the enterprise would like to offer the stability of their job positions, preserving the jobs under the same period of time.

Afraid of how our people would react, D.I.Co's executives could never imagine how grateful its employees would respond to the emergency proposal. Instead of seeing the worried faces at the beginning, they were replaced by the long and silent relief present in each smile while video cameras started turning on. This gratitude appeared in the testimonies during the remote conference in real time and in messages sent after end of the call.

During the video conference, a region procurement specialist said: "Amazing, I did not have any idea what to expect from this call, but I know the company that I had chosen. It means a lot to me. My husband and my daughter have lost their jobs and there is no more income in my house. My eternal gratitude to this company." More than the spontaneous declaration, it was possible to see tears in her eyes. Complementing her, a regional business manager said: "I have been working here for more than 20 years, I've never seen something like that. So proud to be part of this team." The declarations continued. The members from engineering continued to say "That's the reason we are here, that's the reason that we wake up every morning, that's the reason I never doubted that we are in the right place." In the last few minutes, something unexpected and exciting happened. A sincere thanks came back directly to HR director from the majority of the group members, attributing to him and recognizing the human resource leadership in moving this initiative forward and it was so exciting. In fact, he felt that he had done the job as a part of the leadership team, supporting the business and promoting dignity as people/the employees could feel that people are really important to D.I.Co.

Other posts came from the professional and nonprofessional social media. The announcement and communication expanded the local horizons. Other regions and employees that worked in other country groups were totally surprised and very thankful. Families, sons, daughters, and parents posted their messages onto the net (internal and external) recognizing the company and its efforts during these tough times. It created a positive wave which encompassed the company along the entire value chain from the shop floor to the C-level. It did not take long for the results to improve significantly. No more than 30 days after, the net sales and operating performance monthly results achieved 15% higher to the same month in the previous year and they are getting better month by month. At this moment, the forecast appoints an annual increase of 10% to 15%, i.e., the best EBIT margin in the last 10 years.

The good news does not stop there. In the last quarter, the enterprise launched its engagement survey in order to identify the progress and areas of opportunities. Considering that the survey is strictly voluntary and totally confidential, benchmarking says that 75% of participation is usually considered a great result. After two weeks, we achieved 95% of respondents, of almost 3000 employees in the region. One of the best participations across the globe when comparing to other regions and functional areas. Finally, the results were issued during the quarter and our engagement was improved tremendously.

The general engagement results improved from 75 to 80% which shows that the satisfaction rate rose from 80 to 86%, comparing year by year. This survey considers a hierarchy of employee needs, broken down in four topics: basic needs, individual contributions, teamwork and growth. All categories rates have increased significantly while the basic needs improved 7 pp, the individual contribution improved 10 pp, teamwork 6 pp and growth 10 pp. It is very impressive when considering that D.I.Co is in the middle of the pandemic, dealing with complex situations and putting unpopular actions in place. Despite this tough scenario, more than 90% of the total population recommends our company to others as a great place to work.

This journey and experience show to the entire company the power of managing the people, treating others with dignity and recognizing how important the employees are when driving results. There is no doubt that we are navigating through this uncertainty and ambiguous period of time successfully because the internal labor force sees how/in what way they are able to lead the change. The marginal and indirect results are getting better day by day too. Absenteeism, overtime, and turnover rates are decreasing month by month. The processes are more connected across the company between areas. Solutions, contributions, and new ideas are springing from the bottom to the top without any additional recognition program. The watercooler conversations have almost disappeared, counter-arguments are presented during the meetings without fear of any retaliation, which means that people are really feeling they are part of the company, they are dealing with problems firmly and in a timely manner, are not allowing problems to fester, they are reviewing their performance and holding timely discussions. They can make negative decisions when all other efforts fail, and they can deal with troublemakers effectively. This new era means that the relationship between the enterprise and employees raised the bar, moving to the next level. It is healthier, more fair and more balanced. More than running the business, how effective companies are when they deal with the agenda combining the people's well-being with entire society. These approaches will connect across the enterprise, sharing their values, trust, cooperation, and reciprocity across the end-to-end value chain, adding value to the entire stakeholders.

10.4 Implications for Management

This narrative is presented with the expectation that it could inspire other human resources leaders, other companies and other managing directors to review their bias and paradigms related to the people management. We hope that lessons learned here help companies to avoid mistakes and drive their results aligned with improving engagement rates.

With this narrative, it is possible to learn that to put people in the center of business agenda is not an easy task, mainly when the company is not going through a good results period. It is necessary to be creative, courageous and able to deal with contradictory institutional logics. Determination, persuasion, and negotiation ability are other requirements to improve the dignity preservation and promotion.

There is no doubt that people are the main asset inside the company and as they are the principal element in the system, looking for alternatives and finding solutions is essential not only in a tough time but also on a regular basis. It is not possible to achieve better results without connecting the business imperative to the people agenda. There is no way out. This is the symbiosis which promotes unexpected and amazing upshots from the shop floor to the top management. Respect, dignity, empowerment, diversity, and honesty are the words that will compose the business agenda more than ever from now on.

10.5 Final Remarks

This narrative shows that moving from economic to humanistic paradigm is not an easy task. The process is not linear. Pirson and Lawrence (2019) proposed some procedures to move from one archetype to another. To move from economism archetype to bounded economism, it is necessary for company to respect the human rights and to preserve dignity. From bounded economism to enlightened/masked economism, it is fundamental to put the promotion in the center of business agenda. In this paradigm, each human being needs to be recognized in his/her uniqueness with a potential and capability to be developed. To move toward humanistic archetypes means to connect the business with welfare, focusing on well-being outcomes. To reach the "bounded humanism" archetype, it is important to consider the impact of emotions, compassion, entrepreneurial activity, and well-being. The attention is not only on the company but also on society's institutions. Finally, to the humanism archetype, organizations have to focus on the promotion of well-being and social welfare creation. In bounded humanism and humanism archetypes, to measure the well-being outcomes is important. However, the process is not linear. To survive, a company can move forward and back depending on the situation it faces.

As could be learned in the narrative presented in this chapter, to reach a humanism archetype takes a long time. When pressured by COVID pandemic D.I.Co, even in the new management stage, came back to economism discussing job positions with focus on efficiency. This means that this institutional logic lives inside company, but the fact that the company aligned business imperative to the people agenda means that the predominant institutional agenda is winning the war. This agenda is connected partially to enlightened/masked economism, as the main goal is economic, but not only this. Dignity is the center of management aligned with economic outcomes. On the other hand, D.I.Co shows signs that is in the process of moving to humanism paradigm, as it is putting not only the well-being but also the social welfare in the management agenda. Different institutional agendas are living together. To move toward humanism archetype, it requires efforts to reinforce the well-being and social welfare agenda (about institutional agendas see Pache & Santos, 2010; Smets et al., 2015; Mangen & Brivot, 2015; Glaser et al., 2016; Bertels & Lawrence, 2016; Zietsma & Toubiana, 2018; Kyratsis et al., 2017).

References

Bertels, S., & Lawrence, T. B. (2016). Organizational responses to institutional complexity stemming from emerging logics: The role of individuals. *Strategic Organization, 14*(4), 336–372.

Caram, B., & Resende, T. (2020, May 28th). *Business.* Retrieved from Folha de São Paulo: https://www1.folha.uol.com.br/internacional/en/business/2020/05/brazil-loses-11-million-formal-jobs-in-two-months-of-the-pandemic.shtml.

Donaldson, T., & Walsh, J. P. (2015). Toward a theory of business. *Research in Organizational Behavior, 35*, 181–207. http://dx.doi.org/10.1016/j.riob.2015.10.002.

Gani, A., & Sharma, B. (2009). The effects of the business environment on pollution. In *International Trade and Finance Association, 19th International Conference Working Papers*, paper 6.

Glaser, V. L., Fast, N. J., Harmon, D. J., & Green, S. E., Jr. (2016). Institutional frame switching: Ow institutional logics shape individual action. *Research in the Sociology of Organizations, 48A*, 37–69.

Hodson, R. (2004). The dignity of research. *Contemporary Sociology, 33*(1), 17–20. https://doi.org/10.1177/009430610403300109.

Jackson, I., & Nelson, J. (2004). *Profits with Principles—seven strategies for delivering value with values*. New York: Currency Doubleday.

Kyratsis, Y., Atun, R., Phillips, N., Tracey, P., & George, G. (2017). Health systems in transition : Professional identity work in the context of shifting institutional logics. *Academy of Management Journal, 60*(2), 610–641.

Mangen, C., & Brivot, M. (2015). The challenge of sustaining organizational hybridity: The role of power and agency. *Human Relations, 68*(4), 659–684.

Mele, A. R. (2003). *Motivation and Agency*. Oxford University Press.

Mele, A. R. (2009). *Effective Intentions: The Power of Conscious Will*. Oxford University Press.

McGEEVER, J. (2020, May 28th). *Emerging Markets*. Retrieved from Reuters: https://www.reuters.com/article/us-brazil-economy-unemployment-idUSKBN23422O.

Pache, A. C., & Santos, F. (2010). When worlds collide: the internal dynamics of organizational responses to conflicting institutional demands. *Academy of Management Review,* 35(3), 455–476.

Pirson, M., & Lawrence, P. (2010). Humanism in business: Towards a paradigm shift? *Journal of Business Ethics, 93*(4), 553–565.

Pirson, M., & Lawrence, P. M. (2019). A humanistic perspective for management theory: Protecting dignity and promoting well-being. *Journal of Business Ethics, 159*, 39–57. https://doi.org/10.1007/s10551-017-3755-4.

Ponce, D. (2020, July 16th). *Nature reviews nephrology*. Retrieved from Nature Reviews : https://www.nature.com/articles/s41581-020-0327-0.

Prates, I., & Barbosa, R. (2020). The impact of COVID19 in Brazil: Labour market and social protection responses. *The Indian Journal of Labour Economics*.

Saez, E., & Zucman, G. (2014). Wealth Inequality in the United States since 1913: Evidence from Capitalized Income Tax Data. https://gabriel-zucman.eu/files/SaezZucman2014.pdf.

Sikula, A., Sr., Olmosk, K., Kim, C. W., & Cupps, S. (2001). A "New" theory of management. *Ethics & Behavior, 11*(1), 3–21.

Smets, M., Jarzabkowski, P., Burke, G., & Spee, P. (2015). Reinsurance trading in Lloyd's of London: Balancing conflicting-yet-complementary logics in practice. *The Academy of Management Journal, 58*, 932–970.

Zietsma, C., & Toubiana, M. (2018). The valuable, the constitutive, and the energetic: Exploring the impact and importance of studying emotions and institutions. *Organization Studies, 39*(4), 427–443. https://doi.org/10.1177/0170840617751008.

Part III
Organizational Dignity in Customer Perception

Chapter 11
Dignity and Power Relations Between Call-Center Companies and Clients

Jones Carlos Louback

Abstract The empirical research presented in this chapter aimed to discuss the power relations between a call center company and its customers, in a Foucauldian perspective. The study emphasizes the management performed by the company, constituting customers in productive and docile customers. Speeches of dignity reside on two levels: claiming rights and attempting government. The claiming of rights includes the right to information about the status of orders, correct information, respectful treatment, the right to compliance with the time of delivery, and the right to have moments of life free of the company's effect of power. Government attempts range from claiming compensations for financial, psychological, and social damages to interference on the company management. The most forceful refusal, however, is in retaliation of the company. Retaliation takes different forms, from reporting in newspapers, discouraging friends from consuming the company's services, suing the company in court, and rupturing with the company. As a theoretical contribution, it addresses the organization's search for control and regulation of the customer. As a practical contribution, it seeks to shed light on a relationship that affects the daily lives of customers, in a society of consumers that is permeated by uneven power relations and ownership of resources.

Keywords Call center · Power · Customers

11.1 Introduction

According to some authors, the growth of call center organizations is a reflex of a search for a strategy to improve customers' services, upon the differentiated delivery of services. Others, however, point out strong dissatisfaction of customers with the call center services, making them even resist against what is proposed in the relationship of consumption (Peñaloza & Price, 1993; Fournier, 1998; Shankar et al., 2006; Roux, 2007; Izberk-Bilgin, 2010; Valor et al., 2017), considering the strategies

J. C. Louback (✉)
São Paulo, Brazil
e-mail: jonesslouback@gmail.com

M. L. Mendes Teixeira and L. M. B. de Oliveira (eds.), *Organizational Dignity and Evidence-Based Management*, https://doi.org/10.1007/978-3-030-68560-7_11

of companies to ensure markets and win the consumers and their trust (Anderson, 1987; Dowling & Uncles, 1997; Kantola et al., 2019; Valor et al., 2017).

In recent years, in Brazil and abroad, authors have proposed including in organizational studies the reflections and questions proposed by Foucault, involving themes such as power relations, resistances, government, constitution of docile, and productive subjects (Burrel, 1998; Motta & Alcadipani, 2004; Alcadipani, 2005; Souza et al., 2004; Amorim & Martins, 2007; Mendes & Ichikawa, 2008; Tadajewski & Jones, 2016).

Authors who investigate the business–customers relationship from a Foucauldian perspective highlight the effects of organizational actions on customers, in the perspective of power relations, in a dynamic of consumers' constitution (Shankar et al., 2006), considering the market the locus of construction of this identity (Roux, 2007).

For Roux (2007), the company in its relationship with customers uses management strategies: stratagems, pressures, and manipulations; promises, injunctions, and seductions that affect the freedom and autonomy of consumers; and consumption practices contrary to the consumers' systems of representations and values. Resistance arises in the face of those strategies.

Kasabov (2004), from a Foucauldian perspective, argues that studies on consumer behavior have disregarded the importance of discipline and power, and that traditional marketing discourse about the centrality of customer brings with it a naive view of the business-to-consumer relationship. In his studies with dissatisfied consumers, he discusses the issues of power and control, seeking to shed light on what he calls the 'dark side of marketing.' 'Power is not a universal monolithic entity with universal, definite, permanent features that operates according to pre-established rules' (Kasabov, 2004, p. 5). In his study on consumers in cities in Ireland and Bulgaria, he identified what he calls four types of power: direct power, gender-related power, power related to inequalities in holding information, and disciplinary power.

Kasabov (2004), in interviews with call center operators, observed that the operators somehow controlled customers, with a multitude of repeated questions. That way, the call center structure took on a role of a 'buffer zone,' preventing the consumer from having access to other areas of the organization. The disciplinary power in this case is camouflaged by 'carefully formulated phrases, questions and suggestions aiming to put the dissatisfied customer 'on the right track" (p. 7). The conclusion of that study was that dissatisfied consumers are aware of the veiled control measures and the observations about them, and aware of the government exercised over them. However, they are aware that the reactions are singular, discontinued, superficial, due to the short resources and information they hold. In addition to these limitations, the author observes that the increase in social visibility and the emphasis on consumer reactions allow institutions to develop new and refined forms of accruing information, thus facilitating monitoring and normalization of customers' behavior.

Although Kasabov (2004) refers to the call center environment in his surveys, few studies approach this type of organization from a Foucauldian perspective, with a focus on customers, and when they do it they highlight the effects of power relations mainly on employees (Silva et al., 2007; Ramalho et al., 2008; Knights & McCabe, 2003; Bain & Taylor, 1999). Studies involving the relationship with other stakeholders are still incipient. This finding in our understanding justifies the survey presented in this study.

The empirical research presented herein aimed to discuss the power relations between a call center company and its customers, in a Foucauldian perspective, with emphasis on the management performed by the company, constituting customers in productive and docile customers.

As a theoretical contribution, it addresses the organization's search for control, standardization, and regulation of the customer. As a practical contribution, from the customer's perspective, it seeks to shed light on a relationship that affects the daily lives of customers, in a society of consumers that is permeated by uneven power relations and ownership of resources (Bauman, 2001; Arendt, 2010).

11.2 The Star Company

The Star Company (fictitious name) is a young call center company, with a decade and a half of existence, well established in the market. It has more than 20 thousand customers, an annual average of 150 thousand orders served, specialized in the meal delivery. It defines itself as a differentiated form of delivery, different from pizza delivery, working with restaurants specialized in different types of cuisine, such as Mediterranean, Portuguese, German, Mexican, Moroccan, and Indian, and offering customers the possibility to place their orders directly on the Web site or by calling the call center. It receives the orders in a single delivery, in a pre-established time, ensuring quality and speed.

The company's customers are considered differentiated, with purchasing power enough to consume in the good restaurants. The message conveyed to customers suggests that they are special rather than customers of a common delivery. They are customers of restaurants renowned in their specialties, and whenever they wish they can choose a company that is also special, differentiated in the market. This company has been built over the years in partnerships with renowned restaurants in the market and matching with the social and economic level of customers.

Although the company positions itself as of a social level equivalent to that of its customers, it certainly does not cease to be a commercial relationship: on the one side the customers with the financial resources for consumption, and on the other side the company fighting for those resources in the market. These are power relations exercised from numerous points and in the midst of unequal and mobile relationships (Foucault, 1988). The economic differences, skills, and competencies involved in these relationships allow and enable acting on the others' action (Foucault, 1995).

This speech of differentiation entails results to the organization since, despite being young, it is an outstanding company in the market, in its segment, with a large number of customers and annual services used as a business card to attract new customers with purchasing power.

11.2.1 Organizational Efficiency in Practice

From the moment that the company receives an order, it estimates the delivery in 70 min. The company relies on technology resources that monitor and make the records from the moment the order is placed by the customer. In their daily operation, and especially on weekends or special dates, it is almost routine having the number of orders received exceeding the capacity of service. When the number of delayed orders exceeds two or three times the number of available deliverers, new orders are suspended. However, despite the suspension of orders, the Web site remains available to be accessed by customers, giving rise to further complaints.

In urban cultures, the practice of shopping by phone or Internet is a practice. These purchases require trust in the supplier, since payment is made in advance (Aiken & Boush, 2006; Cheung & Lee, 2006). But the purchase of meals has some special features. When you order a meal, you are experiencing a physiological need and/or a social need, represented by a moment shared with family, friends, celebrations, among others. If there is any problem with the delivery, the advance payment inhibits the customer from canceling the order. Canceling the order implies a new attempt that may take another hour, delaying the time to have the so-longed meal. If the order takes longer to be delivered, the search for new alternatives becomes more difficult, because it will take even longer to get the meals. The anticipation of payment retains the customer and brings about an imbalance in the relationship, even if temporarily.

11.2.2 Government Strategies in the Face of Abnormal Services Provided

For orders that exceed the company's capacity of service, the company must call every customer and explain the reasons for the cancelation of the order. Order cancelations are managed through calls to customers to explain the reasons why orders cannot be fulfilled.

That proactivity is part of the organization's discourse that exposes the impossibility of providing the service but, at the same time, seeks to maintain a relationship of trust. That discourse produces different effects for the customer, showing concern for them and, at the same time, moving the relationship in the company's favor. Those speeches try to exempt the company from the responsibility for the impossibility of delivering because of unforeseen weather events such as 'unfortunately due to the rain we have no way to make the delivery,' or 'unfortunately, due to the excess of demand, the order had to be canceled.' Here, the inability to provide the service is hidden in the competence highlighted and proven by the strong attraction exercised on customers, generating excessive demand and, as an undesirable consequence, the cancelation of orders and their justification.

The different discourses of the organization intend to transmit to customers the respect they deserve, trying to hide potential flaws in the provision of the service. These are speeches that make up a greater speech of demand management, allowing to work, sometimes, with a number of orders higher than the capacity of delivery, but also allowing the cancelation of exceeding orders, and the provision of service of other customers waiting for the delivery of their meal.

When the customer's proactivity surpasses the company's proactivity, and they call asking for the delivery of their orders, the company's agents try to gain time with answers like 'your order is coming,' 'your order has already left the restaurant,' 'your order is already on the way.' When referring to other problems such as misunderstandings with deliverers, and missing or changing products, and the customer requests the reversal of the amount paid with the card, first the operator asks the customer information about what actually occurred to further accept the amount reversal or tries to persuade the customer to accept some kind of compensation. In these cases, the company almost always offers financial compensation, starting with the waiving of the delivery fee, going through partial credits of the order, and may reach a credit of 100% of the order, giving the order as a courtesy.

When we analyze the relations between customers and the call center company in the perspective of power relations proposed by Foucault in his analytics of power, first of all, one perceives the existence of systems of legal, social, economic differentiation, allowing the company to act on the action of customers as an exercise of power (Foucault, 1995). These systems also allow the company to keep the Web site running, even with the delivery system suspended, regardless if this occurs due to technical limitations, management flaws, or as a deliberate strategy. The fact is that the company can do it because 'living in society is, in anyway, living in such a way that some can act on the action of others' (Foucault, 1995, p. 245), and that action on the action of the others as an art of governing (Foucault, 2006). Power relations bring power strategies that seek to gain an advantage over others, and deprive them of the means to fight, so as to lead them to give up the struggle (Foucault, 1995).

However, as Foucault puts it, power relations do not represent states of domination, because resistances are always present (Foucault, 1988), and are enabled by confrontation in a constant manner (Branco, 2008). If it is true that in the core of power relations, and as a permanent condition of their existence, there is an 'insubmission' and essentially reluctant freedoms, there is no power relation without resistance, with no way out or escape, free of eventual inversion; every power relation implies, then, at least in a virtual way, a strategy of fight (Foucault, 1995).

Since power and resistance are different sides of the same coin, we could ask: How do customers react, how do they resist, how do they refuse the company's speeches of government? What are their speeches of refusal and their speeches of dignity? In the following topics, we will try to answer these questions.

11.3 The Discursiveness of Customer's Reactions to Abnormality in Service Delivery

Customers react to corporate government in different ways, ranging from acceptance of corporate government to attempting to govern the company.

11.3.1 Accepting the company's Government

Reaction: 'Never Mind'

Among the reaction speeches identified when the company calls the customer canceling their order due to excess of demand, there are those who do not complain. These are speeches that range from a laconic 'it's fine,' 'it's OK,' 'it´s fine, thanks,' to the inquiry if the delivery is really impossible, complemented with an 'OK,' or inquiries about the reversal of the value, 'Wasn't it charged on my card?', 'so it won't be put down from the card, right?'. They are statements of a compliance speech in face of the company's government. Nogueira (2001) identified this type of conformed reaction, of acceptance, in his studies on discrimination, and interpreted it as a denial of the need for resistance (Nogueira, 2001).

Considering what Nogueira (2001) tells us, that in Foucault's perspective the consciousness of the action of power implies resistance, we can assume that this type of reaction may represent a non-consciousness of the government by the company over them and their interests, implying no need for resistance, with cancelations taking on a natural role in the daily commercial relations with the company, as a natural component of those relations.

A type of reaction close to this was also found by Roux (2007) in his study on consumer's resistance, characterized by a choice of 'see nothing, hear nothing, speak nothing' (Roux, 2007, p. 606). That would be the choice for voluntary ignorance, implying some awareness, because an exposure to threats, risks, and tensions present in the relationship with the other would imply a necessary effort seeking for protection. It would be an action of 'never mind,' an expression that characterizes what happens in ordinary situations, a reaction speaking to the self 'better this way' (Roux, 2007).

Reaction: Excusing the Company

In cases of changed orders, missing items, and lack of quality, we find records in which customers speak in a perspective of cooperation. They defend the deliverers who supposedly could have made a mistake, and attribute the mistake to restaurants, releasing the company from responsibility. Here too, in this kind of perceived behavior, customers seem to be unaware of the company's government over them, putting themselves as supporting actors in the business or, when they are aware, they take on the tactic of 'not seeing, not hearing, not speaking' (Roux, 2007, p. 606). The non-consciousness about government, pointed out by Nogueira (2001), reminds us of the effort of organizations in the search for customers' trust and loyalty.

Many researchers in the area of marketing and management, acknowledging the importance of trust in the relations between consumers and companies (Hosmer, 1995; Rousseau et.al., 1988; Aiken & Boush, 2006; Al Abdulrazak & Gbadamosi, 2017), defend the winning of consumer's trust as a constant goal. This is the case of Daffy (2011), who proposes the search for 'true loyalty' of the customer, despite the offers and the competing market. Trust is built based on engagement and affinity with the company, bearing emotional components, resembling relationships of trust between friends and family members. The discourse of affinity seems productive in these cases, as well as the many speeches of the docile and cooperative consumer, partner, polite. That is so these customers show to be faithful to the organization, accepting what the relation puts in the relation, including themselves in given situations, displacing responsibility to other individuals or companies that appear in the relation.

Customers, as well as companies, are constituted in a culture of consumption (Peñaloza & Price, 1993), and since they are engaged in multiple power relations, with strategies and tactics that interchange and renew themselves at every meeting, throw by throw, blow by blow (Certeau, 2009), they bring the lack of trust in the other to this sphere.

11.3.2 Feeling Powerless to React Over Corporate Government

Another set of speeches shows that the company's government is perceived by customers, but they feel powerless in face of that government. In that case, refusal is not only a matter of awareness about government, but the perception of powerless also falls within the field of possibilities.

Perceiving the Company in a Context of Deteriorating Service Quality

In the face of irregularity in the delivery of their orders, some customers perceive the imperfections of the service and place them in the context of quality of services in the country 'the problem that is happening is that all the services in our country are increasingly deteriorated.'

By attributing the drop in the quality of services received from the company to a broader, social context, customer justifies their own powerlessness to act on the company's action, because the way the company acts is not unique to it, but the result of forces that are beyond it. The action by the company, and its government, becomes a result of the government of the context.

Not knowing what to do, the customer vents 'what they are making me go through...' The customer recognizes the company's government over them and is aware of this government that leaves them without the expected food, hindering and limiting their decision. They do not know if they cancel the order and if they go out to have a snack in the street. So does a customer who declared 'Wow! It will take an hour and a half, won't it? [...] Can't cancel, right?' as if they depended on approval to make the cancelation. These and other statements that implicitly bring impotence to act on the company's action. They bring with them some conformism, acceptance of a situation that they cannot change, a tone of discouragement.

These speeches, while expressing an awareness of powerlessness to act on the company, do not fail to outline resistance to its government. However, although they outline resistance, these speeches do not constitute speeches of refusal, and so one cannot consider that these speeches underlie speeches of dignity. Dignity in light of Foucault can only be understood as a refusal to be governed. It is worth recalling the concept of strategy for Foucault (1995), as a set of procedures used in a confrontation to deprive the opponent from their means of fighting, and thus, the company's strategies can produce in customers the 'consciousness' of impotence, although resistance is always possible (Foucault, 2006).

11.3.3 Claiming Rights

This part analyzes the customers' speeches of refusal in face of government situations that affect them and their respective speeches of dignity about rights to: information, true information, be consulted in decisions that affect them, be respected, the right of immediate return of amounts incorrectly charged, the fulfillment of the negotiated deadline, the preservation of moments of life of the effects of government.

Claiming the Right to Information

Those who complain manifest no intention to perform any other action in relation to the company; some limit themselves to requesting clarification as to the reasons for the cancelation, 'but, why?' and/or requests for clarification on the reversal of the amount charged on the card: 'and the money, will you return?'.

Requesting information shows resistance to the company's government, even if diffuse, not incisive, but that presents a customer's refusal to the operator's silence about the reversal procedure. That refusal hosts a speech of dignity that claims the right to obtain information about the process of repaying the amount charged.

Claiming the Right to Proper Information, to Not Being Considered Stupid or Naive

Some of the speeches pointed out reactions against the company's failure to fulfill what was previously promised, and of justifications that are not clear:

> Excuse me, I live two minutes away from the restaurant... How could [the deliverer] be fifteen minutes away? [...] It's been over an hour; I can't wait fifteen minutes anymore. [...] I live five blocks from the restaurant, how can it take fifteen minutes by motorcycle... You didn't make the food, is that it? [...] Do you think I'm an idiot? Do you have a manager there?

These customers' statements have unmasked the supposed truthfulness of the information they are given, reminding the strong refusals mentioned by Foucault

(2006) when he talks about throw at the face of power what one considers unfair, here, denouncing untrue information.

Claiming the Right to Be Respected as Customer

Other customers react to the company's decision of canceling the order in different ways, expressing their dissatisfaction in more intensive tones, accusing the company of not taking them seriously 'You're kidding me!', 'A mockery, a lack of respect, leaving the website active without deliverers'. These are reactions denouncing that company made the customer silly, because they left their website on the air, when the delivery was already suspended, 'I'm waiting a fool for 24 min, and they call me saying they have no biker?!', or even customers who have a previous history with the company, who talk about their growing dissatisfaction, 'Wow, you are getting worse! I am very dissatisfied with your service.' Some do not scream, do not offend the operator, and simply hang up before the operator continues with the explanations. Others manifest that they will no longer use the company's service. These speeches point to the customer's refusal to be treated with disrespect, with neglect 'You should shut the website down, then. Not let people order. Well, now you have lost a customer for good. Because I will never make an order on your website again.'

It is to the constitution of a docile and useful customer that some resist and refuse to be governed this way by the company. That refusal has underlying speeches of dignity, claiming what they deem to be the right, to be treated with respect, assuming this respect different traits: right to information on how their resources will be handled, right to not having these managed differently from what they allowed, right to receive reliable information about the facts.

Claiming the Right to Compliance with the Delivery Time Established

There are many customers who not only complain, but refuse to be governed and decide to make decisions regarding the ongoing fact, whether these are delays in delivery or other types of irregularity. When they are told by the company that the delivery will not occur in the estimated time, they limit themselves to cancel the order, not accepting the delivery, not presenting any additional justification other than the situation itself.

If there are speeches of customers that decided taking a decision about the company's action, such as canceling the request without major justification, there are those who opted for a retaliation speech against the company, such as writing to newspapers or making advertising against the company among friends, or yet the search of consumer protection authorities to make complaints against the company.

Customers who choose to speak badly due to the delay warn that they will talk to their fellows and tell what happened on the Internet, and ask for confirmation if the company is recording what they are saying, 'I'll tell it to all my fellows, I'll make a chain on the Internet to show your [negative] quality, okay?' 'I will make a formal complaint from you in the newspaper [name of the newspaper],' 'I will tell everyone that I am disappointed.'

Not all speeches refusing to have the delivery time governed by the company beyond what had been agreed bring the decision of cancelation or retaliation to the company's action. These are speeches of refusal to the effects of government on the moment that is being experienced, effects that the customer makes a point of making explicit when deciding on the cancelation.

Claiming the Right to Have Moments of Life Preserved from the Effects of Corporate Government

Some cases end with the cancelation of the request, considering the problems, but presenting the reasons for the cancelation they are making, justifying their action. They justify the cancelation and their complaints for the presence of small children, who are waiting to eat, denouncing that the agreed deadline was not met, suggesting that they even tolerate the delays, the issues, but children do not, 'I don't want to wait anymore. You are disrespecting the contract. You have a time period for delivery. That period expired. I have two hungry children. I'm leaving home to have something to eat. It's over.'

Testimonials show effects of the company's government on customers, effects that are unwanted at that moment, in that situation, like that of the person leaving for his wedding, accompanied by the godparents, and who waited until the last moment for the delivery of a meal: 'Cancel it. I'm getting married in 40 min, so you have an idea. And I ordered [the meal] two hours ago for some of the best men who were here with me. They're all gone now. I want a refund.'

These are speeches that claim rights and show the customer's action over the company's action by canceling the requests, justifying the decision. These justifications bear underlying speeches of dignity claiming the right to have moments of their lives preserved from the effects of corporate government.

11.4 Trying to Govern the Company

As in the cases cited by Roux (2007), there are speeches of customers who complain, refuse, in some situations retaliate against the company, but they advance in their refusals and start trying to exercise government over the company. Attempts to govern occur in various ways: insinuating, suggesting, confronting, demanding, depending on personal negotiation styles. These government attempts do not show clear standardization or strategy but are directed at the government. Resistance acts in the most diverse ways without constituting a strategy to dominate the other powers. If resistances establish a strategy, they cease to be resistance and become power (Souza et al., 2006).

These are discourses of refusal accompanied by requests or demands for financial compensations, as in the case of the customer who reacts to the action of cancelation by the company, saying 'The service you provide is a shame,' 'I don't want any kind of explanation, I want you to tell me how you will pay me off.'

Some try to convince the company to act toward reducing the effects of power on them, instructing how the operator should proceed, 'Ask the guys to hurry up, send the motoboy to pick [the food at the restaurant].' Or when, besides delay in delivery, the customer complains about the services got from the delivery guy, ‘You can fire him. He doesn’t deserve to work anywhere.’

Other customers deal with values, insinuating or determining, as rewards for inconvenience, compensation for problems, changes, and even replacement for the traditional apology, ‘You could give me the meal for free… I’ve been waiting almost 2 h…’, ‘What discount will you give me? You’re going to give me the food for free!’, ‘I’m not paying for it, you’re going to deliver it and you’re not going to charge me.’ Others refuse the operator’s apologies and condition receiving order to receiving the food for free, ‘It’s okay [you can deliver], but only if it’s free. I want my order reversed. I don’t want your apologies.’

Among these speeches of customer’s government over the company, one of them particularly called attention. In an apparent speech of dignity, of claiming rights, mentioning issues of commitment and ethics, complaining and demanding information about the company’s commitment to providing the service, the customer says ‘I won’t argue for money, this is not my intention. I’ll discuss about commitment, respect and ethics in dealing with your company’s customers. The fact of being dealing with a human being, in principle, should be respected,’ but complements ‘you don’t know with whom you are talking!’. If they only wanted to effectively present themselves as a human being, they would not refer to their social status. By referring to it, the customer brings an attempt of government because of their supposedly differentiated social status, trying to intimidate the operator with whom they talk, because the operator belongs to a social stratum lower than theirs. A government strategy is part of the authoritarianism of the Brazilian culture, pointed out by Matta (1981).

The customer’s government speeches about the company show another form of speeches of dignity. The customer acts over the company, claiming the right to be compensated for the financial, emotional, and social losses suffered as consequence of the effects of power. Also, in confrontations, by claiming rights and promising to act over the company by retaliating it, an attempt of the government is implicit, regardless of the type of retaliation (reparation via legal or social apparatus, trying to dissuade other customers or potential customers from acquiring the company’s services).

Power is not a property that can be either sold or exchanged. Power and resistance walk hand-in-hand, and power relations assume perpetual confrontation (Maia, 1995). Customers are not confined to an inflexible position of resistance, but their practices may cease exercising resistance and become government (Zanette & Brito, 2019).

11.5 A Continuum of Dignity Discourses

The analysis of the speeches by customers who participated in the survey shows that there is a continuum of intensity of resistance, which can become government. That continuum occurs as customers become aware of the company’s government and their willingness to react to it. Dignity discourses are present only as customers react. The perception over the government on the subject is a condition for resistance (Nogueira, 2001).

The continuum of dignity speeches ranges from non-recognition of corporate government, recognition of diffuse government embedded in a broader context of service delivery, claiming rights, and attempts of government over the company.

At the first two levels—non-recognition of corporate government and recognition of diffuse government—there are no speeches of dignity. At the first level, the customer accepts corporate government and does not complain about the problems caused. At the second level, the customer understands that problems caused by the company are not specifically caused by it, but by the context of the service quality in which the company is inserted. The company acts like all the others within a deficient service standard. The customer feels powerless and even tries to help the company to solve the problems found regarding the delivery of meals.

Speeches of dignity reside on the last two levels: claiming rights and attempting government. The claiming of rights includes the right to information about the status of orders, correct information, respectful treatment, the right to compliance with the time of delivery, and the right to have moments of life free of the company's effect of power. Government attempts range from claiming compensations for financial, psychological, and social damages to interference on the company management. The most forceful refusal, however, is in retaliation of the company. Retaliation takes different forms, from reporting in newspapers, discouraging friends and fellows from consuming the company's services, suing the company in court, and rupturing with the company.

However, of all the refusals the one that seems to have an effect is the refusal to be a customer of a company that does not recognize the rights of customers. While there is no rupture, the speeches of dignity placed in the refusals to the company's government are managed by it. That management is via financial compensation; especially if the offer is voluntary and associated with empathy, it will have greater calming effect (Desmet et al., 2010; Wei et al. 2020).

Although loss of customers who are dissatisfied is part of the curves of normality of companies, as well as the incoming of new customers, rupture brings something of imponderable and may evolve into the organization of collective resistance pools. Collective resistance pools can be facilitated by the dissemination and speed of social networks or consumer support groups (Kozinets, 2002; John & Klein, 2003).

11.6 Implications to Management

Managing demands in call centers has ethical implications if the possibility of placing orders is left open, and there is no possibility of making deliveries on time. Deliberate failure to meet the deadline agreed with customers is a violation of dignity. Managers need to be aware that receiving orders should be compatible with the possibility of meeting the standard time of delivery.

When a violation of dignity by the company in relation to customers is detected, genuine compensation is necessary. A behavior of bargaining by the company's operators or an attempt to convince the customer to wait longer for the delivery of the order constitutes a violation of dignity.

The violation of customers' dignity breaks the relationship of trust with the company and promotes resistance that is translated into speeches of dignity. Resistance can affect the company's reputation as customers can publicize the poor quality of services on social networks and promote boycotts.

It is important to emphasize, however, that keeping worthy relationships with customers should be a guiding principle of the business, rather than only because customer reactions can affect the company. Call center companies or other industries should maintain a policy of zero violation of dignity, in addition to instruments for monitoring dignity in relationships with stakeholders that allow stakeholders to monitor these relationships.

11.7 Final Remarks

In the face of actions that violate their dignity, customers react by refusing to the company's government. These refusals are characterized as resistance and can take various forms. One of these refusals is the demand for respect for rights and the attempt to reverse the situation through actions of corporate government. These are simple rights, such as the right to correct information about the service rendered, right to have one's dignity respected as a human being, right to not having moments of life affected by the government of the company. Meals with family or friends, or even alone, are moments of break in the midst of daily agitation. Not complying with the commitment to deliver meals within the standard of time and quality is to negatively intervene in the life of customers and affect their sacred moments of having a meal.

Basing commercial relations on dignity must be a commitment of all companies, regardless if the customer is aware of the company's government and reacts to it or not. It is suggested that companies adopt policies of zero violation of the customer's dignity, as well as of other stakeholders.

From a theoretical point of view, this chapter sought to contribute with knowledge about the dignity of customers characterized as refusals to corporate government.

References

Aiken, K. D. & Boush, D. M. (2006). Trustmarks, objective-source ratings, and implied investments in adversiting: investing online trust and the context-specific nature of internet signals. *Journal of the Academy of Marketing Science, 34*(3).

Alcadipani, R. A. (2005). *Michel Foucault: poder e análise das organizações*. São Paulo: Editora FGV.

Al Abdulrazak, R., & Gbadamosi, A. (2017). Trust, religiosity, and relationship marketing: A conceptual overview of consumer brand loyalty. In *Society and business review* (Vol. 12, 3rd ed., pp. 320–339).

Amorim, M. C. S., & Martins, R. H. P. (2007). Poder e liderança, as contribuições de Maquiavel, Gramsci, Hayek e Foucault. In *Encontro da Associação Nacional de Pós- Graduação em Administração e Pesquisa em Administração,* XXXI, Rio de Janeiro/RJ.

Anderson, J. V. (1987). Power marketing: Its past, present, and future. *The Journal of Services Marketing, 1*(2), 27–35.

Arendt, H. (2010). *A condição humana.* Tradução de Roberto Raposo e revisão técnica e apresentação de Adriano Correia. 11a. ed. rev. Rio de Janeiro: Forense Universitária.

Bain, P., & Taylor, P. (1999). Employee attitudes, worker attitudes and trade union representation in call centres. In *Paper to 17th Annual International Labour Process Conference, London.*

Bauman, Z. (2001). *Modernidade líquida.* Rio de Janeiro: Jorge Zahar Ed.

Branco, G. C. (2008). Atitude-limite e relações de poder: Uma interpretação sobre o estatuto da liberdade em Michel Foucault. *Revista Verve, 13,* 202–216.

Burrell, G. (1998). Modernism, post modernism and organizational analysis 2: The contribution of Michel Foucault. *Organization Studies, 9*(2), 221–235.

Certeau, M. (2009). *A invenção do cotidiano.* Petropólis/RJ: Vozes.

Cheung, C. M. K., & Lee, M. K. O. (2006). Understanding consumer trust in internet shopping: A multidisciplinary approach. *Journal of the American Society for Information Science and Technology, 57*(4).

Daffy, C. (2011). *Once a customer, always a customer: How to delivery customer service that creates customers for life.* Ireland: Oak Tree Press, Ebook.

Da Matta, R. (1981). *Carnavais, malandros e heróis.* Rio de Janeiro: Zahar.

Desmet, P. T., De Cremer, D., & van Dijk, E. (2010). On the psychology of financial compensations to restore fairness transgressions: When intentions determine value. *Journal of Business Ethics, 95,* 105–115. https://doi.org/10.1007/s10551-011-0791-3

Dowling, G. R., & Uncles, M. (1997). Do customer loyalty programs really work? *MIT Sloan Management Review, 38*(4), 71–82.

Foucault, M. (1988). *História da sexualidade I: a vontade de saber*. Rio de Janeiro: Edições Graal.

Foucault, M. (1995). O sujeito e o poder. In H. Dreyfus, & P. Rabinow (Eds.), *Michel Foucault, uma trajetória filosófica: para além do estruturalismo e da hermenêutica* (pp. 231–249). Rio de Janeiro: Forense Universitária.

Foucault, M. (2006) A "governamentalidade". In M. B. Motta (Org.), *Ditos e Escritos IV: estratégia, poder-saber* (pp. 281–305). Rio de Janeiro: Forense Universitária.

Fournier, S. (1998). Consumer resistance: Societal motivations, consumer manifestations, and implications in the marketing domain. *Advances in Consumer Research, 25,* 88–90.

Hosmer, L. T. (1995). Trust: The connecting link between organizational theory and philosophical ethics. *Academy of Management Review, 20*(2), 379–403.

Izberk-Bilgin, E. (2010). An interdisciplinary review of resistance to consumption, some marketing interpretations, and future research suggestions. *Consumption Markets & Culture, 13*(3), 299–323.

John, A., & Klein, J. (2003). The boycott puzzle: Consumer motivations for purchase sacrifice. *Management Science, 49*(9), 1196–1209.

Kasabov, E. (2004). Power and disciplining: Bringing Foucault to marketing. *Irish Marketing Review, 17*(1), 2.

Kantola, A., Seeck, H., & Mannevuo, M. (2019). Affect in governmentality: Top executives managing the affective milieu of market liberalization. *Organization, 26*(6), 761–782.

Kozinets, R. V. (2002). Can consumers escape the market? Emancipatory illuminations from burning man. *Journal of Consumer Research, 29,* 20–38.

Knights, D., & McCabe, D. (2003). *The American dream: Organisation, innovation and change management*. Milton Keynes: Open University Press.
Maia, A. (1995). Sobre a analítica do poder de Foucault. *Tempo Social-Revista De Sociologia Da USP, São Paulo, 7*(1–2), 84–103.
Mendes, L., & Ichikawa, E. Y. (2008). As ações de um programa governamental na constituição do sujeito pequeno produtor rural: uma análise à luz de Michel Foucault. In *V Encontro de Estudos Organizacionais da Anpad, Anais*... Belo Horizonte/MG.
Motta, F. C. P., & Alcadipani, R. (2004). O pensamento de Michel Foucault na teoria das organizações. *Revista de Administração, 39*(2), 117–128.
Nogueira, C.(2001). Análise do Discurso. In L. Almeida & E. Fernandes (Eds.), *Métodos e técnicas de avaliação: novos contributos para a prática e investigação* (pp. 15–48). Braga: CEEP.
Peñaloza, L., & Price, L. L. (1993). Consumer resistance: A conceptual overview. *Advances in Consumer Research, 20,* 123–128.
Ramalho, C. C., Arruda, F. A. A. M., Sato, L., & Hamilton, L. F. T. (2008). Viver na baia: dimensões psicossociais da saúde e do controle no trabalho de teleatendimento. *Cadernos de Psicologia Social do Trabalho, 11*(1), 19–39.
Rousseau, D. M., Sitkin, S. B., Burt, R. S., & Camerer, C. (1988). Not so different after all: A cross-discipline view of trust. *Academy of Management Review, 23*(3), 393–404.
Roux, D. (2007). Ordinary resistance as a parasitic form of action: a dialogical analysis of consumer/firm relations. *Advances in Consumer Research, 34.*
Shankar, A.; Cherrier, H., & Canniford, R. (2006). Consumer empowerment: a Foucauldian interpretation. *Emerald—European Journal of Marketing, 40*(9–10), 1013–1030.
Silva, M. F.; Borini, F. M., & Trevisan, L. N. (2007). Práticas organizacionais dos call centers. In *Encontro da ANPAD, 31.* 2007, Anais... Rio de Janeiro.
Souza, E. M., Bianco, M. F., & Machado, L. D. (2006). Análises sobre poder: comparativo entre a perspectiva foucaultiana e funcionalista. In *Encontro da Associação Nacional de Pós-Graduação em Administração e Pesquisa em Administração,* XXX, Anais... Salvador/BA.
Souza, E. M., Machado, L. R., & Bianco, M. F. (2004). Poder disciplinar: a analítica foucaultiana como uma alternativa as pesquisa organizacionais sobre poder. In *Encontro da Associação Nacional de Pós-Graduação em Administração e Pesquisa em Administração,* XXVIII, Anais... Curitiba/PR.
Tadajewski, M., & Jones, D. G. B. (2016). Hyper-power, the marketing concept and consumer as 'boss.' *Marketing Theory, 1*(4), 513–531. https://doi.org/10.1177/1470593116666408.
Valor, C., Diaz, E. M., & Merino, A. (2017). The discourse of the consumer resistance movement: Adversarial and prognostic framings through the lens of power. *Journal of Macromarketing, 37*(1), 72–84. https://doi.org/10.1177/0276146715627851.
Wei, C., Liu, M., & Keh, H. T. (2020). The road to consumer forgiveness is paved with money or apology? The roles of empathy and power in service recovery. *Journal of Business Research, 118*, 321–334.
Zanette, M. C., & Brito, E. P. Z. (2019). Fashionable subjects and complicity resistance: Power, subjectification, and bounded resistance in the context of plus-size consumers. *Consumption Markets & Culture, 22*(4), 363–382. https://doi.org/10.1080/10253866.2018.1512241.

Chapter 12
Customer-Perceived Organizational Dignity

Mauro Silva Ferreira and Ronaldo de Lucio

Abstract The dignity of customers is a topic that has not generally been the subject of scholars' attention, despite the emergence of several institutions and laws that takes care of consumer protection, worldwide. This chapter argues that dignity is not only related to the human being, since groups of individuals behave differently in relation to one of their individual components; in this sense, we understand that organizations arise from associated social forms and norms that hold organizations responsible for customer dignity. In this context, inequalities in relations between companies and consumers arise, becoming sources that generates indignity. Thus, we present the process of validating a scale of organizational dignity practices and a scale of organizational values, both from the perspective of customer perception, making it possible to identify how the relationship of organizations and their customers is in aspects of practices related to dignity. Thereby, the PRADOC and VOPC-R scales can be used in periodic applications designed to monitor the culture of organizational dignity perceived by clients and through the results of these assessments contribute to outline strategies for improving the culture of dignity.

Keywords Customers · Organizational dignity · Organizational values

12.1 Introduction

Customers' dignity has been discussed mainly in relation to vulnerable individuals such as elderly (Dobarro & Villaverde, 2016) and disable individuals (Eskytė, 2019). It is astonishing that studies on dignity, consumers, and clients in general have not deserved the attention of scholars, as several international organizations and laws were established to protect the rights of consumers, such as the International Consumer Protection and Enforcement Network (ICPEN) and the European Consumer Organization (BEUC).

M. S. Ferreira · R. de Lucio (✉)
São Paulo, Brazil
e-mail: ronaldodelucio@uol.com.br

M. L. Mendes Teixeira and L. M. B. de Oliveira (eds.), *Organizational Dignity and Evidence-Based Management*, https://doi.org/10.1007/978-3-030-68560-7_12

The International Consumer Protection and Enforcement Network, ICPEN, was founded in 1991 and gathers several countries. It aims to cooperate to solve problems of consumers of goods and services in cross-border transactions (https://www.icpen.org). BEUC was founded in 1962 and gathers 44 organizations from 32 countries. It aims at advocating for the interests of the European consumers (https://www.beuc.eu/). The large scope of the types of trade in the last few years has generated a wide range of documents aimed to protect consumers, like in e-commerce deals (OECD, 2016). In Brazil, the consumer's protection law dated 1990, updated in 2009 (New Consumer's Rights Code), sets forth the rules to defend consumers, and the Consumer Protection and Defence Program works to meet the consumers' demands ensuing from conflicts in the relationship with product and service providers.

International and national authorities and laws about the protection of consumer' rights are ultimately aimed to protect the consumer's dignity in their consumption relationships. The demands ensuing from conflicts with different defective services or products delivered to consumers disclose flaws in the relationship. That relationship should be reviewed to establish new levels of respect and dignity, based on values that go beyond pursuing for profits. This pursuing, many times irresponsible, brings about conflicts and demands in consumer defense authorities and the judiciary system.

The study about dignity in organizations has its origin in studies comprising employees and approaching topics such as: maintenance of dignity at work (Hodson, 2004); dimensions related to job activities (Naughton & Laczniak, 1993; Berg & Frost, 2005); control at work (Ottensmeyer & Heroux, 1991); exploitation at work (Avery et al., 2010); work's objectivation (Marx, 2010); worker's valuation (Ledur, 1998); and influence of the individual's self-respect and dignity in their self-esteem (Calhoun, 2004). Despite these studies, for Pirson and Kostera (2017) the role of dignity in the economy and in the environment of associations has still been largely neglected (Pirson et al., 2016; Pirson, 2019). The concept of dignity in organizations developed to the point of starting approaching the relationship between corporations and their stakeholders, employees, customers, shareholders, investors, suppliers, community, and public authorities. Organizational dignity is expressed by means of worthy practices in the relationship between companies and stakeholder (Teixeira et al., 2014).

This chapter has the aim of presenting the results of a qualitative study about the customer-perceived services provided by the company wherever a telephone-related issue arises. Moreover, this study aimed to present the validation of the Organizational Dignity Practices Perceived by the Client (PRADOC) scale aimed to measure the practices of organizational dignity perceived by customers, and the Organizational Values Perceived by the Client (VOPC) scale as a way to evaluate the customer-perceived organizational values. Finally, it identifies the relationship between practices of organizational dignity in the customer's standpoint and the customer-perceived organizational values. The qualitative study was carried out during conciliation hearings between attorneys of companies and customers, mediated by conciliators. The other studies were quantitative. Data were collected from a sampling of 205 end customers from several business segments. Most of the participants were male (58.5%), half the sampling was made up by youth of 17–35 years old (49.5%), and almost all participants held undergraduate degree (98%). The exploratory factorial analysis (EFA) was used for the quantitative data analysis aimed at validating the PRADOC scale. The VOPC scale was validated through confirmatory factorial analysis (CFA). The practices of organizational dignity were analyzed in the standpoint of customers and customers-perceived organizational values. The analysis employed the structural equation modeling (SEM) through partial least square (PLS).

Results suggested that customer-perceived organizational values affect the perception of organizational dignity practices found in the relationship between customers and the company.

12.2 Objective Responsibility of Organizations

Some believe that dignity is related exclusively to the human being, as they have capacity of acting and, therefore, can be rendered liable for their acts. However, it was found that groups of individuals demonstrate typical behaviors that differ from the behaviors of their components individually. When approaching organizations, including companies, they present other features than natural persons (individuals) and are known by the society as "legal entities."

Organizations are created from social institutions that, in turn, come to life from social forms and associated social norms (Whetten & Mackey, 2002). The legal devices used to handle with the relationship between the society and private and public institutions assign individuals' characteristics to companies. The **objective responsibility** stands out among those legal devices.

The objective responsibility of public and private legal entities is established in articles and ordinary laws in the Brazilian Federal Constitution that provided for the administrative and civil liability of legal entities. The Constitution grants the rights to people damaged by any practice or willful misconduct by a legal entity.

The state treats organizations as autonomous elements, rendering them liable for damages practiced by their agents and recognizing that agents and legal entities have different identities. Moreover, conducts harmful to the environment are subject to penal and administration sanctions, involving both natural and legal entities, regardless the liability toward repairing the damages caused. This reaffirms the position of organizations as entities endowed with autonomy and sovereignty, holding responsibility in relation to their practices.

For example, the sentence by the Brazilian Highest Court (Supremo Tribunal Federal, 2013) imposed practice of environmental crime to the legal entity, even without investigation of the natural persons' responsibility for the activities that triggered the environmental crime. Although going against the prevailing position by then, that any penal procedure against legal entity should only be applicable if the effective participation of one or more agents in the practice of environmental crime was effectively ascertained (Silva & Trevizan, 2013). The decision has set a paramount precedent. In addition to sanctions of civil and administrative nature, the companies may be that penal penalization does not depend if managers or other employees were directly responsible for the environmental crime. That decision discloses an important change on how the Brazilian and the international societies perceive public and private organizations (Silva & Trevizan, 2013).

Organizations' essence is not a simple sum of the people making it up; rather, it is an independent structure (Hirsch, 2002) that supports the practice of blaming the firms, regardless the attributions of individual responsibilities. Culpability could be avoided if the company established controls to hinder a criminal policy.

When it comes to crime, the Brazilian criminal law adopts the finalist theorist developed by Welzel (2003) that considers that all the behaviors of individuals have a purpose, in which the conduct is a final activity, where the will does not come out of nowhere, it has an objective, and the conduct takes place when the actions are directed toward that objective. Therefore, in the Brazilian criminal scope, the objective responsibilization is unfeasible. In England, however, the principle *societas delinquere potest* prevails. It challenges the finalist theory and allows playing an organization as an active element of the crime (Souza, 2007).

Companies increasingly perform harmful action, mainly related to economic and environmental crimes. This has led to the need for the criminal responsibilization of the legal entity. According to Smanio (2001), economic and environmental crimes in our society are a reality, there is increasing involvement of companies, and this situation that added to aspects related to economic growth and globalization stimulates the depersonalization of events related to legal entities, which suggests discussions on the importance of criminal accountability of offending organizations.

During the VI Congress on Prevention of Crime and the Treatment of Offenders, the UN met in New York in July 1979 to approach crime and power abuse. The UN recommended the State Members to establish the principle of criminal responsibility of the societies (Smanio, 2001).

By considering the organization as liable for its acts, the objective indictment applied to corporations proves to be crucial to maintain the economic order, and the relationships between organizations and customers. The nonexistence of such a mechanism would hinder the state from controlling the consumption relations and enforcing sanctions to organizations. This would make the society hostage of any action taken by the companies.

Moreover, in light of dignity organizations hold moral obligations to the market and their customers. Therefore, organizations can no longer be accepted as an extension of their leaders and employees, considering the enormous power, mainly economic, they have on the society. When referring the relationships between the many stakeholders, Teixeira (2008) emphasizes the need for organizations to try to understand and establish businesses driven not only by financial values, but also by moral and ethical values. Therefore, it could build up a fairer society and reaffirms the trend toward rendering the companies liable for their actions.

12.3 Dignity in the Relation Between Company, Consumers, and Customers

The definition of consumer should not be confounded with that of customer. To be a consumer, all a person has to do is to purchase products and services from supplier companies (Decker, 2017). The companies that are in vulnerability in their relationships with suppliers may also be considered as consumers (Antunes, 2013). Those who are not final consumers of the products cannot be considered as consumers (Oliveira, 2010). Client, in turn, holds links with the service provider. Companies invest efforts through marketing actions and operations to establish and sustain long-lasting links and earn profits by means of that link (Hoekstra et al., 1999). However, the literature not always clearly establishes that difference. This is this chapter does not differentiate consumers and customers.

Serving customers demands some care such as self-control of emotions during the service and lack of discretion. Activities demanding emotional engagement with customers require from professionals a subtle balance so they can perceive respect. This does not imply coldness or undesired closeness. Self-control and limited expression of emotions are important when dealing with customers. Customers trust more in professionals that are in control of themselves. Likewise, discretion and confidence are important. Social skills and emotional intelligence can lead to genuine quality services perceived by customers. These behaviors contribute to a worthy relationship with the customer (Sayer, 2007).

Consumers' dignity has deserved little attention by scholars, in both Brazil and abroad. In Brazil, Julio and Hemais (2019), when studying the meaning of health plans to the low-income population, found dignity as one of the main categories of meaning. To that population, having a health plan means social inclusion and by feeling included that population perceives themselves as worthy. This is an acquired dignity. Acquired dignity is mentioned by Tadd, Vanlaere and Gastmans (2010) as the dignity associated with achieving better positions in the society by virtue of the individuals' merit.

However, life is not a bed of roses when it comes to the relation between consumers and society. There is inequality in relations between professionals representing companies before consumers, and that inequality is a source of indignity both for the first and for the last. Treating consumers as sovereigns or, in opposition, submitting customers to the companies will bring about feelings of indignity (Sayer, 2007).

Vulnerability is an assumable condition of all consumers. The consumer defense codes based on social justice and human dignity foster the defense of consumers as they lack assets (Dias Simões, 2011). The actions by the society toward establishing rules to equal the relationships between consumers and companies suggest that vulnerability and lack of assets are factors of indignity in the relation between consumers and companies.

In the study about negotiation between consumers and companies of phone services, consumers tried to solve their issues with the companies, and when they failed in getting a solution, they suited the company. Some statements show how the relation can shift "*They are great when we are buying. [...] When we are buying, they provide us great services, but when we complain about anything, it is not possible [to solve the complaint].*"

The interviews disclosed the consumers' efforts toward finding solutions: "*I called thousands times, talked to thousands people in there[...],*" "*I tried by letter, chat, phone,* "*We get really stressed, it seem nobody wants to solve your problem[...].*" The company considers consumers as a means to reach an end, namely the profit. The image of a company that excels for profit in detriment to services delivered to consumers gives rise to an image of a consumer in "*[...] neglect, lack of respect [...].*" The consumer that fulfills their duties, but is neglected, being harmed and tired of trying to solve the issue with the company, perceives themselves as vulnerable and powerless in the weakest side of the relation. Vulnerability is a condition for violation of dignity (Jacobson, 2009).

Seeking the Judiciary Branch to solve the issue is the last resource, when all the other means of solving the problem with the company are exhausted. "*We filed a suit because we could not solve it at administrative level.*" By seeking the justice to find a solution, consumers recognize themselves as holders of rights and try to protect their dignity by refusing the company's government (Louback, 2012) "[...] *I've tried countless times to solve it on the phone, now I'll only accept an agreement in a conciliation hearing, I don't want to accept anything by phone.*" When they perceive that the company disregards their problems, consumers seek means to pay off the waste of time, of feeling such as anger and stress, and also the financial losses springing from the problem with the company.

Conciliation hearings are held before the Judiciary Power reviews the customer's claim. The hearings are held in the presence of the customer, the company's attorney, and a conciliator. The attorney is a representative of the company exclusively assigned to attend the audience to which they were hired. The company gives these attorneys limited powers to negotiate monetary values with the customer. In the perception of customers participating in the survey, the attorneys are unskilled and, therefore, finding solutions is restricted.

"*[...] I believe the conciliation hearing should exist, but with powers. Because [the attorney] was very limited [in his power of negotiation] and results were disappointing.*" "*I should be working, and not here losing my money.*" Effectively, the attorneys proved they are there only to bring the company's proposals: "*[...] I'm here to bring the company's proposal. So, we don't effectively act on the case itself.*". "*We [bring] a standard proposal. [...]So, I have that template [...],*" "*[...]I'm hired to act on the hearing in the terms they ordered.*" Thus, if the consumer does not accept what the company proposed through the attorney, there will be no solution responsive to the consumer's needs.

The attorneys rely on the conciliator to close the deal with the client. They regard conciliators as important players to reach that end. "*He tries to interfere, but he interferes to help both parts,*" "[...] *the conciliator explains [to the consumer] that we have nothing to do with the company, he is just bringing a proposal, there's nothing we can do,*" "*[...] the conciliator's word is very important,*" "*The consumer listens more [to the conciliator], trusts more in the conciliator than in the other part [attorney].*" The conciliator's intervention is even considered by attorneys as something part of their work in heading the conciliation hearing, as depicted in the following report: "*That conciliator who intervenes in the sense of advising the consumer, [...] that conciliator helps*" [when closing a deal within the terms of the company's proposal]. The conciliator's impartiality is something perceives as useless for the attorney b y the time of negotiation. "*There's that [conciliator] who takes literally, he is neutral there, there he can't [help the attorney], this [conciliator], I believe, he takes to nothing.*" In other words, the attorney perceives their limited work by the time of negotiation, and that they are supported by the conciliator's work to close a deal. When a conciliator is not impartial, they work in favor of the company by intervening on the negotiation in such a way as to have the company's proposal accepted.

In brief, the study showed that conciliation hearings are built in a way to induce customers to accept the proposal offered by the company. Attorneys are nothing but messengers of the company, with very little freedom of negotiation, and count on the support of conciliators to persuade the customer to accept the deal. The inequality of powers between companies and customers promotes the consumer's vulnerability. That consumer, in turn, has their dignity violated even in the conciliation hearings.

According to Jacobson (2009), the elements of violation of dignity are manifested through indifference, disrespect, objectivation, and exploration, among others. In this study, consumers' dignity violation takes place when they seek for different means to solve their problems and are not duly heard by the company to solve the problem. Non-hearing is through the transfer of calls, by waiting on the line, and even by shutting down the connection. Violation by the company is manifested by the disrespect to consumers, by changing the values of the phone service plans initially hired, with no previous notice. In the conciliation hearing, the company continues violating the consumer's dignity, showing indifference when it sends an attorney with little freedom of negotiation. The conciliation hearing then becomes nothing but a bureaucratic act that delays an attempt of solving the problem experiences by the consumer.

12.4 How Dignity in an Organization Can Be Measured in the Customers' Perspective

To measure organizational dignity in the customers' perspective, the PRADOC scale was developed based on the original version of the Organizational Dignity Practices (EPRA-DO) scale (Teixeira et al., 2011) aimed to evaluate organizational dignity in the employees' standpoint. It may seem weird the development of a scale to evaluate the organizational dignity in the customers' standpoint based on a scale used to evaluate it in light of employees. What happens is that the EPRA-DO scale was developed based on a qualitative survey on people's concept of worthy company. The survey targeted people at large, disregarding any role they performed in the society. The same set of items serves as grounds to generate a scale for evaluation in the customer's standpoint.

Organizational dignity was defined as "practices of organizational values that serve the many stakeholders, and are perceived and evaluated by them, assigning them distinction, respect to free will, and that meet the universal maxim that 'what is good for one must be good for all'" (Teixeira et al., 2014, p. 4).

The 31 items of the EPRA-DO scale version developed by Teixeira et al. (2011) were applied to 205 customers, for them to assess the dignity of a company of their choice. Responses were subjected to the EFA, resulting in a 26-item scale, split into five factors: Practices of Promotion of the Participatory Development of the Employee (DO1), Practices of Responsibility with Customers and Society (DO2), Practices of Respect to the Rights of Employees (DO3), Non-deceiving Practices in Relation to Stakeholders (DO4), and Practices of Appraisal of Performance (DO5). All factors achieved reliability indexes higher than 0.7 (Hair Jr. et al., 2009).

The factor **practices of promotion of the participatory development of the employee (DO1)** refers to actions that allow employees to develop and participate in the company, so they develop and share actions to improve the productive activities. These practices seem to reflect to which extent the company knows the potential contributions its employees can offer, appraising aspects of technical and administrative merit, and avoiding political interferences on the productive activities. This factor comprises the following items:

Allows the participation of employees in the processes of change.
Allows the participation of employees in the processes of promotion.
Offers opportunities to employees.
Promotes based on merit.
Empowers employees.
Hires based on competence.
Acknowledges the employee's value.
Promotes teamwork.

The factor **practices of responsibility with customers and society (DO2)** is concerned with activities favorable to the community and the individuals of a society, showing concern about public well-being through the production of quality goods, and cooperation to sustain a healthier environment. This factor comprises the following items:

Puts in practice philanthropic actions.
Invests in the environment.
Assists the third sector.
Fulfills its obligations with the society.
Offers environment-friendly products and services.
Offers quality products and services.

The factor **practices of respect to the rights of employees (DO3)** is related to the company's commitment toward complying with legal and financial rules, showing respect and commitment with legal agreements. The following items are part of the factor:

Recognizes the right to vacation.
Pays on time.
Hires through the Brazilian labor laws.
Prioritizes the settlement of its labor-related liabilities.

The factor **non-deceiving practices in relation to stakeholders (DO4)** is negatively related to actions aimed at putting the company's interest above the interests of employees and the society, through practices that exploit internal professionals, and of evading taxes. The following items make up the factor:

Exploits employees.
Tries to deceive the employee.
Tries to deceive the customer.
Evades taxes.

The factor **practices of appraisal of performance (DO5)** concerns the company's procedures aimed to improve the quality of services internally delivered, as a means to offer better products and services externally. Following are the items:

Assesses employees.
Disseminates the employees' assessments.
Invests in training.
Offers conditions for the professional development.

The scale PRADOC brought about two new factors different from the EPRA-DO scale. These are factors DO5 and DO2. The other factors are similar to those of the EPRA-DO scale, showing that customers also valuate organizations that respect the rights of their employees, promote their participatory development, and do not use deceitful practices in relation to stakeholders.

12.5 Relation Between Customer-Perceived Organizational Dignity and Customer-Perceived Organizational Values

One of the most quoted organizational value approaches in the international literature is that by O'Reilly III et al. (1991). The scale presents seven dimensions: innovation, stability, respect to people, results-oriented, details-oriented, teams-oriented, and aggressiveness.

In Brazil, the studies on organizational values were fostered by the surveys by Tamayo and collaborators. Tamayo and Gondim (1996) developed a scale of organizational values based on empirical procedures, with five dimensions: efficacy/efficiency, interaction at workplace, management, innovation, and respect to employee. Tamayo et al. (2000), based on the Schwartz's (1999) theory on cultural values, have identified that the three bipolar dimensions proposed by the theory, namely autonomy versus conservatism, hierarchy *versus* egalitarianism, and harmony versus domain, were not completely confirmed by the organizational value inventory developed by them. The dimensions of autonomy versus conservatism and domain versus harmony proved to be adjacent, while in Schwartz's theory on cultural values they are opposite.

Imbued with the purpose of building a scale of organizational values based on a theory of values, and considering that the scale developed by Tamayo et al. (2000) failed in fully reflecting the theory of cultural values by Schwartz (1999), Oliveira and Tamayo (2004) developed a new scale of organizational values based on the theory of baseline values of Schwartz (1992). The scale aimed to identify the organizational values in the employees' perception.

Organizational values are those perceived by workers as representative of the organization and are based on the building of the organizational identity (Tamayo, 1998). Organizational values ensue from personal values, as they are introduced by individuals: the founder, managers, workers themselves (Oliveira & Tamayo, 2004). Therefore, Oliveira and Tamayo (2004) developed the Inventory of Organizational Values Profile (IPVO, in Portuguese) that reflected the theory of baseline values proposed by Schwartz (1992). The IPVO comprises eight factors:

- Autonomy: Corresponds to self-determination and stimulus, and aims to offer challenges and variety at work and foster curiosity, creativeness, and innovation.
- Well-being: Hedonism-related, it tries to promote satisfaction, well-being, and quality of life at work.
- Fulfillment: Corresponds to fulfillment and tries to value the workers' competence and success.
- Domain: Power-related, aims at profits and competitiveness, and corners the market.
- Prestige: Power-related, aims to gain prestige, be acknowledged and admired by all, and offer products and services that are satisfactory for customers.
- Tradition: Tradition-related, aims to sustain tradition and respect the organization's customs.
- Conformity: Conformity-related, aims to promote righteousness, courtesy and good manners at the workplace, and respect to the rules of the organization.
- Concern with collectivity: Related to benevolence and universalism, aims to promote justice and equality in the organization, as well as tolerance, sincerity, honesty.

The organizational value inventory gave rise to the customer-perceived organizational values (VOPC, in Portuguese).

12.5.1 Customers-Perceived Organizational Values

Based on the works by Tamayo and Gondim (1996), Tamayo (1998), Tamayo et al. (2000) and Oliveira and Tamayo (2004), Guardani (2008) exposes that the work started from the understanding that the organizational values perceived by clients are characteristics of an organization that served as principles or beliefs, related to ways of knowing the reality and responses to organizational matters; they are organized hierarchically; guide the objectives of the organization, its functioning and the relationship with the environment; they guide behavior and are shared by their members.

As Guardani (2008) points out, values reflect distinctive traits of each culture and guide individuals, as it provides them with an organized concept about nature, on the human being's place in it.

To carry out the study, Guardani (2008) adjusted the Inventory of Organizational Values Profile IPVO (Oliveira & Tamayo, 2004), generating the VOPC, a 41-item and 5-factor scale:

A. Respect to stakeholders—including its customers, employees and organizations, and the community.
B. Domain and power—trying to corner the market and employees.
C. Well-being of employees—appraising them.
D. Tradition and prestige—reinforcing achievements before the society and the market.
E. Aversion to changes—not providing changes in how it works.

The VOPC scale factors correspond to the following factors in the IPVO scale: Respect to stakeholders corresponds to concern with collectivity, conformity, fulfillment, autonomy; domain and power correspond to domain; well-being of employees corresponds to the same IPVO factor; tradition and prestige correspond to the factors tradition and prestige in the IPVO; and aversion to changes corresponds to tradition.

12.5.2 The Influence of Customers-Perceived Organizational Values on the Customers-Perceived Organizational Practices

In order to identify the influence of customers-perceived organizational values on the customers-perceived organizational dignity practices, the convergent and discriminant validity were firstly performed through partial least squares path modeling (PLS-PM).

The PLS-PM measurement model implies assessing the construct validity, through the assessment of convergent and discriminant validities. The convergent validity is assessed through the average variance extracted (AVE) that must be equal to or higher than 0.5 (Fornell & Larcker, 1981); composite reliability equal to or higher than 0.7

(Bido, 2012); and t value between each indicator and related latent variable at a minimum level of 0.5 (Gefen & Straub, 2005). The discriminant validity is assessed by means of the analysis of each factor's factor loading, which must be higher in the latent variable to which it belongs, and lower in the other variables. Gefen and Straub (2005) mention, for illustration purposes, that if the loading of an item is 0.7 in the expected variable, it should not exceed 0.6 in the remaining variables. The square root of AVE of each latent variable must be higher than the correlation between the LVs (Chin, 1998).

The VOPC validation resulted in a 26-item scale (VOPC-R) distributed over 5 factors, meeting the convergent validity criteria, reliability indexes ranging from 0.62 to 0.94, and factor loading higher than 0.7. Comparing the square root of average variance extracted (AVE) with the correlations of latent variables, all correlations are lower, corroborating the discriminant validity.

The VOPC-R factors are made up by the following items:

Factor: Respect to stakeholders

1. Sincerity among individuals is encouraging for this organization. Being true to the others is important to it.
2. To this organization, everyone must be fairly treated. In its view, people deserve equal opportunities.
3. This organization values competence. It considers important for employee to show their skills and knowledge.
4. This organization encourages the professional success of employees. It encourages them to work in a competent way.
5. This organization believes in the value of honesty. It honors its commitments with people and organizations to which it relates.
6. It is important for this organization that individuals are treated in a fair way. Respecting the others' rights is important for it.
7. What minds in this organization is that employees deeply know what they do. It recognizes the competent employees.
8. This organization believes in the importance of being loyal to its employees and customers. It fulfills its commitments with them.
9. This organization appraises employees that seek for fulfillment at work. It recognizes when an employee has professional goals.
10. This organization believes that people should be honest in all situations. Telling the truth is part of the principles of this organization.
11. This organization considers that loyalty is important. It is loyal to people and organizations surrounding it.

Factor: Domain and Power

12. For this organization, planning goals is crucial. It considers that achieving goals is an evidence of competence.
13. This organization believes that being competitive is important. It wants to win new markets.

14. This organization considers business security as a very important factor. It is attentive to the market threats.

Factor: Well-being of Employees

15. This organization finds that helping its employees is very important. It wants to take care of their well-being.
16. This organization offers opportunities of amusement to its employees. It believes that feeling pleasure at work is important.
17. For this organization, keeping clubs for the leisure of its employees is important. It considers that amusement is an important piece of the employees' lives.
18. This organization is concerned with the quality of life of its employees. It develops social projects that contribute to their well-being.
19. This organization proposes activities that amuse employees. In its view, the employee must feel satisfied with him/herself.

Factor: Tradition and Prestige

20. Tradition is a brand of this organization. It has practices that sustain its customs.
21. This organization influences other organizations. It is very prestigious.
22. This organization preserves old customs. It respects tradition.
23. This organization is prestigious in the society. It believes that being admired by all is important.
24. This organization is influent in the society. It believes that being respected by all is important.

Factor: Aversion to Change

25. This organization avoids changes. It prefers keeping its way of working.
26. This organization tries to maintain widely accepted practices. It believes that working always in the same way is important.

In the study to identify the influence of customer-perceived organizational values and customer-perceived practices of organizational dignity, after individually reviewing the PRADOC and VOPC-R scales, the analysis of relations between those constructs was performed. Observing the relationships between the factors of organizational values and factors of practices of organizational dignity, it was found that some relations did not present significant loads, were below 1.96, and were excluded.

Factors related to respect to stakeholders and well-being of employees justified 47% of the existence of the practices of promotion of the participatory development of the employee. The factors respect to stakeholders, well-being of employees, and tradition and prestige justified 41% of the factor practices of responsibility with clients and the society. The factor respect to stakeholders explained 20.3% of the factor practices of respect to the rights of the employee. The factors of respect to stakeholders and aversion to change explained 30.6% of the factor non-deceiving practices in relation to stakeholders. The factor practices of valuation of performance was influenced in 38.6% by the factors respect to stakeholders and well-being of employees. The only factor of customer-perceived organizational values that did not influence the perception of practices was that of domain and power. Results showed that customer-perceived practices of dignity are influenced by their perception of the organizational values.

12.6 Implications to Management

The main contributions of this chapter to management rely on the potential application of the scales customers-perceived values and customer-perceived practices of dignity, in addition to reflecting over the violation of customers' dignity. Managers are expected to put themselves in the customers' shoes when they outline policies to receive complains. After all, they are customers as well.

The factors customers-perceived values influence the perception of practices of dignity, except for the value domain and power. Practices of dignity and the organizational values sustaining it reflect an organizational culture that prioritizes dignity in the organization. This culture of dignity fosters managers to invest in it.

The PRADOC and VOPC-R scales may be applied to planned regular applications with customers to monitor the customer-perceived culture of organizational dignity. The PRADOC scale may complement the other instruments aimed to evaluate and monitor the customers' satisfaction with products and services delivered.

The results of the assessments performed by customers can contribute to outline strategies to enhance the culture of dignity, enabling the development over time.

12.7 Final Remarks

This work aims to contribute with organizations seeking to establish relationships with customers that are based on practices of dignity guided by values in tune with an ethical and well-balanced society. A relationship between companies, consumers, and customers prioritizes the common well-being, with gains for companies and for consumers and customers. Secondarily, these relations are expected to reduce conflicts in the relationships of consumption, favoring the society as a whole.

Also worthy of attention from scholars is the influence of customer-perceived organizational values. Studies on organizational values have been oriented to the workers' perception. One could imagine that customers, for missing direct access to the inner organizational life, could not perceive the organizational values. This, however, was contradicted in this study. Customers can have perceptions about the organizational culture, but do not perceive it the same way as the organization's workers.

The factors of employee-perceived organizational values partially differ from those perceived by customers. While employees perceive valuation of employees, customers, and society in separate, customers perceive them as part of one single block: respect to stakeholders. Differently from workers, clients differentiate tradition related to customs from tradition in the sense of rejection to change. Customs-related traditions are associated with prestige by customers.

We hope this work fosters scholars to investigate factors that influence worthy relationships between companies, consumers, and customers, in addition to relations that could be established between customer-perceived practices of organizational dignity and other constructs like intention to purchase, reputation, and trust of customers in the company that produces goods or provides services.

References

Antunes, T. C. (2013). *Apontamentos sobre a definição legal de consumidor e a jurisprudência contemporânea*. Jus Navigandi. Retrieved September 10, 2020, from https://jus.com.br/artigos/24358

Avery, D. R., Tonidandel, S., Volpone, S. D., & Raghuram, A. (2010). Overworked in America? How work hours, immigrant status, and interpersonal justice affect perceived work overload. *Journal of Managerial Psychology, 25*(2), 133–147.

Berg, P., & Frost, A. (2005). Dignity at work for low wage, low skill service workers. *Relations Industrielles / Industrial Relations, 60*(4), 657–682. Retrieved September 29, 2020, from https://www.jstor.org/stable/23077680

Bido, D. S. (2012). *Modelagem de Equações estruturais com estimação PLS*. Retrieved November 10, 2020 from https://www.anpad.org.br/diversos/enanpad2012/minicursoequacoes_estruturais.pdf

Calhoun, C. (2004). An apology for moral shame. *The Journal of Political Philosophy, 12*(2). 127–146. Retrieved September 25, 2020.

Chin, W. W. (1998). The Partial Least Squares approach to structural equation modeling. In G. A. Marcoulides (Ed.), *Modern methods for business research* (pp. 295–336). Mahwah: Lawrence Erlbaum Associates Inc.

Decker, C. (2017). Concepts of the consumer in competition, regulatory, and consumer protection polices. *Journal of Competition Law & Economics, 13*(1), 151–184. https://doi.org/10.1093/joclec/nhx005.

Dias Simões, F. (2011). O Conceito De Consumidor No Direito Português (II) (The Definition of Consumer in Portuguese Law - September 30, 2011). Retrieved November, 25, 2020, from https://ssrn.com/abstract=1935738

Dobarro, S. L. C., & Villaverde, A. (2016). A vulnerabilidade agravada do consumidor idoso à luz do princípio da dignidade da pessoa humana. *Revista Jurídica Luso-Brasileira, 3*, 1371–1391. Retrieved November 15, 2020 from https://www.cidp.pt/revistas/rjlb/2016/3/2016_03_1371_1391.pdf

Eskytė, I. (2019). Disabled people's vulnerability in the European single market: The case of consumer information. *Journal of Consumer Policy, 42*, 521–543.

Fornell, C., & Larcker, D. (1981). Evaluating structural equation models with unobservable variables and measurement error. *Journal of Marketing Research, 18*(1), 39–50.

Guardani, F. (2008). *A relação entre os valores organizacionais, as práticas e a confiança dos clientes em organizações do setor de serviços*. Tese de doutorado, Administração de Empresas. Universidade Presbiteriana Mackenzie, São Paulo, Brasil.

Gefen, D., & Straub, D. (2005). A practical guide to factorial validity using PLS-graph: Tutorial and annotated example. *Communications of the Association for Information Systems, 16,* 5.

Hair Jr., J. F., Black, W. C., Babin, B. J., Anderson, R. E., & Tatham, R. L. (2009). *Análise multivariada de dados* (6th ed.). Porto Alegre: Bookman.

Hirsch, H. J. (2002). *Derecho penal. Obras completas.* Buenos Aires: Rubinzal-Culzoni.

Hodson, R. (2004). *Dignity at work.* Cambridge: Cambridge University Press.

Hoekstra, J. C., Leeflang, P. S. H., & Wittink, D. R. (1999). The customer concept: The basis for a new marketing paradigm. *Journal of Market-Focused Management, 4,* 43–76. https://doi.org/10.1023/A:1009856028285.

Jacobson, N. (2009). A taxonomy of dignity: a grounded theory study. *BMC Int Health Hum Rights, 9*(3), 1–9.

Julio, L. F. F., & Hemais, M. W. (2019). Significados de Planos de Saúde para Consumidores de Baixa Renda. *Pretexto, 20*(4), 60–74. https://doi.org/10.21714/pretexto.v20i4.5517

Ledur, J. F. (1998). *A realização do direito ao trabalho.* Porto Alegre: Sergio Antônio Fabris Editor.

Louback, J. C. (2012). *Dignidade e relações de poder: um estudo em um call center à luz de Foucault.* Tese de doutorado Administração de Empresas, Universidade Presbiteriana Mackenzie, São Paulo, Brasil.

Marx, K. (2010). *Crítica à filosofia de direito de Hegel* (2ª ed.). São Paulo: Boitempo.

Naughton, M., & Laczniak, G. R. (1993). Theological context of work from the Catholic Social Encyclical Tradition. *Journal of Business Ethics, 12,* 981–994.

OECD. (2016). *Consumer protection in E-commerce: OECD recommendation.* Paris: OECD Publishing. https://doi.org/10.1787/9789264255258-en

Oliveira, J. M. (2010). *20 anos do Código de Defesa do Consumidor. A evolução do conceito de consumidor.* Jus Navigandi. Retrieved September 10, 2020, from https://jus.com.br/artigos/17948

Oliveira, A. F., & Tamayo, A. (2004). Inventário de perfis de valores organizacionais. *RAUSP Management Journal, 39*(2), 129–140.

O'Reilly, C. A., III., Chatman, J., & Caldwell, D. F. (1991). People and organizational culture: A profile comparison approach to assessing person-organization fit. *Academy of Management Journal., 34*(3), 487–516.

Ottensmeyer, E., & Heroux, M. A. (1991). Ethics, public policy, and managing advanced technologies: The case of electronic surveillance *Journal of Business Ethics, 10*(7), 519–526. Retrieved September 29, 2020, from https://www.jstor.org/stable/25072180

Pirson, M. (2019). A humanistic perspective for management theory: Protecting dignity and promoting well-being. *Journal of Business Ethics, 159*(1), 39–57. https://doi.org/10.1007/s10551-017-3755-4.

Pirson, M., Goodpaster, K., & Dierksmeier, C. (2016). Guest editors' introduction: Human dignity and business. *Business Ethics Quarterly, 26*(4), 465–478.

Pirson, M., & Kostera, M. (2017). Introduction to dignity and organization. In M. Kostera & M. Pirson (Eds.), *Dignity and the organization* (Chap. 1, pp. 1–9). London: Palgrave Macmillan.

Sayer, A. (2007). Dignity at work: Broadening the agenda. *Organization, 14*(4), 565–581.

Schwartz, S. H. (1992). *Universals in the content and structure of values: Theoretical advances and empirical tests in 20 countries.* In M. P. Zanna (Ed.), *Advances in experimental social psychology* (Vol. 25, pp. 1–65). New York: Academic.

Schwartz, S. H. (1999). A theory of cultural values and some implications for work. *Applied Psychology: An International Review, 48*(1), 23–47.

Silva, E., & Trevizan, V. P. (2013). STF muda critérios para processo de pessoa jurídica. Consultor Jurídico. Retrieved September 15, 2020, from https://www.conjur.com.br/2013-set-01/decisao-stf-altera-criterios-processo-penal-pessoa-juridica?imprimir=1

Smanio, G. P. (2001). A Responsabilidade Penal da Pessoa Jurídica. In: Escola Superior do Ministério Público de São Paulo (Ed.), Caderno Jurídico: Novas Formas de Criminalidade 1(3), 163–176.

Souza, A. D. (2007). Direito Penal: responsabilidade objetiva e teoria da imputação objetiva do resultado. Âmbito Jurídico. Retrieved September 15, 2020, from https://ambitojuridico.com.br/cadernos/direito-penal/direito-penal-responsabilidade-objetiva-e-teoria-da-imputacao -objetiva-do-resultado/
Supremo Tribunal Federal. (2013). Recurso Extraordinário nº 548.181, Órgão Julgador: Primeira Turma. Responsabilidade Penal da Pessoa Jurídica.
Tadd, W., Vanlaere, L., & Gastmans, C. (2010). Clarifying the concept of human dignity in the care of the elderly: A dialogue between empirical and philosophical approaches. *Ethical Perspective, 17*(1), 253–281.
Tamayo, A. (1998). Valores organizacionais: sua relação com satisfação no trabalho, cidadania organizacional e comprometimento afetivo. *RAUSP Management Journal, 33*(3), 56–63.
Tamayo, A., & Gondim, M. D. G. C. (1996). Escala de valores organizacionais. *RAUSP Management Journal, 31*(2), 62–72.
Tamayo, A., Mendes, A. M., & Paz, M. G. T. (2000). Inventário de valores organizacionais. *Estudos de Psicologia (Natal), 5*(2), 289–315.
Teixeira, M. L. M. (2008). *Dignidade Organizacional: valores e relações com stakeholders*. In M. L. M. Teixeira (Org.), *Valores humanos & gestão: novas perspectivas* (pp. 81–92). São Paulo: Editora SENAC.
Teixeira, M. L. M., Domenico, S. M. R., & Dias, S. M. R. C. (2011). Proposta e validação de um modelo de Dignidade Organizacional. *Relatório parcial de pesquisa (Tech. Rep.)*. Mackenzie Presbyterian University.
Teixeira, M. L. M., Domenico, S. M. R., Dias, S. M. R. C., & Mendes, L. H. L. (2014). Práticas de Dignidade Organizacional Percebidas por Trabalhadores na Relação entre Organizações e Stakeholders. In *XXXVIII ENANPAD, Rio de Janeiro/RJ*
Welzel, H. (2003) *Direito Penal*. Campinas: Ed. Romana
Whetten, D. A., & Mackey, A. (2002). A social actor conception of organizational identity and its implications for the study of organizational reputation. *Business & Society, 41*(4), 393–414. https://doi.org/10.1177/0007650302238775.

Chapter 13
Dignity in the Application of Microcredit Resources

Gilvanete Dantas de Oliveira Pereira

Abstract This study aimed to understand the application of microcredit resources by members of solidarity groups, in light of dignity. The investigation was carried out through the interpretative approach. A discussion group and 20 face-to-face interviews were conducted with members of solidarity groups, microcredit borrowers. The first relevant result of the survey was that not all microcredit borrowers were popular entrepreneurs, as expected. Among them, there were people who were not entrepreneurs (non-entrepreneurs), who used trickery to deceive microcredit institutions. The second result was that popular entrepreneurs invested the resources: in goods, reservation for payment of microcredit installments, and payment of old bills of the enterprise. The funds received by non-entrepreneurs were to be passed on to entrepreneurs. Dignity in the application of microcredit resources, for different purposes, only makes sense if it is explained as conditional dignity socially and historically constructed varying in space and time. This investigation contributes in a practical way for microcredit organizations to rethink their missions, more updated toward the real needs of popular entrepreneurs.

Keywords Microcredit · Dignity · Resources application

13.1 Introduction

Microcredit aims to eradicate world poverty by 2030 (Microcredit Summit Campaign, 2020). It became known worldwide from the experience of the Grameen Bank in Bangladesh developed by Mahammad Yunus, winner of the Nobel Peace Prize in 2006. Microcredit is a small-value loan (Yunus, 2008), aimed at popular entrepreneurs to help their productive activities (Neri, 2008; Saini et al., 2013). As a guarantee, microcredit uses the social guarantee of solidarity groups (Dantas, 2014).

Besides reducing poverty, microcredit yields benefits such as self-employment (Rahman, 2010; Alves, 2008), women's empowerment (Berlage & Vasudeo 2015)

G. D. de Oliveira Pereira (✉)
Queimadas, Brazil
e-mail: gilvanete.dantas@hotmail.com

M. L. Mendes Teixeira and L. M. B. de Oliveira (eds.), *Organizational Dignity and Evidence-Based Management*, https://doi.org/10.1007/978-3-030-68560-7_13

and the promotion of dignity (Neri, 2008; Yunus 2005). Dignity, in turn, can be understood as what is priceless for man (Kant, 2014) and presents itself in different perspectives, such as the dignities of merit, moral stature, identity, and essence, identified by Tadd et al. (2010).

The dignity subject has spurred the interest of researchers in several areas of knowledge, especially in law (Castilho, 2015; Chan, 2015; Inciarte, 2014; Piosevan, 2010), in nursing (Griffin-Heslin, 2005; Jacobson, 2009), in biotechnology (Chan, 2015; Körtner, 2011), in the universal and positive individual law (Castilho, 2015).

In business, which is the main focus of this work, there are studies, covering issues related to employees, dealing with workers and work dignity (Hodson & Roscigno, 2004; Mattson & Clark, 2011), health and hygiene (Auerbach, 1988), sustainability (Aguado et al., 2015), humanistic business education (Dierksmeier, 2015), job security (Barrett & Thompson, 2012), adaptive business models (Hahn, 2012), moral harassment (Heloani, 2004), alienating work and its reflexes both in the worker's life and at work (Agassi, 1986), dignity at the firm level (Aguado et al., 2017) in the relationship with stakeholders (Teixeira, 2016). Little attention has been given to the issue of dignity in the application of microcredit resources.

Microcredit funds should be invested in working capital or fixed assets (Parente, 2003; Dantas, 2014), but there are reports of investments in general family expenses and home renovations (Shahiar & Shepherd, 2019) and cultural needs (Hulme, 2008). Can the diversion of resources to purposes other than the specific purpose of microcredit be considered a decent behavior on the part of entrepreneurs? In order to address this issue, this study aimed to understand the application of microcredit resources by members of solidarity groups, in light of dignity.

The investigation was carried out through the interpretative approach. A discussion group and 20 face-to-face interviews were conducted with members of solidarity groups, microcredit borrowers in the State of Paraíba, Brazil. The State of Paraíba is located in the Northeastern region of Brazil. It consists of 223 municipalities; it has a surface of 56,468.4 km^2 and an estimated population, in 2020, of 4.1 million inhabitants, according to data of the Brazilian Institute of Geography and Statistics (IBGE, 2020). Microcredit for Solidary Groups has existed in Paraíba since 1994, when the Support Center for Small Enterprises of the State of Paraíba (CEAPE/PB) was founded. The research findings constitute the content of this chapter that aims to reflect on dignity within the scope of microcredit. The analysis and interpretation of the data was carried out through the analysis of interpretative content.

13.2 Microcredit

Microcredit consists of a small loan (Yunus, 2008), geared to poor people (Neri, 2008; Saini et al., 2013), for self-employment (Rahman, 2010), with specifics regarding the form and purpose of the loan (Parente, 2002). The term small value was pointed out as a characteristic of microcredit by several authors (Abdul Khir et al., 2013; Alves, 2008; Carpenter & Williams, 2010), but, as stated by Brown (2010), there are no maximum nor minimums parameters to actually characterize what should be defined as microcredit.

Microcredit is aimed at poor people (Alam, 2013; Alves, 2008; Carpenter & Williams, 2010; Hernandez & Torero, 2013), and what is a poor person? In the microcredit literature, works that are concerned with defining what a poor person is are not frequent. Yunus (2008) considered as poor a person who had a per capita income of less than a dollar a day and claimed that this is the same parameter adopted by the United Nations Organization UN.

Microcredit allows enhancement and creation of self-employment (Alves, 2008; Barone et al., 2002). It makes funds available with the objective of strengthening or creating changes in self-employment, and it contributes to the reduction of unemployment rates (Alves, 2008) and promotes the economic development of the country (Brown, 2010), in addition to providing individual and/or collective benefits to the people involved. It is estimated that, for each entrepreneur given microcredit, four more people are directly benefited (Yunus, 2008).

When a company needs a loan, it has to offer some form of collateral to the financial institution. In the microcredit realm, the business or the entrepreneurs financed do not have, for the most part, assets that can be used as collateral for loans (Barone et al., 2002). And the solution found by the organizations was the release of funds through the Solidarity Groups, which were to be seen as a social guarantee.

The Solidarity Group emerged to replace the current guarantees demanded in other types of financing (Dantas, 2014), as well as the strengthening of its members, acting in a supportive solidarity to expand the business. According to *Accion International*, an institution that brings together the Microcredit Organizations in Latin America, the Solidarity Group is made up of five to eight underprivileged microentrepreneurs who live in urban areas and who are engaged in similar activities within the informal economy and that are organized to lending and other associated benefits such as training and technical assistance (Otero, 1986). Although each member of the group is responsible for his own loan, the group functions as a small social network that provides stimulus, psychological support to deal with the debt (Yunus, 2008).

Unlike the banking logic, in which the customer goes to the bank, in microcredit, a completely revolutionary element was incorporated, in the words of Dantas (2014). Customer service is right there, on the spot. A credit agent, a professional trained by the microcredit institution, goes to the client. He goes to the entrepreneur in the location where he lives and works (Parente, 2002).

In Brazil, microcredit resources are used for economic activity (Dantas, 2014; Parente, 2003), with the immediate objective of investments to be made in working capital or fixed assets (Barone et al., 2002; Dantas, 2014; Parente, 2003). The release of credit for working capital aims to provide the entreprencur with the expansion and diversification of inventories, the reduction of costs and the financing of installment sales (Parente, 2003). Fixed assets financing occurs when funds are allocated to the small company's fixed assets. In this modality, financing is geared to small renovations in the establishment, furniture, utensils, machines, equipment, vehicles, among other items that make up the company's fixed assets (Sá & Sá, 2009).

The purpose of microcredit is the production activity (Barone et al., 2002), not in the strict sense of lending to a company in the industrial sector, but to release funds to be applied in economic activity, to thousands of poor families in the world (Yunus, 2008) or for unemployed people (Alves, 2008), as an alternative for generating employment and income. The release of resources in the form of microcredit constitutes a means to achieve specific purposes, such as the opening of new businesses (Alves, 2008), strengthening of self-employment (Ahmed & Siwar, 2014; Lensink & Pham, 2012) and eradicating world poverty by 2030 (Microcredit Summit Campaign, 2020).

Finally, the ultimate purpose of microcredit is to promote dignity, by enabling entrepreneurs to break their dependence on aids, donations, and other financial supports generated by individual solidarity thus promoting their autonomy (Alves, 2008).

13.3 The True Application of Microcredit Resources

The first relevant result of the survey was that not all microcredit borrowers were popular entrepreneurs, as expected. Among them, there were not entrepreneurs (non-entrepreneurs), who had no business, and thus, they should have not been granted microcredit funds.

According to the survey, non-entrepreneurs used trickery to deceive microcredit institutions, since they were aware of how the organizations worked. They knew what the microcredit agents asked and what documents they asked for during the on-site visit. One of the interviewees, a non-entrepreneur, reported that she had applied for two microcredits for a church friend to help her avoid problems with her husband. According to the interviewee, her friend was in need of microcredit funds because she owed money to a money lender, and if she did not pay, they would tell her husband. The interviewee explained to her friend that she did not know how microcredit worked, but her friend informed her about the whole procedure, including telling her that she would be visited by a credit agent and that she would lend some goods from her business, so that in the interview she could pretend she had an economic activity in the informal market. Other stories of tricks, which hurt the organizational dignity of microcredit institutions, were noticed during the survey, having as their common motivation, helping others on account of family ties or friendships.

Let us see how credit applications were made by popular entrepreneurs (Fig. 13.1).

The popular entrepreneurs interviewed stated that they were aware that the resources should be invested in the purchase of merchandise for business development. Despite this, it was found that, in general, funds had other destinations serving different purposes. Even in the testimonies of those popular entrepreneurs who claimed they invested the resources in the business, contradictions were noticed. One of the indications of these contradictions was the fact that they obtained resources in several microcredit institutions and that they were reticent to explain in what and how they applied the resources.

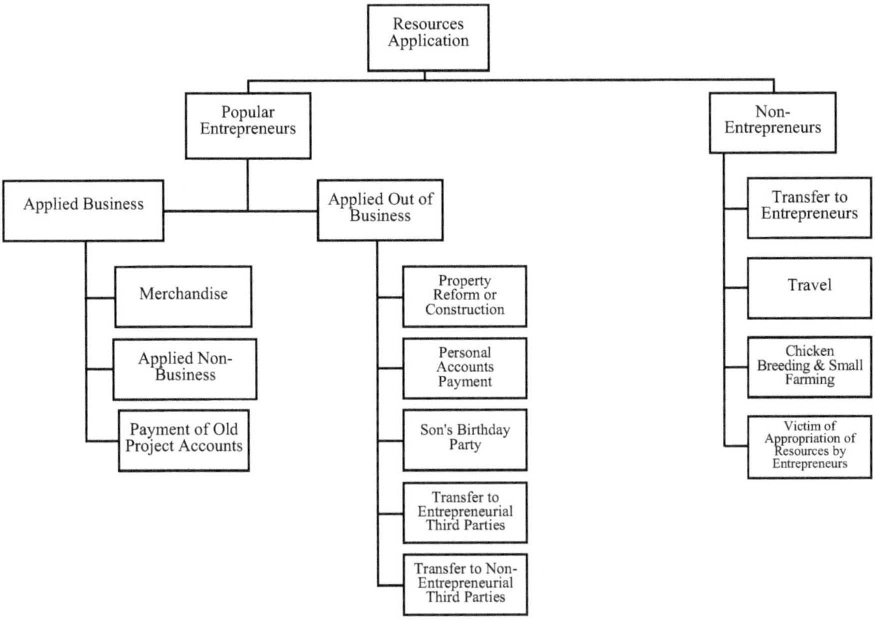

Fig. 13.1 Application of microcredit resources

According to the survey, popular entrepreneurs invested the resources: in goods, reservation for payment of microcredit installments and payment of old bills of the enterprise.

Entrepreneurs who invested the funds in their own business reported that the amount of credit obtained was not invested only in goods, but also for protection against the risk of default or to pay old business debts. As a way of minimizing the risk of not being able to pay the microcredit installments when due, because they could be unable to sell the purchased merchandise, some interviewees stated that they invested the funds in stages. Others said that in order not to run the risk of default, they did not apply all the credit in the purchase of goods, separating the amount of the first installment to be paid as a reserve. Still others said that when they received the funds, they paid bills for goods purchased before they had received the microcredit.

Other interviewees reported that they used the resources not only to invest in their own business, but for other purposes as well, such as remodeling or building houses; payment of personal bills; son's birthday party; transfer of funds to third parties small entrepreneurs; and transfer of funds to non-entrepreneurial third parties.

One respondent stated that she invested the resources in goods, but that she left a reserve to form a "nest egg" for the payment of the installments. During the interview, it was found that the purpose of the "nest egg" was the building of two residential properties, one for her daughter and the other for the interviewee herself. But this was not the only case of investing resources in residential properties. Two other respondents also undertook construction and/or acquisition of properties. One of them mentioned the construction of several properties in order to obtain income through rents, and another for the acquisition of two business sites close to his undertaking. However, the purchase, construction and/or renovations of residential properties that are not related to improving the quality of service provision should not be performed using the microcredit resources (Almonacid & Zuluaga, 2012).

Some entrepreneurs asked for credit amounts higher than what they really needed for the business and used the surplus to pay personal bills necessary for survival, such as water, electricity, and the purchase of medicines. But, there were also cases where the part of the credit that exceeded the business needs was used for purposes that were not related to personal survival, such as having a debutant party for one of her daughters.

Another use by popular entrepreneurs is to transfer funds, either to other small entrepreneurs or to non-entrepreneurs. The transfer of resources to entrepreneurs usually occurs within the solidarity groups themselves. This happens when a member of the group petitions for a higher amount of funds than what he needs and transfers the excess money on to other members of the group or to entrepreneur relatives. This case is also common when a popular entrepreneur does not have a good financial standing and cannot be granted microcredit, so a close relative (brother, husband, mother, father), who is a popular microentrepreneur, petitions for a microcredit and transfers the funds. In this investigation, it was found that the transfer of resources to people in the same group or to people who are not part of the group is based on kinship criteria (son, nephew, grandson, daughter-in-law) or friendship. The transfer to non-entrepreneurs involved close relatives, such as the case of an aunt (popular entrepreneur) who transferred funds to her nephew (non-entrepreneur) to help him set up the room of the baby that was about to be born.

Although all respondents were borrowers of microcredit resources, not all were popular entrepreneurs, as mentioned earlier. Let us see how the investment of funds by non-entrepreneurs developed.

In the investigation, it was found that the funds received by non-entrepreneurs were to be passed on to entrepreneurs. The reason was the need for more resources; that is, entrepreneurs needed more resources than those allowed under the microcredit rules. One of the alternatives found was the setup of solidarity groups that would obtain the financing and pass on the funds entirely to those entrepreneurs who were in need. In other words, the transfer of microcredit resources had been premeditated by the members of the Solidarity Groups, since the setup of the Solidarity Group; the microcredit funds to be received had already been earmarked for not investing in the main objectives of microcredit, which can be configured as an ethical problem.

Another case of investment of resources by a non-entrepreneur detected in the survey was reported by a woman who had received the microcredit funds and allocated them for a trip. The reported reason was that she had made a friendship with someone over the Internet and that she would like to meet him in person and had the opportunity to join a solidarity group and withdraw the funds. She petitioned for the microcredit and was able to fulfill her desire to meet her friend. The microcredit resources should be invested in activities in the urban area, but one of the respondents, a non-entrepreneur, revealed that he used the resources in chicken breeding and in small farming (planting of beans and corn).

In the investigation, the appropriation of resources by a component of a group was observed. The misappropriation of funds occurred through the authority exercised in the relationship between boss and employee. A beauty parlor's employee set up a solidarity group with her employer, and the funds were released to the group leader, in this case, the employer. According to the employee, the employer did not transfer the funds to her. This case can be considered a case of misappropriation of funds.

According to the literature, microcredit should be the credit that supports entrepreneurship (Berlage & Vasudeo, 2015), since its global goal is to eradicate poverty by strengthening self-employment (Daley-Harris, 2007), but the investigation revealed that, according to the interviewees, microcredit is the "credit that works," that is, it is the credit in which the funds that were collected from the microcredit organizations were paid within the term agreed upon between borrowers and the institution. Perhaps this connotation enhances an aspect of microcredit, that of a system that lends resources to those who have no real guarantees to offer, as stated by Dantas (2014), so that the investment of resources in the business is no longer the main focus.

This last perception was reinforced during the holding of the Discussion Group (DG), when one of the participants mentioned that "the resources are granted to purchase goods, but you can use them in whatever you want, because afterward they (the lenders) don't come here." In other words, borrowers of microcredit loans understand that they can use the resources for any purpose they want, as there is no post-credit monitoring. Also, according to the DG, microcredit institutions, after the release of funds, do not monitor where the credit was used, they are only interested in receiving back the installments on time.

13.4 Reflections on Dignity and Microcredit

Since borrowers are not monitored and since post-credit inspection does not exist, but only the charge for payment on time, the borrowers of microcredit funds understand that their commitment with the credit institution is to honor payments within the agreed term. This is a dubious situation from the point of view of dignity. If, on the one hand, borrowers should invest the amounts received in the business and they do not, on the other hand, they are concerned with paying on the due date. Saying that the individual is recognized by others as a person who honors his commitments with third parties and pays within the agreed term can be understood as one of the dimensions of dignity proposed by Tadd et al. (2010), the dignity of the moral status, which among other meanings, means that the individual is recognized as a person who honors his commitments. But on the other hand, the fact that the funds are invested with a purpose that is not the one to which the person has committed, we cannot say that this behavior can be framed in moral dignity. But from the interviewees' point of view their behavior is not unworthy. The fact that the credit institution does not monitor the use of the credit makes them feel free to apply the funds as they wish.

A situation illustrated by one of the interviewees stirs other reflections on the issue of dignity and microcredit. This is the case of a person who transferred part of the credit funds to his nephew to help him set up the room of the child that was about to be born. As an underemployed employee, he would not obtain the required amount from a bank. There is evidence that microcredit can contribute to improving the social status of the individual for, being recognized in society as a person with resources is one of the dimensions of dignity proposed by Tadd et al. (2010), which is the dignity of merit.

Another case that surfaced in the investigation was that of a woman, who was using the microcredit resources to build two "little houses," one for her and one for her daughter. The right to dwelling is indirectly addressed in the Brazilian Federal Constitution. In practice, the government does not have public policies in place that support the poorest in the acquisition or construction of housing. When obtaining microcredit resources and applying part of the funds to housing construction, can it be said that people's behavior is unworthy? The criticism that could be made would be that considering the purpose of microcredit, improvement in the quality of life is occurring directly when it should happen indirectly, that is, building houses through the resources obtained from a business and not directly through the use of microcredit funds. But, there is evidence that microcredit improves quality of life, and this is one of the dimensions of dignity posed by Tadd et al. (2010), which is the dignity of identity, means that the individual has his rights ensured.

Microcredit is an "object of desire" not only by entrepreneurial people, in order to invest in their business and other needs, but also by other people, to meet other needs or to invest in the dream of having a small business. Still, reflecting on decent and unworthy behaviors in microcredit, we display a case observed during the investigation. A man needed a small amount of money to open a small business, but the microcredit institution was unable to assist him, since the microcredit is not intended for opening businesses. The story drew the investigators' attention regarding the aspect of exclusion. The man was 53 years old, was separated, and his profession was bricklayer. For some reason that he did not want to reveal, he could not continue working in the profession until reaching retirement. Considering the way he walked, it is believed that he had some health problem in his spine. His greatest desire, at that time, was to have a small business that would guarantee income for his basic needs (food, water, energy, and gas). Meeting basic needs is guaranteed in the Federal Constitution and is also one of the dimensions of dignity proposed by Tadd et al. (2010), which is the dignity of identity, but the institution could not help him, since he needed the funds for purposes that are not the specific purpose of microcredit.

From the cases exposed, there is an investment of funds that brings dignity to individuals, depending on the dignity approach that is used to assess the situation. In this work, we chose to use the approach proposed by Tadd et al. (2010). These authors, when carrying out a study on human dignity and care for the elderly, found four types of dignity: dignity by merit, dignity of moral status, dignity of identity and *menschenwürde* or essence dignity. Dignity by merit is that which the individual enjoys by obtaining a prominent role or position in society. The dignity of the moral status is about the person's moral autonomy and how he deals with the respect for himself and for others. The dignity of the identity deals with the individual's self-esteem when relating with other individuals. *Menschenwürde* or essence refers to a person's inalienable value. This approach includes both dignity as an inalienable value and acquired dignity. The dignity acquired through actions can be understood as conditional dignity, while the dignity that deals with human rights, as unconditional (Pirson, 2019). *Menschenwürde* dignity (Tadd et al., 2010) corresponds to the unconditional dignity proposed by Pirson (2019).

Unconditional dignity is mostly perceived when the vulnerable parties cry out for protection. This vulnerability can be physical, psychological, social, economic conditional dignity, on the other hand, is related to self-esteem or self-respect, and is better perceived when people feel the need to be valued (Pirson, 2019). It can be said that in the face of a State that does not protect the most vulnerable, it violates the dignity of its citizens and that, in this context, the population that perceives itself as unprotected tries to promote their self-esteem and self-respect through dignity of merit, identity, and morals in the conception of Tadd et al. (2010). These dignities are socially built and have historical roots.

Human dignity should not only be considered as a dignity inherent to the human being, but also with the cultural meaning constructed throughout the history of a society. Dignity stems from the interaction of ontological and intersubjective dimensions involved in historical and cultural aspects and incorporates the social and moral development of society (Sarlet, 2009).

Dignity in the investment of microcredit resources, for different purposes, only makes sense if it is explained as conditional dignity (Pirson, 2019) socially and historically constructed varying in space and time (Sarlet, 2009). The use of microcredit funds for taking a trip, for example, can be better explained if we understand that the dignity of this action is defined by the culture in which borrowers are inserted. Therefore, the concept of the correct application of microcredit resources, from the perspective of borrowers, will vary from culture to culture.

From the above, it can be said that the historical–cultural dimension (Sarlet, 2009) overlaps the dimensions put forward by Tadd et al. (2010). It can also be said that the investment of microcredit resources, under the historical–cultural perspective of dignity, can be carried out for any purpose, since dignity is morally constructed through culture and the development of society itself.

According to the historical–cultural dimension, microcredit borrowers can ignore the rules imposed by microcredit institutions and start trying to find alternatives to obtain microcredit, in order to use it in what gives them dignity, since they do not receive from the State respect for their rights as human beings from the perspective of unconditional dignity (Pirson, 2019).

13.5 Implications for Management

The theoretical assumption is that all solvent customers invest the microcredit resources according to the rules, but the reality is different. Microcredit borrowers invest resources not only in the business, but to satisfy other life needs. The first question that arises is about the management of microcredit by microcredit institutions, but we can say nothing about how this management is done. What in fact occurs in the management of the process is that people who do not develop any economically productive activity take resources and pass them on to third parties. What can be deduced is that the management process is fragile. And here a question arises: Is this fragility intentional, or not? Or perhaps there is a shortage of funds to manage it properly? In any case, it seems unlikely that the institutions are unaware that credit is not always applied in the business, as planned. It seems that what is most important is perhaps to lend and receive the installments on the scheduled dates and that is how the surveyed microcredit borrowers understand that, in fact, this is what the institutions want. And considering that the default rate in microcredit is low, it means that the credit analysis that has been carried out is satisfactory.

Could it be that in financing the different needs of the business and the family, microcredit institutions would actually be taking on a new mission to promote dignity by acting as microfinance institutions and doing so with the resources of microcredit? Would not the reality of investing microcredit resources signal for the institutions the need to steer activities toward microfinance and to promote the dignity of credit borrowers?

The investigation leads us to reflect that the behavior of microcredit borrowers can be considered unworthy when observing what they are doing considering microcredit institutions' rules, showing that it is necessary to evolve toward microfinance, serving not only entrepreneurs, but low-income people who do not have access to microfinance services in general.

13.6 Final Remarks

The aim of this investigation was to understand the application of microcredit resources by members of solidarity groups in light of dignity. Conducting the investigation through a discussion group and face-to-face interviews with people who took out microcredit in the solidarity group modality made it possible to understand that people when applying microcredit resources experience their dignity, under different perspectives, such as merit dignity, moral status or identity (Tadd et al., 2010). These dignities are conditional (Pirson, 2019), and in the case of the credit borrowers interviewed, they reflect the concept of dignity shared by the Northeastern Brazilian society, since the conditional dignity is historical–cultural, woven by society.

This investigation contributes in a practical way for microcredit organizations to rethink new missions, more updated toward the real needs of popular entrepreneurs.

Who knows, they may seek to expand their operations to different businesses or social products such as microfinance for example?

Considering the limitations of this investigation, interviews were only conducted with borrowers of microcredit resources. This is not enough to list the potential (in) dignities of microcredit organizations. Investigation is necessary to understand the dignity of institutions in the relationships created with credit borrowers, in order to obtain a broader view of organizational dignity.

The theme of dignity includes several other studies in the field of microcredit and microfinance, targeting both clients and microcredit organizations. We suggest: dignity meetings in solidarity groups; organizational dignity in microcredit institutions; dignity and leadership in solidarity groups, and dignity as a variable in the analysis of microcredit.

References

Abdul Khir, M. F., Bahroddin Badri, M., & Hussain, L. (2013). Critical appraisal of Rahn-based Islamic microcredit facility from Shari'ah perspective. *American-Eurasian Journal of Sustainable Agriculture, 7*(3), 221–231.

Agassi, J. B. (1986). Dignity in the workplace: Can work be dealienated? *Journal of Business Ethics, 5*, 271–284.

Aguado, R., Alcañiz, L., & Retolaza, J. L. (2015). A new role for the firm incorporating sustainability and human dignity: Conceptualization and measurement. *Human Systems Management, 34*(1), 43–56.

Aguado, R., Retolaza, J. L., & Alcañiz, L. (2017). Dignity at the level of the firm: beyond the stakeholder approach. In M. Kostera & M. Pirson (Eds.). *Dignity and the organization* (Humanism in Business Series, pp. 81–97). Palgrave Macmillan.

Ahmed, F., & Siwar, C. (2014). Impact of microcredit programme on poverty alleviation: A comparative study in Bangladesh and Malaysia. *Advances in Environmental Biology, 8*(7), 2487–2496. https://www.researchgate.net/publication/289363028

Alam, S. (2013). The impact of credit and non-credit aspects on self-employment profit: A comparison of microcredit programs and commercial lenders in rural Bangladesh. *The Journal of Developing Areas, 47*(1), 23–45.

Almonacid, J. A., & Zuluaga, U. (2012). *Manual Genérico Grupos Solidarios Rurales.* (Proyecto BID Rural, Componente 1). Centro ACCIÓN Microempresarial. https://silo.tips/download/manual-generico-grupos-solidarios-rurales

Alves, M. B. (2008). Com o microcrédito, devolver mais dignidade às pessoas. *Revista Migrações, 3*, 271–280. https://www.om.acm.gov.pt/documents/58428/183863/Migr3_Sec3_Art6_PT.pdf

Auerbach, J. (1988). Organized labor: Toward a new dignity in the workplace. *Journal of Career Development, 15*(1), 65–72.

Barone, F. M., Lima, P. F., Dantas, V., & Rezende, V. (2002). *Introdução ao microcrédito.* Conselho do Comunidade Solidária. https://www.bcb.gov.br/htms/public/microcredito/microcredito.pdf

Barrett, J., & Thompson, L. (2012). Returning dignity to labour: Workplace safety as a human right. *New Zealand Journal of Employment Relation, 37*(1), 82–89. https://hdl.handle.net/11072/1499

Berlage, L., & Vasudeo, N. (2015). Microcredit: From hope to scepticism to modest hope. *Enterprise Development and Microfinance, 26*(1), 63–74.

Brown, G. (2010). When small is big: Microcredit and economic development microcredit and economic development. *Open Source Business Resource,* (Novembrer 2010), 14–20. https://timreview.ca/article/392

Carpenter, J., & Williams, T. (2010). Moral Hazard, peer monitoring and microcredit: Field experimental evidence from Paraguay. *Federal Reserve Bank of Boston Working Papers, 10*(6). https://hdl.handle.net/10419/55582
Castilho, R. (2015). *Direitos humanos* (5th ed.). Saraiva.
Chan, D. K. (2015). The concept of human dignity in the ethics of genetic research. *Bioethics, 29*(4), 274–282.
Daley-Harris, S. (2007). *Informe del Estado de la Campaña de la Cumbre de Microcrédito 2007.* Microcredit Summit Campaign. https://www.ruralfinanceandinvestment.org/sites/default/files/State_of_the_Microcredit__ES_pdf.pdf
Dantas, V. A. (2014). Microcrédito e cidadania. In F. Matos, J. Macambira, J., & M. C. Cacciamali. *A atividade e a política de microcrédito no Brasil: visões sobre sua evolução e futuros desafios* (pp. 159–176). IDT, USP.
Dierksmeier, C. (2015). Human dignity and the business of business. *Human Systems Management, 34*(1), 33–42.
Griffin-Heslin, V. L. (2005). An analysis of the concept dignity. *Accident and Emergency Nursing, 13*(4),251–257.
Hahn, R. (2012). Inclusive business, human rights and the dignity of the poor: A glance beyond economic impacts of adapted business models. *Business Ethics: A European Review, 21*(1), 47–63.
Heloani, R. (2004). Assédio moral: um ensaio sobre a expropriação da dignidade no trabalho. *RAE – Eletrônica, 3*(1), 1–8.
Hernandez, M. A., & Torero, M. (2013). Parametric versus nonparametric methods in risk scoring: An application to microcredit. *Empirical Economics, 46*(3), 1057–1079.
Hodson, R., & Roscigno, V. J. (2004). Organizational success and worker dignity: Complementary or contradictory? *American Journal of Sociology, 110*(3), 672–708.
Hulme, D. (2008). The story of the Grameen Bank: From subsidised microcredit to market-based microfinance. *BWPI Working Paper, 60,* 1–11. https://doi.org/10.2139/ssrn.1300930
IBGE. (2020, November 28). *Cidades e Estados: Paraíba.* https://www.ibge.gov.br/cidades-e-estados/pb.html
Inciarte, F. (2014). Contingencia y libre voluntad: observaciones sobre el concepto de la dignidad humana. *Anuario Filosofico, 47*(1), 27–73. https://hdl.handle.net/10171/35628
Jacobson, N. (2009). A taxonomy of dignity: A grounded theory. *BMC International Health and Human Rights, 9*(3), Article 3.
Kant, I. (2014). *Fundamentação da metafísica dos costumes.* Translation A. P. Carvalho. Companhia Editora Nacional.
Körtner, U. H. J. (2011). Human dignity and biomedical ethics from a Christian theological perspective. *HTS Teologiese Studies/Theological Studies, 67*(3), 1–9.
Lensink, R., & Pham, T. T. T. (2012). The impact of microcredit on self-employment profits in Vietnam. *Economics of Transition, 20*(1), 73–111.
Mattson, D. J., & Clark, S. G. (2011). Human dignity in concept and practice. *Policy Sciences, 44,* 303–320.
Microcredit Summit Campaign (2020). *Committed organizations.* https://microcreditsummit.org/featured-commitments.html
Neri, M. (Org.). (2008). *Microcrédito: o mistério nordestino e o Grameen Bank: perfil e performance dos clientes do CredAmigo.* FGV.
Otero, M. (1986). *El concepto del Grupo Solidario: características y significado para las actividades del sector informal.* PACT.
Parente, S. (2002). *Microfinanças: saiba o que é um banco do povo.* AED.
Parente, S. (2003). *Microfinanças passo a passo: saiba como implantar e gerenciar uma organização de microcrédito.* AED.
Piosevan, F. (2010). *Direitos humanos e o direito constitucional internacional* (11th ed.). Saraiva.
Pirson, M. (2019). A humanistic perspective for management theory: Protecting dignity and promoting well-being. *Journal of Business Ethics, 159,* 39–57.

Rahman, S. (2010). Consumption difference between microcredit borrowers and non-borrowers: A Bangladesh experience. *the Journal of Developing Areas, 43*(2), 313–326.
Sá, A. L., & Sá, A. M. A. L. (2009). *Dicionário de contabilidade.* Atlas.
Saini, B., Kumar, M., & Singh, R. (2013). Empowerment of rural women by micro-finance & microcredit scheme. *International Journal of Management, IT and Engineering, 3*(4), 205–218. https://www.indianjournals.com/ijor.aspx?target=ijor:ijmie&volume=3&issue=4&article=017
Sarlet, I. W. (2009). As dimensões da dignidade da pessoa humana: construindo uma compreensão jurídico-constitucional necessária e possível. In Sarlet, I. W. (Ed.), *Dimensões da dignidade: ensaios de filosofia do direito e direito constitucional* (2nd ed., pp. 15–43). Livraria do Advogado.
Shahiar, A. Z. M., & Shepherd, D. A. (2019). Violence against women and new venture initiation with microcredit: Self-efficacy, fear of failure, and disaster experiences. *Journal of Business Venturing, 34*(6), Article 105945.
Tadd, W., Vanlaere, L., & Gastmans, C. (2010). Clarifying the concept of human dignity in the care of the elderly: A dialogue between empirical and philosophical approaches. *Ethical Perspective, 17*(1), 253–281. https://doi.org/10.2143/EP.17.2.2049266.
Teixeira, M. L. M. (2016). Organizational dignity theory: a proposal. *Proceedings of the SemeAd – Seminários em Administração FEA-USP*, São Paulo, SP, Brazil, 19. https://login.semead.com.br/19semead/arquivos/1237.pdf
Yunus, M. (2005). *O banqueiro dos pobres: a revolução do microcrédito que ajudou os pobres de dezena de países.* Ática.
Yunus, M. (2008). *Um mundo sem pobreza: a empresa social e o futuro do capitalismo.* Ática.

Part IV
Dignity in the Relationship Between Suppliers and Customers

Chapter 14
Dignity as Perceived by Suppliers in the Business-to-Business Segment

Guilherme Kosmann and Ronaldo de Lucio

Abstract The business relationship between companies is influenced or even governed by factors such as power, hierarchical position of involved professionals, size, and level of financial dependence between them. In B2B relationships, suppliers can be neglected and considered interchangeable, with prioritization for relationships based on dominance increased profits. Companies tend to have bargaining power over suppliers and customers, and a symmetrical relationship leads to a violation of dignity. This study presents how suppliers evaluate the dignity of customers. For this, the supplier-perceived dignity scale DIGC-B2B was developed and validated. Thereby, with the objective to investigate the concept of what a worthy customer is in the B2B relationship, 109 companies participated. In this way, we sought to expand theoretical knowledge about dignity and contribute to companies in their commercial relations. The periodic monitoring of organizational dignity through the DIGC-B2B scale allows companies to know and monitor how their suppliers perceive them as a dignified company. The dignified relationship between companies can affect purchasing conditions, price, and terms, in addition to the quality of products, and helps associations to evolve in the stages of organizational dignity practices.

Keywords Suppliers · Business to business · Dignity · Firm's dignity

14.1 Introduction

The commercial relationship between legal entities is influenced or even governed by factors such as power, hierarchical position of the professionals involved, size of the companies, and level of financial dependence between them. Such factors can be decisive on how deals are closed.

Companies that are major players in their areas of activity tend to have bargaining power over suppliers and customers. Small companies or companies with a low level of differentiation in their areas of activity tend to be the weakest part of the

G. Kosmann · R. de Lucio (✉)
São Paulo, Brazil
e-mail: ronaldodelucio@uol.com.br

M. L. Mendes Teixeira and L. M. B. de Oliveira (eds.), *Organizational Dignity and Evidence-Based Management*, https://doi.org/10.1007/978-3-030-68560-7_14

business relationship. A supplier's strong dependence on a customer can have a direct impact on the way business is conducted. There are companies that impose long-term payment to their suppliers as a condition for doing business, which clearly favors to a great extent the purchasing company over the selling company. Other organizations impose commercial conditions in relation to the prices charged that can impact the form and quality of products or services offered. Information and power asymmetric relations lead to the violation of dignity (Jacobson, 2009).

The concept of organizational dignity was first used by Margolis (1997), who stated that organizations need other values besides economic values, such as ethics, contribution to the community, and dignity. The author first used the term "organizational dignity" when proposing a model for organizations that would respect and promote their workers' dignity. Teixeira (2016) extended the scope of organizational dignity to all stakeholders outside the organization and did not restrict his analysis to the company's employees.

Organizational dignity (OD) must be assessed by different stakeholders (Teixeira, 2016). A literature review showed studies in which the OD was evaluated from the perspective of employees (Santana, 2011; Medeiros & Teixeira, 2017), end customers of service companies (Ferreira, 2014), and members of communities that surround companies' sites (Araujo, 2011).

This study proposed a different approach: to identify how suppliers evaluate the dignity of customers in the business-to-business relationship. For this purpose, it was necessary to initially identify what characterizes OD from the suppliers' perspective, and then develop a measurement scale that would allow an assessment to be carried out and finally apply it to suppliers of a service company.

This study aimed at expanding the theoretical knowledge about dignity and contributing with companies that are interested in improving their relationships with suppliers, by monitoring the dignity of business activities as perceived by their suppliers.

14.2 Dignity of the Company

In order to assess and implement human dignity practices and address issues related to morality within organizations, Aguado et al. (2017) present a model to allow companies to discuss these issues in the business context. To provide guidance on the development and use of this approach, the authors relied on Integrative Social Contracts Theory (ISCT), Maslow's hierarchy of needs, and Herzberg's two-factor theory and stakeholders' theory. The recommendation is based on the understanding that considering human dignity and morality, as key elements, when developing business strategies, operations, and daily decision-making, can help align social interests with the behavior of companies.

As a result of current discussions on the role of organizations in society and after the 2008 financial crisis, as pointed out by Aguado et al. (2017) a new positioning of companies in the social context was proposed. This discussion stems from the loss of organizations' legitimacy due to the predominance of the short-term profit maximization concept; there is still a belief that maximizing profits is the only possible strategy, leaving no room for moral discussions regarding the company's objectives or participation in social issues. However, in the authors' perception, human dignity and social well-being should be placed at the core of the organizations' economic activity and should be part of the business outcome.

Certainly, proposing the concept of human dignity within the organizations has great relevance, according to Milczarczyk (2017); this concept has a high value and stands above any price thought; dignity is not a gift, it is not donated, and the individual does not need to offer or do anything in exchange to deserve it; the individual is born with dignity which is inherent to the human being, and when dignity is under attack, it is necessary to act to recover it. Hodson (2001), also cited by Aguado et al. (2017), argues that life demands dignity and it represents the individual's ability to establish value and self-respect, in addition to recognizing and giving importance to the respect of others.

Furthermore, for those authors, dignity is based on politics, economics, and work; it is based on politics through the pursuit of democracy and justice, on economy when seeking decent wages and equal opportunities at work, through actions that seek to curb abuse and the desire to be proud of the daily work.

Along the same line, Bolton (2007) states that dignity, in the field of social sciences, has always been used to express concerns in aspects such as work and, according to him, dignity should be understood as a human need. He reports that the first writings related to human aspects in the work setting vaguely dealt with the dignity revealed by the Maslow's hierarchy of needs and later by the supporters of work humanization, underscoring that more recently, more dignity in work conditions has been demanded.

In parallel, in order to use the ISCT guidance, Aguado et al. (2017) reexamined the theory with the objective of positioning the relationship between society and companies as a macrosocial contract subject to moral conditions; thus, for the contract to be considered moral, it must be consistent with the hypernorms, which, in turn, protect human dignity and social well-being. Hypernorms are based on established universal principles, such as the Universal Declaration of Human Rights, International Covenant on Civil and Political Rights, as well as other global scope initiatives. Thus, through the development of micronorms in line with hypernorms and the macrosocial contract, companies can adapt these concepts to their own culture and activities. Scholz et al. (2019) also consider ISCT to be a significant way of approaching business ethics, besides serving as a way to assist managers to review business ethics; for those authors, through hypothetical social contracts, the ISCT establishes a basis for moral legitimacy in business decision-making processes and this legitimation is complete when obligations are fulfilled.

Donaldson (2013) showed that the objective of ISCT is to use the concept of social contracts in economic activities, as a way to facilitate the understanding of commercial responsibilities and obligations. As a result of the combination of two types of social contracts, the micro and the macro, the author added to the theory the wording integrative, considering them as the main components of the established principle, yielding macrosocial and microsocial contracts. Still according to Donaldson (2013), the ISCT defines three types of hypernorms: the procedural hypernorms that express the conditions of the macrosocial and microsocial contracts, the substantive hypernorms that characterize the elementary principles of right and wrong, good and bad, being exogenous to the macrosocial and microsocial contracts, and the structural hypernorms that identify and ensure essential rights and principles, such as the right to property.

The macrosocial contract is a hypothetical agreement to understand all economic arrangements between contracting parties and contractors based on morality to guide preferences and basic values; based on the community, it can help to optimize economic and social interests. Norms of ethical behavior are established through microsocial contracts, generating contracts that establish rules for its members, becoming authentic when they reflect attitudes and behaviors agreed by the community; thus, the ethical and practical rules guide the economic communities. However, even if a standard is considered authentic and if it does not respect the universal principles, called hyper-standards, it ceases to create a binding obligation for the members of the community. According to Donaldson (2013), hypernorms are principles that constitute norms by which all other norms must be judged. Therefore, norms compatible with hypernorms become totally legitimate and create morally binding obligations.

Aguado et al. (2017) use Maslow's hierarchy of needs to incorporate the concept of human dignity within organizations, so that it is possible to convert hypernorms into micronorms and enable the monitoring of the implementation and evolution of human dignity at the microlevel. From the authors' perspective, human dignity, once incorporated in the companies, occurs when interested people who interact with the business are enabled to reach the state of self-realization; in this way, the results obtained on the development of the concept are evaluated.

Therefore, Aguado et al. (2017), established three stages in the monitoring of human dignity, based on Maslow's hierarchy of needs: (1) correcting the terms of dignity—when organizations are still unable to meet the physiological and security needs of individuals; (2) improve dignity—when social needs and self-esteem needs are not met; and (3) maintain dignity terms—when companies are able to meet the self-fulfillment needs of individuals. In this case, the hypernorm is converted into a micronorm, so that human dignity is linked to the level of self-realization of people who are part of or interact with the company. Thus, in the context of the hierarchy of needs, it is possible to interconnect the company's management systems and assess whether there is respect and promotion of human dignity. The authors also consider that regardless of the situation, whether they are meeting or not, whether partially or not, in relation to promoting human dignity, the most important point is the opportunity for change. Individuals according to Dye (2013) can be motivated by natural and universal human needs and still ordered hierarchically. Thus, one need may be more important than another due to the environment, allowing a need to be fulfilled only after the previous deprivation needs are fulfilled. The author suggests that understanding employees' needs can help motivate, as they are supposed to be motivating. Maslow's work shows that human beings share needs established through a hierarchy of satisfaction, represented in the form of a pyramid (physiological, security, social, esteem, and fulfillment needs); the needs at the bottom of the pyramid represent the most basic needs; that is, the physiological needs and without these being met, there will be no motivation to pursue higher-up tier needs. The second tier involves security needs, covering an environment of physical, emotional, and stable security (e.g., stable employment, benefits to take care of personal and family health). Once this second tier of the pyramid is overcome, the employee finds motivation to continue his ascension. The sequence of social needs includes the need of belonging, which involves affection and relationships with others. At this point, Dye (2013) exposes that managers who are aware of this hierarchy level can promote an organizational culture that facilitates coexistence and creates a feeling of belonging.

The next need categorized by Maslow represents the need for esteem which refers to the need for personal and social fulfillment such as rewards and recognition. This category involves internal and external organization's environment, encompassing internal needs that refer to feelings of accomplishment and self-respect and external needs that refer to external recognition of success and social status. At the top of the pyramid, the last need is self-realization, a situation in which the individual can affirm that he is what he could be, having met his/her highest needs, and feels fulfilled as a person and as a professional (Dye, 2013).

Regarding Herzberg's two-factor theory—the two-factor theory or motivation-hygiene theory, Aguado et al. (2017) state that the use of Herzberg's theory in this context, in parallel with the Integrative Social Contracts Theory—ISCT and Maslow's hierarchy of needs, contributes to making it possible to differentiate companies that are oriented toward promotion of human dignity. According to Basset-Jones (2013), the theory is based on two distinct categories: The first one lists the sources of job satisfaction that include the nature of the work itself, the achievements of employees, recognition by the hierarchy and co-workers, possibilities of promotion, and opportunities to take on new responsibilities; the category related to dissatisfaction occurs when there are no adequate management policies or processes, absence of supervision and work conditions, in addition to lack of adequate compensation, cleanliness, and security, among other factors. The sources of satisfaction were named by Herzberg "motivating factors" and the sources of dissatisfaction "hygiene factors"; the hygiene factors, when not available, besides causing dissatisfaction can neutralize the motivating factors. Thus, companies that work on motivating and hygiene factors have more committed, engaged, and satisfied employees; there is less turnover, and employees have opportunities to reach the top of the Maslow pyramid (Aguado et al. 2017).

Finally, Aguado et al (2017) include the theory of stakeholders, arguing that all people who interact with the company should have a treatment based on dignity. According to Phillips (2003), managing stakeholders goes beyond simply seeking maximum return to shareholders; he emphasizes that paying attention to the interests of those who contribute to the results of the organization is the core objective of the theory, in addition to addressing morals and values as central characteristics of an organization. According to Phillips et al. (2019), business is the result of relationships between different groups that have genuine interests in the activities of organizations and on which organizations depend to achieve their goals. Thus, stakeholders, customers, suppliers, employees, and shareholders work to create value. In addition, they enhance the role of standards, values, and ethics which are essential and indispensable to the theory of the stakeholders. The model presented by Aguado et al. (2017) has a verticalized sequential orientation, in which human dignity, absorbed as a hypernorm, directs the entire order related to activities within organizations that seek to promote this concept. In this way, human dignity becomes a basic and reference concept to guide decisions in organizations, and it becomes a hypernorm of universal scope, thus becoming a common tool among all specific norms, that is, macronorms and micronorms. The macrocontracts, on a global level, represent the relationships between contractors from different communities, are influenced by the hypernorms, and influence the microcontracts. Microcontracts, at the level of specific communities, represent companies, national and international economic organizations, professional organizations, departments of companies, and industries, and are influenced by hypernorms and macrocontracts. These agreements reflect shared understandings about moral norms—micronorms.

The implementation and control tools suggested by Aguado et al. (2017) are based on Maslow's hierarchy of needs, Herzberg's two-factor theory and stakeholder theory as set out below (Basset-Jones 2013; Dye 2013; Phillips 2003; Phillips et al. 2019):

> Maslow's hierarchy of needs: three levels of monitoring human dignity practices: (1) in the stages in which psychological and security needs are still not met, it is necessary to correct the terms related to dignities; (2) in a stage in which social and esteem needs are not yet met—improve dignity; and (3) when met or when searching to meet the needs of self-realization—maintain the terms of dignity in organizations.
>
> Herzberg two-factor theory: It contributes to making it possible to differentiate companies that are oriented toward the promotion of human dignity. Based on two separate categories, the first related to sources of job satisfaction: nature of work, employees' achievements, recognition by the hierarchy and co-workers, possibilities of promotion, and opportunities to take over new positions; sources of dissatisfaction: perceived absences of adequate management policies or processes, absence of supervision, work conditions, and inadequate compensation.
>
> Stakeholders' theory: The analysis of the self-realization concept must go beyond the company's employees and involve the entire group of people affected by the company's actions or omissions. All interactions between people and the company must be treated based on dignity.

The promotion of an organizational culture with internal policies and standards designed and aligned with the model's proposal, that is, focusing on the universal moral proposition that is the established hypernorm, with the hierarchy of needs as an initial internal guide and work based on the theories of the two factors covering all stakeholders, should align the company with the promotion of human dignity as advocated by Aguado et al. (2017).

14.3 Business to Business—B2B

Business to business (B2B) is transaction carried out between companies in the most different branches of activities, products, and services. These activities take place from the relationship arising out of a single sale, generally of materials that are not included in the buyer's production process, accessory materials for use, among others, in administrative tasks, a continuous supply of products and services. The commercial relationship that involves the supply of products that are part of the production process and/or products has different specificities; in this case, we seek more lasting relationships, the demand can be greater and more complex, a longer sales process is required, and in some situations, even investments to win the customer, as well as many visits, meetings, folders, tests, prototypes, among others are required. Therefore, in the sales processes aspects related to the needs to be fulfilled by the products, demographic and economic characteristics aligned with the offer, in addition to personal and behavioral aspects, should be considered; on the other hand, in addition to a professional buyer, there are also situations that require negotiation skills. Despite the B2B seller often having a greater negotiation margin, a buyer under pressure by the organization can conduct tense, detailed and uninteresting negotiations from the financial and economic standpoint.

According to van Zeeland et al. (2018), differences between the B2B and B2C (business to consumer) markets have been emphasized, specifically with regard to purchasing behavior. One of the typical differences between consumer and industry purchasing behavior is the number of players involved in the process; industrial purchasing is characterized mainly as performed by several people that is made up of buying groups instead of individual buyers. The authors also point out that there is a difference in relation to the character of the purchasing process—industrial purchasing behavior is considered to be more professional and more regulated by decision guidelines.

In view of the above, in the context of B2B no impulse buying occurs, as in the case of electronic retail businesses or street shops, malls, etc. All purchases are based on defined needs, strict technical specifications, well-designed and standardized purchasing processes, and in cases involving long-term supply, the cost–benefit of the transaction is assessed and contracts, rules, and assigned responsibilities exist. As reported by van Zeeland et al. (2018), purchasing decisions may involve the participation of other employees, besides the buyers: These are the employees who will use the products or services; thus, they can contribute to the negotiation and evaluation, which requires an advisory sales process.

In addition, the complexity of the decision and the risk involved is seen as another difference between consumer (B2C) and industrial (B2B) purchases, according to van Zeeland et al. (2018). The industrial buyer often has to deal with a higher level of complexity, both in the product and in the process, than a consumer. In the business-to-business relationship, Harrison-Walker and Neeley (2004) emphasize the parties' interest in maintaining long-term relationships, since transactions carried out in B2B settings are generally of high added value. Several authors have focused on the business-to-business segment in their studies (Gorla, Chiravuri & Chinta, 2017; Subramanian, 2018; Flanigan & Obermier, 2016; Skjølsvik, 2016), but none of them conceptualized what the business-to-business market is. Winch (2008), although also not conceptualizing the business-to-business market, points out that this market can be composed of high value-added services, such as accounting, legal, design and advertising services, as well as some lower added value, such as cleaning.

Purchasing companies need regular supply, and the type of relationship and the supplier's selection is essential to avoid interruptions and losses in their business. In the business relationship between companies, there is no room for mistaken purchases or defects; errors in this process, in addition to putting at risk the production progress, can cause losses and could mar the corporate image. Thus, organization cooperation is essential for their success.

Borella et al. (2017) enhance that in all formats of supply chains there is the presence of B2B relationship, especially the importance of cooperation. They argue that a supply chain is successful when there is a good relationship between suppliers and customers, in addition to all logistic and operational guidance.

Thus, as a seller, we should evaluate the customer's acquisition cost, the sales process time, the strategies aimed at a lasting relationship and that bring recurring revenues to the business, with higher added value sales, new commercial opportunities that will occur if the relationship is based on trust and transparency. Long-lasting relationships are developed when scalability, predictability, innovation, and competitive prices are offered in order to contribute to the clients' improved results. In addition to permanently caring for the image and reputation and presenting adequate values, it is important to be a facilitator with optimized sales processes, offering alternative contact channels, efficient workflows, quality of service, and continuous investments in innovation.

In the framework of B2B, there are many studies on the relationship between suppliers and customers; according to Hudnurkar and Ambekar (2019), most of them mainly focused on the performance and development of suppliers with a buyer-oriented approach; however, the suppliers' satisfaction with their customers has been little studied and ascribes this divergence to the existence of a power imbalance between these two agents; however, they emphasize the importance of this knowledge, since supplier satisfaction affects the quality of the relationship in the aspects of trust and communication between the parties.

They emphasize that, according to the evolution and competition within a supply chain, the relationship between buyer and supplier gains importance, since, as mentioned, a strategic relationship, an approach with a long-term view, helps to improve the results for buyers. However, the purchasing companies should look at suppliers as partners, so that any change in the dynamics of commercial relations creates a win–win situation.

Another key point in the B2B relationship is trust; as Frederico and Ferreira (2018) put it, trust brings the conviction that all responsibilities in the commercial relationship will be fulfilled by the parties involved; trust is built over time, based on behaviors that demonstrate cooperation, performance, and the absence of opportunistic occurrences that harm or exploit the other party; thus, over time, trust becomes an instrument that will contribute to the solution of conflicts in a more favorable way. According to those authors, behavioral aspects, such as integrity, intentions, predictability, openness, description, ethics, as well as operational competence, are characteristics that build trust in the B2B relationship. The lack of trust prevents the development of strong and long-lasting partnerships, especially when there is an imbalance of power as dealt with by Habib et al. (2015), because in the buyer–supplier relationship, both agents invest in the commercial relationship; however, when a stronger player explores his position to the detriment of the weaker player, an unproductive relationship develops with potential permanent damage to a partnership that could have been very productive for both.

14.4 Worthy Customer in the Suppliers' Conception

In order to investigate the conception of what a worthy customer is in the B2B relationship, Kosmann (2018) interviewed procurement professionals from 109 companies located in the city of São Paulo, Brazil. These companies operate in different fields and have different sizes. A total of 70 managers and 39 professionals participated in the survey, all of them with seniority and experience in the sales area. One professional per company, qualified to offer his/her opinion about what is a worthy customer in the B2B relationship, participated. To conduct the investigation, these professionals were asked by means of a form to be filled out electronically, what they considered to be a worthy customer in the B2B relationship.

The responses collected were treated through content analysis (Bardin, 2011). This procedure generated 223 sentences, which were grouped into 11 categories: (1) respect: 41 expressions (18%); moral/ethics: 39 expressions (17%); compliance: 39 expressions (17%); commitment: 29% expressions (13%); collaboration: 19 expressions (9%); appreciation: 8 expressions (4%); honor: 8 expressions (4%); transparency: 6 expressions (3%); loyalty: 6 expressions (3%); admiration: 1 expression, without percentage representation; and 27 expressions that could not be categorized. To continue with the analysis, categories were selected with a minimum concentration of 15 expressions, resulting in 167 expressions subdivided into four categories.

- Compliance: action to comply, to perform;
- Respect: reverence;
- Commitment: agreement, adjustment, obligation;
- Moral/ethics: set of rules of conduct/branch of knowledge that studies human conduct.

The allocation of sentences in the five categories enabled a better understanding of what suppliers understand to be a worthy customer in the B2B relationship. Below are the phrases that represent each of the categories.

Compliance: They honor commitments on time; pay their bills; fulfill the orders requirements in their entirety; fulfill their responsibilities; fulfill their part of the negotiation; fulfill the obligations agreed in the contract; fulfill their rights and duties; fulfill their obligations; fulfill their role in the chain (payment); comply with the agreement; and fulfill their commitments.

Respect: They base their relations with the company on fair values and consistent with good practices; treat employees who offer services with dignity; make honest and sincere comments about products and services; respect the service and safety protocol for the quality of the service provided; treat everyone with respect; respect the rules of the contracted service; respect their employees; respect their suppliers; and respect customers.

Commitment: They seek to purchase products/services from an ethical and sustainable company; value all the work that the company develops to serve the customer in the best possible way; value respect and professionalism; value the capacity, knowledge, and commitment of the entire team of the supplying company through the person of the seller; value the service provided; know that their supplier must be treated as a business partner; and carry out all negotiations, focusing both the interests of the company they work for, and the interests of their supplier. Honor the commitments assumed with the supplier.

Moral/Ethics: They act honestly regardless of the situation; focus their responsibilities ethically; pay for the service provided in a fair manner; tell the truth; work with personality; act correctly; do not seek to take advantage of the supplier's company to the point of making a good relationship unfeasible; and use ethics as a guideline in the relations with suppliers.

The four categories indicated by the suppliers can be considered as the hypernorms referred to by Aguado et al. (2017) that will guide macrocontracts and microcontracts. According to the result of the survey, suppliers consider worthy customers who are guided by hyper-standards in carrying out contracts with their suppliers. They are worthy customers who honor their commitments (compliance); they respect employees, customers, and suppliers (respect), and carry out all negotiations, targeting both the interests of the company they work for, and the interests of their supplier (commitment); they act honestly regardless of the situation (morals/ethics).

14.5 How to Assess the Dignity of Customers in the B2B Relationship

Kosmann (2018), from the qualitative survey presented in the previous section, following the procedures suggested by Hinkin (1998), developed a scale to assess the dignity of customers in the B2B relationship. The DIGC-B2B scale consists of 22 items and includes the categories identified in the qualitative survey.

Fulfillment

- Fulfills his responsibilities;
- Does his part of the negotiation;
- Complies with his duties;
- Fulfills his obligations;
- Complies with what he has agreed with the company;
- Complies with his commitments.

Compliance

- Complies with established deadlines;
- Complies with the service protocol to achieve the quality of the service provided;
- Treats everyone with respect;
- Respects the agreements entered into.

Commitment

- Values the service provided;
- Knows that his supplier must be treated as a business partner;
- Honors his commitments;
- Honors deadlines;
- Honors payments;
- Honors contracts.

Moral/Ethics

- Acts honestly regardless of the situation;
- Fulfills his responsibilities with ethics;
- Pays fairly for the service provided;
- Tells the truth;
- Works with personality;
- Acts correctly.

Each item is evaluated using a 6-point Likert scale response: 1—Does not reflect the organization at all; 2—does not reflect the organization; 3—reflects the organization a little; 4—reflects on average the organization; 5—reflects the organization; and 6—reflects the organization a lot. Points 5 and 6 are the only ones that reflect a positive assessment of dignity practices toward suppliers. Points 1 to 4 indicate the need for improvement. The scale is composed of a single factor called "complies with his responsibilities," summarizing the understanding of what suppliers consider a worthy customer in the B2B relationship.

The DIGC-B2B scale was applied to evaluate an institution in the educational field—IESM (fictitious name)—located in the city of São Paulo. The educational institution has undergraduate and graduate courses in distance learning. At the undergraduate level, at the time of the survey, the institution deployed 46 courses concentrated in colleges and 13 postgraduate courses covering different areas of knowledge, from humanities to technological sciences. Such a multiplicity of offers translates into a large volume of purchases (totaling 21 thousand acquisitions in 2017), distributed in 114 purchasing categories and a roster of its suppliers that includes more than 13 thousand entries.

The reasons behind IESM suppliers' selection for this investigation were the extent of supplier's categories, corresponding to the purchase categories, which allowed suppliers from different segments to be included in the study. The investigation used an accidental and convenience non-probabilistic sample, in which the elements are chosen according to the researcher's convenience (Aaker et al., 2008). The sample was composed of business contacts from companies with active registration (with at least one business transaction in the last two years) with the database of the educational institution in question, and who held different positions (salespeople, sales representatives, supervisors, coordinators, C-level managers, and executives), depending on the size of the company and the type of business relationship established between the parties.

Data collection was performed electronically, resulting in 108 suppliers participating in the survey. The data were analyzed using the SPSS software (Statistical Package for the Social Sciences), by calculating Cronbach's alpha reliability index (0.990), descriptive analysis, and main components.

The principal component analysis showed a KMO (Kaiser–Meyer–Olkin-measure of sampling adequacy—MAS) of 0.964 and Sig 0.000, commonality ranging from 0.697 to 0.932, with no need to exclude items from the scale. The principal component analysis and the varimax rotation indicated that the scale is composed of a single factor with an eigenvalue of 18.306, explaining 83.208% of the variance. The dimensionality of a measure refers to the homogeneity of items, with unidimensional measurements in which a single factor or latent variable explains most of the variation associated with the interrelationship between items. In the case of a supposedly unidimensional construct, the unidimensionality of a scale that operationalizes it is a requirement for its reliability and validity (Ribeiro & Veiga, 2011).

The DIGC-B2B scale developed by Kosmann (2018) allows the assessment of organizational dignity from the standpoint of suppliers in relation to their corporate clients in the B2B context.

14.6 Assessment of Organizational Dignity: The Actual Case of IESM

In view of the unidimensionality of the DIGC-B2B scale, to assess the perception of suppliers who participated in the IESM survey, the responses to the items that comprised the categories compliance, respect, commitment, morals, and ethics were reviewed. This procedure allowed for a diagnosis that generates support for improving dignity practices in relation to suppliers.

The data indicated that the compliance category registered 86.88% of the responses concentrated in points 5—reflects the organization and 6—reflects the organization a lot, with 31.64% and 55.25%, respectively. The other categories showed the same pattern of responses, with concentrations in points 5 and 6. The respect category presented 31.48% and 53.24%, respectively; commitment 27.78% and 57.41%; and moral and ethics 25.93 and 59.26%.

Analyzing the score distribution for each of the sentences presented, the large concentration of evaluations 5 and 6 becomes evident. This concentration can be explained by the characteristics inherent to transactions in the B2B segment. According to van Zeeland et al. (2018), industrial buying behavior is considered to be more professional and more regulated by decision guidelines and, according to Harrison-Walker and Neeley (2004), enhances the parties' interest in maintaining long-term relationships.

IESM is an organization with more than 100 years of existence, with a solid reputation that makes it one of the most admired companies in its segment. It is positioned publicly as a solid institution guided by ethical and Christian principles. You do not build a reputation overnight or from a relationship with one type of stakeholder. Over time, IESM has had the opportunity to build a relationship with its suppliers, which does not mean that there is no opportunity for improvement. In the case of IESM, two items show potential for improvement: "complies with established deadlines" and "provides fair payments."

Despite the high rate of responses indicating that IESM is assessed positively by its suppliers, it is important to look for points where improvement in organizational dignity practices can be obtained, reviewing the items that were given the lowest evaluation rates.

14.7 Dignity Perceived by Suppliers: Implications for Management

The periodic monitoring of organizational dignity through the application of the DIGC-B2B scale allows the client company to know and monitor how its suppliers perceive it as a dignified company. The diagnosis is made through the score obtained by the company in the categories compliance, respect, commitment and morals and ethics, identifying in which categories it is best and worst evaluated. The improvement points are found using the mean of the evaluations obtained for each item of the scale. From there, it becomes possible to list which practices will be the focus of attention, with a view to improvement and to monitor development.

The dignity of a company as perceived by its suppliers could influence the purchasing conditions such as price and term and even the quality of the products sold. The recognition of a dignified behavior by a client company in relation to its suppliers can contribute to obtaining better price and payment terms with suppliers, since it strengthens trust relationships over time.

Assessing the dignity of the relationship between suppliers and customers in the B2B context can be a complementary dimension to the performance assessment of the purchasing areas and an ancillary management tool.

14.8 Final Remarks

In B2B commercial relations, depending on the asymmetry of power, suppliers may be neglected. Client companies may consider that suppliers are interchangeable, giving priority to the lowest price in relationships based on dominance, dictating business terms and implying threats in reluctance situations, with an evident interest in increasing their own profits to the detriment of the other party (Sisodia et al. 2018). The firm's dignity model proposed by Aguado et al. (2017) contributes to equating B2B relationships.

The International Covenant on Economic, Social and Cultural Rights and even the Guide for CEOs on Sustainable Development Goals can form the hypernorms, essential in the model of Aguado et al. (2017), containing guidelines exogenous to macrocontracts and microcontracts established by organizations. The categories identified by Kosmann (2018) can be considered as micronorms, establishing rules of ethical and moral behavior capable of guiding the microcontracts established between suppliers and customers in B2B relationships. In the categories listed by Kosmann (2018), the issue of morality with conduct guided by ethical principles is included, with consequent treatment within the concepts of human dignity according to the model presented by Aguado et al. (2017).

The categories identified by Kosmann (2018) contribute to the operationalization of the Aguado et al. (2017) model in the B2B relationship. The compliance category, which means fulfilling an obligation, involves fulfilling the responsibilities in the negotiation, duties, and obligations in relation to an agreement, complying with the commitment assumed. The respect category covers the established deadlines, the service protocols, the treatment with respect for all involved, and the deals made. The commitment category expands the view of a worthy customer by displaying the value of the service provided (besides the price and the product), adding the knowledge, commitment, respect, and professionalism of the sales team, considering the supplier as a business partner. Morals and ethics compose a set which precedes all the actions involved and underlies the other categories. Suppliers expect from a relationship in the B2B context, initiatives that involve honesty regardless of the situation, as well as responsibility and transparency.

Monitoring the assessment of a client's organizational dignity in the B2B relationship through the categories proposed by Kosmann (2018) helps organizations to evolve in the stages of organizational dignity practices in order to become companies on keep the terms of dignity stage, which (in humans) is equivalent to the self-actualization stage proposed by Maslow (see Aguado et al. 2017).

References

Aguado, R., Retolaza, J. L. & Alcañiz, L. (2017). Dignity at the level of the firm: Beyond the stakeholder approach. In M. Monika Kostera & M. Pirson (Eds), *Dignity and the organization* (pp. 81–97). Palgrave Macmillan.

Aaker, D. A., Kumar, V., & Day, G. S. (2008). *Pesquisa de Marketing*. São Paulo: Atlas.

Araujo, B. F. V. B. (2011). *Dignidade no âmbito da relação entre Empresas e Comunidade*. São Paulo, SP, Brazil: Tese de Doutorado. Universidade Presbiteriana Mackenzie.

Bardin, L. (2011). *Análise de conteúdo*. São Paulo: Edições 70,

Basset-Jones, N. (2013). Two-factor theory (and job enrichment). In E. H. Kessler (Ed.), *Encyclopedia of Management theory, 2* (pp. 907–910). Thousand Oaks: Sage.

Bolton, S. C. (2007). Dignity in and at work: Why it matters. In S. C. Bolton (Eds.), *Dimensions of dignity at work* (pp. 3–16). Butterworth-Heinemann–Elsevier

Borella, M. R. C., Barcellos, P. F. P., Sachdev, H., Merz, G. R., & Galelli, A. (2017). Organizational structure, service capability and its impact on business performance of logistics providers in the B2B context. *Revista Gestão & Produção., 24*(2), 355–369. https://doi.org/10.1590/0104-530x1538-16.

Donaldson, T. J. (2013). Integrative social contracts theory. In E. H. Kessler (Ed.), *Encyclopedia of management theory, 1* (pp. 387–389). Thousand Oaks: Sage.

Dye, K. (2013). Needs hierarchy. In E. H. Kessler (Ed.), *Encyclopedia of management theory, 2* (pp. 503–505). Thousand Oaks: Sage.

Ferreira, M. S. (2014). *Dignidade e Valores Organizacionais Percebidos pelo Cliente*. São Paulo, SP, Brazil: Dissertação de mestrado. Universidade Presbiteriana Mackenzie.

Flanigan, R. L., & Obermier, T. R. (2016). An Assessment of the use of social media in the industrial distribution business-to-business market sector. *The Journal of Technology Studies, 42*(1), 18–28.

Frederico, E., & Ferreira, M. P. C. (2018). Determinantes da intenção de continuidade no relacionamento entre pequenos varejistas de materiais de construção hidráulicos. *Remark - Revista Brasileira de Marketing, 17*(2), 237–250.

Gorla, N., Chiravuri, A., & Chinta, R. (2017). Business-to-business e-commerce adoption: An empirical investigation of business factors. *Information Systems Frontiers, 19*(3), 645–667.

Habib, F., Bastl, M., & Pilbeam, C. (2015). Strategic responses to power dominance in buyer-supplier relationships. *International Journal of Physical Distribution & Logistics Management, 45*(1/2), 182–203.

Harrison-Walker, L., & Neeley, S. (2004). customer relationship building on the internet in B2B marketing: A proposed typology. *Journal of Marketing Theory and Practice, 12(1)*, 19–35. Retrieved June 20, 2020, from https://www.jstor.org/stable/40470122

Hinkin, T. R. (1998). A brief tutorial on the development of measures for use in survey questionnaires. *Organizational Research Methods, 1*(1), 104–121.

Hodson, R. (2001). *Dignity at work*. Cambridge: Cambridge University Press.

Hudnurkar, M., & Ambekar, S. S. (2019). Framework for measurement of supplier satisfaction. *International Journal of Productivity and Performance Management, 68*(8), 1475–1492.

Jacobson, N. (2009). A taxonomy of dignity: a grounded theory study. *BMC International Health and Human Rights, 9*(3). https://doi.org/10.1186/1472-698X-9-3.

Kosmann, G. (2018). *Dignidade organizacional na Relação entre Fornecedores e Clientes em Contexto Business to Business* [Dissertação de Mestrado. Universidade Presbiteriana Mackenzie, São Paulo, SP. Brazil].

Margolis, J. D. (1997). *Dignity in the balance: Philosophical and practical dimensions of promoting ethics in organizations* [Doctoral thesis, Harvard University, Cambridge, USA].

Medeiros, A. L., & Teixeira, M. L. M. (2017). Limites da dignidade de docentes nas práticas de gestão em universidades brasileiras. *Revista Gestão Universitária na América Latina - GUAL, 10*(2), 134–154.

Milczarczyk, A. (2017). Dignity restoration: The indirect goal of social enterprises' activity. In M. Kostera & M. Pirson (Eds.), *Dignity and the organization* (pp. 125–148). Palgrave Macmillan.

Phillips, R. (2003). *Stakeholder theory and organizational ethics*. San Francisco: Berrett-Koehler.
Phillips, R. A., Barney, J. B., Freeman, R. E., & Harrison, J. S. (2019). Stakeholder theory. In J. S. Harrison, J. B. Barney, R. E. Freeman, & R. A. Phillips (Eds.), *The Cambridge handbook of stakeholder theory* (pp. 3–18). Cambridge University Press.
Ribeiro, J. A., & Veiga, R. T. (2011). Proposição de uma escala de consumo sustentável. *Revista de Administração, 46*(1), 45–60. https://doi.org/10.5700/rausp0997.
Santana, M. M. (2011). *Dignidade Organizacional: um estudo em uma organização financeira* [Dissertação de mestrado. Universidade Presbiteriana Mackenzie. São Paulo., SP, Brazil].
Scholz, M., De los Reyes, G., & Smith, N. (2019). The enduring potential of justified hypernorms. *Business Ethics Quarterly*, *29*(3), 317–342
Sisodia, R. S., Henry, T., & Eckschmitd, T. (2018). *Capitalismo Consciente - Guia Prático*. Voo: Curitiba.
Skjølsvik, T. (2016, March). Business-to-business professional service relationships under multiple logics. *Service Industries Journal*, *36*(5–6), 163–182.
Subramanian, H. (2018). Decentralized blockchain-based electronic marketplaces. *Communications of the ACM, 61*(1), 78–84.
Teixeira, M. L. M. (2016). Organizational dignity theory: A proposal. *XIX Semead*, São Paulo, SP, Brazil. Retrieved June 02, 2020 from https://login.semead.com.br/19semead/arquivos/1237.pdf
van Zeeland, V., der Holst, E. M., & Henseler, J. (2018). Thinking outside the box: A neuroscientific perspective on trust in B2B relationships. *IMP Journal, 12*(1), 75–110.
Winch, G. M. (2008). Internationalisation strategies in business-to-business services: The case of architectural practice. *Service Industries Journal, 28*(1), 1–13.

Chapter 15
(In)dignity in Restaurant–Supplier Relationships: The Perspective of Managers

Lucia Maria Barbosa de Oliveira, Maria Luisa Mendes Teixeira, and Vera Lúcia da Silva Cabral

Abstract This chapter aims to contribute to answering this question: what criteria managers involved in business-to-business relationships apply to evaluate the dignity of suppliers? The study comprised 29 restaurant managers in Recife, Pernambuco; one of the most important gastronomic centers in Brazil. By the time of the study, the restaurants were operational for at least 10 years, and customers ranged from 100 to more than 5000 a day. The restaurant managers pointed out three categories of problems related to the relationship with their suppliers: product delivery time and schedule; flexibility to change and return products; control of the quality and quantity of products. The findings have shown that vulnerability is inherent to the context of business-to-business restaurants and suppliers, but this condition is not enough to characterize a violation of dignity. It depends on the suppliers' intention of taking advantage of the restaurant managers. Business-to-business relationships of dignity depend on the alignment between micro-norms and hyper-norms, high trust and reliance between managers involved in the micro-contracts, and the intention of managers of not taking advantages of each other. This study innovates by putting the subject of dignity in the heart of the organizations–suppliers relationship.

Keywords Suppliers · Restaurant · Dignity in the managers perspective

15.1 Introduction

Suppliers are part of the value chain of organizations and, therefore, can be considered as partners. Partnerships are presented as an efficient and effective approach to the relationship between companies and suppliers. Companies that work close to their suppliers can improve the quality of their products because cooperation prevails in working together, and positive and negative results, if any, are shared. (Kashmanian, 2015).

L. M. B. de Oliveira (✉) · M. L. M. Teixeira · V. L. da Silva Cabral
Recife, Brazil
e-mail: lmbdo@terra.com.br

M. L. Mendes Teixeira and L. M. B. de Oliveira (eds.), *Organizational Dignity and Evidence-Based Management*, https://doi.org/10.1007/978-3-030-68560-7_15

In the restaurant industry, suppliers play a core role that influences performance and affects the organization's survival. Cooperative relationships with suppliers play a crucial role in establishing robust financial performance (Kim, 2006). Grácia et al. (2016), for example, found that bovine ground meat used in a Brazilian university restaurant was not compliant with the legal standards. Belaya and Hanf (2014) studied power issues and conflicts in processor–supplier relationships in the Russian agri-food industry. They found several types of conflicts, as well as suggestive power asymmetries.

Power asymmetries constitute one of the conditions that can give rise to violations of dignity (Jacobson, 2009), affecting the organizational competitiveness (Hodson & Roscigno, 2004). Dignity means being in control of one's own actions. However, autonomy is fragile, as human beings are dependent on others (Sayer, 2007), and so are companies, as they are managed by people.

Human interactions hold the potential to violate or promote dignity. These interactions take place in public and private social environments and can involve individuals or collectivities. Dignity encounters can result in violations when one of the actors is in a position of vulnerability in relation to the other, or in the social order when there is inequality, harsh circumstances, antipathy, and/or power asymmetry. Conversely, dignity can be promoted when one actor is in a position of confidence, and the other in a position of compassion, in spite of vulnerability, and there is solidarity between the actors (Jacobson, 2009).

In the scope of organizations, dignity at work has been studied mainly with a focus on worker's dignity (Hodson & Roscigno, 2004). More recently, the concept has evolved to incorporate organizational dignity, including other stakeholders than workers, which means that the concept of organizational dignity takes both workers and stakeholders into account (Teixeira, 2008). However, organizational dignity is a concept that is still under construction (Teixeira & Bilsky, 2015; Teixeira, 2016). A new approach to dignity and organizations beyond stakeholders was proposed by Aguado et al. (2017) based on the discussion about the social contracts' theory (Donaldson & Dunfee, 1994), and the concept of Human Rights Dignity. It refers to dignity at the level of the firm (Aguado et al., 2017). Firms can be classified into stages of dignity, according to the self-actualization of their employees and groups that are affected by the firm's actions and omissions (Aguado et al., 2017). However, a question remains: What criteria managers involved in business-to-business relationships apply to evaluate the dignity of suppliers? This chapter aims to contribute to answering this question.

The reality of the Brazilian Restaurants is particularly suitable for the purpose of this study, as the Brazilian society has a high standard of social complexity, meaning there are several ways in which people can deal with the situations (Stankov & Saucier, 2015). In this specific kind of society, dignity is more likely to be violated.

The study comprised 29 restaurant managers in Recife, Pernambuco, one of the most important gastronomic centers in Brazil. By the time of the study, the restaurants were operational for at least 10 years, and customers ranged from 100 to more than 5000 a day.

This study innovates by putting the subject of dignity in the heart of the organizations–suppliers relationship. This innovative approach can bring another perspective for studying and improving business-to-business theoretical and practical approaches. Moreover, this study expands the contexts of the theoretical and empirical studies about dignity.

15.2 Organizational Dignity and Stakeholder Relationships

The literature on organizational dignity has been expanding since 1997, focusing on the relationships between organizations and their employees (Margolis, 1997). Teixeira (2008) conceptualized organizational dignity from a different standpoint, considering it as the relation between people "of the organization and others," i.e., the stakeholders. The model of dignity presented by Teixeira (2008) expands the concept, since it deals not with certain specific relationships, such as organizations and workers as in Margolis (1997), but rather with all the actors internal and external to organizations—the stakeholders. These relationships, though, should be based on communications among agents, i.e., what they say and think and is understood and accepted by the other with whom they relate. More broadly, established relationships have no intention to use the other as a means of attaining one's own ends. Organizational dignity is established in the practice of acts that involve mutual benefits, since there is intelligibility and common ground between those involved in the interaction. Subsequently, Teixeira et al. (2014) created an index of organizational dignity to contribute to the improvement of the relationship between organizations and their various stakeholders. They defined it as being composed of practices of organizational values that serve different stakeholders, that can be perceived and evaluated by them, giving them distinction and respect for the free will, being in line with the universal maxim that what it is good for one is good for all (Teixeira et al., 2014).

The advancement of studies on organizational dignity resulted in the proposal of a theory of organizational dignity culture, regarding Facet's theory. According to that theory, the concept of organizational dignity has been redefined as the dignity of an organization. It is reflected in the values and practices of an organization and is oriented toward stakeholders' interests, justified by deontological ethics. Moreover, it is evaluated in terms of moral, legal, or pragmatic standards by the stakeholders who influence it, directly or indirectly (Bilsky & Teixeira, 2015).

Comparing the concepts of organizational dignity proposed by Teixeira (2008), Teixeira et al. (2014), Bilsky and Teixeira (2015) and Teixeira (2016), one can realize that the focus has changed. In the first one, the focus was on how stakeholders perceive they are treated by the organization, regarding the respect to their free will, understood as respect to stakeholders' autonomy. The last three focus on the organizational dignity culture, without shedding light on stakeholders' autonomy. Respect for the autonomy of stakeholders and trust are fundamental concepts that should be considered in the culture of organizational dignity. Louback (2012), in a study about a food delivery company, pointed out the strategies used by the organization to control the autonomy of customers when delivery was late, violating the customers' dignity. In the same study, the author identified the strategies used by customers to defend their dignity. Similarly, Carrijo (2017) demonstrated strategies used by cell phone operators that violate the customers' dignity by controlling their autonomy to cancel their contracts.

In sum, the organizational dignity theoretical approach needs to be improved to be more useful for organizations and stakeholders, resulting in benefits for both. Moreover, as one can see in the next section, it is a matter not only of incorporating stakeholders to the theory of organizational dignity, but also of organizational dignity at the firm level, and its implications for business-to-business relationships.

15.3 Organizational Dignity in Business-to-Business Relationships

A business-to-business relationship is supported in the long term, as it is a commercial transaction of high added value (Harrison-Walker & Neeley, 2004), and reliance and trust are important to build this type of relationship. Trust is an interpersonal emotional construct, while reliance is related to rational relationships between organizations. Regarding relationships between organizations and suppliers, reliance is crucial to protect the management autonomy to run a business without being negatively affected by the other parties in the agreements. Moreover, some organizations maintain their interorganizational relationships based on interpersonal trust. If trust and reliance between organizations are low, relationships are fragile. If trust is high and reliance is low, relationships are personally supported. Moreover, if reliance is high and trust is low, the relationship can be supported. However, if both trust and reliance are high, the relationship is stable (Mouzas et al., 2007). How can the approach of dignity helpful relationships between organizations?

Aguado et al. (2017), based on the integrative social contracts' theory (Donaldson & Dunfee, 1994), proposed a tool for firms to enhance human dignity regarding micro- and macro-contracts and their alignment with hyper-norms. Hyper-norms are universal ethical principles of human dignity addressed to the human universal rights of every human being, regardless of the conditions that need to be practiced in the organizational context and operations. Micro-contracts reflect implicitly shared moral micro-norms present in agreements that are relevant to economic interactions between communities, which could be national or international organizations, economic organizations, and others. These micro-contracts between organizations evolve toward macro-contracts when they are extrapolated to other firms in different communities. Macro-contracts share macro-norms. Both micro- and macro-contracts are ruled by hyper-norms.

Regarding hyper-norms (Aguado et al, 2017), reliance and trust are not enough to guarantee relationships of interorganizational dignity supported by ethical principles.

Reliance and trust can be understood as the way in which dignity can be operationalized in business-to-business relationships and assure autonomy for both organizations, what means mutual respect for the partner's autonomy. On the other hand, interorganizational relationships can be characterized by asymmetry of information and power, what is a favorable condition for violation of dignity (Jacobson, 2007). Violation of dignity negatively affects business management, mainly regarding the relations between organizations and suppliers.

Regarding meanings, dignity can be classified into two categories: concrete and abstract. Concrete dignity meanings and concepts have their roots in the Ancient Age and have been supported by several concepts regarding humans as social beings immersed in social realities, and affected by these, as demonstrated by Marx, Max Weber, Durkheim (Hodgkiss, 2013), Jacobson (2009) and Sayer (2007).

The abstract meaning is implicit on Kant dignity approach: it is an absolute and inherent human value that allows human beings to make moral choices. Reason is the source of that value. There is a tension between the meanings of concrete and abstract dignity that have been transversal to the different scopes in which the core issue of dignity arises: autonomy to make decisions. The abstract meaning is embedded in the concept of worker dignity in the sense of universal human rights, and the same can be found in the organizational dignity either regarding stakeholders or business-to-business relationships, in this last in the form of hyper-norms (Aguado et al., 2017) aimed to protect the human rights. However, that purpose is not achieved only per se. Human beings, regardless of the role they play in the organizations' scope—workers, stakeholders or managers—are involved in concrete vulnerable asymmetric relationships. Those relationships demand trust or strategies by the more vulnerable part to protect its dignity.

15.4 (In)dignity in Restaurant–Supplier Relationships

The restaurant managers pointed out three categories of problems related to the relationship with their suppliers: product delivery time and schedule; flexibility to change and return products; control of the quality and quantity of products. As shown in the following sections, restaurant managers reported that some suppliers do not respect the agreements, thus affecting the business management. Suppliers do not respect the managers' rights established in their agreements and behave untruthfully, thus affecting managers' dignity and behaving unreliably toward the organization. Those behaviors demonstrated that the micro-contracts between restaurants and suppliers are not ruled by hyper-norms of human and organizational dignity (Aguado et al., 2017).

15.4.1 Product Delivery Time and Schedule

Issues related to product delivery were reported to occur very frequently. The late delivery of products can hinder serving customers, often requiring a change of the menu in the restaurant or even impairing restaurants from offering some dishes. These issues can cause customer's dissatisfaction or loss of customers. In addition, late delivery combined with an upset manager can cause discomfort to customers and consequently to the restaurant as a whole. All these constitute a behavior of violation of dignity (Jacobson, 2009) on the part of suppliers toward managers and exert a negative impact on business management, as reported by a manager "If the supplier does not deliver it to me, then it spoils all my schedule; it affects the customer." Restaurant managers have to take measures to avoid consequences for customers and the risk of losing them, as said one respondent "As I cannot let it mess up my relationship with the customer, I end up looking for other units, other suppliers. I often pay even more for this." However, managers not always attribute the problem to the absence of micro-norms (Aguado et al., 2017), but refer to the lack of suppliers' capacity, as pointed out by one of the managers interviewed: "There are problems of delivery time, off-route, personnel missing accurate logistics." Another manager pointed out that it is not just a matter of not following micro-norms; it depends on how suppliers manage the situation when they cannot deliver the product on time: "If they cannot deliver the product, they can communicate with us in advance, and then we have time to look for another supplier." It means that it is not the fact that the product has not been delivered on time that makes one consider the situation as violation of dignity or untrustworthy suppliers; one should analyze the suppliers' behavior regarding the fact. It is indispensable to determine if the suppliers wanted to take advantage of the managers' vulnerability in the management of their business (Sayer, 2007) when they failed to deliver products on time. It is necessary to ascertain whether the fact stems from the intention of taking advantage of the partner, resulting in disrespect for the party's autonomy.

It appears that not receiving the products from suppliers on time is usual. Some managers try to minimize this problem by having more than one supplier of the same product, or by keeping a larger stock than necessary, already anticipating a delay in delivery. This can be observed in a respondent's remarks: "Then I have a slack in the stock of all items: groceries, canned goods, meat, chicken, fish. So, I don't have this problem because I'm wary, I have a small regulating stock"; "we have a stock we call 'lung stock'; on this basis, we can guarantee regularity in the supply." Another manager stated: "And when I buy from a supplier and it does not deliver to me, then I already have recourse to my portal, and see which of my suppliers offer similar price and quality, and I already buy directly from it." Another small company manager indicated that the company has no problems with suppliers, and that it has worked with the same suppliers for a long time, because they know the company rules. Those supply management strategies suggest that restaurant managers are dependent on suppliers, which means a condition that can give rise to violation of dignity (Jacobson, 2009), but it is not a determinant, as it depends on whether micro-contracts are oriented by shared understanding of the micro-norms (Aguado et al., 2017).

15.4.2 Control of the Quality and Quantity of Products

There were many complaints that suppliers often do not deliver the requested quantity of products within the specified standards. This can cause major inconvenience. All participants considered quality as a key factor, since it reflects on the product offered to the customer. In the case of quantity, such issues will generate stress for being unable to offer products on the menus. In this case, there is a violation of dignity in the encounters between suppliers and restaurant managers/owners. There is also a tricky element, as emphasized by Jacobson (2009). That is, suppliers are seen as lying and manipulating products to gain material advantage. As one manager complained "Another very serious problem that happens with the sale of meat is when you buy a box of meat with a certain weight, and you do not have time to check it upon delivery. Another problem that is sometimes related to quality of products "When we bought raw material from a supplier, and it was not of good quality, it affected us. We stopped producing some items, to avoid delivering a poor-quality product to our customers said one manager.

Regarding the quality and quantity of products delivered by suppliers, it does not seem that the managers who took part in the research need to understand the intention behind the facts, because it is clear that the intention is to take advantage of the vulnerability of managers, as a manager said: "So, the question of being able to trust people is something very complicated." Another stated, "If the supplier's product is not of the ideal quality, they know they can tell us in advance, and explain that the product is out of our specified quality, then we can choose other suppliers, no problem." There are clear rules (micro-norms) that should be respect by suppliers, and when those norms are not met by them the dignity in the relationships with restaurants is violated.

15.4.3 Flexibility to Change and Return Products

Another problem highlighted was the constant errors in relation to products purchased. However, the process of returning them is always very complicated and entails problems of time waste, cost, and great stress for managers of most restaurants surveyed. Errors imply loss to managers; in this way, their dignity is violated. Jacobson (2009, p. 5) called this exploitation "using an actor or viewing him or her only as a means to an end." One manager commented "The process of returning a product it is not easy, it is demanding to many sections: the financial section, procurement section, stock section. When the delivery is not done as we want, it involves several people."

Other managers made the same claim and said that this is a usual situation. However, one manager of a small company reported a more positive experience: "We talk with the suppliers. We explain that we have norms, we work in compliance with the law, everything with established patterns." Therefore, dignity is promoted as there is respect and clear communication between suppliers and restaurant managers.

Taking into account the flexibility to change products, we could not identify whether managers considered the situation attributable to the suppliers' intention or capacity. Nevertheless, it was clear that suppliers make the process difficult, and this could be a form of controlling the managers' will of changing the products and limiting their autonomy that is a fundamental element of dignity (Hodson, 2001).

As can be observed, in most cases, the relationship between suppliers and managers presents many problems. There are reports of lack of trust, late delivery, and products incompliant with what has been ordered. A violation of dignity occurs, since there is a breach of the contract established. As stated by authors such as Amato Neto and Marinho (2014), Kashmanian (2015), and Kim (2006), suppliers should be allies of the company managers; but the reality found was not quite that. There is a process of trying to deceive the restaurant as buyer company, what is probably due to their vulnerability due to their dependence on suppliers.

There are situations in which violation of dignity is quite clear in face of vulnerability, as Jacobson (2009) has indicated, and lack of conditions to build trust (Sayer, 2007). Despite that, some managers pointed out the importance of understanding the intentions behind contract breaches in some situations, what could be understood as a lack of suppliers' capacity. In that sense, those breaches are not sufficient to establish whether the act could be understood or not as violation of dignity. On the other hand, it was found that dignity can be promoted if the suppliers' behavior is supported by the micro-norms implicit in micro-contracts, which need to be aligned with the hyper-norms (Aguado et al., 2017).

These findings are different from the solidarity proposed by Jacobson (2009) as an essential condition for promoting dignity. There is no question of solidarity in the business-to-business relationships. It is about fulfilling hyper-norms that are reflected in the micro-norms provided in the micro-contracts, as Aguado et al. (2017) pointed out. However, that is not all. It depends on the supplier's intentions when breaches of contracts occur.

In order to defend their dignity, and the operations of their restaurants, managers use strategies such as keeping larger stock of products, having easy access to other suppliers in an emergency situation, or terminating the contract and changing the supplier. These strategies are different from those used by workers do defend their dignity at work (Hodson, 2001) or those adopted by retail customers (Louback, 2012). One of the most important strategies used by workers is resistance through small acts that not always are perceived by their managers (Hodson, 2001). Retail customers of delivery food learn how to take advantage of the suppliers (Louback,

2012) or go to the court (Carrijo, 2017). Business to business is a different situation, and the strategies are those that can preserve the organizations.

The findings of this research indicate that, from the restaurant managers' point of view, evaluating dignity in the restaurant–suppliers relationships demands more than considering the micro-norms in the micro-contracts according to hyper-norms, as proposed by Aguado et al. (2017). In the context of restaurant business to business, it is important to consider the intention of suppliers when their actions do not conform to the hyper-norms. The intention perceived by managers is part of the construction of trust with their suppliers that, in association with reliability, operationalize the approach of dignity to relationships between organizations proposed by Aguado et al. (2017). The intentions perceived and monitored by managers bring the solution for the tension between the abstract meaning of dignity, as proposed by Kant (Hodson, 2001), and the concrete meaning aimed by some authors like Durkheim, Marx Weber, and Marx, according Hodgkiss (2013), and others as Jacobson (2009) and Sayer (2007), in the everyday managerial life in relationships with suppliers.

15.5 Implications for Management

The findings have shown that vulnerability is inherent to the context of business-to-business restaurants and suppliers, but this condition is not enough to characterize a violation of dignity. It depends on the suppliers' intention of taking advantage of the restaurant managers.

The results pointed out even the importance of considering the influence of intentions perceived behind the facts on the perception of violation or promotion of dignity. It is very important for management, as it includes the possibility of empathy in the relationships between customer firms and their suppliers. This empathy can help both customers and suppliers in business-to-business relationships to overcome restrictions in the activity of supplying. Empathy is an important element for developing relationships of trust and cooperative business to business.

Another finding is that, in spite of vulnerability, the dignity of restaurant managers can be promoted if suppliers follow the micro-norms established in micro-contracts, pursuant to the hyper-norms. It means that an advantaged position of a supplier in the supply chain is not a sufficient condition for violating the dignity of a vulnerable customer company.

In sum, in the business-to-business context, it is important to realize and understand what intentions are behind suppliers' actions in order to decide if there is or not enough room for building relationships of dignity in supply.

15.6 Final Remarks

In light of the findings of this study, some propositions can be made in order to contribute to operationalize the approach of relationships of dignity in the business-to-business context:

(a) Vulnerability is not a necessary condition for violation of dignity, as proposed by Jacobson (2009). It depends on the supplier´s intention. The necessary condition for violation of dignity is the intention of one manager of taking advantage of the other partner business' manager.
(b) High trust and reliance between managers involved in contracts do not guarantee business-to-business relationships of dignity. It depends on the alignment between micro-norms that rule the contract and hyper-norms.
(c) Business-to-business relationships of dignity depend on the alignment between micro-norms and hyper-norms, high trust and reliance between managers involved in the micro-contracts, and the intention of managers of not taking advantages of each other.

Organizational dignity at the firm level depends on the intentions of managers of the businesses involved in the micro-contracts. As intentions are dependent on values and attitudes, one can say that organizational dignity at the firm level depends on the values and attitudes related to hyper-norms in the sense proposed by Aguado et al. (2017), what means valuating universal ethics principles and favorable attitudes toward them, as these will be reflected in micro-contracts and micro-norms.

References

Aguado, R., Retolaza, J. L., & Alcañiz, L. (2017). *Dignity at the level of the firm: Beyond the stakeholder approach.* In M. Kostera & M. Pirson (Eds.), Dignity and the organization. (Humanism in Business Series). London, England: Palgrave Macmillan.

Amato Neto, J., & Marinho, B. L. (2014). *Estratégias de fornecimento: Panorama e conceitos fundamentais.* In J. Amato Neto, B. L. Marinho, G. M. Correia, & L. F. Amato (Orgs.), *Gestão estratégica de fornecedores e contratos: uma visão integrada.* São Paulo, BR: Saraiva.

Belaya, V., & Hanf, J. H. (2014). Power and conflict in processor-supplier relationships: Empirical evidence from Russian agri-food business. *Supply Chain Forum: An International Journal, 15*(2), 60–80.

Carrijo, F. A. (2017) *A dignidade em audiência de conciliação: um estudo com consumidores, conciliadores e representantes de empresas de telefonia* [Dissertation, Universidade Presbiteriana Mackenzie, UPM, Brazil].

Donaldson, T., & Dunfee, T. W. (1994). Toward a unified conception of business ethics: integrative social contracts theory. *Academy of Management Review, 19*(284), 65–91.

Grácia, M. A., Freitas, R. J. S., Perussello, C. A., Frizoniet, C. N. T., Hoffman-Ribani, R., & Garcia, C. E. R. (2016). Quality indicators of ground beef purchased by bidding in a Brazilian university restaurant. *African Journal of Food Science, 10*(4), 54–60. https://doi.org/10.5897/AJFS2015.1388.

Harrison-Walker, L. J., & Neeley, S. E. (2004). Customer relationship building on the internet in B2B marketing: A proposed typology. *Journal of Marketing Theory and Practice, 12*(1), 19–35.

Hodgkiss, P. (2013). A moral vision: Human dignity in the eyes of the founders of sociology. *The Sociological Review, 61*(3), 439–471
Hodson, R. (2001). *Dignity at work*. New York: Cambridge University Press.
Hodson, R., & Roscigno, V. J. (2004). Organizational success and worker dignity: Complementary or contradictory? *American Journal of Sociology, 110*(3), 672–708.
Jacobson, N. (2007). Dignity and health: A review. *Social Science and Medicine, 64,* 292–302.
Jacobson, N. (2009). A taxonomy of dignity: A grounded theory study. *BMC International Health and Human Rights, 9,* 292–307.
Kashmanian, R. M. (2015). Building a sustainable supply chain: Key elements. *Environmental Quality Management, 24,* 17–41.
Kim, B. I. (2006). The impact of supplier development on financial performance in the restaurant. *International Journal of Hospitality & Tourism Administration, 7,* 81–103.
Louback, J. C. (2012). *Dignidade e relações de poder: Um estudo em um Call Center à luz de Foucault* [Doctoral dissertation, Universidade Presbiteriana Mackenzie, UPM, Brazil].
Margolis, J. (1997). *Dignity in balance: philosophical and practical dimensions of promoting ethics in organizations* [Doctoral dissertation, Harvard University, Cambridge, MA].
Mouzas, S., Henneberg, S., & Naudé, P. (2007). Trust and reliance in business relationships. *European Journal of Marketing, 41*(9), 1016–1032.
Sayer, A. (2007). Dignity at work: Broadening the agenda. *Organization, 14*(4), 565–581.
Stankov, L., & Saucier, G. (2015). Social axioms in 33 countries: Good replicability at the individual but less so at the country level, *46*(2), 296–325.
Teixeira, M. L. M. (2008). Dignidade organizacional: Valores e relações com stakeholders. In M. L. M. Teixeira (Ed.). *Valores humanos e gestão: Novas perspectivas.* São Paulo, Brazil: Senac.
Teixeira, M. L. M. (2016). Organizational dignity: A proposal. In *Seminários em Administração – SEMEAD, São Paulo, SP, Brazil,* 19.
Teixeira, M. L. M., & Bilsky, W. (2015). Faceting organizational theory. In *Facet Theory Conference, Nova York, NY, USA,* 15.
Teixeira, M. L. M., Domenico, S. M. R., Dias, S. M. R. C., & Mendes, L. H. de L. (2014). Práticas de Dignidade organizacional por trabalhadores na relação entre organizações e stakeholders. *Encontro da Associação Nacional de Pós-Graduação em Administração – EnANPAD.* Rio de Janeiro, RJ, Brazil, 38.

Part V
Relationship of Dignity with Other Constructions

Chapter 16
The Relationship Between Stress and Organizational Dignity in a Financial Institution

Jonathan Borges de Melo Valença and Lucia Maria Barbosa de Oliveira

Abstract This study aimed to identify the degree of association between the level of stress perceived by bank workers and their perception of organizational dignity practices. The survey was conducted at "Bank X." It is one of the largest banks in Latin America. Bank X advocates social and environmental responsibility through business practices. The study is the result of a quantitative survey with 401 employees. Two measurement scales were applied—the work stress scale (Paschoal & Tamayo, 2004) and the organizational dignity practices (EPRA-DO) scale (Teixeira et al., 2004). The results suggest that Bank X implements practices that help bank workers deal with stress, despite perceiving it, such as organizational dignity practices. There is an association between organizational dignity and stress in the banking work setting, indicating that the more bank workers perceive that the company is acting in a dignified way through its practices in relation to stakeholders, the less they perceive a stress and suffer therefrom. The main lesson learned from the investigation is that in order to reduce workers' stress, it seems to be important investing in dignified relationships with stakeholders emerges as one of the potential antidotes against bank workers' stress.

Keywords Stress · Organizational dignity · Financial institutions

16.1 Introduction

Since last century, stress has assumed a relevant proportion among the topics of concern in people's lives. There is a strong link between stress and professional life, or occupational stress, so that it is difficult to think about stress without making an immediate connection with the workplace. Although stress has positive features, it is usually linked to a negative aspect that affects professionals' performance.

In admittedly stressful activities, it is not always possible to mitigate the level of stress the employee is exposed to, which goes against a worthy model of business

J. B. de Melo Valença · L. M. B. de Oliveira (✉)
Recife, Brazil
e-mail: lmbdo@terra.com.br

M. L. Mendes Teixeira and L. M. B. de Oliveira (eds.), *Organizational Dignity and Evidence-Based Management*, https://doi.org/10.1007/978-3-030-68560-7_16

performance. Quick et al. (1998) point out that organizational stress is inevitable; therefore, it cannot be simply eliminated. The authors also reveal that organizational stress is desirable as long as it remains a eustress.

Organizational dignity is a theme that has a deep adherence to the need for responsibility that has been attributed to organizations. The dignity level of organizations can be assessed by different stakeholders based on the organization's worthy practices. Teixeira (2008) conditions the dignity of organizations to the congruence between espoused and shared values, through practice. Thus, an organization's practices become the result of its values, validating the perception of such practices as a way of observing them.

The financial system harbors different stress factors, both individual's and associated with work (Garg & Yajurvedi, 2017). In Brazil, stress in the National Financial System (NFS) is endemic. As the NFS depends on the stakeholders' trust, a perception of dignity practices becomes necessary. Datz (2002) draws attention to the dependence on reliability by the NFS when reporting the existence of a significant impact for any event that reduces confidence in the system, including with financial consequences. Thus, phenomena with potential for negative interference in the perception of dignity practices, such as stress, can trigger devastating effects on the system.

Banks are one of the main participants in NFS. This study aimed to identify the degree of association between the level of stress perceived by bank workers and their perception of organizational dignity practices. The survey was conducted at "Bank X".[1] It is one of the largest banks in Latin America. Bank X advocates social and environmental responsibility through business practices. In this way, it fits into a company's reality that, immersed in NFS, which is admittedly stressful, seeks to be known for its socially responsible practices. In view of the fact that social responsibility practice is one of the factors of organizational dignity (Teixeira et al., 2014), Bank X was considered of interest for this study.

The study is the result of a quantitative survey with 401 employees of Bank X, who answered a questionnaire containing two measurement scales—the work stress scale (Paschoal & Tamayo, 2004) and the organizational dignity practices (EPRA-DO, *Escala de Práticas de Dignidade Organizacional*) scale (Teixeira et al., 2014).

16.1.1 Stress Concepts and Approaches

Stress studies commonly face difficulties in correctly defining the stress concept (Vargas, 2010; Filgueiras & Hippert, 1999; Stefano & Roik, 2005; Contratada, 2011). This difficulty is revealed from the first precursor studies of the subject. After some time, a review of own nomenclature occurs and is corrected, calling such stimuli "stressors," categorizing stress as an effect. So far, several approaches are present in

[1]The identification of the institution surveyed was omitted in compliance with its own rules, therefore, the data were put showing the reason for the choice and the relevance for this work.

the literature, and this multiplicity of options imposes to the investigator in this area the need to choose which approach to use.

Stress has been approached in the literature in different forms, the most well known of which are: stimulus, response, and transational process (Stefano & Roik, 2005; Vargas, 2010; Lazarus & Folkman, 1984; Cotti, Haley & Miller, 2017; Makkar & Basu, 2018; Akinola et al., 2019).

Following the line of some authors (Paschoal & Tamayo, 2004; Pandey et al., 2011; Uchino & Birmingha, 2011; Rauch, Fink, & Hatak, 2018; Pathmaseelan & Mendis, 2019), this work approaches the stress as the transactional process triggered by stressors that are perceived as such by the inidviduals, demanding some type of reaction. This view positions stress between external or internal stressors and the individuals' cognitive aspects. A reaction will then be fostered depending on how much the stressor was perceived and had an impact on the person's affective and cognitive notions. With this approach, the possibility of analyzing the construct based on perception is clear. The resulting reactions will have consequences depending on how they are channeled.

When stress reactions are positively directed, eustress occurs; otherwise, the distress phenomenon surges (Quick et al., 1998; Pandey et al., 2011; Mende et al., 2017). In eustress, the result is positive for the individuals and usually occurs when they are able to identify the stressor and feel able and motivated to react to the demand (stressor). When the opposite occurs—distress—the feeling of incapacity and demotivation in the face of demand generates an inactivity or escape reaction, which, in itself, becomes another stressor and generates a devastating chain effect.

Among the stressors that commonly trigger distress processes, those that occur in the workplace stand out (Albrecht, 1990; Pandey et al., 2011; Kahn, 2019). It is precisely for this reason that many studies on stress, such as this one, are directed to the setting where people work. This subdivision is known as occupational stress, activity stresses, or work stress.

16.1.2 Occupational Stress

Occupational stress is related to the stress that involves the individual in the occupational setting through occupational stressors (Ayres et al., 2001; Levi, 2011; Mota et al., 2008; Pandey et al., 2011; Siva Kumar et al., 2018; Wushe & Shenje, 2019). According to Paschoal and Tamayo (2004), occupational stress is a process in which individual sees the work demands as stressors and cause negative reactions as he/she could not coping skill.

This concept brings two important contributions. The first one is that it inserts the work demands as stressors, confirming our understanding reported this study. The other is to admit the possibility of stress-generating negative results, when the individual lacks coping skills, which also opens up some possibilities for exploration with other constructs that are capable of improving those skills. It is possible to infer, therefore, that the individual's skills are decisive for channeling toward eustress, as seen before. Occupational stress goes along all line of work with category. It is a great alarm to management and all other stakeholders. (Siva Kumar et al., 2018). Furthermore, occupational stress could bring different types of both psychological and physiological pressures to employees at workforce. (Wushe & Shenje, 2019).

Although some stress is desirable, working at high levels of occupational stress has undesirable consequences for the companies' people (Ayres et al., 2001; Pandey et al., 2011; Vargas, 2010; Naeem, 2018; Dhawan, 2017). The very existence of a concept of occupational stress denotes the inevitability of stress in companies. Regarding excessive stress in the organization, Vargas (2010) reports decrease in productivity, increase in absenteeism, lack of motivation at work, and so on. This implicates in a non-productive direction.

According to Pandey et al. (2011), these problems reflect in different ways in people, such as different forms of severe psychological and physiological distress, drop in commitment with the organization, intolerance, aggressiveness and different forms of violence. Moreover, Naeem (2018) Naeem (2018) reinforce that stress could bring changes in work performance or in behavior.

In addition to the consequences for people, organizations can also be affected (Ayres et al., 2001; Pandey et al., 2011; Vargas, 2010). Authors, such as Vargas (2010), differentiate the effects of stress on individuals and on the organizations. Other authors (Ayres et al., 2001) use the organization analogy as a living being, which is also affected by stress. However, there is a report that deserves to be highlighted because it is especially interesting for this study. Pandey et al. (2011) reported the negative effect of occupational stress on organizational citizenship behavior.

As a result of the concern of organizations with the individuals that compose them and with their own health, different models have specifically studied organizational stress Cooper, 1998; Paschoal &Tamayo, 2004; Vargas, 2010; Veloso & Pimenta, 2005). The quantitative vastness of models makes it difficult to study the subject when these studies are not interested in isolating its facets. As an example, Cooper (1998) alone reports more than ten models. It is worth mentioning here that the line of this author, which has been adopted in this work, called functionalist (Veloso & Pimenta, 2005), is only one of the known aspects. In their research, Veloso and Pimenta (2005) mention the existence of two currents that have a greater projection in Brazilian research: Cary Cooper and his collaborators, from Anglophone countries (mainly USA and England), and Christophe Dejours, from Francophone countries (part of Canada and France).

Among the functionalist models, the dynamic stress model and the stress preventive management theory stand out in this work (Cooper, 1998; Moser, 2008; Quick et al., 1998; Veloso & Pimenta, 2005). These models, besides being compatible, because they bring views that complement each other in explaining the construct, are sufficient for the connections intended in this work. Moser (2008) summarizes the first model, reporting that the authors, advance their studies on the topic, developing the dynamic stress model, which includes stressors, personal characteristics, individual and organizational manifestations, and strategies to combat stress. As can be seen, the authors emphasize the validity of the model and its applicability for understanding stress caused by the organizational stressors. As for the theory of preventive stress management, its contribution to this work is underscored, as it assumes: (a) interdependence between the health of the individual and that of the company; (b) the manager's responsibility for the health of the individual and the organization; (c) individualized reactions to stress; d) organizations and their dynamics, constantly changing; and (d) concludes about the inevitability of stress, directing the focus toward maximizing eustress, and not about stress elimination (Quick et al., 1998).

Following the line of these models, stress can be reduced by avoiding stressors, by a process called primary prevention (Quick et al., 1998; Kompier & Kristensen, 2003). This type of prevention consists of reducing, eliminating, or changing organizational stressors. When possible, it is especially effective on young employees, as it primarily tries to avoid their exposure to stressors (Pandey et al., 2011). However, as already mentioned, and, based on Paschoal and Tamayo (2004), the stressor is a stressor to the individual from the moment that he, the collaborator, perceives it as a stressor. Therefore, it is explained that the same event causes stress in some workers and not in others. Thus, it is possible to infer that interventions in the individual's cognitive domain, demystifying the event and making it non-stressful, can also be seen as a primary prevention, since, from a different perspective, they delete the stressor (Pandey et al., 2011).

It is also possible to reduce the negative results of stressors by improving people's ability to react or secondary prevention (Quick et al., 1998; Kompier & Kristensen, 2003; Dhawan, 2017). This type of action aims at preventing workers from succumbing to the inevitable stress, by increasing their coping capacity. Included in the scope of this prevention are, among others, the support strategies for the individual, degree of autonomy, time management, protection mechanisms, definition of roles, and communication clarity (Pandey et al., 2011; Uchino & Birmingha, 2011). It is a type of prevention that fits well the organizations (Paschoal & Tamayo, 2004). The models also bring a third form of prevention—tertiary—more focused on the symptomatic treatment of stress and, therefore, outside the scope of this work.

The banking area is known to have high levels of occupational stress (Ayres et al., 2001; Veloso & Pimenta, 2005; Garg & Yajurvedi, 2017). Stressed organizations, as defined by Ayres et al., are conducive for individuals' stress and for their own organization stress. Veloso and Pimenta (2005) detect, in their research in banking stress, results that call into question the strategies of primary prevention of occupational stress in banks:

Some specific characteristics of banking work define some of the sources of pressure and, therefore, cannot be understood as being organizational dysfunctions, but elements inherent to the type of work performed. Some of these characteristics cannot be understood as variables to be changed at the level of the organizational structure in order to reduce stress, since, in some cases, they are part of the banking work (Veloso & Pimenta 2005).

Apparently, in these organizations, primary prevention seems to be more difficult, requiring new approaches and auxiliary constructs capable of resolving stress.

As seen, the negative impact of stress on organizations generates undesirable results that go against values-based business performance models (Ayres et al., 2001; Veloso & Pimenta, 2005; Garg & Yajurvedi, 2017; Luturlean et al., 2019).

16.2 Discussion on Stress Level in Banking

In order to measure the respondent's stress level, we chose to use Paschoal and Tamayo's short work stress scale (WSS) which measures the individual's perception of occupational stress. It is 13 quantitative items, with a Cronbach's alpha of 0,85. The answers are given by the level of agreement for each of the questions, as follows: 1 (strongly disagree), 2 (disagree), 3 (partially agree), 4 (agree), and 5 (strongly agree).

The use of this scale is due to three characteristics that are rarely found in other instruments: 1—treating occupational stress specifically: other instruments that have been reviewed and which are widely disseminated include reaction and physiological aspects, which do not fit the objectives of this study. 2—be directed to occupational stress: for the approach intended in the investigation, scales that consider the individual's stress without a direction toward occupational activity could reduce the reliability of the relationships possibly found. 3—have a reduced size, and a good consistency coefficient: the size of the scale is very relevant for the success of data collection.

In the specific case of this study, two factors were addressed: stress level at work (SLW) and perceived stress level (PSL). The SLW factor has as an assumption the measuring of stress at work based on the feelings of the respondents about some stressors (Paschoal &Tamayo, 2004). On the other hand, the PSL factor (perceived stress level) reflects how much people realize that their activity is stressful. This factor does not go into the merit of people's suffering due to the stress level of the activity.

The findings of this study regarding the level of activity stress (PSL—perceived stress level) indicated a high level of perceived stress in Bank X activity. These data endorse the findings of Stefano and Roik (2005) who concluded that the perceived stress is significant, even causing concern; other authors also recognized the banking area as bearing high levels of occupational stress (Ayres et al., 2001; Veloso & Pimenta, 2005). Stress level at work (SLW) presented an average index of stress at work, which at first goes against the outcome presented by the authors mentioned in the previous paragraph. The data found in the SLW variable seem to differ from the results of the PSL variable; however, a few considerations need to be made in this regard.

If the activity stress level, identified by PSL, was high and the level detected from people's suffering (SLW) was not so high, it is possible that the level of coping with the situation is high in the group investigated, or at least in part of it. Some authors have already described such situations when referring to secondary stress prevention (Quick et al., 1998; Kompier & Kristensen, 2003). That is, stress is present and people recognize this fact, but they are not greatly affected by its presence.

The way the bank workers surveyed identified the stress, does not indicate a primary, but a secondary prevention. That is, there is evidence of factors that minimize the effects of stress on people. Both Pandey et al. (2011) and Uchino and Birmingha (2011) reported some factors that contribute to such minimization, such as support to the individual, autonomy, time management, protection mechanisms, role definitions, and communication clarity. These results suggest that Bank X possibly implements practices that help bank workers deal with stress, despite perceiving it, such as organizational dignity practices.

16.3 Discussion of the Findings on Organizational Dignity

The EPRA-DO scale comprising 24 items and 5 factors was used, namely F1-Practices of Promotion of Employees, F2-Practices of Social Responsibility, F3-Practices of Respect to the Rights of Employees, F4-Practices of Offer of Quality Products and Services, F5-Non-misleading Practices (Transparency).

The level of organizational dignity pointed out by Bank X respondents was considered high. Likewise, factors of organizational dignity practices indicated scores above average. This last indicator adds to the first, showing that it is a company with dignity practices recognized by employees.

The strength of the correlations between factors of organizational dignity practices and the level of organizational dignity was significant, with all factors showing positive correlations. This finding reveals adherence to Teixeira's proposition (2008, p. 91): "The organizational practices associated with the stakeholders (employees, customers, suppliers, government, and community) reflect the organizational dignity practiced by the organization."

Santana et al. (2015) conducted a study with the objective of verifying any differences in the practices related to organizational dignity perceived considering bank workers and Brazilian workers in general. The survey results indicated that, with the exception of the F1 factor—Practices of Promotion of Employees, the level of organizational dignity perceived by the employees of the surveyed bank was significantly higher than the level of organizational dignity perceived by workers from other economic segments.

The findings of this research with workers at Bank X compared to the data found by Santana (2015) indicated that practices at Bank X obtained higher scores than those obtained by that author with the exception of the F5 factor—Non-misleading Practices (Transparency).

At Bank X, no difference was found between men and women mean scores regarding practices of organizational dignity. The outcome is different from that found by Santana (2015), who identified a tendency for women to perceive fewer opportunities to promote dignity than men. It is a fact that both Santana's investigation (2015) and this one does not have scope that allows generalizations. But knowing that reality changes from bank to bank can be a sign that inclusion policies may be linked to organizational dignity practices.

16.4 Association Between Stress and Organizational Dignity

The results obtained with the workers of Bank X indicated that they had a higher perception than other workers regarding the practices of employee promotion, including no difference between men and women regarding this perception. This could be one of the reasons why despite perceiving a high level of stress in banking activities (PSL), they exhibit a lower level of stress at work (SLW).

The analysis of the association between stress and organizational dignity was performed using Pearson's correlation calculation. The results indicated that both the PSL and SLW factors presented significant negative correlations with all factors of organizational dignity practices. This indicates that the more the organizational dignity is perceived, the less is the banking stress observed, as well as the stress experienced at work and vice versa.

Although other studies reviewing the association between stress and dignity have not been found, the outcome of this survey are consistent with Pérez-Rodríguez et al.'s (2019) studies, who report that emotions related to work justice mediate stress at work. Positive emotions associated with justice at work presented a negative impact on stress, while negative emotions generated a positive effect. Gomes et al. (2020), in a study with bank employees, also found a relationship between perception and organizational justice and stress, showing that the higher the perception of organizational justice, the lower the stress.

Pandey et al. (2011) highlight the potential undesirable results of stress in organizations regarding the incompatibility of values-based business performance models. Ayres et al. (2001) identified that communication problems, lack of participation in decision making are the most common symptoms of stress in the organization. Our findings are consistent with the results of that investigation since Organizational Dignity, as an assumption of the existence of communication (Teixeira, 2008).

Veloso and Pimenta (2005) reported the impossibility of adequately serving the customer in the bank's stressful environment, which corroborates the negative relationship between stress and the organizational dignity factors. The same authors also identified the lack of training as a source of stress-generating pressure which also confirms the opposite relationship between stress and the factor "promotes employees' development."

In short, one can state that there is an association between organizational dignity and stress in the banking work setting, indicating that the more bank workers perceive that the company is acting in a dignified way through its practices in relation to stakeholders, the less they perceive a stress and suffer therefrom.

16.5 Implications for Management

The stress phenomenon has generated financial and productivity losses (Hassardet al., 2017). Different studies have been carried out to identify the factors that cause stress at work and others studies have been focusing in the investigation of factors that can contribute to the reduction of stress, which is the context in which this work is inserted.

The most recent works aimed at identifying factors that contribute to reduce stress perception include mindfulness (Fisher, 2004), leaders' humor (Guenzi et al., 2019), physical activation (Vite & Amparo, 2019), organizational justice (Pérez-Rodríguez et al., 2019) and Gomes et al. (2020), sustainable HRM (Savaneviciene & Stankeviciute, 2019).

Individual factors, such as mindfulness, leave little room for managers or organizational action to reduce stress. In contrast, organizational justice, leaders' humor, and HR practices are the appropriate space for management strategies and actions that enable stress reduction. However, these spaces focus attention only on the worker. The results of the association between organizational dignity and workers' stress at Bank X suggest that stress can decrease as workers perceive worthy company practices concerning respect to their rights and the possibility of promoting their dignity through their participation in decision-making processes, especially those that affect their life and autonomy, but this is not all.

The main lesson learned from the investigation at Bank X is that in order to reduce workers' stress, it seems to be important that the workers perceive the company's practices aimed not only at employees, but also at customers, whether through the offer of quality products and services and customer service, and to society through practices worthy of social responsibility. Investing in dignified relationships with stakeholders emerges as one of the potential antidotes against bank workers' stress.

16.6 Final Remarks

This study aimed to identify the degree of association between the level of stress perceived by bank workers and their perception of organizational dignity practices. The investigation was carried out in one of the largest banks in Latin America (Bank X), with bank workers who develop their activities in branches located in different geographical regions of Brazil.

Before reviewing the association between the two constructs in question, the level of stress perceived and experienced by workers was assessed. The level of stress proved to be high, but certainly less than imagined considering the literature entries. Perhaps exposure, over the years, has enabled people to develop coping tools to deal with the stress of banking activities. The level of organizational dignity practices perceived by workers, however, brings us other clues. The analyses indicated a mature company in its dignity practices, which even stood out in relation to other companies in the same industry to which the investigation had access. In the view of its employees, Bank X placed itself above the averages accessed in other surveys.

When analyzing the association between dignity practices and the level of stress, the results indicated an inverse correlation; that is, the more Bank X workers perceive dignity practices targeting them as well as the customers and society, the less they perceive and feel they are experiencing stress in performing activities. These findings allow us to clarify why despite the perceived high level of stress (PSL), the level of stress experienced at work (SLW) is recognized as less intense.

The investigation at Bank X brought innovative findings by showing that not only the practices of dignity that result from the employees' rights and promotion defense, affect stress negatively, but also the practices of dignity directed at customers, through service and product offerings and quality services. These findings open new perspectives for future studies on stress reducers as well as new possibilities for stress management in the banking segment.

References

Akinola, M., Kapadia, C., Lu, J. G., & Mason, M. F. (2019). Incorporating physiology into creativity research and practice: The effects of bodily stress responses on creativity in organizations. *Academy of Management Perspectives, 33*(2), 163–184.

Albrecht, K. (1990). *O gerente e o estresse: faça o estresse trabalhar para você* (2nd ed.). Rio de Janeiro: Zahar.

Ayres, K. V., Cavalcanti, G. A., & Brasileiro, M. C. E. (2012). Estresse Organizacional: o caso das empresas de base tecnológica incubadas da Região Nordeste. In *Encontro da ANPAD, 25., 2001*, Campinas. Trabalho apresentado... Rio de Janeiro: ANPAD, 2001. Disponível em: https://www.anpad.org.br/login.php?cod_edicao_subsecao=50&cod_evento_edicao=5&cod_edicao_trabalho=2781. Acesso em: 24 set. 2012.

Contratada, R.J. (2011). Stress, adaptation, and health. In R. J. Contratada & A. Baum (Eds.), *The handbook of stress science: Biology, psychology, and health*. Springer Publishing Company.

Cooper, C. L. (1998). Introduction. In *Theories of organizational stress* (pp. 1–4). Oxford University Press.

Cotti, C. D., Haley, M. R., & Miller, L. A. (2017). Assessing the impact of different workplace flexibilities on workplace stress in the presence of varying degrees of job control. *Applied Economics Letters, 24*(3), 198–201. https://doi.org/10.1080/13504851.2016.1176108

Datz, M. D. X. S. (2002). *Risco Sistêmico e Regulação Bancária no Brasil*. Rio de Janeiro, 2002. 103 f. Dissertação (Mestrado em Economia) - Escola de Pós-Graduação em Economia, Fundação Getúlio Vargas, Rio de Janeiro.

Dhawan, N. (2017). Coping mechanism to manage stress: An empirical analysis. *Delhi Business Review, 18*(2), 87–96.

Filgueiras, J. C., & Hippert, M. I. S. (1999). A polêmica em torno do conceito de estresse. *Psicologia Ciência e Profissão*, Brasília, v. 19, n. 3, Disponível em: https://www.scielo.br/scielo.php?script=sci_arttext&pid=S1414-98931999000300005&lng=en&nrm=iso. Acesso em: 22 jun. 2013.

Fisher, A. (2004). *The logic of real arguments*. Cambridge University Press.

Garg, P., & Yajurvedi, N. (2017). Assessing the impact of stress on the work-life of bank employees—A case study of Meerut Region. *ITIHAS—The Journal of Indian Management, 7*(1), 13–18.

Gomes, T. C., Estivalete, V. F. B., & Ramadam, A. O. (2020). Organizational justice and stress at work of bankers. [online]. *Rev. Psicol. Organ. Trab., 20*(2), 994–1001. ISSN 1984-6657. https://doi.org/10.17652/rpot/2020.2.17739
Guenzi, P., Rangarajan, D., Chaker, N. N., & Sajtos, L. (2019). It is all in good humor? Examining the impact of salesperson evaluations of leader humor on salesperson job satisfaction and job stress. *Journal of Personal Selling & Sales Management, 39*(4), 352–369. https://doi.org/10.1080/08853134.2019.1598267
Hassard, J., Teoh, K., Visockaite, G., & Dewe, P. (2017). The cost of work- related stress: A systematic review. *Journal of Occupational Health Psychology, 23*(1).
Kahn, W. A. (2019). Dynamics and implications of distress organizing. *Academy of Management Journal, 62*(5), 1471–1497. https://doi.org/10.5465/amj.2016.0319
Kompier, M. A. J., & Kristensen, T. S. (2003). As intervenções em estresse organizacional: considerações teóricas, metodológicas e práticas. *Cadernos de Psicologia Social do Trabalho*, v. 6, p. 37–58, Disponível em: https://revistas.usp.br/cpst/article/view/25850/27582. Acesso em: 5 dez. 2012.
Lazarus, R. S., & Folkman, S. (1984). *Stress, appraisal and coping*. New York: Springer Publishing Company.
Levi, L. (2011). Preface: Stress in organizations, theoretical and empirical approaches. In R. J. Contratada & A. Baum (Eds.), *The handbook of stress science: Biology, psychology, and health*. New York: Springer Publishing Company.
Luturlean, B. S., Prasetio, A. P., &Saragih, R. (2019). Increasing employee's job satisfaction through the implementation of transformational leadership and work stress level management. *Journal of Management & Marketing Review (JMMR), 4*(3), 209–217. https://doi.org/10.35609/jmmr.2019.4.3(6)
Makkar, S., & Basu, S. (2018). Influence of emotional intelligence on workplace behavior among bank employees in Mumbai, India: An assessment of the moderating role of job stress. *South Asian Journal of Management, 25*(3), 135–158.
Mende, M., Scott, M. L., Jo Bitner, M., & Ostrom, A. L. (2017). Activating consumers for better service coproduction outcomes through eustress: The interplay of firm-assigned workload, service literacy, and organizational support. *Journal of Public Policy & Marketing, 36*(1), 137–155. https://doi.org/10.1509/jppm.14.099
Moser, P.C. (2008). *Estresse ocupacional em profissionais de tecnologia da informação e sua relação com a prática de mentoria:* um estudo em Pernambuco, Recife, 2008. 241 f. Dissertação (Mestrado em Administração) – Faculdade Boa Viagem, Recife.
Mota, C. M.,Tanure, B., &Carvalho Neto, A. (2008). Estresse e sofrimento no trabalho dos executivos. *Psicologia em Revista*, [S.l.], *14*(1), 107–130. Disponível em: https://periodicos.pucminas.br/index.php/psicologiaemrevista/article/view/291. Acesso em: 7 Nov. 2012.
Naeem, F. (2018). Antecedents of organisational stress among bank executives. *Jaipuria International Journal of Management Research, 4*(2), 82–91. https://doi.org/10.22552/jijmr/2018/v4/i2/177080
Pandey, A., Quick, J. C., Rossi, A. M., Nelson, D.L., & Martin, W. (2011). Stress and the workplace: 10 years of science, 1997–2007. In R. J. Contratada & A. Baum, A. (Eds.), *The handbook of stress science: Biology, psychology, and health*. Springer Publishing Company.
Paschoal, T., & Tamayo, A. (2004). Validação da escala de estresse no trabalho. *Estudos de Psicologia*, Natal, v.9, n.1: p.45–52, Disponível em: https://www.scielo.br/scielo.php?script=sci_arttext&pid=S1413-294X2004000100006&lng=pt&nrm=iso. Acesso em: 2 dez. 2012.
Pathmaseelan, S. K., & Mendis, T. (2019). The impact of positive psychology on occupational stress in banking sector employees of Sri Lanka. *Sri Lankan Journal of Management, 24*(1), 30–59. https://doi.org/10.33939/SJLM.24.01.02.2019
Pérez-Rodríguez, V., Topa, G., & Belendez, M. (2019). Organizational justice and work stress: The mediating role of negative, but not positive, emotions. *Research Gate*. https://doi.org/10.1016/j.paid.2019.04.047.

Quick, J. D., Quick, J. C., & Nelson, D. L. (1998). The theory of preventive stress management in organizations. In C. L. Cooper (Org.), *Theories of organizational stress* (pp. 246–268). New York: Oxford University Press.

Rauch, A., Fink, M., & Hatak, I. (2018). Stress processes: An essential ingredient in the entrepreneurial process. *Academy of Management Perspectives, 32*(3), 340–357. https://doi.org/10.5465/amp.2016.0184.

Santana, M. M. (2015). *Dignidade Organizacional*: um estudo em uma organização financeira, São Paulo, 2011. 104 f. Dissertação (Mestrado em Administração de Empresas) – Universidade Presbiteriana Mackenzie, São Paulo.

Siva Kumar, S. V., Prasad, A. V. V. S., & Kumar, P. V. (2018). Impact of occupational stress on personal life: A study on private sector life insurance companies in Telangana state. *BVIMSR Journal of Management Research, 10*(2), 225–232.

Santana, M. M., De Domenico, S. M. R., & Teixeira, M. L. M. (2015). Organizational dignity: A study in a financial organization. *Revista de Administração da UNIMEP, 13*(1). ISSN: 1679-5350

Stefano, S. R., & Roik, A. (2005). Estresse Bancário e Sistemas de Administração de Pessoas: um estudo exploratório na cidade de Irati/PR. *Revista Capital Científico, Guarapuava, 3*(1), 111–128.

Savaneviciene, A., & Stankeviciute, Z. (2019). *Human resource management and performance: From practices towards sustainable.* Competitive Advantage. Disponível em: Acesso em: 20 mai.2020.

Teixeira, M. L. (2008). M. Dignidade organizacional: valores e relações com stakeholders. In M. L. Teixeira (Org.), *Valores Humanos e Gestão: novas perspectivas* (pp. 81–94). São Paulo: Senac São Paulo.

Teixeira, M. L. M., Domenico, S. M. R., Dias, S. M. R. C., & Mendes, L. H. L. (2014). Práticas de Dignidade Organizacional Percebidas por Trabalhadores na Relação entre Organizações e Stakeholders. In *XXXVIII ENANPAD, Rio de Janeiro/RJ*.

Uchino, B. N., & Birmingha, W. (2011). Stress and support processes. In R. J. Contratada & A. Baum (Eds.), *The handbook of stress science: Biology, psychology, and health.* Springer Publishing Company.

Vargas, T. I. (2010). *Qualidade de Vida no Trabalho (QVT) e stresse profissional:* influência da variável sexo e estudo das relações entre as dimensões da QVT e o stresse profissional, Lisboa, 2010. 43 f. Dissertação (Mestrado Integrado em Psicologia) - Secção de Psicologia dos Recursos Humanos, do Trabalho e das Organizações, Universidade de Lisboa.

Veloso, H. M., & Pimenta, S. M. (2005). Análise do estresse ocupacional na realidade bancária: um estudo de caso. *Revista de Administração da FEAD*, Belo Horizonte, Capa, v. 2, n. 1, pp. 111–128.

Vite, O., & Amparo, G. (2019). Research proposal for the implementation of a physical activation program to reduce work stress in professors at the Higher Polytechnical School of Chimborazo. *Dilemas Contemporaneos Educacion Política* Y Valores, Volume: 7, Edição especial. Número do artigo: 3

Wushe, T., & Shenje, J. (2019). An analysis of the relationship between occupational stress and employee job performance in public health care institutions: A case study of public hospitals in Harare. *South African Journal of Human Resource Management, 17*(1), 1–11. https://doi.org/10.4102/sajhrm.v17i0.1079

Chapter 17
The Relationship Between Spirituality and Dignity Perceived by Managers and Non-Managers

Lindevany Hoffimann de Lima Mendes and Lucia Maria Barbosa de Oliveira

Abstract The work presented in this chapter aimed at expanding knowledge about the relation between spirituality and dignity in the work context. The main objective was to review the relation between organizational dignity and spirituality. The analysis of the difference between spirituality and the organizational dignity perceived by managers and non-managers was a complementary objective. The research comprised 610 managers and 546 non-managers in corporations of different segments in the Northeast region of Brazil. The study was based on the scales by Spirituality of Rego et al. (2005), and of practices of dignity, EPRA-DO by Teixeira et al. (2014). The results pointed out that spirituality and organizational dignity are positively related and managers perceive organizational dignity and experience of spirituality more positively than non-manager employees. This research demonstrates the crucial role of monitoring the employees' evaluation about the alignment of their values with those of the company, and their perception about the practices of promotion of employees oriented to them. Other results have pointed out the different perceptions about the factors of spirituality and organizational dignity considering gender, age group, education, length of work, type, and size of the company.

Keywords Spirituality · Organizational Dignity · Managers

17.1 Introduction

The organizational environment has raised concerns about the relationship between men and their work. Therefore, some issues are stressed in the discussions about what is effectively essential for professionals to be both productive and happy at the same time (Renesch et al., 1994). Academics and managers should no longer disregard spirituality in organizations. Creativity and innovation at the workplace now demand

L. H. de Lima Mendes · L. M. B. de Oliveira (✉)
Recife, Brazil
e-mail: lmbdo@terra.com.br

M. L. Mendes Teixeira and L. M. B. de Oliveira (eds.), *Organizational Dignity and Evidence-Based Management*, https://doi.org/10.1007/978-3-030-68560-7_17

people to be present in body, mind, and spirit (Tecchio et al., 2016). Therefore, spirituality is increasingly perceived as an important element at the workplace (Ashmos & Duchon, 2000; Karakas, 2010; Eginli, 2017).

People work not only with their hands, but with their hearts as well (here, heart is associated with the spirit). When people work with their heart or spirit, they find meaning and purpose, a sort of satisfaction and fulfillment for doing their jobs. That means to say that workplace may be a place where people can absolutely express and be themselves. In there, human experience can be expressed in its deepest level—the spiritual level. All that may not only reduce stress, conflict, and absenteeism, but also improve job performance (Petchsawang & Duchon, 2009), well being, and quality of life (Karakas, 2010).

Spirituality plays a genuine role in the workplace, and one can hardly bear the idea that organizations could offer best-in-class products or services through an emotionally depleted or spiritually impoverished labor force (Mitroff, 2003). Corporations are attaching attention to the immaterial, and aiming at spiritualization through the adoption of practices driven by respect, moral, and ethics. By treating workers in a human way, their vendors as true partners, and trying to build empathy with customers, they show spiritual wisdom (Hunter, 2006) and practices of organizational dignity (Teixeira, 2016). Spirituality may be the main component of all managerial systems (Mitroff, 1998), in the same vein as organizational dignity (Teixeira, 2016).

Studies about spirituality in the workplace have mainly approached its impacts, notably the influence between spirituality and commitment (Jena & Pradhan, 2018) and satisfaction in the workplace (Walt & Klerk, 2014). The work presented in this chapter aimed at expanding knowledge about the relation between spirituality and dignity in the work context. Bearing this purpose, the main objective of the study was to review the relation between organizational dignity and spirituality. The analysis of the difference between spirituality and the organizational dignity perceived by managers and non-managers was a complementary objective.

The research comprised 610 managers and 546 non-managers in corporations of different segments in the Northeast region of Brazil. The study was based on the scales by spirituality of Rego et al. (2005), and of practices of dignity, EPRA-DO by Teixeira et al. (2014).

The scale by Rego et al. (2005) reviews the dimensions of spirituality comprising the following factors: sense of community; individual's alignment with the organization's values; sense of service to the community (meaningful work); happiness at work; and opportunities for the inner life. The scale by Teixeira et al. (2014), in turn, approaches the dimensions of dignity and addresses the practices of organizational dignity in light of the Brazilian workers, based on the following factors: F1—Practices of Promotion of Employees; F2—Practices of Social Responsibility; F3—Practices of Respect to the Rights of Employees; F4—Practices of Offer of Quality Products and Services; and F5—Non-misleading Practices (Transparency). Data were processed with descriptive, bivariate, and inferential statistic.

The results pointed out that spirituality and organizational dignity are positively related, and managers perceive organizational dignity and experience of spirituality more positively than non-manager employees. By the end of the chapter, some considerations about the results of the research are presented, as well as their implications on the corporation management.

17.2 Spirituality at Organizations

The term '*spirituality*' is derived from the Latin word '*spiritus*' or '*spiritualis*' that means breath, blow, air, or wind (Karakas, 2010).

Spirituality in the workplace goes beyond the mere survival through work (Paul & Saha, 2016). It could be translated by a search in the transcendental sense (Dehler & Welsh, 2010), and demands leaders to recognize that employees have an inner life that feeds and is fed by the performance of meaningful work in a community context (Ashmos & Duchon, 2000; Milliman et al., 2003).

Based on a review of literature that found the terms connection, compassion, consciousness, meaningful work, and transcendence as the most frequent ones, Petchsawang and Duchon (2009) have defined workplace spirituality as the capacity of feeling connected to it, be compassionate to the others, experiencing a state of inner consciousness in the search for meaningful work that allows for transcendence. To those authors, workplace spirituality is multi-dimensional, and each dimension or component is deeply connected with the other dimensions, and cannot be considered individually. Engagement is one of the consequences of experiencing workplace spirituality (Karakas & Sarigollu, 2019).

One of the main contributions about workplace spirituality is found on the works developed by Ashmos and Duchon (2000) that served as input for further research. The authors have developed and validated an instrument to measure workplace spirituality that approached the dimensions of meaningful work; sense of community; individual's alignment with organizational values.

Based on Ashmos' and Duchon's scale (2000), Milliman et al. (2003) established a relationship between the three dimensions of spirituality and five attitudes at work (organizational commitment: intention to leaver; inherent satisfaction at the workplace; engagement with the function; organization-based self-esteem) in an attempt to explain the relationship between them.

Deepening the empirical studies on the construct of spirituality, Rego et al. (2005) ratified the results found by Ashmos and Duchon (2000). Beyond the previously tested and validated dimensions, they created their own scale of measure with two additional dimensions (sense of happiness and respect for inner life).

Quantitative studies about spirituality in organizations received the contribution by Rego et al. (2005), with the development of a scale that gave rise to five dimensions:

(a) **Sense of Community of the Team**
This dimension comprises factors related to the team spirit, meaning to which extent the organization members have experienced strong connection or relation to other individuals that are part of the same work environment. This

approach also includes mutual care among members and, above all, the sense of community and common purpose. This dimension is marked by a strong process of interaction between co-workers:

(b) **Alignment with the Organization's Values**
The dimension 'alignment with the organization's values' refers to which extent individuals feel there is compatibility and congruence between their personal values and the organization's mission and purpose. This alignment takes place when managers and employees in an organization are deeply aware of and concerned about the collective. Individuals feel inside they are more aligned to organizations whose leaders try to be helpful and are concerned about the society as a whole, rather than exclusively concerned with the interests of the organization or its shareholders.

(c) **Sense of Service to the Community**
This dimension basically corresponds to the sense the job makes to the individual and could be strengthened by the sense of usefulness to the self and to the others. The word 'community' dates back to the Indo-European baseline word *mei* that means 'change' or 'exchange.' That root was joined to another root, *kom* that means 'with,' to give rise to the Indo-European word *kommein*: shared by all. The idea of 'change or exchange shared by all' is very close to the sense of community in current organizations. Building a community is a core strategy to share among all members the duties and benefits of change and exchange (Senge, 1995).

(d) **Happiness at Work**
This dimension portrays the human beings' needs of living a sense of happiness and joy at work.

(e) **Opportunity for the Inner Life**
This dimension comprises items related to how the organization respects spirituality and the spiritual values of the individual, including inner awareness and search for meaning.
Spirituality at companies has gone beyond the relationship with workers and may be defined as raising the company's awareness about the reason for its existence and mission before customers and workers. Any company willing to experience its dimension of spirituality should review its moral and ethical values, focusing on serving life. The company's roster of values and beliefs determine the development of its management policies (Rego et al., 2007).

17.3 Organizational Dignity

The term 'organizational dignity' was used for the first time by Margolis (1997). The author, however, approached dignity in the intra-organizational context, by outlining the conditions required to promote the dignity of the organizations' employees. The model created by Margolis emphasizes that, for organizations to respect the dignity of their workers, there should be no physical, intellectual, and emotional harm to employees. Moreover, to promote dignity the company must pay attention to three conditions: autonomy, respect for the contributions by employees, and opportunities for growing and developing.

In an endeavor to expand the academic studies about the organizational context, Teixeira (2008) proposes a concept of organizational dignity that comprises not only the internal context of organizations, but dignity in the relations between internal and external stakeholders.

Organizational dignity consists in the attributes of dignity of a given organization, perceived by the stakeholders, and assigned by them to the organizations. It is a multi-dimension and multi-faceted concept. A dimension concerns to whom the practices of dignity are oriented and that, in turn, evaluates the dignity of an organization. This dimension varies in dimensionality depending on the direct–indirect influence of each stakeholder on the organization. Another dimension refers to the 'extent of dignity,' and ranges from particular to universal dignity. Universal dignity denotes that organizations may be driven by dignity based on Kant's categorical imperative. The companies driven by particular dignity are oriented by moral values shared by the society in which they exist and that may be aligned or not with the values of universal dignity. The third dimension joins values and practices. Values are part of the abstract dignity, while practices are part of the concrete dignity. The organizational values embraced by an organization may be grounded either on the particular or universal dignity. However, they are not part of the organizational practices and, therefore, are included in the abstract dignity. In opposition, the practices of dignity represent values, are visible, and may be directly evaluated, setting up the concrete dignity.

In order to measure dignity assigned by stakeholders to organizations, Teixeira et al. (2014) developed a scale of practices of organizational dignity (EPRA-DO) made up by five factors that represent employees, customers and society: F1—Practices of Promotion of Employees: gathers practices of people's management and valuation oriented to the development and promotion of employees; F2—Practices of Social Responsibility: concerns practices of care with the environment and the less protected individuals; F3—Practices of Respect to the Rights of Employees: practices of labor relation aimed to protect the rights of employees; F4—Practices of Offer of Quality Products and Services: refers to practices of respect and consideration with consumers and customers; and F5—Non-misleading Practices (Transparency): gathers practices of respect and transparent relationship with the many stakeholders.

17.4 Spirituality and Organizational Dignity in the Perception of the Sampling

Before comparing the spirituality of organizational dignity perceived by managers and non-managers, the reliability of the scale factors was analyzed. *Espiritualidade* by Rego et al. (2005) and *Práticas de Dignidade*, EPRA-DO by Teixeira et al. (2014) were applied in a survey. The data were treated considering the total sample (1156 managers and non-managers). All factors both scales achieved Cronbach's alpha factors above 0.7; an index recommended to measure the reliability of a construct (Hair et al. 2007).

Another stage consisted of identifying the factors of spirituality and organizational dignity that stood out in the evaluation of the whole sampling, followed by the analysis of the means statistical difference performed using the *t* test for independent samples, ANOVA and Scheffe test. Those tests were applied to the variables gender, age, education, length of work, managerial position, type, and size of the company.

The total sampling was comprised of 652 (56.3%) women, and 507 (43.7%) men, half of them (50.6%) aged up to 40 years, most of them holding undergraduate and graduate degree, 52.8% managers and 47.2% non-managers, working for the company for up to 11 years (70.5%), mainly employed in private (65.4%), big-sized and multinational companies (59.1%).

The factors of spirituality with the highest means were 'happiness at work' and 'sense of service', while the best evaluated factors of dignity were 'offer of quality products and services,' and 'respect to the rights of employees.'

The inferential analysis pointed out that men and women evaluate differently 'happiness at work' and 'alignment with values'. Men evaluated these factors more positively than women. Significant differences were also found between men and women regarding the evaluation of the practices of organizational dignity 'promotion of employees,' 'offer of quality products and services' and 'social responsibility.' Results suggested that men evaluate these practices of organizational dignity more positively than women.

Significant differences were found regarding age groups both for factors of spirituality and for factors of organizational dignity. The group aged up to 30 years old differed from the other age groups regarding the factor of spirituality 'sense of service,' and from the groups of more than 40 years old regarding 'Happiness at Work.' The youngest ones were more skeptical in relation to the others, assigning lower scores in relation to the companies in which they worked. This group has also assessed the factors 'Respect to the Rights of Employees' and 'Social Responsibility' more negatively than the other groups.

These results related to age group can be explained by the different thirst for life between younger generations, like the Y and Z generation, and the older generation. The younger ones are more worried about helping the world, are more skeptical in relation to the existing ethics, and are also more oriented to the short time, and to living life in their own way (La Taille & Menin (2009). On the other hand, the older generations tend to be more satisfied with their jobs than the youngest ones and seem less willing to leave the company they work for (Costanza et al., 2012). Therefore, it seems natural that they are less skeptical than the younger respondents when they evaluate the spirituality experienced and the organizational dignity perceived.

Education was found to have impact on the evaluation of spirituality and organizational dignity. More educated individuals (Master's—Doctor's degree) better evaluated the factor 'sense of service,' 'promotion of employees,' and 'social responsibility' than the less educated respondents. The evaluation of the factor 'sense of service' was also affected by respondents' length of work. Those with seniority in the company have better evaluated this factor than those employed more recently and also ranked better the organizational dignity factor 'social responsibility.' Length of work is a variable that proved to be important to predict commitment. Senior employees tend to show more behaviors of organizational citizenship and to engage in discretionary behaviors than the others with less length of work (Ng & Feldman, 2010), suggesting that senior workers are more willing toward less skeptical evaluations regarding spirituality and organizational dignity.

In the survey, the micro and small businesses offered to employees the best possibilities of experiencing the factors of spirituality. Only the factor 'sense of service' had no significant difference in the evaluation of employees from companies of different sizes. Regarding the factors of practices of organizational dignity 'offer of quality products and services', micro and small businesses were better ranked; on the other hand, the multinational companies excelled in the factor 'social responsibility' and, paradoxically, were evaluated as those with more misleading practices in the relationship with stakeholders. Cooperatives and other third-sector associations were best evaluated regarding the factor of spirituality 'inner life.' The employees from public organizations were more skeptical when evaluating their organizations both regarding practices aimed at the promotion of employees and regarding the offer of quality products and services in comparison with employees from private companies. Likewise, the employees from public organizations were more skeptical in relation to the practices of respect to the rights of employees compared not only with private companies, but also with the other types of organization.

In brief, results suggested that the variables gender, age, education, length of work, type, and size of the company influence the perception of workers about spirituality and the practice of organizational dignity developed by the companies. Women, employees with less length of work, the employees of public companies were more skeptical, while men, older employees, more educated individuals, and those with longer length of service were less skeptical.

17.5 Spirituality and Organizational Dignity in the Perception of the Sampling of Managers and Non-managers

The study comprised 609 managers and 545 non-managers. In the sampling of managers, most participants were men (51.1%), while in the non-managers sampling, most participants were women (64.2%). Regarding age, most managers were aged 41 years or more (55.3%), and most of non-managers (57%) were younger than 40 years old. As regards education, most managers (84.4%) and non-managers (57.5%) had concluded graduation courses. Managers and non-managers were mainly from private companies, 73.3% and 56.9%, respectively. Regarding the company size, the ratio of non-managers working in big and multinational companies was significantly higher than managers, respectively, 68% versus 51.2%. Length of work, an important variable to the perception of organizational dignity, was equivalent for both samplings: 52.5% for managers and 52.9% for non-managers, both working for at least six years to the same company. Therefore, the sampling of managers was mainly made up by men of more than 40 years old, with graduation degree, who worked in big and multinational private companies. The sampling of non-managers, in turn, was mainly made up by women of less than 40 years old, with graduation degree, who worked in private or public companies.

The descriptive analysis of means showed that both managers and non-managers evaluated 'sense of service' and 'happiness at work' as the main factors of spirituality experienced at work. 'Sense of community' and 'alignment of values' received intermediary evaluations, and inner life was the factor with lowest mean. Both managers and non-managers evaluate 'respect to the rights of employees' and 'offer of quality products and services' as the best organizational dignity practices. The factor 'Misleading practices' was evaluated in a intermediary position and the factors 'practices of promotion of employees' and 'social responsibility' received the lowest mean.

Managers and non-managers significantly differ in relation to all factors of spirituality (inferential analysis t test for independent samples). Managers considered they experienced more intensively all factors of spirituality than those who did not hold management positions. As with the factors of spirituality, managers and non-managers presented significant differences regarding the perception of organizational dignity. Managers evaluated all factors of organizational dignity more positively than non-managers.

Kangas et al. (2018) identified that lay-off, career challenges, dissatisfaction with the job or organization, organizational change, and decreased well being/motivation are the main factors that may lead managers to separate from their companies. Half of the managers participating in the survey presented in this chapter had been employed for at least six years in their companies. That suggests they were likely to be satisfied enough to stay in the company. This could justify the more favorable evaluation of the factors of spirituality experienced at work and of the factors of organizational dignity. Moreover, managers are tasked with the duty of preserving the culture of their organizations (Kane-Urrabazo, 2006).

17.6 Relation Between Factors of Spirituality and Practices of Dignity as Evaluated by Managers and Non-managers

The relation between factors of spirituality and practices of organizational dignity was studied based on Spearman's correlations analysis. Three analyses were performed using the total sampling data and data of the two samplings of managers and non-managers, finding similar results: all the factors of spirituality showed positive correlations with the factors of organizational dignity.

For the three samplings, the factor of spirituality with highest indexes of correlation with factors of organizational dignity was 'alignment of values,' while the one reporting the lowest indexes was 'inner life.' The highest correlation indexes were found in the relation between the factor 'alignment of values' and the organizational dignity factors 'promotion of employees,' 'offer of quality products and services,' and 'social responsibility.'

For the sampling of managers, the correlation index between the factor 'alignment of values' was 0.68 with 'promotion of employees'; 0.58 with 'offer of quality products and services'; 0.56 with 'social responsibility', and –0,45 with 'misleading practices.' The lowest index was in the correlation with 'respect to the rights of employees' (0.40). Non-manager sampling has shown the same trend. The correlation between 'alignment of values' and 'promotion of employees' was 0,63; 0,45 with 'offer of quality products and services'; 0,48 with 'social responsibility'; 0,31'respect to the rights of employees'; and with –0,45 with misleading practices. The correlation index between 'alignment of values' and 'respect to the rights of employees,' although still positive was lower for both samplings but lowest for non-managers. It suggests that in non-managers sampling the respondents' perception of being aligned with the company's values is less influent on the perception about the respect of the company for their rights than in the sampling of managers. This results suggest that managers' perception about the alignment with the values of the company affects more their perception about practices of respect to the rights of employees than among employees that do not hold managerial positions.

The correlations between the spirituality factor 'inner life' and organizational dignity factors were significant for both samplings (0,31 for managers and 0,25 for non-managers, but can be considered as negligible (Hair et al., 2007), suggesting that inner life has little or no influence on the practices of organizational dignity developed in the organization.

Regardless whether the research subjects held or not managerial position, the results point out correlation between the factors of spirituality and organizational dignity.

17.7 Implications to Management

The first implication to management lies in the fact that managers have evaluated more favorably the factors of spirituality than the non-managers. Although data collected refer to the Brazilian workers in the Northeast region of the country, they give rise to an alert that could be useful for companies in other geographic regions and other countries, notably countries with similar cultural characteristics. When managers evaluate their company more positively, they may fail to notice that non-managers may evaluate spirituality and practices of dignity in a less favorable way, mainly women and younger employees. These different perceptions may be sharpened when managers are men, older, and with longer length of service.

It is worth observing that the factors 'sense of community,' which concerns team spirit, connection between team members, and the factor 'alignment with values' did not report the highest means, either for managers and for non-managers. However, in the correlation with factors of organizational dignity, 'alignment with values' reached the highest indexes of correlation with factors of organizational dignity. Therefore, these results point out the relevance of monitoring this factor of spirituality, considering its influence on the evaluation of organizational dignity.

Another point that deserves attention refers to the factor 'promotion of employees' that is not among the best evaluated factors of organizational dignity. However, the relation between this factor and the factor of spirituality 'alignment with values' had the highest index both for managers and non-managers. Therefore, if in a given company these factors are not among the best evaluated ones by employees, this may indicate that the human resources strategic management should develop a work to align values and invest in practices of promotion of employees that consist in investing in a career and development plan for the employee, respecting their autonomy.

In short, the results of this research demonstrate the crucial role of monitoring the employees' evaluation about the alignment of their values with those of the company, and their perception about the practices of promotion of employees oriented to them.

17.8 Final Remarks

This study aimed to analyze the relation between dignity and spirituality, comprising managers and non-managers of organizations in different segments, located in the Northeast of Brazil. Results show positive correlations between factors of spirituality and organizational dignity, regardless the managerial or non-managerial position held.

The factor of spirituality 'alignment of values' reached the highest indexes of correlation with the factors of organizational dignity, mainly regarding the development of employees, quality services to customers, and practices of environmental and social preservation. The holders of managerial position presented higher indexes of correlation between those factors, suggesting that they directly associate the factors of organizational dignity with their alignment of values. This is quite different with the non-managers that associate their alignment of values mainly with the practices of organizational dignity addressing their development. The results suggest that the more managers perceive they experience spirituality, notably in the alignment of values with the organization, the more they perceive the organization as promoting practices of organizational dignity.

Other results have pointed out the different perceptions about the factors of spirituality and organizational dignity considering gender, age group, education, length of work, type, and size of the company. Women and young employees proved to be more skeptical than men and older employees. Managers, older and more educated employees were less skeptical than the others.

Results advanced studies both about spirituality and about organizational dignity, as they enabled identifying the relation between both constructs.

References

Ashmos, D. P., & Duchon, D. (2000). Spirituality at work: A conceptualization and measure. *Journal of Management Inquiry, 9*(2), 134–145.

Costanza, D. P., Badger, J. M., Fraser, R. L., Severt, J. B., & Gade, P. A. (2012, December). Generational differences in work-related attitudes: A meta-analysis. *Journal of Business and Psychology, 27*(4), 375–394.

Dehler, G. E., & Welsh, M. A. (2010).The experience of work: Spirituality and the new workplace. In A. Giacalone & C. L. Jurkiewicz (Eds.), *The handbook of workplace spirituality and organizational performance* (2nd ed., pp.59–72). M.E. Sharpe.

Eginli, A. T. (2017). Spirituality in the workplace: What does it mean? A literature review. *Advances in Social Sciences Research Journal, 423,* 82–97.

Hair, J. F., Jr., Anderson, R. E., Tatham, R. L., & Black, W. C. (2007). *Análise Multivariada de Dados* (5th ed.). Porto Alegre: Bookman.

Hunter, J.C. (2006).*O Monge e o Executivo: uma história sobre a essência da liderança.* Rio de Janeiro: Sextante.

Jena, L. K., & Pradhan, S. (2018). Workplace spirituality and employee commitment. *Journal of Enterprise Information Management, 31*(3), 380–404. https://doi.org/10.1108/JEIM-10-2017-014

Kangas, M., Kaptein, M., Huhtala, M., Lämsä, A. M., Pihlajasaari, P., & Feldt, T. (2018). Why do managers leave their organization? Investigating the role of ethical organizational culture in managerial turnover. *Journal of Business Ethics, 153,* 707–723. https://doi.org/10.1007/s10551-016-3363-8

Karakas, F. (2010). Spirituality and performance in organizations: A literature review. *Journal of Business Ethics, 94,* 89–106. https://doi.org/10.1007/s10551-009-0251-5

Karakas, F., & Sarigollu, E. (2019). Spirals of spirituality: A qualitative study exploring dynamic patterns of spirituality in Turkish organizations. *Journal of Business Ethics, 156*(3), 799–821. https://doi.org/10.1007/s10551-017-3619-y

Kane-Urrabazo, C. (2006). Management's role in shaping organizational culture. *Journal of Nursing Management, 14,* 188–194.

La Taille, Y. L., Menin, M.S.S. (2009). Crise de Valores ou Valores em Crise. São Paulo: Artmed.

Margolis, J. D. (1997). *Dignity in the balance: Philosophical and practical dimensions of promoting ethics in organizations* [Doctorate thesis in Philosophy, Harvard University, Cambridge, Massachusetts].

Milliman, J., Czaplewski, A. J., & Ferguson, J. (2003). Workplace spirituality and employee work attitudes: An exploratory empirical assessment. *Journal of Organizational Change Management, 16*(4), 426–477.

Mitroff, I. I. (1998). On the fundamental importance of ethical management: Why management is the most important of all human activities. *Journal of Management Inquiry, 7*(1), 68–79.

Mitroff, I. I. (2003). Business not as usual: Reflections on spirituality in the workplace. In O. F. Williams (Ed.), *Business, religion and spirituality: A new synthesis* (pp. 187–200). Notre Dame: University of Notre Dame Press.

Ng, T. W. H., & Feldman, D. C. (2010). The relationships of age with job attitudes: A meta-analysis. *Personnel Psychology, 63,* 677–718. https://doi.org/10.1111/j.1744-6570.2010.011.

Paul, M., & Saha, P. (2016). Spirituality as a potential psychological capital tool to deal with academic stress among management students. *IUP Journal of Organizational Behavior, 15*(4), 46–65.

Petchsawang, P., & Duchon, D. (2009). Measuring workplace spirituality in an Asian context. *Human Resource Development International, 12*(4), 459–468.
Renesch, J., et al. (1994). *Liderança para uma Nova Era: Estratégias visionárias para a maior das crises do nosso tempo.* SP: Editora Cultrix Ltda.
Rego, A., Cunha, M. P., & Souto, S. (2005). *Espiritualidade nas Organizações e Empenhamento Organizacional:* Um estudo empírico. Área Científica de Gestão, [S.1.], n.6, pp 4–5, 2005. Retrieved from: http://www.egi.ua.pt/Wp_gestão./Wp6_Espiritual_Empenhamento.pdf. Accessed on: January 2012. Universidade de Aveiro.
Rego, A., Cunha, M. P., & Souto, S. (2007). Espiritualidade nas Organizações e Comprometimento Organizacional. *RAE-eletrônica, 6*(2), Art. 12, jul./dez. https://www.rae.com.br/eletronica/index.cfm?FuseAction=Artigo&ID=3840&Secao=ARTIGOS&Volume=6&Numero=2
Senge, P. R. (1995). *A Quinta Disciplina: Caderno de campo.* Rio de Janeiro: Qualitymark.
Tecchio, E. L., Cunha, C. J. C. A., & Santos, F. B. (2016). Spirituality in organizations? *Organ. Soc., 23*(79), 590–608. Retrieved from https://www.scielo.br/scielo.php?script=sci_arttext&pid=S1984-92302016000400590&lng=en&nrm=iso
Teixeira, M. L. M. (2008). *Dignidade Organizacional: Valores e relações com stakeholders.* In M. L. M. Teixeira (Org) *Valores Humanos & Gestão : novas perspectivas.* Sao Paulo: SENAC.
Teixeira, M. L. M. (2016).Organizational dignity: A proposal. In *Seminars in Administration—XIX SEMEAD.* FEA-USP. Sao Paulo: SP, Acesso. https://login.semead.com.br/19semead/anais/resumo.php?cod_trabalho=1237
Teixeira, M. L. M., Domenico, S. M. R., Dias, S. M. R. C., & Mendes, L. H. L. (2014). Práticas de Dignidade organizacional por trabalhadores na relação entre organizações e stakeholders. *Encontro da Associação Nacional de Pós-Graduação em Administração – EnANPAD* (Vol. 38, pp. 1–15). Rio de Janeiro: RJ. Retrieved from www.anpad.org.br/admin/pdf/2014_EnANPAD_EOR1880.pdf
Walt, F. V. D., & Klerk, M. (2014). Workplace spirituality and job satisfaction. *International Review of Psychiatry, 26*(3), 379–389. https://doi.org/10.3109/09540261.2014.908826.

Chapter 18
The Role of Trust in Building Relationships of Dignity: A Case Study on the Street Market in Vulnerable Conditions

Francilene Araújo d e Mbrais

Abstract This chapter aims to present how trust contributes to the construction of dignity relationships between marketers and customers in street markets and the contribution of trust to build relationships of solidarity to overcome vulnerability and preserve the marketers' dignity. The street market of Campina Grande, in the Brazilian Northeast region, was elected to this study. This traditional street market exists in precarious conditions and dates back to the city's origin. To develop the work presented in this chapter, we used ethnographic methods with immersion in the street market experience, observations, in addition to 35 interviews with marketers and customers. Results show that people in vulnerability situations are likely to get together in relationships of solidarity to overcome vulnerability and preserve their dignity. These relations are enabled by relationships of trust and friendship. This study proves that even in adverse conditions of vulnerability people seek alternatives to preserve their dignity, despite the disrespect and unworthy treatment the disadvantaged ones receive by those in advantageous positions. This chapter contributes to the readers' consideration about the power of trust to overcome the conditions of vulnerability and build dignity relationships.

Keywords Vulnerability · Trust · Dignity

18.1 Introduction

Market as a social construction observed throughout the History of Humanity is immersed/interwoven in economic and social actions that intertwine and influence one another (Granovetter, 1985, 2007). These actions comprise different and countless segments of the economy where businesses and/or organizations are mainly pooled in terms of services and/or products they deliver (Rosseti, 2002).

Market is permeated by the presence of social players (competitors, marketers, suppliers, farmers, government representatives, among others) that try to fulfill their

F. A. de Morais (✉)
Campina Grande, Brazil
e-mail: francilene.morais7@gmail.com

M. L. Mendes Teixeira and L. M. B. de Oliveira (eds.), *Organizational Dignity and Evidence-Based Management*, https://doi.org/10.1007/978-3-030-68560-7_18

objectives and meet their legitimate interests (Freeman, 1984; Donaldson & Preston, 1995) through the establishment of relationships that highlight their weaknesses and strengths (Granovetter, 2007). Moreover, concrete and networked personal relationships give rise to trust in market, as a way to control bad faith (Granovetter, 2007).

Street market is an important means of trading, and also room for meetings and leisure, since people gather together in a given site to sell or exchange products, and to establish dialogues. Up to these days, it is a relevant economic and social activity (Sá, 2010; Gomes et al., 2013; Sales et al., 2011; Araújo, 2011). As it is an open-air space, street market allows the interaction of several marketers, customers, suppliers and/or farmers, and government agents in the same physical space. Thus, if facilitates these players' contact. We could say that street market is a unique and socially built market.

Street market dates back to the antiquity and is part of the economic and social lives of a wide range of peoples in all continents. In some countries, street markets take place in extremely vulnerable environments that violate the dignity of workers and users of the service, notably in some Latin American and African countries.

Vulnerability is conceived as a condition favorable to violation of dignity, where the vulnerable being is at the mercy of the other person of whom he depends to have his dignity promoted. (Jacobson, 2007, 2009). Vulnerability, however, is also inherent to the relationships of trust. Trust can be understood as a subjective state of the human being, inherent to the positive expectations of a person in relation to another (Mcallister, 1995; Mayer et al., 1995). Trust minimizes uncertainties and complexities and risks inherent to the workplace, thus reducing their impacts by dimensioning future expectations of interpersonal, inter-group, and institutional relationships (Luhmann, 2005).

This chapter aims to present how trust contributes to the construction of dignity relationships between marketers and customers in street markets, and the contribution of trust to build relationships of solidarity to overcome vulnerability and preserve the marketers' dignity.

The street market of Campina Grande, in the Brazilian Northeast region, was elected to this study. This traditional street market exists in precarious conditions and dates back to the city's origin. To develop the work presented in this chapter, we used ethnographic methods with immersion in the street market experience, observations, in addition to 35 interviews with marketers and customers.

This chapter is intended to contribute to the readers' consideration about the power of trust to overcome the conditions of vulnerability and build dignity relationships.

18.2 Street Market: Unique Place of Trade and Meetings

The emergence of market streets can be pictured since the human groups left behind the nomadic lifestyle and started living a sedentary life, accumulating production. One can imagine a place where people go to satisfy their basic needs regarding, for example, food, drink, resting after long hours of work. This site can be a crossroad, the margin of a river, stream, lake or roads that served for long time as passage to a wide range of passers-by. These sites could host a street market where sheep, bulls, chickens, ducks can be exchanged for barley, wheat, oat, manioc, primitive tools, or leather coat, boots or sandals, among others.

Whoever exercises their ability of imagining can mentally view a space of meetings and leisure when people started to assemble to exchange their products. Therefore, over time these sites developed and improved, starting to play a relevant role in the building of cities, and their respective historical, social, and cultural consolidations (Huberman, 1976; Maior, 1978).

Today, street markets are still open spaces that enable meetings, chats, connecting, and amusement for marketers, buyers, suppliers, and persons at large, despite the competitiveness imposed by big-size entrepreneurs installed in urban centers (Ferreira et al., 2011; Souza et al., 2014).

It is a diversified and busy environment, abounding in sounds, colors, smells, etc. Aromas are mixed: the scent exhaled by fruits and flowers blend with the smell of fish. Rich, poor, white, black people, tourists, educated individuals—everyone circulate around the street markets (Ferreira et al., 2011; Cavedon, 2002).

In relation to its particularities and peculiarities, the street market is a unique environment of trade, because of a wide range of characteristics such as offer of differentiated and quality products; friendship and trust relationships established between marketers and customers that enable marketers to know their customers' needs and desires, thus improving aspects of production and sale to continuously meet those needs; intrinsically playful environment that goes beyond the trading space (Sales et al., 2011).

Although it is a space for jokes and fellowship, friendship and opportunities for customers to acquire new, good quality, and safe products, the street market is a business that should be managed with care, efficiency, efficacy, and devotion. This would ensure not only the marketers' survival in the competitive market they are inserted, but would also ensure the possibility of expanding their businesses. It could become a strong instrument of public policies, and a powerful generator of job and income to the municipality (Sales et al., 2011).

The street market environment is permeated by contradictions, while allying the features of hard work and drudgery to a work that offers satisfaction, fulfillment and well-being, among others (Sá, 2010; Cavedon, 2002; Gomes et al., 2013; Souza & Tolfo, 2009).

Therefore, the work is extremely meaningful to workers, as it is marked by values and beliefs found in the context of street market. Most times, the work is associated to family values, as it is a professional activity primarily handed from generation to generation (Souza & Tolfo, 2009).

Street market plays a relevant role in the marketers' lives as it is an environment favorable to their social identification, psychological well-being and provides the individual with opportunities to produce, create, and create value to the society. The street market's professional is a worker that has a specific *modus operandi*; i.e., each one tries to show up in a different way, making use of their creativity and imagination. This is shown by how they fix their booths and display their products (Souza & Tolfo, 2009).

18.3 Vulnerability in Campina Grande Street Market

The central street market of Campina Grande dates back to the origin of the city that gave its name to the market. It has even been confounded with the settlement of the city, when it was still a village. The street market has more than 150 years. It occupies 75,000 m^2 spread over nine streets and has a central market with 4400 trading posts (Araújo, 2004). Easily accessible on foot or by urban transportation, the street market of Campina Grande is located in the center of the city. It is largely visited by the city's inhabitants and inhabitants from the surrounding cities.

The market has several entries delimited by streets, also known as "entry gates." The open-air street or entry gate is selected depending on the good to be acquired. Each street is named after the main product sold on it, like street of flowers, street of fish, street of candies, street of tobacco, street of roots, street of clothes and shoes, among others. However, it does not mean that only flowers are sold on the street of flowers, for example. There visitors also find jars, domestic appliances, fruits, vegetables, roots, among others. The same happens with the other streets in the market area. There is no inspection in the street market regarding new booths, but there is a code of respect to the spaces established.

In the market, we commonly find marketers who are also farmers and/or suppliers and/or customers. Considering such a multiplicity of roles played by the same player, we can assume this is one of the reasons for the permanence of those individuals in the street market, added with the willing to keep the family in the businesses.

The Association of the Central Market's is an additional player in this scenario. It is a local non-governmental organization, constituted as private legal entity for undefined time, non-for-profit, of charitable, welfare, promotional, and educational character, apolitical and non-partisan (Afemec, 2012).

Since the creation of the Campina Grande central street market to these days, the municipal government plays a structuring role in its dynamic regarding both the occupation and organization of spaces and the operation of the street market itself. Government is represented by the street market's general management. It works in the municipal public market with one street markets' general manager, and the team of effective employees and service providers. As official agent of the city hall, the street market's management holds the main purpose of: *taking care of cleaning, safety in terms of monitoring, and updating the permits, whenever required.*

The search for information about the main difficulties faced to manage the street market unveiled the lack of inspection by public authorities. Each street of the market has countless booths and/or stands and/or parcels where marketers display their merchandises. This crowding narrows the streets and hinders mobility. Added to the overcrowding of facilities, there are people walking around, people riding motorcycles or cars or bikes and people carrying baskets on their heads.

As the Health Inspection does not inspect the street market, it contributes to increase and enhance diseases. Moreover, it favors the building and equipping of booths and/or stalls with different materials, hindering cleaning and sanitizing. The absence of the Public Prosecutor's Office at the street market supports child labor exploitation, expands the number of cases of prostitution, and also favors increased abuse of drugs and alcohol. All that creates outrage among marketers and the population at large.

Besides the lack of inspection from public authorities, there is no healthcare unit in the street market: *If someone feels sick here, we can't help… We have no healthcare unit, not even to take care of a cut. If someone gets hurt, we take the person to the hospital.*

The policing system leaves much to be desired. The police station on the street market cannot cope with the high demand. To meet the security needs, marketers pay alternative private monitoring services. For the marketers, security, sanitation, hygiene, policing, and healthcare unit are urgent measures that cannot wait. They say: *the market is crying for help.* In this context of vulnerability, and despite of it, marketers build and preserve dignity relationships through solidarity and trust.

18.4 Solidarity and Trust to Overcome Vulnerability

Amidst the situation of vulnerability that marketers, customers, and other stakeholders face, the marketers built interwoven relationships of solidarity as a way to preserve their dignity.

As vulnerable beings, human beings are also dependent as mutual cooperation is crucial to satisfy their needs. Solidarity springs from the belief that success is not a consequence of competition, but of cooperation. Solidarity makes the parties support one another in face of adversity (Cannon et al., 2000).

Some authors like Sezen and Yilmaz (2007), and Douwes et al. (2018) point out trust as antecedent of solidarity. Trust can be understood as a subjective state of the human being, inherent to the positive expectations of a person in relation to another (Mcallister, 1995; Mayer et al., 1995). It allows minimizing uncertainties and complexities and risks inherent to the workplace, thus reducing their impacts by dimensioning future expectations of interpersonal, inter-group, and institutional relationships (Luhmann, 2005).

In the organizational context, trust comprises relationships established between peers, mainly unfolding into two dimensions: affective and cognitive. The affective dimension is based on elements internal to the individual (insights) and is grounded on the emotional bonds built between peers. The cognitive dimension, in turn, is of rational nature and is built through elements external to the individual, i.e., the evidence expressed by a given individual's behavior (Mcallister, 1995). Trust relationships assume emotional investments by stakeholders, where some genuinely care about the others (Mcallister, 1995; Monteiro & Teixeira, 2009), a typical trait of friendship relationships.

The building of trust in interpersonal relationships depends on how these are structured. According to Granovetter (2007), regardless the players involved in these relationships the following levels of trust are evident: (a) lack of information about the person with whom one is trading (lowest level of trust); (b) person indicated to make economic transactions; (c) knowledge about the person with whom one will trade by means of previous business experience with that person (highest level of trust).

The Campina Grande's marketers resort to the three levels of trust suggested by Granovetter (2007). When they miss information about customers and/or suppliers, new marketers make use of "test experiments." The individuals' behavior in the "text experiments" that characterize them as reliable will enable the building of new relationships of trust.

Whenever possible, marketers try to get information about the individual with whom they intend to establish relationships of trust. They try to find if the person is credible, has solid record; if the person is a customer, they try to find if the person is the paying kind, an honest person.

Previous business transactions also facilitate building trust, since a successful previous experience of trading supports new sales and/or purchases: *You know the person... You bought from or sold to her, and got paid (Marketer, oral information).*

The relationship with marketers disclosed some aspects that antecede and/or influence the building of trust. Among these, a highlight is the regular presence at the street market and the building of friendship relationships. Sharing confidences, intimacies, and pouring out were other aspects observed in the relationships with marketers and that were construed here as ways of enabling the building of friendship ties toward trust. When people talk about intimacies, leaving behind the superficial links inherent to relationships with strangers or little-known persons, they start relating with each other in a closer way. This proximity contributes to enhance ties that used to be weak in the relationship.

Vulnerability or risk, aspects inherent to the relationships of trust (Luhmann, 1996), are present in the relationships between marketers and customers, marketers and suppliers, and among marketers. If, on the one hand, relationships of trust serve as antidote to vulnerability in the relationships, then on the other hand it paves the way toward relationships of friendship, reciprocity, and solidarity.

The advance of relationships contributes to strengthen friendship bonds, enabling the customers to enter the marketers' lives: *The relationships of formal and/or informal godfather and godmother are very common in the street market.* The relationship between friends gives rise to loyalty both from customers to the marketer and from the marketer to the customer. This loyalty is grounded on honesty and enables each marketer to build their own customer base: *Darling, this starch is cut, it is not good for selling. "I have been D. J.'s customer for years, and I know she will never sell scrap. Darling, this starch is cut, it is not good for selling.*

Friendship relationships among marketers bring about reciprocity, but also tension as they are also competitors. These friendship relationships are imbued with the trust gradually built over time, thus giving rise to reciprocity. As a marketer said: Today [after time] we start feeling we are true friends, that we are not competing here, trying to tear the other competitor down, but to help one another... That's a horse of a different color. Today I fell I'm respected in the street market.

As friendships are built and become mature, the resulting trust can be enhanced and play a structuring role in the business and social relationships. It brings about reciprocity and solidarity.

Solidarity among marketers led them to get together and hire private security services to cope with the insufficient policing provided by the government. The security services hired are in charge of strolling around the street market, watching if someone did anything wrong and, if that happens, take the person to the police station.

Solidarity acts are translated into actions of cooperation among marketers in multiple situations, for example, when a marketer sells all his products, and he lends his stall to another marketer who is displaying his products on the ground. Likewise, when the marketer does not have the product the customer wants, he promptly recommends the customer to another marketer who, in principle, is a competitor. Moreover, marketers talk to each other, exchange information about a given customer and/or supplier, trying to obtain references about them.

Other forms of solidarity are materialized as help, like when a marketer needs to leave to solve any problem, and another marketer takes care of his stall; or when a marketer needs help to carry the merchandises from a stall to another; or even when a marketer helps looking after the children of a marketer who had to take the children to the market.

The solidarity established in the relationship among marketers, and between marketers and customers, enables the creation and strengthening of bonds since, among other aspects, they understand their needs, and mutually help one another, overcoming the conditions of vulnerability typical to their business context. Solidarity contributes to build friendships, reinforcing the concept that economic action is a form of social action (Raud-Mattedi, 2005; Steiner, 2006; Granovetter, 2007). Solidarity is a crucial condition to promote dignity meetings capable of promoting that solidarity (Jacobson, 2007).

18.5 Solidarity: Crucial Condition to Promote Dignity

The concept of dignity as human being's integrity or identity corresponds to the meaning of social dignity that, among others, comprises two types of dignity: that of the self and the relational dignity. Dignity of the self-corresponds to self-respect and self-value and can be identified in the relationships through traits of trust and integrity. Relational dignity is built in the interactions among individuals, groups, and the society. It refers to the presence of respect and appraisal for the other and can be expressed by individual and collective behaviors. Both types of dignity are subject to violations that cause traumas in people's lives as their identity is affected, as well as their sense of responsibility and autonomy. Dignity violation can occur in asymmetric relationships, i.e., when the power and authority of one is stronger than the other's (Jacobson, 2007, 2009).

Integrity dignity is promoted when one of the involved individuals is self-confident and in a position of trust in relation to the other and also feels hopeful and deserver of good things. The other player, in turn, is in a position of compassion, "open" minded, honest, and with good intentions. As such, the meeting of players holding these characteristics is more prone to result in the promotion of dignity, considering that their relationship is of solidarity, reciprocity, empathy, and trust. Moreover, social contexts that contemplate income provision, proper housing, access to education and health, and social investment in public goods are more likely to promote dignity. (Jacobson, 2009).

Dignity violation, in turn, occurs in asymmetric relationships, i.e., when the power and authority of one is bigger than those of the other, placing the other in a situation of vulnerability. To illustrate the situations of vulnerability experienced by one of the players that could lead to violation of dignity, Jacobson (2009) points out the following aspects: ignorance, disease, poverty, shame, and positions of antipathy (ambition, prejudice). These aspects can be manifested through behaviors such as psychological insults, humiliations, physical lesions, emotional damages, among others. (Jacobson, 2007, 2009).

The relationships between the stakeholders at the Campina Grande's street market are marked by vulnerability for many reasons, whether it is in the relationship between marketers and government agents, marketers and suppliers, marketers and customers. That is so because of the existing asymmetry of information in these relationships. There are many ways to overcome that vulnerability, depending on the stakeholders.

In the specific relationship between government and marketers, considering the shortage of governance by the government, marketers come together to solve problems of physical, structural, and social nature. This unity empowers them to manage their own business and, thus, prevent them from being contaminated by the essentially degrading work conditions at the street market: *Here at the street market, work conditions, are subhuman.*

Among the many ways to avoid getting accustomed to the lack of governance, we could mention the marketers' organization, and further hiring of private security: *We have to protect ourselves, our families, and our customers here at the street market.*

Another aspect refers to some marketers' care about their businesses regarding cleaning, hygiene when handling food, and the aesthetic of their booths. *I am not an animal and don't want to live like one. I have to take care of the environment in which I work... It is where I make a living.*

The marketers' organization to build the Marketers' Association is yet another way to get organized to solve the degrading problems that strike the central market. Marketers build dignity relationships by setting strong ties to "control" the vulnerability they experience in their everyday working lives. This way, they minimize the vulnerability ensuing from potential bad faith, deciding to respond with dignity to the essentially undignified working conditions in the street market.

In face of a degrading physical context that abounds in social issues, marketers get together, express their solidarity with their counterparts, adopt behaviors of reciprocity by taking care and protecting each other, protecting themselves even against violence in the market, in a collective way, by hiring private security services. Acting this way, they not only preserve the dignity of the self and of integrity (Tadd et al., 2010), but also build social dignity (Jacobson, 2007, 2009).

The conditions of vulnerability experienced by marketers in the central market and the way they get organized to try to overcome these conditions are not limited to this context. Rather, these reflect the history of the Northeastern people themselves, marked by endless struggles for survival. Many times, survival is made possible through the overcoming of existing climate/geographic, economic, social, and political problems. Due to the lack of economic and social policies, the living conditions of most Northeastern people place them in situation of vulnerability.

A question arises when we consider the difficulties faced by the Northeastern people, and by the marketers at the central street market of Campina Grande: where does this resilience come from? The *cordel* literature provides some answers when talking about the attempts to make a dream come true, persistence, hard work, solidarity, and moral values. The Northeastern people do not give in to the difficulties inherent to their context. Rather, they seek ways out to overcome their difficulties and are strongly marked by persistence: "There is little rain in the Northeast. I know it since I was a child. Still, the Northeastern man. Works hard, and is restless. Because each drop of water. Renews their hope" (Unicampo, 2010, p. 13, free translation).

The paths to follow comprise the optimistic dream that preserves the enthusiasm about a better life; the use of positive lenses to interpret the everyday difficulties; the hard work to conquer the dream; the solidarity in relationships; and, friendships building.

The symbolic value of work is associated both to how people understand their insertion in the labor market and how they perceive the activity they perform and the respective context—physical, social, and psychological. (Muchinsky, 2004; Zanelli et al., 2004).

Solidarity, one of the ways to overcome difficulties found in the relationships between marketers, is deeply rooted in the Northeastern culture: Solidarity is a bread that is fairly shared. That being fairly shared. Feeds humanity. Selfishness and vanity, anger, pride, and curse. All these are like throwing away the pleasure of hugging, loving, smiling. Whoever dos not live to be useful, is not useful for living (Monteiro, 2012).

I'll be nothing alone.
I'm nothing without friends,
There's no way without love;
Everything comes down without peace,
And I take much care
To not let bad feelings
Get the best of me.
I try to be careful

To be harmonious
As peace depends on me.
(Acopiara, 2009)

Moreover, the marketers' willingness to overcome problems can also spring from the moral status dignity, acquired through the moral decisions made by individuals in their interpersonal and social relations (Tadd et al., 2010).

Moral dignity is acquired in the individual's socialization process that comprises several institutions, including the family, community, religion, labor, communication means. Therefore, marketers seek or recover moral dignity in themselves as a way to preserve the dignity of integrity.

Socialization is a process of construction, deconstruction, and reconstruction of identities related to the multitude of activities experienced by individuals throughout their lives. These experiences take place in a given cultural context, either at the personal, family, or professional level. In the socialization process, individuals learn to be a player, i.e., active subjects of their faith, as they learn and (re)apprehend the knowledge that allows them to build autonomy of thinking. In this sense, the socialization process is closely related to learning the culture of a group (Dubar, 2005).

The dignity relations at the Campina Grande's central street market are curiously built from the vulnerability found in those relationships. Jacobson (2007, 2009) points out vulnerability as the key condition for violation of human dignity, while solidarity would be the condition supportive to dignity promotion. However, Jacobson (2007, 2009) approaches solidarity in the scope he calls "dignity meetings" between two parties, when one is in a more favorable position than the other, because the first holds information and powers the last does not have and, therefore, is placed in a vulnerable position. Here, solidarity concerns how the social player in advantageous position treats the disadvantaged player.

The dignity meetings proposed by Jacobson (2007, 2009) leave no option for the disadvantaged social player to preserve his dignity, except for depending on the solidarity of the advantaged player.

Regarding the relationship of vulnerability with government, marketers overcome it through the mutual support upon solidarity and reciprocity in relationships, facilitated by relations of trust established in the course of coexistence. In the relationships with customers, vulnerability is overcome by the construction of trust relationships.

In brief, dignity in the relations between stakeholders at the Campina Grande's central street market is built by overcoming vulnerabilities in many ways, depending on the stakeholders and the cultural context in which they were socialized. For relationships with the government, the ways to overcome vulnerability are deeply rooted in the Northeastern culture.

18.6 Implications to Management

Times of crisis of any nature, be it political, economic, social, ecological, spiritual, among others, can allow personal, professional, and organizational growth and development. The human being's ability of overcoming intrinsic and extrinsic conflicts, making use of their ability of resilience at individual and/or community level, could be one of the factors supportive to that growth. In situations of vulnerability, we find that union, friendship, and solidarity among people contribute to preserve and promote dignity.

Managing or leading people in an organizational context of vulnerability demands an altruistic standing of managers. Above all, they must believe that despite the crisis, personal and organizational developments are a possibility if they overcome the difficulties or challenges experienced. Believe they can win. "roll up our sleeves." Bravely face difficulties. Preserve faith, love, hope, solidarity to the self and to the other are crucial aspects in interpersonal relationships. These aspects minimize vulnerability, preserving and/or promoting human dignity.

Therefore, managers should build strategies to bring collaborators closer, make them more compassionate to each other, also strengthening ties with customers. Work hard and focused on customers, seeking a respectful relation, understanding their needs, fears, and expectations, working with solidarity, and building/strengthening trust links are key aspects in business transactions, mainly in contexts of uncertainties and adversities.

The current scenario of the COVID-19 pandemic that affects the world population illustrates the personal and organizational growth in contexts of vulnerability and adversity.

Added with other aspects, the pandemic caused the world to literally stop in terms of economic growth. Social isolation was and still is needed to fight the COVID-19. All countries of the world, of all continents, were affected as much as all people, regardless their color, gender, race, age group, social level, or religion. Generally speaking, to a greater or lesser extent the global population, and their respective public or private institutions and organizations, were affected or struck.

However, in the chaotic scenario that emerged all over the world because of the COVID-19 transmission, marked by the high number of deaths, and scenarios of deep soreness, fear, and concern, massive episodes of solidarity also emerged. Solidarity was and remains present in human relationships, in different ways. It comprises from simple actions like trying to relieve the other's suffering by delivering food to economically disadvantaged individuals, to more robust actions like, for example, business actions that, regardless their field of work, spared no effort to produce surgical masks, hand sanitizers, and respirators. The world stopped, but the COVID-19 boosted solidarity and, therefore, the dignity relationships.

18.7 Final Remarks

The study presented in this chapter aimed to present how trust contributes to the construction of dignity relationships between marketers and customers in street markets and the contribution of trust to build solidarity relations to overcome vulnerability and preserve the marketers' dignity. Results show that people in vulnerability situations are likely to get together in relationships of solidarity to overcome vulnerability and preserve their dignity. These relations are enabled by relationships of trust and friendship. Trust also plays a structuring role in the relationships between sellers and customers, overcoming the vulnerability embraced in this relation, either on the customers' side or on the marketers' side.

The case being reviewed, the Campina Grande's street market, highlights the relevant role of local culture to the building of relations of solidarity. Campina Grande is a city in the Northeast region of Brazil. For decades, this region has urged persistence and resistance from its inhabitants, so they can survive amidst aridity and water shortage. The Northeast region misses conditions and, according to Jacobson (2007), this shortage leads to a context favorable to the violation of people's dignity.

This study proves that even in adverse conditions of vulnerability people seek alternatives to preserve their dignity, despite the disrespect and unworthy treatment the disadvantaged ones receive by those in advantageous positions.

Managing the organizational dignity in organizations like the street markets in situation of vulnerability is reshaped. In this context, managing organizational dignity is characterized by shared management, enabled by the relations of trust built by the concerned social players. These players build personal relations of friendship, solidarity, and mutual support.

Extrapolating the objectives and respective results found in this study and comparing with the current political, economic, and social scenario experienced by the world population by virtue of the COVID-19 pandemic, we find that humanity is in a state of vulnerability. And, once again, the solidarity present in the relationships between individuals, organizations and/or corporations and/or institutions, generally are actions that minimize human suffering and possibly preserve the human dignity.

References

Acopiara, M. (2009). *A paz depende de mim* (p. 3). São Bernado do Campo: Cordel Literature Leaflet.

Afemec. (2012). *Certificate of the statutory reform of the central market's marketers association.* Campina Grande.

Araújo, G. A. F. (2011). *Continuidade e descontinuidade no contexto da globalização: um estudo de feiras em Portugal e no Brasil (1986–2006)* [Doctoral thesis in History)/ Specialization in Contemporary Age (UMINHO) and Social History (Federal University of Bahia). Co-tutelage regime, Minho University].

Araújo, G. A. F. (2004). *Feira livre: memória "viva" da cultura do povo campinense, ao final do século XX*. Campina Grande: Agenda.

Cavedon, N. (2002). "Pode chegar, freguês": A cultura organizacional do mercado público de Porto Alegre. In: *Enanpad,* Porto Alegre.
Cannon, J. P., Achrol, R. S., & Gundlach, G. T. (2000). Contracts, norms, and plural form governance. In *Journal of the Academy of Marketing Science, 28*(2), 180–194.
Douwes, R., Stuttaford, M., & London, L. (2018). Social solidarity, human rights, and collective action: Considerations in the implementation of the national helath insurance in South Africa. *Health and Human Rights Journal.*
Donaldson, T., & Preston, L. (1995). The stakeholder theory of the corporation: Concepts, evidence and implications. *Academy of Management Review, 20*(1), 65–91
Dubar, C. A. (2005). *Socialização: construção das identidades sociais e profissionais* (A. S. M. da Silva, Trans. Into Portuguese). Sao Paulo: Martins Fontes.
Ferreira, C. M. A., Wanderley, D. M. A., Ferreira, D. J. L., Maia, H. J. L., Medeiros, M. C. S., & Lima, V. L. A. (2011). Percepção dos impactos ambientais na feira central de Campina Grande-Pb. *Revista Educação Agrícola Superior, 26*(1), 3–6.
Freeman, E. R. (1984). *Strategic management: A stakeholder approach.* Boston: Pitman.
Gomes, A. F., Silva, J. S. F., Santos, A. A., Santana, W. G. P. S., & Santos, J. A. G. S. (2013). Perfil socioeconômico de mulheres feirantes : um estudo no interior baiano. In *4th Meeting of Politial Administration,* Vitória da Conquista (pp. 1–16).
Granovetter, M. (2007, January to June). Ação econômica e estrutura social: O problema da imersão. Forum - Economic Sociology. *RAE-eletrônica, 6*(1), Art. 9, ISSN 1676-5648.
Granovetter, M. (1985). Economic action and social structure: The problem of embeddedness. *American Journal of Sociology, 91*(3):481–510.
Huberman, L. (1976). *História da riqueza do homem.* Rio de Janeiro: Zahar.
Jacobson, N. (2009). A taxonomy of dignity: A grounded theory study. *BMC International Health and Human Rights, 9*(3), 1–14.
Jacobson, N. (2007). Dignity and health: A review. *Social Science & Medicine, 64,* 292–302.
Luhmann, N. (1996). *La ciencia de la sociedad* (p. 613). México/Barcelona: Universidad Iberoamericana/Herder.
Luhmann, N. (2005). *Confianza.* México: Universidad Iberoamericana.
Maior, A. S. (1978). *História geral.* Sao Paulo: Sao Paulo.
Mayer, R. C., Davis, J. H., & Schoorman, F. D. (1995). An integrative model of organizational trust. *The Academy of Management Review, 20**(3), 709–734.
Mcallister, D. J. (1995). Affect- and cognition-based trust as foundations for interpersonal cooperation in organizations. *Academy of Management Journal, 38*(1), 24–59.
Monteiro, M. (2012). *Lição de cidadania e mais 3 poemas.* Campina Grande: Cordel Literature Leaflet.
Monteiro, R. S., & Teixeira, M. L. M. (2009). O papel da confiança na concessão de crédito para empresas em recuperação. *RAM- Revista de Administração Mackenzie, 10*(1).
Muchinsky, P. (2004). *Psicologia organizacional.* Sao Paulo: Thomson.
Raud-Mattedi, C. (2005). Análise crítica da sociologia econômica de Mark Granovetter: Os limites de uma leitura do mercado em termos de redes e imbricação. *Política & Sociedade, 6*(6), 59–82.
Rosseti, J. P. (2002). *Introdução à economia.* Sao Paulo: Atlas.
SÁ, M. G. (2010). Feirantes: Quem são? Como administram seus negócios? In *XXXIV Encontro da ANPAD, Rio de Janeiro.*
Salcs, A. P., Rezende, L. T., & Sette, R. S. (2011). Negócio feira livre: um estudo em um município de Minas Gerais. In *3rd Meeting of Human Resources and Labor Relations, Joao Pessoa* (p. 15)
Sezen, B., & Yilmaz, C. (2007). Relative Effects of dependence an trust on flexibility, information exchange, and solidarity in marketing Channels. *Journal of Business & Industrial Marketing, 22*(1), 41–51.
Souza, D. H. B., Dantas, J. C., Matias, T. B. O., & Moreira, E. (2014, August 10–16). Feira Livre e cultura popular: Espaço de resistência ou de subalternidade? In *7th Brazilian Conference of Geographers. Minutes of the 7th CBG.* Vitória/ES. ISBN: 978-85-98539-04-1

Souza, R. M. B., & Tolfo, S. R. (2009). *Significados atribuídos ao trabalho em condições precárias: Um estudo com feirantes do largo da ordem de Curitiba-PR [*Master's degree dissertation defende in the Psychology Graduate Porgram].

Steiner, P. (2006). *A sociologia econômica.* Sao Paulo: Atlas.

Tadd, W., Vanlaere, L., & Gastmans, C. (2010). Clarifying the concept of human dignity in the care of the elderly: A dialogue between empirical and philosophical Approaches. *Ethical Perspectives, 17*(1), 253–281.

Unicampo. (2010). *Flor de mandacaru.* Campina Grande: Cordel Literature Leaflet (collective production).

Zanelli, J., et al. (2004). *Psicologia, organizações e trabalho no Brasil* (p. 2004). Porto Alegre: Artmed.

Chapter 19
Dignity and Well-Being at Work

Maria Luisa Mendes Teixeira, Maria das Graças Torres Paz, and Sarah Santos Alves

Abstract Traditionally, studies on dignity at work have been developed a qualitative approach. For this reason, little is known about the relationship between dignity in the workplace and other constructs. In 2018, Thomas and Lucas developed a workplace dignity measurement scale, which allows investigating the following issue: what is the influence of dignity at work and personal organizational well-being? To answer this research question, the study had to identify the influence of dignity at work on employees' personal organizational well-being. Dignity at work consists in own and others' acknowledgement of the value acquired by the individuals engaging in work in a setting of interaction with other people. Personal organizational well-being is a dynamic process in connection with work that presupposes reciprocal relationships between workers and organizations. The investigation was carried out with 211 Brazilian workers from different business segments. The results pointed out that organizational dignity influences the personal well-being significantly. The greater the breadth of the employees' dignity perception, the greater their level of well-being in the organization. If managers want to improve the employee's well-being, it is important to improve organizational dignity.

Keywords Well-being at work · Workplace dignity measurement · Employees

19.1 Introduction

The knowledge and information age dynamics has required new institutional changes that force new ways of understanding and intervening in the reality. The socio-political-economic development conception of these new times carries a complex thought and an ecological rationality that includes the well-being, a movement that begins to take shape in the occupational world as well. One of the most important organizations' impacts lies in promoting workers' quality of life (Thomas & Lucas, 2018). Quality of life and well-being are closely interconnected concepts (Skevington

M. L. M. Teixeira (✉) · M. das Graças Torres Paz · S. S. Alves
São Paulo, Brazil
e-mail: malluluisa@gmail.com

M. L. Mendes Teixeira and L. M. B. de Oliveira (eds.), *Organizational Dignity and Evidence-Based Management*, https://doi.org/10.1007/978-3-030-68560-7_19

& Böhnke, 2018), and well-being is related to performance at work (Warr & Nielsen, 2018).

Several studies have been developed on well-being, considering individual, group, organization, and leadership aspects. Among the organizational aspects, HR practices stand out in the form of compensation-based schemes, training, career-supporting activities, performance appraisal, P-O fit, and autonomy (Nielsen et al., 2017).

Autonomy is a central element of dignity at work (Hodson, 2001). Dignity is a topic that has received some attention in organizational studies, especially with regard to dignity violation. Little is known, however, about the role that dignity plays in the management of organizations (Bal, 2017). Margolis (1997) argues that to foster the competitiveness of organizations and the well-being of employees, three conditions must be met: autonomy, respect for the contribution of employees, and the opportunity to learn and develop. Dignity has been approached as a new paradigm for management (Donaldson & Walsh, 2015).

Traditionally, studies on dignity at work have been developed a qualitative approach. For this reason, the relationship between dignity in the workplace and other constructs is almost unknown. In 2018, Thomas and Lucas developed a workplace dignity measurement scale, which allows investigating the following issue: what is the influence of dignity at work and personal organizational well-being? To answer this research question, the study had to identify the influence of dignity at work on employees' personal organizational well-being.

Dignity at work consists in own and others' acknowledgement of the value acquired by the individuals engaging in work in a setting of interaction with other people (Lucas, 2017). Personal organizational well-being is a dynamic process in connection with work that presupposes reciprocal relationships between workers and organizations (Paz, 2004).

The investigation was carried out with 211 workers from different business segments, most of whom were men (62%) predominantly white (59%), brown (28%), and black (10%). The workers average age was 35.5 years, and the average working time in the relevant organizations was 6.4 years. Data were collected using an electronic form containing the workplace dignity scale (WDS) (Thomas and Lucas, 2018), the scale of personal organizational well-being (SPOW) (Paz, 2011), and demographic variables (gender, age, and skin color) and organizational (time working in the organization). The WDS is composed of six factors: respectful interaction, recognition of competence and contribution, equality, inherent value, and general feelings of workplace dignity (Thomas & Lucas, 2018). SPOW comprises two factors: professional achievement and work environment conditions (Paz et al., 2012). Data analysis was performed through descriptive, and multivariate analysis, including confirmatory factor analysis and structural equation modeling (SEM) based on partial least squares, using the measurement model partial least squares path modeling (PLS-PM). The results indicated the existence of influence of the workplace dignity on personal organizational well-being.

19.2 Workplace Dignity

Before dealing with workplace dignity, it is necessary to understand the roots of these studies. Dignity is a term that has its origin in antiquity, more precisely in Greece and that throughout history has been used with different meanings and multiple conceptions (Mitchell, 2017). One of the meanings concerns a person's social status in society; in this connection, dignity can be acquired. It has its origin in the Greek and Roman civilizations and has lasted through the centuries until today (Rosen, 2012). The term "dignity" comes from Latin (*dignitas*), which means prestige (Bal & Jong, 2017). From the Christian perspective, dignity is something inherent to human beings, since man is made in the image and likeness of God, or it is still inherent because, God has given man the ability to shape his own destiny, as in the Oration work of Piccolo Della Mirandola, at the time of the Renaissance, or because he is endowed with reason, and therefore is capable of moral choices, as in Kant in the eighteenth century.

The Kantian concept of dignity has had a strong influence on Western culture, mainly with regard to human rights (Bal & Jong, 2017). For Kant, dignity is inherent and unconditional, it cannot be violated, and the autonomy of choice is its sore point since God would have created human beings as free beings, which is priceless, cannot be exchanged for anything equivalent and stands above all prices (Rosen, 2012).

Dignity has received little attention in management studies, but in recent decades, it has been studied in sociology, within the scope of industrial and work relations, (Hodson, 2001), mainly addressing violation of dignity (Bal, 2017). Hodson (2001), in one of his seminal works on dignity at work, also focused on the violation of dignity. From the points of view of Marx, Durkheim, and Weber on the industrial revolution and its harmful consequences for workers, Hodson and Roscigno (2004) show that dignity at work depends on the control exercised by supervisors, on task segmentation processes, norms, automation, and participation in the work environment. Among the negative consequences, Hodson (2001) emphasizes inequality, overwork, the low level of autonomy, and the consequent motivation loss.

Hodson and Roscigno (2004, p.3) for whom "Dignity is the ability to establish a sense of self-worth and self-respect and to appreciate the respect of others," dignity depends on the exercise of agency (Hodson, 2001). Workers devise strategies to protect their dignity, overcoming obstacles by creating alternatives of resistance, citizenship, and development of social relationships at work. On the other hand, workers realize that they have dignity as they perceive themselves as being trustworthy to others and become confident that they can exercise autonomy at work, and that, just as not taking advantage of other people, managers also do not reap advantages over them (Sayer, 2007).

The workplace dignity was defined by Lucas (2017) as "the self-recognized and other-recognized worth acquired from (or injured by) engaging in work activity" (p. 2549). This definition contains four principles. The first one is that dignity depends on the perception that individuals have of their own value and their perception of how much others recognize their value, through respectful interactions (Lucas, 2015).

The second principle is that dignity is subjective and self-built. The third principle concerns the apparent contradiction that dignity is inherent to human beings and is based on the Kantian concept of human dignity, and that, at the same time, it is acquired by merit. In the workplace dignity, the two concepts appear as complementary. The fourth principle deals with the ambivalent nature of dignity. The dignity "tends to be understood and experienced by its absence rather than its presence" (Lucas, 2017, p. 251), which means that people when defining dignity, they do it in opposition to indignity (Thomas & Lucas, 2018). These principles would help the construction of a dignity scale in the work environment (Thomas & Lucas, 2018), making it possible to test Margolis' proposition (1997) that dignity in the work environment positively impacts the workers' well-being.

19.3 Personal Organizational Well-Being

Studies on well-being were not originally restricted to work contexts. Only in the eighties did they intensify, but mostly, following the two theoretical currents that support most studies on the subject in a more general perspective: subjective well-being and psychological well-being. What can be seen in the literature on well-being in the workplace is that the conceptions about the construct are diverse, sometimes with a perspective more pleasure oriented as a representative of hedonism, which characterizes subjective well-being, sometimes with a perspective of self-development and achievement more focused on psychological well-being, in the eudaimonic perspective. Some propositions have a more empirical base, while others are more theoretical. In addition, studies addressing a mix of approaches are available. Demo and Paschoal (2013) consider that there is no consensus on the definition of the phenomenon. Shulte and Vainio (2010), although also agreeing that there is no consensus on the definition of well-being, refer to a convergence of perceptions that well-being is more than the absence of negative factors.

One of the pioneering scholars of well-being at work is Warr. In 1987, the author considered two aspects through which well-being is manifested in the: cognitive and affective work. The cognitive evaluates satisfaction with different work dimensions, such as salary and relationship, among others. The affective refers to the expression of feelings, such as enthusiasm and depression. For Warr (2007), there are strong relations of influence in the workplace on people's well-being, so that organizations must ensure healthy environments, but people must perceive these favorable conditions and also take advantage of them. Another proposal for investigating well-being is presented by Van Horn et al. (2004) with a focus on occupational well-being. In addition to considering the affective aspects, they introduce the motivational, behavioral, cognitive and psychosomatic dimensions in the model presented, emphasizing, though, that the affective aspect constitutes the core of occupational well-being. Studies on the topic continue to be developed while expanding the spectrum of approaches.

Research on motivational types, well-being, and performance has been enhanced since 2005, with studies like that of Deci and Ryan (2008) emphasizing that, when employees are autonomously motivated (intrinsic motivation), they have more persistence, concentration, productivity, effort, engagement in their tasks and experience a higher degree of well-being. But the opposite occurs with employees with controlled regulation, extrinsic motivation, who exhibit low performance and engagement and experience low levels of well-being. At this time, studies also emerged that explored the identification of variables in the work context that could be subject to intervention, such as task characteristics and compensation, among others. With regard to compensation, some authors explored the issue of materialism, financial compensation relating it to personal well-being. In 2010, Deckop, Jurkiewicz, and Giacalione drew attention to the importance of studying this relationship, since, despite organizational efforts to foster autonomy from a materialistic perspective, it may not be embraced by individuals who exhibit a negative relationship with money.

Studies on well-being in the workplace are expanding, but still addressing conceptual issues of the construct and measurement instruments. In 2011, Juniper, Bellamye White developed a new instrument to assesses the performance and well-being of call centers' employees. The purpose of the study was to test the performance of two generic scales that assess the well-being of employees against a new scale of well-being built specifically for the call center sector. The construction method of the new scale was based on the clinical model. The instrument revealed satisfactory validity and reliability, managing to capture specificities of the sector that were not sensitive to the more generic pre-existing scales. The authors emphasize the importance of considering the different work sectors specifics in the assessment of well-being, to enable organizational practices to fit reality in order to be effective.

Paz et al. (2012) present a Personal Organizational Well-Being concept, based on Paz (2004) empirical study. Paz (2004) conceives well-being as part of a dynamic process in the organizational context that includes the following assumptions in its proposition: (a) well-being occurs in an environment marked by reciprocal relations between worker and organization, in a way that well-being is affected by both organizational and individual characteristics. In this perspective, workers must produce adequately for the organization, which, in turn, must assure workers their right to healthy environments and with infrastructure to carry out their activities; (b) the organization is not fully responsible for its employees' health, but it is responsible for encouraging positive relationships and for building and maintaining settings that are suitable for the occurrence of these relationships and the workers' well-being (Forward et al., 1991); (c) the work environment and the corporate structure contribute to make evident behaviors characterized by tension and stress; thus, they are also strong influencers of the worker's well-being (Rossi, 2005); (d) personal characteristics are moderators or mediators of the impact of the organizational environment on the organization's members (Blanch, 2003; Warr, 2007), consequently in the personal organizational well-being. Paz (2004) defined the personal organizational well-being as the satisfaction of the needs and fulfillment of the wishes of individuals who perform their role in the organization, but without disregarding its opposite, malaise. Paz et al. (2012) based on studies that use the scale developed by

Paz (2004) reviewed the definition of well-being and defined it as the satisfaction of needs and fulfillment of the individual's wishes when the individuals play their role in the organization, with emphasis on reciprocity relations between the individual and the organization.

In the last five years, it has become clearer how different areas of knowledge have addressed well-being studies and how different occupations have been considered as an object of investigation. Different research models have been tested, and different meta-analysis were carried out.

The study by Hillage et al. (2014) brings with it the importance of proactive actions by the organization for the construction of the employee welfare process. They consider that employees should seek to adopt a lifestyle that ensures their mental well-being; the organization can provide guidance and support in this process. The dynamics of employee–organization interaction are clear. In turn, Sojo et al. (2015) performed a meta-analysis to examine the relationships between harmful experiences in the context of women's work and occupational well-being. The study by Jones and Guthrie (2016), based on a survey applied to 1242 partners and employees of a public accounting firm, examined the effect of psychological well-being in the work–home conflict, in a bi-directional sense, with flexibility and clarity of the role in the workplace as a moderator. The model test via structural equations confirmed the moderating effect of role flexibility and clarity, reducing the perception of the work–home conflict and contributing to the increase in well-being.

Lomas et al. (2017), when systematically reviewing the literature on mindfulness, well-being and performance, found that there is a positive association among variables in most measures in the study sample. The Journal of Forensic Sciences has published studies on the subject, like the work of Jeanguenat and Droor (2018). The article describes how stress and well-being can affect forensic work. In 2019, Di Fábio & Kenny issued an article with two studies in which they examine individual resources that can foster individual and organizational well-being. The first study confirmed the mediation of personality characteristics between emotional intelligence and hedonic and eudaimonic well-being. And the second also confirmed the mediation of personality characteristics between positive managerial relationship and hedonic and eudaimonic well-being. Cooper et al. (2019) in a study at a Chinese bank identified a positive relationship between social climate and resilience. The authors considered that the relationship is due to the management of employees' practices and performance and to the well-being orientation of human resources.

Indeed, there are different approaches to well-being in different work contexts. In this study, the concept of Paz was adopted (2004), and the scale of Paz (2011) was applied, in order to review the influence of workplace dignity on personal organizational well-being.

19.4 The Influence of Dignity in the Context of Work and Personal Well-Being

The workplace dignity scale (WDS) was submitted to confirmatory factor analysis (CFA) to ascertain if adjustments were needed as it was the first application of WDS in Brazil. The WDS six-factor structure proposed by Thomas and Lucas (2018) was validated considering the criteria of average extracted variance (AVE) with all values above 0.50; composite reliability above 0.70 for all factors and the discriminant validity with the square root of the AVE of each latent variable much larger than the correlation of the specific latent variable with any of the others, indicating that it was adequate to measure the construct of dignity in the workplace for the sampling.

The AFC applied also to SPOW indicated the need for adjustments to increase its precision in the measurement of constructs; two items had to be excluded. After adjusting the SPOW and confirming the adequacy of the WDS to measure the construct of dignity in the workplace, it was possible to ascertain that the WDS factors that were given priority were 'general dignity' (whose items refer to dignity in a broader way, such as, for example, "I have dignity at work,") followed by the 'respectful interaction' factor (this factor refers to the perception of respectful behaviors that respondents received from other people at the workplace). The indignity factor was the one with the lowest average. Bearing in mind that this factor has a negative meaning, the lower the average, the more it contributes to a positive assessment of dignity in the context of work (Thomas & Lucas, 2018). As for SPOW, which has two factors, it was possible to ascertain the level of worker well-being by the variable 'professional achievement' was higher than the variable 'conditions of the work environment'.

The influence of the workplace dignity on the personal organizational well-being was reviewed by multivariate technique of structural equation modeling. The latent second-order variables "dignity" and "indignity" have explained, with statistical significance, the personal organizational well-being level with an R^2 of 0.565, whereas β, was equal to 0.58 ($p < 0.000$) for the relationship between workplace dignity and personal organizational well-being; i.e., the greater the breadth of the employees' dignity perception, the greater their level of well-being in the organization. The variable 'indignity' revealed a $\beta = -0.220$ ($p < 0.01$), which allows us to infer that the greater the perception of indignity, the lower the personal organizational well-being level will be.

With view at investigating the moderating effect of the demographic variables (gender, age, skin color, and education) and the functional variable "time working for the organization," the model was tested again, but it was not possible to identify statistical significance. Despite this result, some demographic and organizational variables influenced the personal organizational well-being variables. This was the case for the variables age and working time in the organization. Age significantly influenced the well-being variable ($\beta = 0.140$; $p < 0.05$), which allows us to infer that the older the worker, the more he/she tends to better assess his level of personal organizational well-being. Likewise, the variable 'working time in the organization' influenced the well-being variable ($\beta = 0.11$; $p < 0.5$), indicating that individuals who have worked for less time in the organization perceive with less intensity the level of personal organizational well-being regarding 'professional achievement' and 'workplace conditions'.

19.5 Implications for Management

The study revealed that the workplace dignity has a moderate explanatory power (Hair et al., 2009) in relation to the personal organizational well-being. In addition to the theoretical contribution of this work, the results point to the practical relevance for people management in the organizations. Considering that dignity:

(a) is subjective and self-built in relation to others (Thomas & Lucas, 2018);
(b) influences personal organizational well-being and, consequently, affects performance (Lomas et al., 2017);
(c) in the workplace is built on the dynamics of the interaction between managers and the team (Yalden & Mccormack, 2010);

then, managers must be aware of their role in preserving the dignity of the workers and their consequent motivation. Excessive control by supervisors is one of the factors that affects the dignity of the worker (Hodson & Roscigno, 2004). Workers need to feel that they deserve trust from their supervisors and maintain a relationship in which neither side seeks to take advantage of the other (Yalden & Mccormack, 2010).

Employees develop strategies not only to protect their dignity, but also to find spaces where they can express and reinforce their identity and well-being. These strategies involve autonomous behavior and aim to reduce the effects of a controlling management (Hodson, 1996). The agency, in the sense of freedom to make decisions, is directly and positively associated with work dignity and well-being at work (Hojman & Miranda, 2015). Opening space for employees' participation in decisions and freedom to perform their work contributes to the perception of workplace dignity and personal organizational well-being, as well as solidarity relationships and time for social relationships among employees (Hodson, 1996).

It is up to managers to open opportunities for participation, for solidarity and for social relationships among employees.

19.6 Final Remarks

This study aimed to identify the influence of the workplace dignity on employees' personal organizational well-being. The main finding of this investigation is the explanatory power that the workplace dignity has in relation to the Personal Organizational Well-Being, which exceeded 50%, a level considered between moderate and substantial for human science and social sciences studies (Hair et al., 2014).

This result offers opportunities for future research that may lead to a broader understanding of the well-being phenomenon, with possible relevant practical contributions, whether considering its substantive value, or considering its instrumental power of well-being in relation to performance.

The WDS developed by Thomas and Lucas (2018) proved to be reliable and valid for a sample of Brazilian workers who participated in the research. SPOW (2011) needed adjustments, with the exclusion of two items, which suggests that there is still room for improvement.

The fact that no moderating effects have been found regarding the variables gender, age, education, and time spent in the relationship between workplace dignity and personal organizational well-being can be explained by the lack of influence of these variables on dignity. The workplace dignity measured by the WDS (Thomas & Lucas, 2018) is mainly anchored in human dignity in the Kantian concept, that is, as an inherent value of the human being (Bal, 2017), thus not depending on demographic or functional variables.

Bearing in mind that well-being affects the workers' performance (Lomas et al., 2017), it can be hypothesized that dignity in the work environment affects performance in a relationship mediated by well-being and constitutes a potential field for future investigation. Future research can be carried out by associating the workplace dignity variable with other antecedents of well-being, in order to obtain the best possible explanation of this construct and to better understand the relationship between antecedents, well-being, and performance.

This study has some limits. The study has focused the State of São Paulo, mainly the city of São Paulo. Another limit is related to the education level of the sample, which included mainly higher education and post-graduate levels. These limits mean opportunity for future investigation. As for the limitations, the main one concerns the application to WDS with five points instead of seven points, according to the original scale. It is suggested that studies be carried out comparing the psychometric properties of both scales, in order to know if, in fact, the seven-point scale can be replaced by the five-point scale. If equivalence is evidenced, then the five-point scale would result in lower costs in research development.

References

Bal, M. (2017). *Dignity in the workplace: New theoretical perspective. Humanism in Business Series*. London, England: Palgrave Macmillan.

Bal, P. M., & Jong, S. B. (2017). From human resource management to human dignity development: A dignity perspective on HRM and the role of workplace democracy. In M. Kostera & M. Pirson (Eds.), *Dignity and the organization*. Humanism in Business Series. London, England: Palgrave Macmillan. https://doi.org/10.1057/978-1-137-55562-5_9

Blanch, M. J. (2003). Trabajar em la modernidad industrial. In M. J. Blanch (Org), *Teoria de las relaciones laborales: fundamentos* (pp. 19–148). Barcelona: UOC.

Cooper, B., Wang, J., Bartran, T., & Cooke, F. L. (2019). Well-being oriented human resource management practices and employee performance in the Chinese banking sector: The role of social climate and resilience. *Human Resource Management, 58,* 85–97. https://doi.org/10.1002/hrm.21934

Deci, E. L., & Ryan, R. M. (2008). Facilitating optimal motivation and psychological well-being across life's domains. *Canadian Psychological Association, 49*(1), 14–23. https://doi.org/10.1037/0708-5591.49.1.14

Deckop, J. R., Jurkiewicz, C. L., & Giacalone, R. A. (2010). Effects of materialism on work-related personal well-being. *Human Relations, 63*(7), 1007–1030. https://doi.org/10.1177/0018726709353953

Demo, G., & Paschoal, T. (2013). *Well-being at work scale: Exploratory and confirmatory validation in the United States comprising affective and cognitive components* (p. 37). Rio de Janeiro, RJ, Brasil: Anais do Encontro da ANPAD.

Di Fabio, A., & Kenny, M. E. (2019). Resources for enhancing employee and organizational well-being beyond personality traits: The promise of emotional intelligence and Positive Relational Management. *Personality and Individual Differences, 151*, Article 109278. https://doi.org/10.1016/j.paid.2019.02.022

Donaldson, T., & Walsh, J. P. (2015). Toward a theory of business. *Research in Organizational Behavior, 35,* 181–207. https://doi.org/10.1016/j.riob.2015.10.002

Forward, G. E., Beach, D. E., Gray, D. A., & Quick, J. C. (1991). Mentofacturing: A vision for american industrial excellence. *Academy of Management Executive, 5*(3), 32–44. https://doi.org/10.5465/ame.1991.4274462

Hair, J. F., Jr., William, B., Babin, B., & Anderson, R. E. (2009). *Análise multivariada de dados* (6th ed., p. 2009). Porto Alegre: Bookman.

Hair, J. F., Hult, G. T. M., Ringle, C. M., & Sarsted, M. (2014). *A primer on partial least squares structural equations modeling (PLS-SEM).* SAGE: Los Angeles.

Hillage, J., Brown, G., Shiels, C., & Gabbay, M. (2014). Exploring future GP referral to fit for work policy lab. In *Health and employment outcomes: Data exploration.*

Hodson, R. (1996). Dignity in the workplace under participative management: Alienation and freedom revisited. *American Sociological Review, 61,* 719–738. https://doi.org/10.2307/2096450.

Hodson, R. (2001). *Dignity at work.* New York: Cambridge University Press.

Hodson, R., & Roscigno, V. J. (2004). Organizational success and worker dignity: Complementary or contradictory? *American Journal of Sociology, 110*(3), 672–708. https://doi.org/10.1086/422626.

Hojman, D., & Miranda, A. (2015). Agency, human dignity and subjective well-being. *Working Papers wp398,* University of Chile, Department of Economics.

Jeanguenat, A. M., Droor, I. E., & Morgan, R. M. (2018). Human factors effecting forensic decision making: Workplace stress and well- being. *Journal of Forensic Sciences, 63*, 258–261. https://doi.org/10.1111/1556-4029.13533

Jones, A., & Guthrie, C. P. (2016). The new normal? Enhanced psychological well-being from public accounting: Mitigating conflict with flexibility and role clarity. *Advances in Accounting Behavioral Research, 19,* 33–68. https://doi.org/10.1108/S147514882016-0000019002.

Juniper, B., Bellamy, P., & White, N. (2011). Testing the performance of a new approach to measuring employee well-being. *Leardership & Organizations Development Journal, 25,* 344–357. https://doi.org/10.1108/01437731111134634.

Lomas, T., Medina, J. C., Ivtzan, I., Rupprecht, S., Hart, R., & Eiroa-Orosa, F. J. (2017). The impact of mindfulness on well-being and performance in the workplace: An inclusive systematic review of the empirical literature. *European Journal of Work and Organizational Psychology, 26*(4), 492–513. https://doi.org/10.1080/1359432X.20-17.1308924.

Lucas, K. (2015). Workplace dignity: Communicating inherent, earned, and reme-diated dignity. *Journal of Management Studies, 52,* 621–646. https://doi.org/10.1111/joms.12133.

Lucas, K. (2017). Workplace dignity. In C. R. Scott & L. Lewis (Eds.), *The interna-tional encyclopedia of organizational communication* (Vol. 4, pp. 2549–2562). Chichester, UK: Wiley Blackwell.

Margolis, J. (1997). *Dignity in balance: Philosophical and practical dimensions of promoting ethics in organizations.* Massachusetts: Harvard University.

Mitchell, L. (2017). Dignity and membership: A route to the heart of how dignity is done in everyday interaction. In: M. Kostera & M. Pirson (Eds.), *Dignity and the organization.* (Humanism in Business Series). London, England: Palgrave Macmillan. https://doi.org/10.1057/978-1-137-55562-5_9

Nielsen, K., Nielsen, M. B., Ogbonnaya, C., Känsälä, M., Saari, E., & Isaksson, K. (2017). Workplace resources to improve both employee well-being and performance: A systematic review and meta-analysis. *Work & Stress, 31*(2), 101–120. https://doi.org/10.1080/02678373.2017.1304463.

Paz, M. G. T. (2004). Poder e saúde organizacional. In A. Tamayo (org), *Cultura e saúde nas organizações.* Porto Alegre: Artmed.

Paz, M. G. T. (2011). Perfil cultural de lasorganizaciones y bienestardeltrabajador. En E. Agulló, J. L. Álvaro, A. Garrido, R. Medina, & I. Schweiger (Eds.), *Nuevas formas de organizacióndeltrabajo y laempleabilidad* (pp. 85–108). Oviedo (Asturias): Universidad de Oviedo.

Paz, M. G. T., Neiva, E.R., & Dessen, M.C. (2012). Bem - estar e felicidade nas organizações: um só fenômeno? Em: M. C. Ferreira & H. Mendonça (Eds.), *Saúde e bem-estar no trabalho.* São Paulo: Casa do Psicólogo.

Rosen, M. E. (2012). *Dignity: Its history and meaning.* Cambridge, MA: Harvard University Press.

Sayer, A. (2007). Dignity at work: Broadening the agenda. *Organization, 14*(4), 565–581. https://doi.org/10.1177/1350508407078053

Shulte, P., &Vainio, H. (2010). Well-being at work: Overview and perspective. *Scandinavian Journal of Work and Environmental Health, 36,* 422–429. https://doi.org/10.5271/sjweh.3076

Skevington, S. M., & Böhnke, J. R. (2018). How is subjective well-being related to quality of life? Do we need two concepts and both measures? *Social Science & Medicine.* https://doi.org/10.1016/j.socscimed.2018.04.005

Sojo, V. E., Wood, R. E., & Genat, A. E. (2015). Harmful workplace experiences and Women's occupational well-being: A meta-analysis. *Psychology of Women Quartely, 40,* 10–40. https://doi.org/10.1177/0361684315599346

Thomas, B., & Lucas, K. (2018). Development and validation of the workplace dignity scale. *Group & Organization Management,* 1–40. https://doi.org/10.1177/1059601118807784

Van Horn, J. E., Taria, T. W., Scchaufeli, W. B., & Scheurs, P. J. (2004). The structure of occupational well-being: A study among Dutch teachers. *Journal of Occupational and Organizational Psychology, 77,* 365–375. https://doi.org/10.1348/0963179041752718

Warr, P. (1987). *Work, unemployment and mental health.* New York: Oxford University Press.

Warr, P. (2007). *Work, happiness and unhappiness.* New Jersey: Lawrence Erbaum Associates.

Warr, P., & Nielsen, K. (2018). Wellbeing and work performance. In E. Diener, S. Oishi, & L. Tay (Eds.), *Handbook of well-being.* Salt Lake City, UT: DEF Publishers.

Yalden, B. J., & Mccormack, B. (2010). Constructions of dignity: A pre-requisite for flourishing in the workplace? *International Journal of Older People Nursing, 5,* 137–147. https://doi.org/10.1111/j.1748-3743.2010.00218.x